THE INTERNATIONAL DIMENSION OF EU COMPETITION LAW AND POLICY

Modern competition law was first employed by countries over one hundred years ago in order to address issues relating to restrictions of trade at the national level. Recent international economic integration has weakened the distinction between the domestic and the international in several fields of economic activity, and consequently the laws which regulate such activity, competition law included. Several attempts to address the paradox of adopting national competition rules to address international issues have been made at the international, regional and (lately) bilateral levels. This book discusses the international dimension of EU competition law and policy, and examines the position taken by the EU in four distinct categories of international agreements which are devoted to competition or include competition provisions. In particular, it analyses the EU's position with regard to bilateral enforcement cooperation agreements, bilateral free trade agreements, plurilateral regional agreements and the long negotiations for the adoption of a multilateral competition regime.

ANESTIS S. PAPADOPOULOS is a Partner of KPP Law in Athens and a teaching fellow at the University of Athens Law School.

THE CAMBRIDGE ANTITRUST AND COMPETITION LAW SERIES

Publications within the Series consider various legal, economic and political developments related to competition law and policy. They also consider the application of competition law and policy in sector-specific as well as cross-sector contexts and deal with policy questions ranging from the formation and adoption of competition law and policy (whether at national, regional or international level) to those dealing with enforcement, and the connection between law and competition in the market place. The Series also accommodates different analytical and interdisciplinary viewpoints, such as law and economics; law and political science; law and economic geography-driven perspectives.

The Series includes publications designed to cater for academic demands as well as practitioner publications catering for the continuously evolving needs of regulators, policy-makers, and practitioners, in particular lawyers and economists (who increasingly provide advice on regulatory questions).

The editorial board of the Series welcome proposals by authors and editors who are interested in contributing to the Series through: academic monographs; revised PhD theses of high quality; practitioner texts and collections; and edited volumes.

THE INTERNATIONAL DIMENSION OF EU COMPETITION LAW AND POLICY

ANESTIS S. PAPADOPOULOS

CAMBRIDGE
UNIVERSITY PRESS

CAMBRIDGE UNIVERSITY PRESS
Cambridge, New York, Melbourne, Madrid, Cape Town, Singapore,
São Paulo, Delhi, Dubai, Tokyo, Mexico City

Cambridge University Press
The Edinburgh Building, Cambridge CB2 8RU, UK

Published in the United States of America by Cambridge University Press, New York

www.cambridge.org
Information on this title: www.cambridge.org/9780521196468

First published 2010

Printed in the United Kingdom at the University Press, Cambridge

A catalogue record for this publication is available from the British Library

Library of Congress Cataloguing in Publication data
Papadopoulos, Anestis S.
The international dimension of EU competition law and policy / Anestis S. Papadopoulos.
p. cm. – (The Cambridge antitrust and competition law series)
Includes bibliographical references.
ISBN 978-0-521-19646-8 (hardback)
1. Restraint of trade–European Union countries. 2. Antitrust law–European Union countries. 3. Restaint of trade. 4. Antitrust law. 5. European Union countries–Economic relations. I. Title.
KJE6459.P37 2010
343.24′0721–dc22
2010033386

ISBN 978-0-521-19646-8 Hardback

This work is dedicated to the memory of my father,
Spyridon S. Papadopoulos

CONTENTS

LIST OF TABLES

ACKNOWLEDGEMENTS

This book is a slightly revised version of my Ph.D. thesis, defended at the London School of Economics in 2008. Writing my Ph.D. and further working on the book has been a long and difficult journey. During this journey, I have greatly benefited from a number of people, and completing the book offers me the opportunity to express my gratitude to them.

First of all, I would like to thank my teacher and supervisor, Professor Imelda Maher, who believed in me, offered me the opportunity to get involved in this project, and has been both an inspiration and a guide. Giorgio Monti and Deborah Cass also supervised my work in different stages of my research, and their help has been significant. I further want to thank my Ph.D. examiners, Professor Barry Rodger and Dr Andrew Scott, who gave me a number of different perspectives on the thesis and offered me a really demanding and fruitful discussion of my work.

I am also grateful to a number of current and former European Commission officials and practitioners, with whom I had the chance to work, or had very useful discussions in the context of my research. I am indebted to Steve Ryan, with whom I had very interesting and challenging discussions in the process of conducting my research. Blanca Rodriguez-Galindo, Georg Roebling, Irina Orssich, Johannes Gorkos, Janne Kankanen, Holger Dieckmann, Andres Font Galarza, Georgios Kiriazis, Dimitri Giottakos, Stefan Amarasinha, Bruno Zanettin, Jean François Bellis, Charles Stark, Jim Venit and Konstantinos Adamantopoulos, have also all been extremely helpful and supportive.

I also have to thank a number of academics and practitioners who agreed to share with me their views on the issues I discuss in the book, and/or offered me the opportunity to become involved in two projects related to this study, carried out under the auspices of UNCTAD and the CEPR (the latter financed by the EU). These include Philip Marsden, Simon Evennett, Peter Holmes, Angus MacCulloch, Lucian Cernat, Anna Maria Alvarez, Anna Sydorak, Peter Whelan, Pierre Horna, Mor Bakhoum, Heba Shahein and Ozgur Kayali.

Last but not least, I want to say a big thank you to my wife Kalliopi, who has patiently helped me to stay focused on the project and accepted my obsession with it, and to my mother Theodora and my uncle Konstantine Kostopoulos, who have supported me throughout.

ABBREVIATIONS

ABA	American Bar Association
ACCC	Australian Competition and Consumer Commission
ACFC	ASEAN Consultative Forum for Competition
ACP	African, Caribbean and Pacific
ACPA	Antitrust Civil Process Act (US)
APEC	Asia-Pacific Economic Cooperation
ASEAN	Association of South East Asian Nations
CACM	Central America Common Market
CAFTA-DR	Central America Free Trade Agreement plus Dominican Republic
CARICOM	Caribbean Community
CDC	MERCOSUR Committee for the Defense of Competition
CFI	Court of First Instance
COMESA	Common Market for Eastern and Southern Africa
COTED	CARICOM Council for Trade and Economic Development
CPDG	APEC Competition Policy and Deregulation Group
CSME	CARICOM single market economy
DIAC	Draft International Antitrust Code
DoJ	Department of Justice (US)
EAC	East African Community
EC	European Community
ECJ	European Court of Justice
ECN	European Competition Network
ECOWAS	Economic Community of West African States
ECSC	European Coal and Steel Community
EEA	European Economic Area
EEC	European Economic Community
EFTA	European Free Trade Area
EMAA	Euro-Mediterranean association agreement
ENP	European Neighbourhood Policy
EPA	economic partnership agreement
EU	European Union
FDI	foreign direct investment
FTA	free trade agreement

FTAA	Free Trade Agreement of the Americas
FTAIA	Foreign Trade Antitrust Improvements Act (US)
FTC	Federal Trade Commission (US)
FTCA	Federal Trade Commission Act (US)
FYROM	Former Yugoslav Republic of Macedonia
GATS	General Agreement on Trade in Services
GATT	General Agreement on Tariffs and Trade
GDP	gross domestic product
GNI	gross national income
IAEAA	International Antitrust Enforcement Assistance Act (US)
IBA	International Bar Association
ICN	International Competition Network
ICPAC	International Competition Policy Advisory Committee
IMF	International Monetary Fund
IPA	Instrument for Pre-Accession Assistance
ITO	International Trade Organization
LAFTA	Latin America Free Trade Association
LDC	least developed countries
MFN	most favoured nation
MLAT	mutual legal assistance treaty
MOU	Memorandum of Understanding
MTC	MERCOSUR Trade Commission
NAFTA	North American Free Trade Agreement
OECD	Organisation for Economic Cooperation and Development
PCA	partnership and cooperation agreement
PTA	preferential trade area
RBP Code	Restrictive Business Practices Code
SAA	stabilisation and association agreement
SACU	Southern African Customs Union
SADC	Southern African Development Community
TAIEX	Technical Assistance and Information Exchange programme
TDCA	trade, development and cooperation agreement
TFEU	Treaty on the Functioning of the European Union
TRIPS	Trade-Related Aspects of Intellectual Property Rights
UNCTAD	United Nations Conference on Trade and Development
WAEMU	West African Economic and Monetary Union
WTO	World Trade Organization

TABLE OF CASES

EU

ECJ and CFI judgments

Commission decisions

United States

WTO

Other

TABLE OF LEGISLATION

EU

Regulations

Guidelines and Notices

OECD

United Kingdom

United States

TABLE OF TREATIES AND AGREEMENTS

Bilateral enforcement cooperation agreements on competition

Bilateral trade agreements of the EU

Agreements with (former) candidate countries

Decision 1/95 of the EC–Turkey Association Council of 22 December 1995 on implementing the final phase of the Customs Union [1996] OJ L35/1 97–9, 106–8, 116, 118–122, 128, 131–3, 135–8, 140

Euro-Mediterranean Agreements

Algeria: Euro-Mediterranean Agreement establishing an Association between the European Community and its Member States and the People's Democratic Republic of Algeria [2005] OJ L265/1 98, 101, 107, 109–112, 116, 122, 125, 127, 131–4, 140

Egypt: Euro-Mediterranean Agreement establishing an Association between the European Community and its Member States and the Arab Republic of Egypt [2004] OJ L304/38 98, 101, 107, 109–111, 116, 118, 123, 125, 128, 132, 134, 140

Israel: Euro-Mediterranean Agreement establishing an Association between the European Community and its Member States and the State of Israel [2000] OJ L147/3 98, 107, 110, 116, 118, 122, 125, 128, 132, 134, 140

Jordan: Euro-Mediterranean Agreement establishing an Association between the European Community and its Member States and the Hashemite Kingdom of Jordan [2002] OJ L129/3 95, 98, 101, 107, 110–1, 117, 122–3, 125, 128, 132, 134, 140

Lebanon: Interim Agreement on Trade and Trade-related Matters between the European Community and the Republic of Lebanon [2002] OJ L262/2 95, 101, 107, 110, 112, 117, 122–3, 125, 129, 132, 134, 140

Morocco: Euro-Mediterranean Agreement establishing an Association between the European Community and its Member States and the Kingdom of Morocco [2000] OJ L70/2 95, 98, 101, 107, 110–1, 117, 122–3, 125, 128, 132, 134, 140

Palestinian Authority: Euro-Mediterranean Interim Association Agreement on Trade and Cooperation between the European Community and the Palestine Liberation Organization (PLO) for the benefit of the Palestinian Authority of the West Bank and the Gaza Strip [1997] OJ L 187/3 98, 107, 110, 118, 122, 124, 133, 138, 140

Tunisia: Euro-Mediterranean Agreement establishing an Association between the European Community and its Member States and the Republic of Tunisia [1998] OJ L97/2 95, 98, 101, 107, 110–1, 117, 122–3, 125, 128, 132, 134, 140

Agreements with Eastern European and Central Asian Countries

Armenia: Partnership and Cooperation Agreement establishing a Partnership between the European Community and its Member States and the Republic of Armenia [1999] OJ L239/3 98, 107, 112–3, 117, 123–4, 129, 135, 140

Azerbaijan: Partnership and Cooperation Agreement establishing a Partnership between the European Community and its Member States and the Republic of Azerbaijan OJ L246/3 99, 107, 112, 117, 123, 129, 135, 140

Georgia: Partnership and Cooperation Agreement establishing a Partnership between the European Community and its Member States and Georgia [1999] OJ L205/3 99, 107, 112, 117, 123, 129, 135, 140

Agreements with Chile, Mexico and South Africa

Plurilateral Regional Agreements (founding Treaties)

1

Introduction, Structure of the Book and Method

1.1 Introduction

Modern competition law is a tool first employed by countries more than a hundred years ago in order to address issues relating to restrictions of trade conducted by private firms. As a legal instrument used to resolve national problems, competition law continues to be employed by countries. The dominance of market-based economies in the last fifty years, especially following the collapse of the Soviet Union, as well as improvements in transport, communications and technology, and trade liberalisation through the adoption of relevant agreements between states, have, however, progressively dismantled national borders and internationalised trade.

Along with trade liberalisation came practices conducted by firms that have an effect on the territories of more than one country. Attempts to address this paradox – namely, the adoption of national rules to address international issues – have appeared on several occasions over the last eighty years at the international, regional and (lately) bilateral level. The general aim of this book is to observe these attempts and analyse the norms that have been developed: bilateral and tripartite enforcement cooperation agreements, bilateral and plurilateral trade agreements that include competition provisions, and attempts at the adoption of a multilateral competition code.

A number of topics related to the internationalisation of competition law have been addressed in the relevant literature, mostly in the last fifteen years, including, amongst others, the types of practices that may have an effect on multiple countries;[1] the relationship between trade law and competition law; and the debate over the possible inclusion of competition law within the World Trade Organization (WTO) framework.[2]

[1] See e.g., UNCTAD (2005), *Exclusionary Anti-competitive Practices: Their Effects on Competition and Development*, UNCTAD/DITC/CLP/2005/4.

[2] See e.g., P. Marsden (2003), *A Competition Policy for the WTO* (Cameron May); E.U. Petersmann (1999), 'Legal Economic and Political Objectives of National and

Lately, a number of studies have focused on the examination of trade agreements with competition elements.[3] The influence of policy networks in the process of internationalisation of competition,[4] the development of principles in the process of the internationalisation of competition,[5] and the relationship between preferential trade agreements and the attempts to conclude a multilateral agreement on competition have also been explored.[6] There are also works which have compared different domestic competition regimes.[7] Finally, there are papers discussing the influence of the International Competition Network (ICN) on the internationalisation of competition processes.[8] All these studies will be reviewed in the context of the discussion in subsequent chapters.

On the other hand, there are only few studies available which observe the way in which particular states and/or polities have reacted with regard to the adoption and application of international agreements on competition.[9] For instance, in the case of the European Union (EU), there are

International Competition Policies: Constitutional Functions of WTO "Linking Principles" for Trade and Competition' 34(1) *New England Law Review* 145; UNCTAD (2003), *WTO Core Principles and Prohibition: Obligations Relating to Private Practices, National Competition Laws and Implications for a Competition Policy Framework*, UNCTAD/DITC/CLP/2003/2; E.M. Fox (1999), 'Competition Law and the Millennium Round' 2(4) *Journal of International Economic Law* 665; B. Hoekman and P.C. Mavroidis (2002), *Economic Development, Competition Policy and the World Trade Organisation*, World Bank Policy Research Working Paper No. 2917; M.D. Taylor (2006), *International Competition Law: A New Dimension for the WTO?* (Cambridge University Press).

[3] L. Cernat (2005), 'Eager to Ink but Ready to Act? RTA Proliferation and International Cooperation on Competition Policy' in P. Brusick, A.M. Alvarez and L. Cernat (eds.), *Competition Provisions in Regional Trade Agreements: How to Assure Development Gains* (Geneva and New York: UNCTAD); OECD (2006), *Competition Provisions in Regional Trade Agreements*, OECD Trade Policy Working Paper No. 31, COM/DAF/TD(2005)3/FINAL.

[4] I. Maher (2002), 'Competition Law in the International Domain: Networks as a New Form of Governance' 29(1) *Journal of Law and Society* 112.

[5] Ch. Noonan (2007), *Emerging Principles of International Competition Law* (Oxford University Press).

[6] S.J. Evenett (2005), 'What Can We Learn from the Competition Provisions of RTAs?' in Brusick, Alvarez and Cernat, *supra* n. 3.

[7] See e.g., G. Doern and S. Wilks (eds.) (1996), *Comparative Competition Policy: National Institutions in a Global Market* (Oxford University Press); E. Elhauge and D. Geradin (2007), *Global Competition Law and Economics* (Hart Publishing).

[8] See M. Bode and O. Budzinski (2005), *Competing Toward International Antitrust: The WTO versus the ICN*, Marburg Papers on Economics 03/2005.

[9] Exceptions to this general observation are a number of papers which discuss the internationalisation of competition law from the perspective of developing countries. See e.g., B. Hoekman (1997), *Competition Policy in the Global Trading System: A Developing Country Perspective*, World Bank Policy Research Working Paper No. 1735; B. Hoekman

only a few papers that discuss the position taken by the polity in particular fields of international agreements with competition elements,[10] while most of the works in this field, in the context of the discussion of international agreements with competition elements, make reference to the position taken by the EU. That said, there is no single work that discusses the EU position in all the levels of international cooperation on competition (i.e. unilateral, bilateral, plurilateral regional, and multilateral). The aim of this book is to observe and evaluate the role of the EU in the development of competition norms at all levels of international cooperation on competition, or put differently, to observe 'The International Dimension of EU Competition Law and Policy'.

In this debate over the development of international competition norms, the examination of the position of the European Union (EU) competition regime is focal, for a number of reasons: first, the regime has been applied for more than fifty years and is considered one of the most mature regimes in the world; secondly and even more importantly, competition law in the EU has been applied on a transnational level, since the EU itself is a regional bloc. As shown later in the book, in the context of this regional bloc, the law is enforced by a centralised regional institution which is the competent body to supervise the regional market and apply the rules in such a way so as to ensure that there is sufficient competition in this market. In this respect, competition law in the EU is applied on a regional level, and such application has an impact on the national markets of its Member States.

Thirdly, the EU has been particularly active in the negotiations of other international agreements which include competition law, and more generally in the process of internationalisation of competition law and policy. As indicated in the book, at least up until ten years ago, negotiations at the international level on competition law had to a certain extent been dominated by industrialised states, and the EU was certainly one of the protagonists in the debate. Furthermore, in the context mainly of its enlargement and its attempts to develop and contextualise its relation

and P. Holmes (1999), 'Competition Policy, Developing Countries and the WTO' 22(6) *The World Economy* 875. Nonetheless, these works are not focused on a particular developing country.

10 For instance, Szepesi has reviewed the competition provisions of the EU trade agreements. See S. Szepesi (2004), *Comparing EU Free Trade Agreements: Competition Policy and State Aid*, ECDPM InBrief 6E (ECDPM, Maastricht); and Damro has examined the way that the European Commission has reacted in the process of negotiation on competition at the WTO. See C. Damro (2006), 'The New Trade Politics and EU Competition Policy: Shopping for Convergence and Co-operation' 13(6) *Journal of European Public Policy* 867.

with its neighbouring countries, the EU has also been particularly active in the last twenty years in the conclusion of bilateral trade agreements, and all these agreements include competition provisions. Finally, being the first bloc to have applied a competition regime successfully, the EU both encourages the development of other similar settings and has been a model on which other similar agreements have been based.

In its attempt to review the position taken by the EU in the various levels of international cooperation on competition, and the development of international competition norms, the discussion carried out in the context of the book encompasses two main concepts: international agreements with competition elements, and the position taken by the EU in the formation of these agreements. As to the former, the book identifies and discusses four main types of agreements, which are further discussed in separate chapters of the book: bilateral and tripartite enforcement cooperation agreements; bilateral trade agreements with competition provisions; plurilateral regional trade agreements; and the negotiations over a possible multilateral agreement on competition. As to the latter, the EU will be the focus of the examination concerning these agreements. With the aim to understand the international dimension of the EU competition regime, the book attempts, first, to review the relevant agreements signed by the EU and, secondly, to observe the environment under which these agreements are negotiated and (where possible) applied in practice.

1.2 Structure of the book and method

Based on these considerations, the book is structured as follows.

Chapter 2 attempts to highlight some of the aspects of national competition laws and policies which may have an effect on the way that competition law and policy operates at the international level. In particular, the chapter includes the historical development of competition law and policy and makes reference to the various economic theories that may have an effect on the particular application of competition law. The chapter also discusses the relationship between competition policies and other national policies that may have an effect on its application, and endeavours to observe the way that competition law and sectoral regulations interact in a given territory of a nation. Finally, the chapter provides a discussion on economic globalisation and the way that this particular phenomenon has had an effect on the operation of competition law. In doing so, the chapter includes particular business practices that may have an effect on the territory of more than one state. In sum, the aim of this chapter is to draw attention to the main factors that have led to the existence of international cooperation between states on competition law and policy, which, in its turn, has led to the negotiation and adoption of international agreements on competition that are discussed in subsequent chapters of the book.

Chapter 3 analyses bilateral and tripartite enforcement cooperation agreements in the field of competition law and policy. Mainly based on the relevant agreements signed between the EU and the United States, the chapter looks at the legal nature and the provisions of the two generations of these agreements, and also attempts to illustrate the debate relating to their usefulness. In the context of this discussion, the chapter analyses the way in which the EU has used this particular legal instrument.

Chapter 4 also looks at bilateral agreements. In contrast to Chapter 3, it examines bilateral trade agreements that include competition law provisions. The analysis is focused on relevant agreements concluded between the EU and a number of countries; this analysis has a dual aim: first, to discuss the way in which competition law co-exists with other commercial policies included in the text of these agreements; and secondly, to evaluate EU policy regarding the use of this particular instrument.

Chapter 5 discusses plurilateral regional trade agreements which include competition provisions. Once more, the starting point of the analysis is the EU Treaty itself, which has been the most successful example of a plurilateral regional trade agreement. The chapter briefly introduces the main features of the EU competition regime and compares it with the competition regimes developed in other similar agreements in various parts of the world. In this context, the chapter also evaluates the role played by the EU in the development of competition regimes in other regional blocs.

Chapter 6 discusses the attempts to adopt a multilateral agreement on competition law and policy, and in particular, it discusses the EU as an actor in the context of these attempts. The discussion includes negotiations over a possible competition agreement in the General Agreement on Tariffs and Trade (GATT), and lately WTO, context, and examines also the alternative forms of multilateral cooperation, particularly the operation of the ICN.

Finally, Chapter 7 provides the overall findings of this study with regard to the development of international norms on competition and the role of the EU in the formation and, where relevant, application of these norms. The major finding with regard to the particular question that this book attempts to address is that depending on the particular category of agreements under examination, the role of the EU in the formation of such agreements varies.

The analysis carried out in the context of the book is doctrinal, in the sense that it is focused on the discussion of legal provisions, by analysing the texts of international agreements and court decisions, where relevant. The discussion is also informed by various theories borrowed from political science and economics. As McCrudden notes:

> much traditional doctrinal legal analysis now relaxes its view of the autonomy of law, drawing on economic and socio-legal insights increasingly easily.[11]

Competition law is one of the areas of law where this interaction of law and economics is clearly visible; hence the book takes into account economic theories in the context of the discussion of the particularities concerning the application of competition law on a national level. In addition, the process of creation of international rules encompasses various features and theories borrowed from the field of political and social science, and in this regard, the book also employs theories, such as policy networks, epistemic communities and isomorphism, to analyse the process of negotiation and final formation of international agreements, either dedicated to, or which include, competition law.

Three main research tools have been employed for the analysis of the theme of this book. These include a review of the relevant literature, which is carried out in the context of the discussion in the chapters which follow. Another analytical tool employed is that of interviews with academics, competition officials and practitioners, which supplement the primary literature. These discussions have been very informative, as they give a broad idea of what experts believe about the issues addressed in this book.[12] This information is further expanded by practical working experience with institutions which are involved in the application of competition norms.[13] Such experience has been of major importance in the context of research undertaken for this book, as it has provided insights regarding the way in which the political and legal issues relating to cooperation at the international level are addressed in practice.

[11] C. McCrudden (2006), 'Legal Research and the Social Sciences' 122 *Law Quarterly Review* 632, particularly at 635 and 644.

[12] In particular, twenty-two interviews were conducted, of which eleven were with EU officials, four with UK academics, two with EU practitioners, two with US practitioners, one with an UNCTAD official, one with a Brazilian official, and one with business representatives.

[13] Such experience includes a six-month internship with the International Affairs Unit of the European Commission's Directorate-General of Competition, and three years' work for the Greek Competition Commission, as the official in charge of international issues. The opinions expressed in the book are those of the author.

2

The National and International Dimensions of Competition Law and Policy

2.1 Origins of competition law

The first known restrictive trade agreement to be examined under common law by the English courts was *Dyer's Case* in 1414[1] where the court denied the collection of a bond for John Dyer's breach of his agreement not to 'use his art of dyer's craft within the town ... for half a year'.[2] Since then, and throughout the following decades, a number of cases were decided by the English courts, and this gradual development of competition-related jurisprudence created an environment in which judicial principles were transformed into statutes. It was England once again which went even further and adopted statutory rules related to restrictive business practices. The Statute of Monopolies[3] was adopted in 1624, following the 1602 decision in the *Darcy* v. *Allein* case,[4] in which the King's Bench unanimously held as void the sole right that Queen Elizabeth I granted to her groom Darcy to import playing cards into England.[5]

The main question the courts had to address was whether to declare as void any restrictive trade agreement for reasons relating to fairness of trade, or whether a distinction should be made between naked and ancillary (otherwise general and particular) restrictions to trade, where the former would be declared void de facto but the latter should be analysed in order to evaluate their positive and negative effects on the market and then a decision made as to their voidness. With the *Mitchel* v. *Reynolds*

1 (1414) 2 Hen. 5, 5 Pl. 26.

2 E. Gellhorn and W.E. Kovacic (1994), *Antitrust Law and Economics in a Nutshell* (West Publishing) 4. For a more elaborate analysis of the way that common law addressed agreements restrictive to trade see F.J. Goodnow (1897), 'Trade Combinations at Common Law' 12(2) *Political Science Quarterly* 212; M. Trebilcock (1986), *The Common Law of Restraint of Trade* (Toronto: Carswell), ch. 1.

3 21 Jac. 1, c.3.

4 (1602) 11 Co. Rep. 84b.

5 Gellhorn and Kovacic (1994), *supra* n. 2 at 10. See also M. Furse (2004), *Competition Law of the EC and the UK* (4th edn, Oxford University Press) 4–5.

decision in 1711,[6] the court upheld such ancillary restraints since these restraints were limited in time and restricted to a geographical place.[7]

Two further developments strengthened the domination of liberalism in England at that time and the consequent development of competition law. The first was the diffusion of the ideas of Adam Smith, who invented the concept of the market economy.[8] The second was the emergence and development of industrialisation. As Gerber puts it, industrialisation 'changed the unit of competition, replacing the individual artisan or group of artisans with salaried labourers and the organised unit of machine-based production'.[9] It also changed the competition process itself, replacing quality and dependability as keys of commercial success with the rationalisation of production: the main aim was to maximise production while minimising cost. A consequence of this phenomenon was that the size of a firm became increasingly important, in the sense that factories demanded increasingly larger organisations.[10]

These changes in the structure of society demanded a relevant response from the law and, thus, a number of statutes were enacted in continental Europe to regulate combinations by large companies which were restrictive to trade. In France, where the social revolution of 1789 was built upon the notion of freedom and its protection, the law of 14–17 June 1791, declared as unconstitutional, hostile to liberty and void agreements of members of the same trade that fixed the price of an industry or its labour.[11] Two main features of French society at the time led to the adoption of such a statute. The first was the belief that the political system should change in order to constrain the king and the government from wielding power according to their discretion. Those who inspired the revolution further believed that law would be the only way to control such power. In the same intellectual context, albeit later, the Austrian Penal Code of 1852, provided that

[6] (1711) 1 P. Wms. 181. See Gellhorn and Kovacic (1994), *supra* n. 2 at 5.

[7] On the development of the 'restraint of trade' doctrine, see S.B.T. (1966), 'Petrol Solus Agreements: British Common Law of Restraint of Trade in a New Context' 52(4) *Virginia Law Review* 690, at 697–702, where the author notes that by the beginning of the twentieth century agreements were only rarely declared void by the courts on the basis of the doctrine.

[8] See 2.2.1 *infra*.

[9] D. Gerber (2000), *Law and Competition in the Twentieth Century: Protecting Prometheus* (Oxford University Press) 22.

[10] *Ibid.*

[11] F. Walker (1905), 'The Law concerning Monopolistic Combinations in Continental Europe' 20(1) *Political Science Quarterly* 13, at 27. It has to be noted that industrial combinations were not per se prohibited. Only combinations injurious to the welfare of the community were prohibited. See *ibid.* at 39.

'agreements ... to raise the price of a commodity ... to the disadvantage of the public' should be punished as misdemeanours. A subsequent law of 7 April 1870 abolished the penalties but still declared such agreements to be void.[12]

Thus, the idea of excessive restriction of trade by dominant private firms and/or legal monopolists[13] was disseminated in some of the important trading countries of continental Europe throughout the eighteenth and nineteenth centuries. That said, there was no international consensus on whether business firms could restrict trade with their practices, or put differently, 'privatise public interest'.[14] In contrast with the examples given above, during this same period, German civil law clearly validated agreements between firms to raise prices.[15] On the other hand, the Depression which emerged in 1873 (the 'Panic of 1873') following the crash of the Vienna stock market, and which spread throughout Europe and the United States, altered once more the conception of the competitive process. Managed competition came to alter perceptions about liberalism in general and consequently ideas of free competition. Under huge pressure concerning prices and profits, firms had to cooperate by forming cartels in order to survive. As Gerber informs us, with the exception of Austria,[16] 'by the 1890s, cartels were considered "natural" parts of the economic landscape in many parts of the Continent'.[17]

2.1.1 Canada and the United States: first modern competition statutes to be enacted

In contrast to continental Europe, where towards the end of the nineteenth century the idea of competition was losing favour, Canada enacted in 1889[18] what is considered as the first competition-related

[12] *Ibid.* at 22 and 38.

[13] F. Braudel (1979), *The Wheels of Commerce: Civilization and Capitalism 15th–18th Century* (New York: Harper & Row) vol. 2, 445–55.

[14] R.A. Brady (1945), 'The Role of Cartels in the Current Cultural Crisis' 35(2) *American Economic Review* 312, at 314.

[15] Walker (1905), *supra* n. 11 at 38.

[16] Where in the 1890s there was a lively debate as to how the problem of cartels should be addressed, and relevant draft legislation was issued. See Gerber (2000), *supra* n. 9 at 54–60.

[17] *Ibid.* at 26.

[18] For an overview of the particular circumstances of the time that led to the enactment of the law, see M. Bliss (1991), 'The Yoke of the Trusts: A Comparison of Canada's Competitive Environment in 1889 and 1989' in R.S. Khemani and W.T. Stanbury (eds.), *Historical Perspectives on Canadian Competition Policy* (Halifax NS: The Institute for Research on

legislation of modern times: the Act for the Prevention and Suppression of Combinations formed in restraint of Trade.[19] More importantly, a year later, the most famous legal statute on competition law, the Sherman Act,[20] was enacted in the United States. The Act took its name from Senator Sherman who at the time expressed the opinion that the statute 'does not announce a new principle of law, but applies old and well recognised principles of common law'.[21] The adoption of the Sherman Act was a reaction to the prevailing domination of trusts. With the conclusion of the American Civil War, a number of changes occurred in the US market: rapid growth of the economy; an explosion of urban communities; the improvement of transportation and communications linked smaller communities; and new technologies enabled manufacturers to meet the increasing demands by exploiting economies of scale.[22] Nonetheless, in subsequent years declining economic growth and continuous entry by new competitors created major problems for big firms. Fixed costs were too high and, as it was very difficult for established firms to cease operation in order to avoid over-production, these firms were seeking ways to limit competition in the markets in which they operated. The solution was to cooperate with rivals in order to fix output, prices and market shares, initially in the form of pools, and when this proved insufficient, in the form of trusts.[23]

The trust phenomenon first appeared in railroads, the first business to experience the modern type of 'big business'.[24] Railroads were capital intensive. Capital requirements of railroad construction precluded competitive services to scarcely settled territories.[25] Given the absence of competition, railroads were able to discriminate on rates imposed and services provided to clients, and to destroy competitors through predation. Furthermore, a consequence of big business was the creation of trusts, which could become dominant in several markets. A typical example was the trust of the Standard Oil Company, which in the 1880s was controlling a number of markets, including fuel oil, sugar, lead and whiskey.[26]

Public Policy) 240–2; J. Benidickson (1993), 'The Combines Problem in Canadian Legal Thought' 43(4) *University of Toronto Law Journal* 799.

19 S.C. 1889, 52 Vic., c. 41.

20 15 U.S.C. paras. 1–7.

21 Quoted in Gellhorn and Kovacic (1994), *supra* n. 2 at 21.

22 E.M. Fox and L.A. Sullivan (1987), 'Antitrust – Retrospective Prospective: Where are We Coming From? Where are We Going?' 62 *New York University Law Review* 936, at 938.

23 *Ibid.* at 938–40.

24 At the time, in the United States as well as in the United Kingdom, railroads were privately owned. See A.D. Chandler (1977), *The Visible Hand: The Managerial Revolution in American Business* (Harvard University Press) 89–91.

25 Gellhorn and Kovacic (1994), *supra* n. 2 at 15.

26 *Ibid.* at 16.

This dominance in the US economy of what Rostow calls 'a tiny group of Titans'[27] led to furious complaints in the country, initially by farmers and subsequently by labourers and small entrepreneurs.[28] Given the vast number of citizens who were affected by these strategies of the big firms, the adoption of an Act which would attempt to mitigate the effects of this situation was among the priorities on the agenda of both major parties – hence the enactment of the Sherman Act in 1890.[29] What is noteworthy is that instead of opting for regulation that would allow the government to intervene extensively in markets and change their structure, Congress took as an assumption that the competitive market itself should be the principal regulator of price and output and of wages, interest and profits.[30]

The Sherman Act, itself also influenced by the common law restraint of trade doctrine,[31] contains two main prohibitions. Section 1 declares illegal 'Every contract, in the form of trust or otherwise, or conspiracy, in restraint of trade or commerce among the several States, or with foreign nations'. Section 2 prohibits monopolies or attempts to monopolise, and combinations or conspiracies to monopolise, any part of interstate or foreign trade. In the next twenty years, and amid considerable reactions by the business side that questioned the ability of the Sherman Act to follow the evolution of 'modern business',[32] courts started shaping the terms of the Act.[33]

Furthermore, in 1914, the Clayton Act was enacted, with specific provisions prohibiting exclusive dealing agreements, particular tying agreements and interlocking directorates, and mergers achieved by purchasing stock.[34] Since then, competition law (or antitrust law as it is termed in the United States) has developed enormously, becoming a central feature

[27] See E. Rostow (1960), 'British and American Experience with Legislation Against Restraints of Competition' 23(5) *Modern Law Review* 477, at 481–2.

[28] *Ibid.*

[29] For a detailed historical analysis of the events that led to the enactment of Sherman Act, see R.J.R. Peritz (1996), *Competition Policy in America, 1888–1992: History, Rhetoric, Law* (New York: Oxford University Press).

[30] See Rostow (1960), *supra* n. 27 at 482.

[31] According to the former Chairman of the Senate Judiciary Committee, G. Hoar, 'We have affirmed the old doctrine of the common law in regard to all interstate and international commercial transactions'. Quoted in W.F. Dana (1902), 'The Supreme Court and the Sherman Anti-Trust Act' 16(3) *Harvard Law Review* 178, at 180.

[32] For an early analysis of the provisions of Sherman Act, see V. Morawetz (1910), 'The Sherman Anti-trust Act' 11(1) *American Economic Association Quarterly* 321.

[33] W.E. Kovacic and C. Shapiro (2000), 'Antitrust Policy: A Century of Economic and Legal Thinking' 14(1) *Journal of Economic Perspectives* 43.

[34] See 15 U.S.C. para. 13.

in the development of the US economy and society and going through several stages of legislative interpretation in the process.[35]

By reviewing the origins and socio-political and economic values behind the development of US competition law and policy, Peritz has argued that the enforcement of competition law in the United States has been built around two (sometimes conflicting) notions of competition, the first being the expression of individual liberty, free of government intervention, and the other reflecting rough equality in the context of a competitive environment free of excessive economic power, and based on arguments of fair competition.[36] In either case, what characterises the application of US competition law (at least in the last seventy years) is the use of various economic theories which, depending on the particular preference of the US governments, have been used to support the particular enforcement agenda of US antitrust. Due mainly to this characteristic, along with its longevity and extended application by US courts and authorities, US antitrust is considered probably the most influential single national competition legislation in the world.[37]

2.1.2 Competition in the twentieth century in Europe

Back in Europe, ideas about competition which lost favour towards the end of the nineteenth century were once more considered in the interwar period, leading to the enactment of the first anti-cartel law in Germany in 1923, and later to such laws in Sweden (in 1925) and in Norway (in 1926).[38]

[35] For instance, Kovacic and Shapiro have identified the following five distinct periods in the development of US competition law. The first, 1890–1914, was where the courts slowly started applying the provisions of Sherman Act without a consistent economic analysis. The second period was from 1915 to 1936, where a rule-of-reason analysis was frequently used by the courts in competition cases. That said, this period was characterised by a lack of competition enforcement. The third period, 1936–1972, was dominated by the Structure-Conduct-Performance paradigm of the Harvard School. From 1973 to 1991, the enforcement of antitrust rules was based on the efficiency explanation for a number of phenomena, as the theories of the Chicago School were dominant in US government and courts. Finally, from 1992 to date, the authors argue that economic analysis in competition cases has been focused on game theory models. In addition antitrust enforcement has also been focused on innovation issues. See Kovacic and Shapiro (2000), *supra* n. 33. For a brief presentation on the main elements of the various economic theories which have dominated US antitrust thought for certain periods, see Appendix 1.

[36] Peritz (1996), *supra* n. 29 at 301.

[37] I. Maher (2004), 'Regulating Competition' in C. Parker, C. Scott, N. Lacey and J. Braithwaite (eds.), *Regulating Law* (Oxford University Press) 187, at 194.

[38] Gerber (2000), *supra* n. 9 at 115 and 155–8. The author also notes that in the 1930s a number of countries, including Czechoslovakia, Poland, Yugoslavia and Denmark, adopted

Nonetheless, the Great Depression of 1929 and the Second World War led to the disappearance of competition law in Europe.

Following the Second World War, the United Kingdom and Germany were the first European countries to adopt competition laws. Both countries adopted such laws under pressure from the United States, nevertheless it has been documented that the extent to which such pressure was the most important factor leading to the adoption of these rules varies. In particular, while in the case of the United Kingdom the adoption of competition law was a response to the need of the country to secure as much US aid as possible,[39] in Germany, the need for competition legislation had been debated since the 1920s, with the development of ordoliberalism (discussed in Appendix 1), and this development, along with pressure from the allies, equally contributed to the enactment of the German competition law in 1958.[40]

On a regional level, following the Second World War, and in particular in 1951, six European countries (France, Italy, Belgium, the Netherlands, Luxembourg and Germany), signed the European Coal and Steel Community (ECSC) agreement, whose main aim was to prevent Germany from re-establishing its dominance in the production of coal and steel. Only ten years previously this domination had contributed to the well-known detrimental effects of the Second World War.[41]

Competition law was included in the list of issues that the signing countries attempted to address with the conclusion of the ECSC Treaty. In particular, Article 65 banned cartels, while Article 66 included a provision on concentrations (i.e. mergers), and another on the abuse of a dominant position by firms. As Gerber argues, while the United States did not officially take part in the negotiations (since the negotiators wanted to avoid the danger that the project would be seen as US-controlled), it played at least a limited role, as it provided the drafters of the Treaty with basic ideas, with which nevertheless (with the exception of the merger-related provisions), they were already acquainted.[42]

some sort of competition law, which was nevertheless not used in practice, or its application was little known outside the borders of these countries. *Ibid.* at 163.

[39] *Ibid.* at 214.

[40] *Ibid.* at 268, where the author notes that by 1947 both the United States and the United Kingdom had in place competition laws which aimed at breaking up the German industrial 'giants'.

[41] G. Bebr (1953), 'The European Coal and Steel Community: A Political and Legal Innovation' 63 *Yale Law Journal* 1.

[42] See Gerber (2000), *supra* n. 9 at 342.

The most important element of the ECSC competition rules was that it was the first time in the relatively short history of competition law and policy that such rules were included in a plurilateral regional agreement. To this end, and despite the fact that the impact of the actual enforcement of the ECSC competition rules on the development of European competition law was limited,[43] the ECSC introduced the 'trans-European' model of competition law[44] and led to the inclusion a few years later of competition rules in the Treaty of Rome, which established the European Economic Community (EEC).

2.1.3 *The Treaty of Rome*

The Treaty of Rome (EC Treaty) was signed in March 1957, and in terms of competition it included a general provision which included the enactment of a competition law as one of the focal aims of the Community. Article 3(g) of the EC Treaty noted that these focal aims included: 'the institution of a system ensuring that competition in the common market is not distorted'.[45] Two other provisions were devoted to private anticompetitive practices. Article 85 prohibited anticompetitive agreements (but also provided a limited exemption in Article 85(3)) and Article 86 prohibited the abuse of a dominant position. Furthermore, and due to the fact that EC competition law was to be applied to the various EU Member States, two articles of the Treaty were devoted to practices conducted by governments, but which could have a substantial effect on competition in the region: Article 90 of the Treaty of Rome included provisions on public undertakings and Article 92 included provisions concerning state aids. Provisions relating to the control of mergers were not included in the Treaty, due to the failure of the founding Members of the Community to find a consensus on this issue. The system of competition in the EU is discussed in more detail in Chapter 5, in the context of the examination of plurilateral trade agreements which include competition, and the EU (international) competition policy will be the focal point of subsequent analysis of this study, in view of the principal topic that this book attempts to address.[46]

[43] *Ibid.* [44] *Ibid.* at 335.

[45] Following the Lisbon Treaty, under which the EC Treaty was redrafted (inter alia) as the Treaty on the Functioning of the EU (TFEU), Art. 3(g) was moved into Protocol No. 27.

[46] See 5.2 *infra*.

2.2 Expansion of competition law and policy worldwide, and factors that lead to varied application of competition law at the national level

In recent years, one after another, a number of states have embarked on the establishment of competition rules, as competition law and policy have been considered one of the most important mechanisms for the successful implementation of liberal national policies; in some cases, as argued in Chapters 4 and 5, particularly with regard to a number of developing countries, competition rules have been adopted in the context of the participation of these countries in bilateral or plurilateral trade agreements which include competition provisions. An updated compilation of the databases created by the University of Halle[47] and the International Bar Association (IBA)[48] (which include the national statutes on competition enacted up to 2005) with the database of the World Bank (which includes all the countries with a population exceeding 80,000 people, and the level of the income of such countries),[49] provides us with useful statistics regarding the expansion of competition rules, and noteworthy observations as to the identity of countries that have adopted such rules. By 2008, 111 countries, accounting for more than 50 per cent of countries with a population exceeding 80,000 people, had competition rules in place.

As Table 2.1 illustrates, 81 of these 111 countries adopted their competition law in the last twenty years. The collapse of the Soviet Union, as well as the expansion of the EU, has definitely had an impact on the increase in the number of countries adopting competition rules.[50] On the other hand, only 21 out of the 111 countries with competition rules had these rules in place thirty years ago. This list includes the United States, Canada, Australia, Germany and the United Kingdom,[51] and some other

[47] This work has been carried out by Franz Kronthaler and Johannes Stephan, in the context of the EU Sixth Framework Programme STREP project 'Competition Policy Foundations for Trade Reform, Regulatory Reform, and Sustainable Development', available at www.iwh-halle.de/projects/competition_policy/db/index.asp (last visited on 2 December 2009).

[48] See www.globalcompetitionforum.org (last visited on 2 December 2009).

[49] See the Classification of Countries on the World Bank website at http://web.worldbank.org (last visited on 2 December 2009).

[50] This argument is based on the discussion in Chapter 4 where it is shown that following the collapse of the Soviet Union, the EU signed a number of agreements with former Soviet Union states and countries which had until then communist regimes in place. In this context such countries adopted competition rules.

[51] Which nevertheless adopted a prohibition model only in 1998 with the enactment of the Competition Act. See D. Morris (2003), 'Dominant Firm Behaviour under UK

Table 2.1 *Adoption of competition rules by decade*

Period	1889–1900	1901–1910	1911–1920	1921*–1930	1931–1940	1941–1950	1951–1960	1961–1970	1971–1980	1981–1990	1991–2000	2001–2008	TOTAL
No. of countries that adopted competition	2	—	—	—	—	3	5	4	7	9	63	18	111

* As noted above, Germany and Sweden adopted some sort of competition rules in the 1920s and another four countries in the 1930s, nonetheless these laws were of little use and therefore Table 2.1 takes into account the date of the adoption of 'modern' competition legislation by these countries.

EU Member States. It also includes India, Pakistan and Chile, where nevertheless competition rules have only recently been used in practice. In addition, as noted in the following chapters, in particular in Chapter 6, in a number of other countries, mainly developing, even though competition law has been adopted, this law has not been applied to date. In any case, these statistics may safely lead us to the conclusion that in most of the countries which have adopted competition legislation courts have not had the time to review many competition cases, relevant academia has not had the time to examine and develop competition-related principles, and agencies have not had much time to apply competition policy widely.

Consequently, the current development of competition law and policy, both in terms of academic literature and in terms of their practical application, has to a great extent taken place in large industrialised countries, which, with greater resources, expertise and longevity, remain an influence and model for new regimes. On the other hand, the development of competition law and policy even in these countries has shown that there is diversity in the way that competition law has been applied at a national level.

This is not to say that there is total disagreement as to the proper content and function of competition law, since most of the industrialised countries accept that provisions on cartels, abuse of dominance, and some sort of merger control should be included in their national legislation. Nevertheless, as the next section argues, on several occasions the understanding about the proper evaluation of particular practices varies, and moreover, there is no universal agreement as to the scope of competition law, in view of the fact that several sectors of national economies are regulated by sector-specific regulations and not competition.

With the increase in the number of anticompetitive practices (discussed in section 3) that may have an effect on multiple national markets, this variety in the application of national competition rules may lead to conflicts in cases where more than one national authority claim jurisdiction over a practice and apply different standards on the evaluation of this particular practice.[52] From a more theoretical perspective, in the context of internationalisation of competition, the discussion over the factors that lead to diverse application of competition rules is of significant importance, and this importance derives from the fact that, as the section notes,

Competition Law', paper presented to the Fordham Corporate Law Institute Thirtieth Annual Conference on International Antitrust Law and Policy, New York City, 23–24 October 2003, at 3–8, available at www.competition-commission.org.uk/our_peop/members/chair_speeches/pdf/fordham2003.pdf (last visited on 2 December 2009).

[52] See e.g, the brief reference to the GE/Honeywell case *infra*.

competition law and policy operate in complex economic, socio-political and legal environments of a given country. Accordingly, negotiations at the international level are rarely exclusively dedicated to competition law. In fact, only bilateral enforcement cooperation agreements (discussed in Chapter 3) are solely focused on competition matters. In all other forms of agreements and prospective agreements, competition is only one of the subjects under negotiation. Throughout the next chapters, this observation will become more obvious, both with regard to the examination of bilateral and plurilateral trade agreements which include competition provisions and, in particular, with regard to the negotiation of a multilateral competition law. Hence, the way in and extent to which competition law and policy operate at a national level is indicative of whether it is considered as a priority by particular states when they negotiate an international trade-related agreement which includes competition provisions.

On the other hand, this diversity in approaches regarding the proper application of competition law may also be seen as a process in which the various ideas about the nature and aims of competition law and policy are exchanged, and the economic, social, legal and political standards according to which national competition laws apply are observed. While it is not intended here to review in detail the different aspects of this process, the chapter identifies four main factors which lead to such a varied application of competition, which in turn become the subject matter of discourse at the international level.

The first one relates to economics and to the fact that a number of sometimes divergent theories have been used to apply the competition-related rules. The second one relates to the fact that certain sectors of national economies are regulated by sectoral regulation and not competition, and such sectors vary from country to country. The third factor is political and has to do with the relationship between competition law and policy and other national policies, which sometimes may have a scope divergent from that of competition law and policy. Finally, the fourth factor is cultural and relates to the social structure and traditions of particular national societies that have an effect on the way that competition law is applied in these countries.

2.2.1 Influence of economics in the application of national competition rules

Probably the most important feature in the application of competition law and policy, at least with regard to industrialised countries such as the

United States and the EU, is the role of economics in the evaluation of particular business behaviour and its effect on the market. Competition has been very much the work of economists (Adam Smith being the intellectual leader), and economic analysis has been of major influence in the application of competition rules ever since.[53] The particular role of economics in competition law is to define the market in which a practice under examination has taken place, as well as the possible effects that this practice may have had on this market.[54]

This is not always an easy task, especially with regard to the evaluation of the effect that alleged anticompetitive practices may have on the market. The main difficulty with the application of economic theories in the field of competition law is that they cannot define *ex ante* the ability of firms to compete with their competitors in a given market. What economic theories are able to do is to provide us with tools to define, measure and evaluate *ex post* the effects of a particular market structure or the effects of a particular practice or strategy by a firm related to prices, outputs, profits and efficiency.[55] Economic theories and models are based on and around assumptions. These assumptions by definition do not cover (all) real world situations. Additionally, when the assumptions are changed the outcomes of the models may look strikingly different, changing for example the price from a monopoly level to a competitive price level.[56] Hence, by definition, economic thinking and economic models are not always perfect guides as to what will be the future effect of a practice (vertical restraint,

53 The first antimonopoly legal instrument which received attention from economists was the 1824 repeal of the Combination Acts of 1799 and 1800, which forbade either employers or employees to influence the wage bargain. Informed by the theories developed by Adam Smith, J.R. McCulloch wrote in strong support of the repeal of the Act, stressing the necessity of an active antimonopoly programme. See G. Stigler (1982), 'The Economists and the Problem of Monopoly' 72(2) *American Economic Review* 1, at 2.

54 See Maher (2004), *supra* n. 37 at 196, where the author also notes that the inadequacy of economics to answer whether a particular conduct is anticompetitive stems from the fact that in such a situation 'competition law is not purely technocratic in nature but raises political issues such as the balancing of public and private (economic) power where competition law acts as a bridge'. In this respect, competition law encompasses legal, economic and political elements.

55 P. Nicolaides (2000), 'An Essay on Economics and the Competition Law of the European Community' 27 *Legal Issues of Economic Integration* 7, at 10.

56 This inability of economics to provide valuable predictions as to the way that markets will operate (i.e. whether a practice by a firm will distort the competitive process) has generated criticism in the relevant literature. It is indicative that as early as 1912, scholars had declared that 'The fundamental reason why nothing has been done ... with reference to improving the antitrust situation, is that there has never been any consistent or satisfactory course which seemed available. On most subjects, at least two distinct

merger, etc.) under examination on the markets. Furthermore, different economic theories may lead to different outcomes when evaluating whether a practice is anticompetitive or not.

In this regard, Appendix 1 briefly reviews the main economic schools and theories that have been used in the analysis of competition cases. It shows that economic theories change over time; therefore the approach to law changes within a system and the way that competition law has been applied even in the biggest economies with commitment to competition is diverse. For instance, as noted above,[57] even in the United States, which is the country with the most mature competition law in the world, five distinct periods of application of competition law may be identified, with at least the last three of them having been influenced by different schools of economic thought.[58]

In fact, in the field of competition law and policy, and more generally, in the field of broader economic policy, the choice of one economic theory or the other as more appropriate also relates to an extent to the ideology one holds about society. As Page notes,[59] there are two competing ideologies that have an effect on the formation of economic policy in general and subsequently competition policy: the evolutionary and the intentional visions. These two ideologies have dominated western culture since the eighteenth century and have an important effect on the economic theories that have been applied to competition law and policy.

According to the *evolutionary vision*, the individual is intellectually limited, motivated by self-interest, or the interest of his household, rather than the interest of the society in general.[60] In social contexts, like the market, individuals form voluntary relationships and contracts based on their self-interest. Thus, the pattern of these relationships is not the

policies are contending for supremacy'. See H. Parker Willis (1912), 'Political Obstacles to Anti-Trust Legislation' 20(6) *Journal of Political Economy* 588. Along the same lines, and some eighty-seven years later, Hughes argued that 'If economics is a science, then economic behaviour must be predictable. All individuals, whatever their background or idiosyncrasies, must respond in the same way to the same economic stimuli. If we know the factors that they must take into account, then we will be able to predict their actions with certainty': E.J. Hughes (1999), 'The Left Side of Antitrust. What Fairness Means and Why it Matters' 77 *Marquette Law Review* 265, at 280.

57 See Kovacic and Shapiro (2000), *supra* n. 33.

58 Harvard School, Chicago School and game theory. See Kovacic and Shapiro, *supra* n. 33 and Appendix 1.

59 W.H. Page (1991), 'Ideological Conflict and the Origins of Antitrust Policy' 66 *Tulane Law Review* 3.

60 R.H. Coase (1979), 'Adam Smith's View of Man' 19 *Journal of Law and Economics* 529, at 534.

result of anyone's plan but the outcome of countless such relationships. Accordingly markets reflect the accumulated preferences of producers and consumers, and thus only the most preferred and most effective patterns will succeed. It follows that a monopoly situation can only occur if government has intervened and created it, since, in the first place, it is not possible for the single will of an individual to create it, and even if that happens, then the market will create self-correcting mechanisms, which would break down this monopoly.

Given the limited intellectual ability of individuals (including those who govern), it is not possible to understand the reasons that led to a specific contract pattern or in a market situation in general. Thus, according to the evolutionary vision, the role of the government should be negative: to protect the process of mutual exchange by setting rules of general application to prevent the use of force and fraud and make sure that the agreements are applied. With regard to monopolies, governments should only remove governmental impediments to entry, such as tariffs and exclusive licences.[61]

In contrast, according to the *intentional vision*, individuals are not motivated by self-interest nor intellectually limited. They will normally act to benefit others. Nonetheless, either corrupted individuals with great power, or disparities in access to information and decisional errors may prevent markets from revealing the true preferences of societies.[62] It follows that according to the intentional view, governments have to intervene in such anomalies (like monopolies) in order to correct false outcomes by restructuring society in accordance with the rational plan.

This analysis merely validates the assumption that as regards economic, political and social sciences there are almost always two or more theories providing one with alternative options as to the proper analysis of a particular issue. In the context of the discussion about competing economic theories that may have an influence on the application of competition law and policy, it has been shown that these theories provide one with guidance as to when the state has to intervene in the market and correct possible anomalies, but that they also create inconsistencies as they may lead to different outcomes concerning the examination of similar, or even identical, practices.

The impact of economics on the particular and sometimes varied application of national competition rules may also be observed in the well-documented divergence as to the way the EU competition rules have been

[61] Page (1991), *supra* n. 59 at 12–14. [62] *Ibid.* at 13.

applied compared to the US rules. This divergence has mainly occurred because of the influence of ordoliberalism on the enforcement of EU competition law, and the market integration goal, which has been the primary economic goal of the European Union.

In particular, as is noted in Appendix 1, according to the ordoliberal school of thought, analysis of restrictive business practices should be focused on whether such practices may reduce the opportunity of other competitors to compete (put differently, reduce their economic and political freedom). In this regard, as opposed to US competition law enforcement,[63] the extent to which these practices have an effect on overall societal efficiency has been on many occasions of secondary importance in the EU.[64]

This trend has been observed in the application of competition rules in the EU on vertical restraints, where the European Commission has been allegedly over-focused on the protection of competitors, rather than protection of competition and efficiency.[65] It should also be mentioned, nevertheless, that the stricter approach followed by the EU in the field of vertical restraints has to a significant extent been attributed to the accomplishment of the single market, which has been one of the major objectives of the Union.[66] In particular, vertical agreements that offer absolute territorial protection to the distributors have been treated by EC competition law as restricting competition by object,[67] since such restrictions could isolate national markets and therefore erect barriers to trade between the Member States.[68] That said, the divergence seems to be decreasing in recent years, with the adoption of the 1999 block exemption (further amended in 2010)[69]

[63] At least following the dominance of the Chicago School.

[64] See UNCTAD (2005), *Exclusionary Anti-competitive Practices: Their Effects on Competition and Development*, UNCTAD/DITC/CLP/2005/4, 100–2; E.M. Fox (2003), 'Antitrust and Regulatory Federalism: Races Up, Down, and Sideways' 75 *New York University Law Review* 1781, at 1785.

[65] B. Hawk (1995), 'System Failure: Vertical Restraints and EC Competition Law' 32 *Common Market Law Review* 973; W. Commanor and P. Rey (1997), 'Competition Policy Towards Vertical Restraints in Europe and the United States' 24 *Empirica* 37.

[66] Article 2 of the EC Treaty.

[67] See Joined Cases 56 and 58/64 *Etablissements Consten SA and Grundig-Verkaufs-GmbH* v. *Commission* [1966] ECR 299.

[68] A. Jones and B. Sufrin (2004), *EC Competition Law: Text, Cases and Materials* (Oxford University Press) 618–19.

[69] Commission Regulation (EC) 2790/1999 of 22 December 1999 on the application of Article 81(3) of the Treaty to categories of vertical agreements and concerted practices [1999] OJ L336/21. On the reform of the EU policy on vertical restraints, see R. Subbioto and F. Amato (2002), 'Reform of the European Competition Policy Concerning Vertical

and the far more rigorous enforcement by the European Commission on cartel cases.[70]

Likewise, in the last five years there has been convergence in the area of mergers, where, as shown below, serious conflicts have arisen between the EU and the United States in recent years.[71] Such convergence was impelled to a certain extent by the Court of First Instance (CFI, now General Court), which first questioned the depth of economic analysis by the Commission on three mergers and annulled the relevant Commission's decisions.[72] In response, the Merger Regulation was amended in 2004 and requires one, in the context of the examination of a merger, to examine whether this commercial deal 'would significantly impede effective competition, in the common market or a substantial part of it' and therefore evaluate whether a particular merger may have an anticompetitive effect on the market, in addition to the 'dominance test', which was exclusively applied until the entry into force of Regulation (EC) 139/2004. It is considered that the amendment of the Merger Regulation and the introduction of the new test was a move by the Commission towards a more economic-based analysis in merger cases, and closer to the policy followed by the United States.[73]

In a broader context, the introduction of more robust economic analysis in the examination of competition cases has been one of the primary aims of former Commissioner for Competition Mario Monti, an economist, and economic analysis now plays a much more important role in the application of competition rules in the EU. The appointment of a Chief Economist at the European Commission is also a strong indication that

Restraints' 69(1) i 147; P. Dobson (2005), *Vertical Restraints Policy Reform in the European Union and United Kingdom*, Loughborough University Research Series Paper No. 2005:2. It is further noted that the European Commission is currently in the process of amending Regulation 2790/1999, which expired in May 2010 and was replaced by Regulation (EU) 330/2010 of 20 April 2010 [2010] OJ L102/3.

70 N. Kroes (2005), 'The First Hundred Days', speech delivered at the Fortieth Anniversary of the Studienvereinigung Kartellrecht 1965–2005, International Forum on European Competition Law, Brussels, 7 April 2005, speech 05/205.

71 See the Boeing/MDD and GE/Honeywell cases discussed at 2.2.1 *infra*.

72 See Case T-310 *Schneider Electric SA* v. *Commission* [2002] ECR II-4071; Case T-342/99 *Airtours plc* v. *Commission* [2002] ECR II-2585; Case T-5/02 *Tetra Laval BV* v. *Commission* [2002] ECR II-4381.

73 See Y. Akbar and G. Suder (2006), 'The New EU Merger Regulation: Implications for EU–US Merger Strategies' 48(5) *Thunderbird International Business Review* 667, in particular at 673–5. In addition, the European Commission issued more economic-based guidelines on horizontal mergers. Commission (EC) Guidelines on the assessment of horizontal mergers under the Council Regulation on the control of concentrations between undertakings [2004] OJ C31/5.

economic analysis is becoming more influential in Brussels,[74] and in this regard, it has been noted that EU law has converged with the relevant US law.

That said, such convergence has not been achieved in the area of unilateral conduct, called abuse of a dominant position by a firm (in the EU), or monopolisation (in the United States).[75] In the United States, the relevant case law takes the view that only rarely should section 2 of the Sherman Act apply, since, on the basis of the principles developed by the Chicago School,[76] what a dominant firm does is almost always rational and good for the market, while even in cases where the dominant firm acts irrationally, the market itself has the inherent ability to correct any anomalies and therefore the role of the enforcement agencies should be minimal.[77]

In the EU, former Commissioner Kroes has stated that '[A]rticle 82 [EC] enforcement should focus on real competition problems: in other

[74] M. Monti (2004), 'A Reformed Competition Policy: Achievements and Challenges for the Future', speech delivered at the Center for European Reform, Brussels, 28 October 2004, speech 04/477; N. Levy (2005), 'Mario Monti's Legacy in EC Merger Control' 1(1) *Competition Policy International* 99.

[75] H. Pate (2004), 'Antitrust in a Transatlantic Context: From the Cicada's Perspective', speech delivered at Antitrust in a Transatlantic Context Conference, Brussels, Belgium, 7 June 2004, available at www.usdoj.gov/atr/public/speeches/203973.pdf (last visited on 2 December 2009); J. Vickers (2005), 'Abuse of Market Power' 115 *Economic Journal* 244; M. Motta and A. De Streel (2003), 'Exploitative and Exclusionary Excessive Prices in EU Law' in C.-D. Elerman and I. Atanasiu, *European Competition Law Annual 2003: What is an Abuse of a Dominant Position?* (Hart Publishing); J. Kallaugher and B. Sher (2004), 'Rebates Revisited: Anti-competitive Effects and Exclusionary Abuse under Article 82' 25(5) *European Competition Law Review* 263, and particularly at 268–72 where the authors discuss ordoliberalism and its influence on EU policy.

[76] See Appendix 1.

[77] See E. Fox (2006), 'Monopolization, Abuse of Dominance and the Indeterminacy of Economics: The US/EU Divide' *Utah Law Review* 725, at 728. See also J.T. Rosch (2007), 'I Say Monopoly, You say Dominance: The Continuing Divide on the Treatment of Dominant Firms, is It the Economics?', speech delivered at the International Bar Association Antitrust Section Conference, Florence, Italy, 8 September 2007, at 5–10, available at www.ftc.gov/speeches/rosch/070908isaymonopolyiba.pdf (last visited on 2 December 2009). It has to be noted that this has been a theme that has recently created serious disagreement even between the two US enforcement bodies, i.e. the Department of Justice (DoJ) and the Federal Trade Commission (FTC). In particular, in September 2008, the DoJ issued a Report on *Competition and Monopoly: Single Firm Conduct under Section 2 of the Sherman Act* in which it repeated the position taken by US authorities and courts that s. 2 of the Sherman Act was in practice to be applied against dominant firms only in exceptional cases (see www.justice.gov/atr/public/reports/236681.pdf). Despite the fact that the FTC participated in the hearings leading to the drafting of the report, the majority of the FTC Commissioners (in particular Commisioners Harbour, Leibowitz and Rosch) issued a statement in which they expressed their disagreement with the DoJ Report and noted that the Report would lead to weakening of

words, behaviour that has actual or likely restrictive effects on the market',[78] therefore opening the door for more robust application of economic analysis in Article 102 TFEU cases, something which is also noted in the 2005 Discussion Paper on the application of Article 82, which notes that 'the essential objective of Article 82 when analysing exclusionary conduct is the protection of competition on the market as a means of enhancing consumer welfare and of ensuring an efficient allocation of resources'.[79] Nevertheless, in contrast to its position under US law, according to the relevant case law of the European Commission and the EU courts on abuse of dominance cases, the dominant firm has a special responsibility to ensure that its conduct does not weaken competition in the common market, and therefore EU competition law, as evolved in the last fifty years, also looks at the structure and openness of the market when it reviews relevant cases.[80] To this end, the application of EU competition

the enforcement in monopolisation cases since it 'erects a multi-layered protective screen for firms with monopoly or near-monopoly power' (see FTC (2008), 'Statement of Commissioners Harbour, Leibowitz and Rosch on the Issuance of the Section 2 Report by the Department of Justice', available at www.ftc.gov/os/2008/09/080908section2stmt.pdf). As a consequence, the DoJ recently withdrew the Report, with Assistant Attorney General Christine Varney stating that 'Withdrawing the Section 2 report is a shift in philosophy and the clearest way to let everyone know that the Antitrust Division will be aggressively pursuing cases where monopolists try to use their dominance in the marketplace to stifle competition and harm consumers'. See DoJ, 'Justice Department withdraws Report on Antitrust Monopoly Law: Antitrust Division to apply more rigorous standard with focus on the impact of exclusionary conduct on consumers', Press Release of 11 May 2009. While these developments clearly show that there are voices requiring more active enforcement of s. 2 of the Sherman Act, it would be premature to take the position at this stage that the overall policy of the US authorities with regard to monopolisation will change in the short term.

78 See N. Kroes (2005), 'Preliminary Thought of Policy Review on Article 82', speech delivered at the Fordham Corporate Law Institute, 23 September 2005, speech 05/537, at 2.

79 European Commission (2005), *Discussion Paper on the Application of Article 82 of the EC Treaty to Exclusionary Abuses*, public consultation document, para. 53. In a similar manner, the Commission more recently stated that 'The aim of the Commission's enforcement activity in relation to exclusionary conduct is to ensure that dominant undertakings do not impair effective competition by foreclosing their competitors in an anticompetitive way, thus having an adverse impact on consumer welfare'. See European Commission (2008), *Guidance on the Commission's Enforcement Priorities in Applying Article 82 of the EC Treaty to Abusive Exclusionary Conduct by Dominant Undertakings*, C(2009)864 final, para. 19.

80 See Fox (2006), *supra* n. 77 at 728; see V. Mertikopoulou (2007), 'DG Competition's Discussion Paper on the Application of Article 82 of the EC Treaty to Exclusionary Abuses: The Proposed Economic Reform from a Legal Point of View' 28(4) *European Competition Law Review* 241. Both authors argue that despite the fact that the Discussion Paper introduces a more economic-based approach regarding the application of Article 82 EC, the relevant case law of the courts should and will continue to take into account the

law in abuse of dominance cases differs from the relevant US practice,[81] and in simple terms, it means that the Commission may continue being more aggressive in the enforcement of competition law on practices conducted by dominant firms than the US authorities and courts.

2.2.2 Legal aspect of competition law: competition law versus sectoral regulation

While the previous subsection has attempted to highlight the extent to which different economic analyses may have an effect on the particular application of competition law, this one briefly introduces the debate over the relationship between competition law and sectoral regulation, with the aim of describing the extent to which competition law regulates national markets. Put differently, the aim of this brief analysis is to highlight the fact that competition law is only one of the legal tools employed by countries to regulate their internal trade conducted by private firms. On the other hand, several sectors of the economy of industrialised countries with mature competition systems are even exempted from the application of competition rules and are regulated by sectoral regulation, instead of competition law. An Organisation for Economic Cooperation and Development (OECD) study has explored such sectors in a number of OECD member states and found that sectoral regulation is common in industrialised countries (members of the OECD) in sectors like media, services, infrastructure, transport and energy. Even more rigid regulation, which sometimes excludes the operation of competition law, is usually applied in sectors such as agriculture, health and employment.[82]

On the theoretical side, the main difference between competition law and sectoral regulation is the following: competition law is based on the presumption that markets generally work well and that operational decisions should be left to the firms involved in the markets. It is therefore concerned with the dispersal and decentralisation of public and private power. On the opposite side, regulation follows the assumption that there

openness and structure of the market factors. See also L. Gormsen-Lovdahl (2010), 'Why the European Commission's Enforcement Priorities on Article 82 Should be Withdrawn' 31(2) *European Competition Law Review* 45, in which the author further notes that the Commission has attempted, by using the form of guidelines, i.e. a soft law instrument, to circumvent case law, and that in this context, by using such a soft law instrument it has acted outside its remit by going beyond the law set by the courts.

[81] See also Rosch (2007), *supra* n. 77.

[82] OECD (2004), *Regulating Market Activities by Public Sector*, OECD Competition Committee, DAF/COMP(2004)36.

is a need for direct or indirect government supervision of the markets; this argument is based on a number of alternative and sometimes overlapping theoretical and practical justifications.[83]

A first such justification is the concept of *market failure*, a situation where markets may not work due to a number of reasons that cannot be addressed by competition law in its narrow sense. For instance, with regard to public goods, such as national defence, public education or lighthouses, the government must assume responsibility for the production of the goods and recover its expenses through the tax base.[84] Another example of market failure is that of natural monopolies, i.e. a situation where due to economies of scale or scope, only one firm can survive.[85] Market failure could also occur in cases where asymmetries of information may enable incumbent suppliers to exploit consumers, either by using these asymmetries to persuade consumers to buy at excessive prices or by creating too high barriers to entry and thus putting themselves in a dominant position in the market. These issues are addressed by consumer protection rules such as labelling, product liability, product safety and deceptive marketing laws.[86] Finally, market failure could occur due to externalities, that is situations where 'the costs and benefits of producing

[83] For instance Prosser argues that there can be 'no single model or objective for utilities regulation'. In other words he suggests that competition cannot replace the complex web of acts and initiatives exercised by the sectoral regulator. T. Prosser (1997), *Law and the Regulators* (New York: Oxford University Press) 4; on the role of regulation in general see R. Baldwin and M. Cave (1999), *Understanding Regulation: Theory, Strategy and Practice* (New York: Oxford University Press). On the role of regulation in various sectors of the economy, see G. Amato and L. Laudati (eds.) (2001), *The Anticompetitive Impact of Regulation* (Edward Elgar Publishing); on energy see M. Albers (2002), 'Energy Liberalisation and EC Competition Law' 25 *Fordham International Law Journal* 909; on postal services, see OECD (2001), 'Promoting Competition in Postal Services' 3(1) *OECD Journal of Competition Law and Policy* 7; on pharmaceuticals, see P. Danzon and Li-Wei Chao (2000), 'Does Regulation Drive Out Competition in Pharmaceutical Markets?' XLIII *Journal of Law and Economics* 311; on air transport, see R. Abeyratne (2001), 'Competition and Liberalisation in Air Transport' 24(4) *World Competition* 607. It should be pointed out nevertheless that the dichotomy between regulation and competition has been questioned in recent years, on the basis that competition law itself may be considered as a form of regulation. See Maher (2004), *supra* n. 37 at 288–9.

[84] P.S. Crampton and B.A. Facey (2002), 'Revisiting Regulation and Deregulation through the Lens of Competition Policy' 25(1) *World Competition* 25, at 32.

[85] Typical examples of natural monopolies were telecommunications, water and natural gas. Nonetheless, with the improvements in technology and the globalisation of markets, traditional natural monopolies (like telecommunications or electricity production and retailing) have been opened up to competition in a number of countries.

[86] Crampton and Facey (2002), *supra* n. 84 at 33; particularly on the EU, see S. Weatherill (2005), *EU Consumer Law and Policy* (Edward Elgar Publishing).

and consuming certain products, are not fully considered or internalized in the production and consumption calculus'.[87]

A second justification for the use of regulation instead of competition law is special interest-based regulation, which occurs on occasions where special interest groups manage to influence the government and secure the adoption of legislation harmful for the average consumer and detrimental to the economy in general.[88] Crampton and Facey provide us with a number of examples of such regulations: supply management schemes (broadly used in agriculture), labour codes, investment and procurement laws, licensing regimes, and foreign ownership restrictions.[89]

Discussing the relationship between competition and regulation, Baldwin and Cave divide competition transition into three phases. The first phase, called the pre-competition phase, refers to those markets where competition has not been used or is just emerging and regulation is used in order to prohibit monopolistic activities by dominant firms.[90] The second phase is that of emerging competitive markets, where regulation (i.e. price regulation) can still exist for the settlement of the remaining monopolistic firms and at the same time competition policy can be used for the competitive parts of the market. Finally in the third phase, fully competitive markets will not need economic regulation and general rules of competition policy can completely control the market.[91] According to this idea, each market should be regulated (by using sectoral regulation, the combination of the former with competition policy or, finally, just competition rules) depending on which phase of transition it is in. [92]

The figures in Table 2.1 clearly show that almost half of the countries with a population exceeding 80,000 people have not yet adopted

[87] Crampton and Facey (2002), *supra* n. 84 at 33–4. A typical example of such a situation is environmental legislation. Another example is supply network externalities, that is a situation where the cost of providing services to additional consumers reduces the total cost of the network. The dominance of Microsoft Windows operating system over the one provided by Apple is a typical example.

[88] G. Stigler (1971), 'The Theory of Economic Regulation' 2(1) *Bell Journal of Economics and Management* 1.

[89] Crampton and Facey (2002), *supra* n. 84 at 35.

[90] See e.g., the Greek experience in OECD (2002), 'Regulatory Reform for Greece' 3(4) *OECD Journal of Competition Law and Policy* 7.

[91] Nevertheless, this distinction is not always an absolute one in practice, since in terms of competition law the enforcement role of competition agencies includes the element of public interference. See Maher (2004), *supra* n. 37 at 204–5.

[92] Baldwin and Cave (1999), *supra* n. 83 at 222–3; see also J. Jordana and D. Levi-Faur (2004), 'The Politics of Regulation in the Age of Governance' in J. Jordana and

competition rules and consequently their markets are in a pre-competitive phase. In addition, competition law has been adopted by 73 per cent of the countries with such law in the last eighteen years. Thus, at least three-quarters of the countries with a competition regime are either in the first phase (pre-competitive phase) or in the second phase (emerging competitive markets). These observations lead us to two main conclusions. First, that on a national level economic activity is regulated much more by sectoral regulation rather than by competition law. Secondly, and most importantly, at the international level differences in national sector-specific regulations can have an effect on the ability of foreign firms to enter a market.[93]

It could be argued that there is a mounting perception that national economic regulations should be framed in such a way so as to allow as much market competition as is politically and socially acceptable.[94] Still, the adoption of common regulatory standards in several sectors of the economy (such as telecommunications, energy, pharmaceuticals and agriculture) has been a priority on the agenda of nations when they negotiate at the international organisations, and more relevantly to the present discussion, there is an ongoing discourse at the international level as to the role of competition policy in the adoption and application of sectoral regulation.[95]

D. Levi-Faur (eds.), *The Policy of Regulation: Institutions and Regulatory Reforms for the Age of Governance* (Edward Elgar Publishing) ch. 1; W. Moschel (2002), 'The Relationship between Competition Authorities and Sector Specific Regulators' in D. Tzouganatos (ed.), *EU Competition Law and Policy: Developments and Priorities, Proceedings from Athens Conference, 19 April 2002* (Nomiki Vivliothiki SA) 19. Further problems may arise in the context of the delineation of competences between the sectoral regulator and the competition authorities. See E. Truli (2009), 'Competition in the Telecommunications Sector: Delineation of Competences Between the NCA and the NRA – the Example of Greece' 8 *Competition in the Telecommunications Sector* 188.

93 S. Ostry (1995), 'New Dimensions for Market Access: Challenges for the Trading System' in OECD, *New Dimensions in Market Access in a Globalising World Economy* (Paris: OECD) 25, at 26.

94 F. Jenny (2001), 'Globalisation, Competition and Trade Policy: Convergence, Divergence and Cooperation' in Yang-Ching Chao, Gee San, Chang Fa Lo and Jiming Ho (eds.), *International and Comparative Competition Law and Policies* (Kluwer Law International) 34–5.

95 For instance, in the case of telecommunications, the relationship between competition policy and sector-specific regulation is an issue discussed under the auspices of the ICN, the OECD and the WTO, while the General Agreements on Trade in Services and the Reference Paper which complements the WTO Telecommunications Agreement include competition provisions.

2.2.3 *Political aspect of competition law: competition policy versus other national policies*

Another important aspect of competition law that has to be examined in the context of the influence of such law on a national socio-political and legal system is the political aspect of competition law, that is, competition policy. It is important to define this concept, which is admittedly a very difficult task. Competition policy has been defined by the WTO working group on the interaction between trade and competition[96] as the policies which 'comprise the full range of measures that may be used to promote competitive market structures and behaviour, including but not limited to a comprehensive competition law dealing with anti-competitive practices of enterprises'.[97] Similarly, Doern defines competition policy as the policy which 'consists of those policies and actions of the state intended to prevent certain restraints of trade by private firms. Stated more positively, it is a policy intended to promote rivalry among firms, buyers and sellers through actions in areas of activity such as mergers, abuse of dominance cartels, ... misleading advertising, and related criminal and economic offences that are held to be anti-competitive'.[98]

Research conducted in the context of this study through interviews with competition officials, academics and practitioners has supported this argument, as there is great variation in the opinions of the interviewees on what competition policy really is. The only standard characteristic of competition policy as opposed to competition law that the discussants pointed out is that competition policy is a wider circle around competition law. Competition policy encompasses competition law as well as a number of other elements, such as the institutions that enforce competition law, competition advocacy and industrial policy concerns. Research by the OECD demonstrates that even more objectives may be included in the concept of competition policy: decentralisation of economic decision-making; promotion of small business; fairness and equity; and other socio-political values.[99] By the same token, Sir Leon Brittan, former Commissioner in charge of competition, once stated that, 'indeed, it can

[96] On the establishment and work of the WTO working group, see Chapter 6.

[97] WTO Working Group on the Interaction between Trade and Competition Policy (1999), *The Fundamental Principles of Competition Policy*, WT/WGTCP/W/127, para. 2.

[98] B. Doern (1996), 'Comparative Competition Policy: Boundaries and Levels of Political Analysis' in B. Doern and S. Wilks (eds.), *Comparative Competition Policy: National Institutions in a Global Market*, at 7.

[99] OECD Global Forum on Competition (2003), *The Objectives of Competition Law and Policy*, OECD Secretariat Note, CCNM/GF/COMP(2003)3, paras. 3 and 22.

be said that positive competition policy should not be determined in isolation; it must be related to and integrated with economic, industrial and also social policy'.[100]

The problem with discussing these various (related to public interest) objectives which lie beneath the broad concept of competition law and policy is that these objectives vary across different countries or regions. That said, a general introduction to some of these indirect objectives of competition policy would be important in the context of our attempt to highlight specificities of national competition regimes that may have an effect on the process of internationalisation of competition law.

As noted above, the notion of public interest has been used to justify the application of sector specific regulations. In a broader context, public interest justifications also allow governments to exempt various practices of private firms from strictly economic approaches and thus minimise the reach of competition law and policy. This is clearly indicated by the OECD study, which points out that all policies taken into consideration in the context of application of competition law are based on the concept of public interest.[101] In this context, public interest is used in a much broader sense. It justifies the exemption of particular practices (and not whole sectors as in the case of sectoral regulation) from the realm of competition rules in accordance with the specific public policy of a government. In some cases, the basis of such exemptions is clearly drafted within the text of the competition laws. In other cases, it cannot be found in the competition-related rules, but derives from the general powers of a government.

Using the competition policy of the EU as an example of the former, Giorgio Monti[102] has reviewed a number of cases that have been exempted from the application of Article 101(1) TFEU, which prohibits anticompetitive agreements between firms. On the basis of Article 101(3), the European Commission has exempted a number of anticompetitive agreements based on arguments that these agreements would have a beneficial effect on EU employment, industrial and environmental policy.[103] As to

[100] Quoted in S.M. Willimsky (1997), 'The Concept(s) of Competition' 18(1) *European Competition Law Review* 53, at 54; in a similar vein, Barry Rodger noted that 'Competition law or policy has no fixed content and is dependent to a great extent upon the particular political and social emphases of the legal system in which it operates'. See B. Rodger, (2000) 'Competition Policy, Liberalism and Globalization: A European Perspective' 6 *Columbia Journal of European Law* 289, at 304.

[101] OECD (2003), *supra* n. 99.

[102] G. Monti (2002), 'Article 81 and EC Public Policy' 39 *Common Market Law Review* 1057.

[103] Monti, *ibid.* refers to the following cases: on employment policy, Case 26/76 *Metro* v. *Commission (No. 1)* [1977] ECR 1875, para. 43; Case 42/84 *Remia and others* v. *Commission*

the latter, it has been documented that a number of Commission decisions to clear mergers in the 1990s have been based on industrial policy concerns and/or political pressure by particular Member States.[104]

2.2.4 *Cultural factors that may have an effect on the adoption and/or application of competition rules*

A relevant, but to a great extent separate, issue that has to be addressed is the influence of the culture of a particular country concerning the operation of markets in general and the reach of application of competition rules. This does not necessarily have to do with pure strategic political decisions, as seen in the previous section, but mostly with the traditions and patterns of a particular society with regard to markets and trade in general, or with regard to a particular sector of society.

Historians, anthropologists and sociologists have examined the relationship between geopolitical characteristics of a society and the particular perceptions of these societies on the nature and operation of the markets.[105] With regard to competition law and policy, Fikentscher has accurately expressed the relationship between cultural factors and competition law and policy:

> Americans are inclined to think that in these days the free market system is on its way to pervade the whole world, and many Europeans share this view. Maybe this is so, and should even be welcomed as a step to worldwide democracy and equal chances for every one. But there is also evidence that other cultures are afraid of this. The Muslim World cannot agree to explicit advertising, the Siberians in their great majority fear democracy more than anything else because it leads to the economic destruction of their habitat, North-American Indians wonder at the

[1985] ECR 2545, para. 42; *Stichting Baksteen* [1994] OJ L131/15, paras. 27–8; *Synthetic Fibres* [1984] OJ L207/17, para. 37. On industrial policy, *BPCL/ICI* [1984] OJ L212/1, para. 37; *ENI/Montedison* [1987] OJ L5/13, para. 31; *Olivetti/Canon* [1988] OJ L52/60, para. 54; *GEC-Siemens/Plessey* [1990] OJ C239/2. On environmental policy, *Exxon-Shell* [1994] OJ L144/21, paras. 67 and 68; *Philips-Osram* [1994] OJ L378/37, para. 25.

104 A. Schmidt (2001), *Non-Competition Factors in the European Competition Policy: The Necessity of Institutional Reforms*, Centre for Globalisation and Europeanisation of the Economy Discussion Paper No. 13, available at www.cege.wiso.uni-goettingen.de/Dokumente/Diskussion/discuss_13.pdf (last visited on 2 December 2009). The author refers to *Nestle/Perrier* [1992] OJ L356/1; *Mannesmann/Vallourec/Ilva* [1994] OJ L192/15; *Kali&Salz/MdK/Treuhand* [1994] OJ L186/38; and *Mercedes Benz/Kassbohrer* [1995] OJ L211/1.

105 For an elaborate review of such studies, see J. Lie (1997), 'Sociology of Markets' 23 *Annual Review of Sociology* 341.

> 'frenzy' (panicking as they call it) that comes with the economy-oriented lifestyle of the 'Anglos', and many traditional societies fear exploitation and assimilation.[106]

Along the same lines, and on a more specific basis, the OECD has documented a number of situations where for cultural reasons various practices in different countries are exempted from the application of competition rules. What the OECD calls 'historical relics' include examples such as the exemption in Norway concerning municipal monopolies of movie theatres, a leftover of a century ago when movie theatres were considered a novelty.[107] In Korea, territorial constraints on rice wine (a national specialty) are allowed, in conformity with long-lasting national policies on this matter.[108]

The most illustrative example with regard to this phenomenon is Japan. As a recent study indicates, in Japan policies that promote product market competition have long been compromised by ministerial guidance and explicit exemptions from competition law.[109] One of the most important reasons which have led in this direction is the traditional Japanese practice of 'Keiretsu', which refers to long-term closely interconnected relationships among Japanese companies through formal and/or informal relations, and hampers foreign investors from entering the Japanese market.[110]

2.2.5 *Competition law in developing and small countries*

Almost the whole of the discussion that has been developed until now refers to industrialised countries and polities with mature competition regimes, mainly the EU. Another important question regarding the operation of competition law and policy on a national level relates to the adoption and application of competition rules by developing and small countries. The statistics in Table 2.2 may provide us with some indications as to the type of countries that have adopted competition legislation.

[106] W. Fikentscher (2001), 'Market Anthropology and Global Trade' 1(1) *Gruter Institute Working Papers on Law, Economics, and Evolutionary Biology* 1, at 12.

[107] OECD Global Forum on Competition (2004), *Regulatory Reform: Stock-taking of Experience with Reviews of Competition Law and Policy in OECD Countries and the Relevance of Such Experience for Developing Countries*, CCNM/GF/COMP(2004), at 21.

[108] *Ibid.*

[109] J. Hoj and M. Wise (2004), *Product Market Competition and Economic Performance in Japan*, OECD Economics Department Working Paper No. 387, ECO/WKP(2004), at 10.

[110] Keiretsu was the practice that prompted the US company Kodak to go to the WTO Dispute Settlement Body against the Japanese company Fuji: *Japan – Measure affecting*

Table 2.2 *Level of income* and competition law*

	Low income	Lower middle income	Upper middle income	High income/ OECD non-member	High income / OECD member	TOTAL
Countries	59	54	40	31	24	208
Countries with competition law	24	30	24	9	24	111
% of countries with competition law	41%	55%	60%	29%	100%**	53%

* According to the World Bank, low income includes countries with a Gross National Income (GNI) of US$905 or less; lower middle income, US$906–3,595; upper middle income, US$3,596–11,115; and high income, US$11,116 or more. See the World Bank Country Classification at http://web.worldbank.org.

** Another six countries with an upper middle income participate in the OECD: Czech Republic, Hungary, Mexico, Poland, Slovak Republic and Turkey. All these countries have adopted competition rules, thus the total percentage of OECD members with a competition legislation remains 100%.

With the exception of countries with high income which are not OECD members, there is a direct link between the level of development of a country and whether this particular country has adopted competition legislation. As Table 2.2 shows, the higher the income of a country the more likely it is that this country has a competition regime in place.[111] For instance, only 41 per cent of countries with a low income have competition rules in place. On the opposite side of the spectrum, all the OECD members have adopted such rules. What therefore are the reasons why developing countries seem reluctant to adopt competition rules?

Consumer Photographic Film and Paper, WT/DS44/R. For a comment on the case, see M. Furse (1999), 'Competition Law and the WTO Report: *Japan – Measures affecting Consumer Photographic Film and Paper*' 20(1) *European Competition Law Review* 9. See also 6.4 *infra*.

111 The only exception to this rule is countries with high income, which are not OECD members. Only 23 per cent of such countries have adopted competition law. Most of these high income countries without competition law are very small in terms of population. Specifically, the countries of this kind that have not adopted competition rules are

A first obvious reason is that competition law may seem a luxury to countries with very low income. As a European Commission official interviewee noted, '[if] you do not have something to eat you should look for a piece of bread and leave competition law aside'.[112] In a recent paper, Emmert *et al.* have identified many other possible reasons.[113] These include import substitution policy arguments, according to which developing countries attempt to change the structure and composition of imports in order to develop specialised domestic industries, and, similarly, infant industry strategies, through which they attempt to support national industries and/or particular companies (national champions) in order to make them stronger and capable of competing in the international markets.[114] Another point raised by the authors is that developing countries fear that the opening of their markets through competition may be detrimental to their companies, as multinational companies would dominate their markets.[115]

On the other hand, recent research has shown that international cartels may have a substantial negative impact on both consumers and producers of developing countries,[116] and the need for adoption of competition rules has been stressed and supported by various international organisations, such as the WTO, the World Bank and the International Monetary Fund (IMF).[117] In any case, this issue (competition law in developing countries) will be further explored throughout the remaining chapters of this book in the context of the examination of the various types of agreements which include competition rules, and especially in relation to the

the following: Andora, Aruba, Bahamas, Bahrain, Bermuda, Brunei, Cayman Islands, Channel Islands, French Polynesia, Guam, Hong Kong China, Isle of Man, Kuwait, Macao China, Monaco, Netherlands Antilles, New Caledonia, Puerto Rico, Qatar, San Marino, Saudi Arabia, United Arab Emirates and Virgin Islands.

112 Interview with EC Commission official, Brussels, 15 July 2003.

113 See F. Emmert, F. Kronthaler and J. Stephan (2005), 'Analysis of Statements Made in Favour of and Against the Adoption of Competition Law in Developing and Transition Economies', paper presented in Brussels, 19 and 20 April 2005, in the context of the EU-financed project Competition Policy Foundations for Trade Reform, Regulatory Reform, and Sustainable Development.

114 *Ibid.* at 31. It has to be noted that such policies have been used by industrialised countries in the past. See H.J. Chang (2002), *Kicking Away the Ladder: Development Strategy in Historical Perspective* (London: Anthem Press) ch. 1.

115 Emmert *et al.* (2005), *supra* n. 113 at 38.

116 M. Levenstein and V.Y. Suslow (2004), 'Contemporary International Cartels and Developing Countries: Economic Effects and Implications for Competition Policy' 71 *Antitrust Law Journal* 801.

117 See e.g., UNCTAD (2005), *Review of Recent Experiences in the Formulation and Implementation of Competition Law and Policy in Selected Developing Countries*,

negotiations over a possible competition agreement in the WTO context, where developing countries have consistently opposed the proposal of the EU for the conclusion of such an agreement.

2.3 International aspects of competition law and policy

To this point, the chapter has dealt with the national dimension of competition law and policy, and more specifically, with the economic, legal and socio-political factors that may have an influence on the application of competition rules in different nation states. As noted in the context of the analysis, these factors vary from country to country, and create differences in the application of national competition laws. On the other hand, as this section attempts to expose, a number of factors have gradually added international features to competition law and policy. A mixture of economic, socio-legal and political developments have played an important role in this process.

2.3.1 Economic globalisation and the appearance of anticompetitive business practices with an international effect

Competition law and policy, along with other forms of commercial law, has acquired international features due to the emergence of economic globalisation.[118] By the term 'economic globalisation' we mean here improvements in technology and communications,[119] liberalisation of

UNCTAD/DITC/CLP/2005/2, at 2, where it is noted that in the case of Thailand, 'the International Monetary Fund imposed this [adoption of competition law] upon the Thai government as one of the conditions under the stand-by arrangement during the economic crisis (1997–2001)'.

118 Economists would rather use the terms 'international economic integration', referring to the extent to which international economic activity has integrated markets. These are probably over-simplified definitions, in view of the debate regarding the meaning, or even the existence of globalisation. See D. Held, D. Golblatt, A.G. McGrew and J. Perraton (1999), *Global Transformations: Politics, Economics and Culture* (Stanford University Press) 2–10, where the authors provide a number of alternative definitions of globalisation; see also S. Piccioto (1998), 'Globalisation, Liberalisation, Regulation', paper presented at the Conference on Globalisation, the Nation-State and Violence, Sussex University, 16 April 1998, available at www.lancs.ac.uk/staff/lwasp/glibreg.pdf (last visited on 2 December 2009).

119 D. Rodrik (1999), 'How Far will International Economic Integration Go?' 14(1) *Journal of Economic Perspectives* 177; D. Archibugi and C. Pietrobelli (2002), 'The Globalisation of Technology and its Implications for Developing Countries. Windows of Opportunity or Further Burdens?' 70(9) *Technological Forecasting and Social Change* 861, in which the authors identify at 864 three main categories of (economic) globalisation: the

international trade,[120] and the subsequent increase of economic flows through the operation of multilateral firms, that has appeared at least in the last decades,[121] and that has weakened the distinction between the domestic and the international in several fields of economic activity.[122]

With regard to competition law and policy in particular, in view of the liberalisation of international trade through the provisions of the GATT and more recently the WTO, which to a great extent opened up national borders to multinational firms, and given the fact that in the late 1980s and early 1990s a number of previously communist states started adopting liberal policies, as well as the vast increase in the number of countries which adopted competition legislation,[123] there have been voices which stress that trade negotiations should not be limited to the regulation of policies applied at the border but should also include issues relating to domestic policies, such as subsidies and sector-specific regulations which may have an effect on international trade.[124]

Competition law and policy has been considered one of these domestic policies.[125] The core idea behind such an argument is that ineffective domestic competition policies could be a substantial obstacle in the process of trade liberalisation,[126] an argument mainly based on the assessment that whereas trade policies and international reforms aim to open up the markets and allow as much competition as possible, the role of competition policy is to prevent private firms from distorting this competitive environment.[127]

international exploitation of nationally produced technology, the global generation of innovation and global technological cooperations.

120 Which has occurred through the abolition of legal barriers on the border and been supported by trade economists. These arguments will be dealt with in some detail in this book, first in this chapter, and more elaborately during the discussion about WTO and competition in Chapter 6.

121 Nonetheless, there has been argument in the relevant literature that the first signs of economic globalisation occurred in the fifteenth or sixteenth century, and became obvious at the beginning of the nineteenth century. See K.H. O'Rourke and G. Williamson (2004), 'Once More: When did Globalisation Begin?' 8 *Journal of European Economic History* 109.

122 K. Jayasuriya (2001), 'Globalisation, Sovereignty, and the Rule of Law: From Political to Economic Constitutionalism?' 8(4) *Constellations* 443, at 446.

123 It is noted that 60 per cent of countries with a competition law adopted such law in the 1990s. See Table 2.1.

124 With regard to these arguments from a critical perspective see P. Krugman (1997), 'What Should Trade Negotiators Negotiate About?' 35(1) *Journal of Economic Literature* 113, at 114.

125 R. Howse (2002), 'From Politics to Technocracy – and Back Again: The Fate of the Multilateral Trading Regime' 96(1) *American Journal of International Law* 94, at 96.

126 OECD (2001), *Trade and Competition Policies: Options for a Greater Coherence* (Paris: OECD).

127 Jenny (2001), *supra* n. 94 at 37.

Along the same lines, it has been observed that efficiency gains from a trade perspective were pursued through the realisation of comparative advantage, whereas competition policy should be used to secure these gains through the elimination of losses created by a single seller who has monopolised the market or by a group of sellers who act in a collusive way.[128] On the other hand, through the opening up of national markets with the limitation of tariffs and other border barriers, the ability of multilateral firms to operate in multiple national markets has also been increased. This assumption may be confirmed by the dramatic increase of foreign direct investment (FDI) in the last few decades.

As figures compiled by the United Nations Conference on Trade and Development (UNCTAD) show, in the last thirty-five years FDI has been multiplied by almost seventy times. In particular, these figures show that global FDI flows in 1974 were US$24,127 million. These flows in 2005 reached US$916,277 million, and this figure was almost doubled by 2007, when they reached the amount of US$1,979 million, before the recent financial crisis which led to the decrease of inward FDI to an amount of US$1,697 billion in 2008.[129] The impact of this increase in the number and influence of multinational firms has become palpable in a number of legal and political fields,[130] competition policy being one of them.

These developments have also been reflected in trade economics, which by the early 1990s was dominated by the classical and neoclassical trade theories that took for granted that labour and capital moving from country to country was immobile and that the comparative advantage was static, and based their results only on the exchanged final products.[131] Another strand of academic literature, known as new international trade theory,

[128] E. Graham (2002), 'The Relationship Between International Trade Policy and Competition Policy' in Z. Drabek (ed.), *Globalization under Threat: The Stability of Trade Policy and Multilateral Agreements* (Edward Elgar Publishing) 225, at 228.

[129] See the UNCTAD database on FDI, available at www.unctad.org.

[130] This statement does not take into consideration the debate over the possible negative effects of multinational companies, a debate that has been developed especially among developing countries. See e.g., N.H. Jacoby (1975), 'Multinational Corporations and National Sovereignty' in P.M. Boarman and H. Schollhammer (eds.), *Multinational Corporations and Governments: Business-Government Relations in an International Context* (New York: Praeger Publishers) 6–7. It should also be pointed out that this book only deals with competition-related issues with regard to business practices. Hence, it will not touch upon (except where relevant) other legal disciplines such as intellectual property, corporate governance, money laundering, telecommunications, energy, environmental, transport, tax and banking regulations which may also deal with business practices.

[131] R. Gilpin (1987), *The Political Economy of International Relations* (Princeton University Press) 177.

pointed out that several other factors have an effect on international trade. According to this line of argument, factors such as research and development, the product lifecycle, oligopoly and economies of scale also have an influence on the creation of each country's comparative advantage.[132]

Thus, the focus shifted from inter-industry trade, that is trade between industries which belong to different domestic markets, to intra-industry,[133] inter-firm[134] and intra-firm trade.[135] These new theories are mainly based on the argument that not only the final products but also intermediate goods as well as technological knowledge are exchanged.[136] The most striking element of these theories is that the analytical tools used for the examination of the international trading system (such as oligopoly and economies of scale) are the same as the ones used for the analysis of competition law and policy issues.[137] In other words, industrial organisation aspects have been introduced into the analysis of international trade.

It was against this background that a number of scholars started looking at the relationship between competition law and policy and international trade. The relevant research agenda includes the examination both of private practices that may have an international effect, and hybrid public-private practices that may have the same effect. These two types of anticompetitive practices are discussed briefly in the following section.

2.3.2 Anticompetitive practices that have an international effect

With the increase of multilateral firms came practices that have an effect on the territory of multiple national markets. Of these practices, the most

[132] These concepts were first introduced by Dixit and Stiglitz in 1977. See A. Dixit and J.E. Stiglitz (1977), 'Monopolistic Competition and Product Diversity' 67(3) *American Economic Review* 297; see also P. Krugman (1983), 'New Theories of Trade Among Industrial Countries' 73(2) *American Economic Review* 343, at 343–4; A. Dixit (1984), 'International Trade Policies for Oligopolistic Competition' 94 *Economic Journal* 1.

[133] For example, it has been shown that in trade between developed countries some countries import some automobile models while exporting other models. See Gilpin (1987), *supra* n. 131 at 176.

[134] That is the trade between firms, irrespective of governmental intervention. These theories are based on the phenomenon of oligopolistic multinational firms and the internationalisation of production in the second half of the twentieth century. See Gilpin *ibid.*

[135] This is a consequence of the creation of multilateral enterprises which are involved through subsidiaries and joint ventures on various levels of production and in several countries.

[136] Gilpin (1987), *supra* n. 131 at 177.

[137] For a brief analysis of these factors, see F.M. Scherer and R.S. Balous (1994), *Unfinished Tasks: The New International Trade Theory and Post Uruguay Round Challenges*, British-North American Committee Issues Paper No. 3, at 9–15.

directly linked to international trade are anticompetitive practices that have an exclusionary effect, thus hindering the entrance and expansion of foreign firms in the markets where the anticompetitive practices take place.[138] This discussion lies at the heart of the debate regarding the international aspects of competition as, apart from more general political concerns and particularities of different free trade settings, the need for international cooperation on competition law, and/or the harmonisation of competition rules exists because of the existence of such practices. The following section reviews three types of anticompetitive agreements that may have an effect on trade: cartels, vertical restraints and cross-border mergers.[139]

(i) International cartels

There has been a growing consensus among academics and politicians in the last forty years that cartels are the most blatant of anticompetitive practices, and prohibition of hard-core cartels (which may be defined as agreements between firms to allocate shares in international markets, increase prices and reduce imports)[140] is included in any modern competition law, as there is widespread recognition that their effects can be very harmful to consumers.

According to the OECD, cartels produce over-charges at a level of 10 per cent and they cause overall harm amounting to 20 per cent of the affected commerce.[141] To give a more specific example, in two cartel cases, the lysine and citric acid cartels, investigated by the US Department of Justice in the 1990s, it was calculated that prices were raised by 70 per cent and 30 per cent respectively,[142] and this is obviously a price difference that may have a substantial effect on consumers. Recent research also indicates

138 P. Marsden (2003), *A Competition Policy for the WTO* (Cameron May) ch. 3, especially at 91–108.

139 The list of these practices is not exhaustive, as it may also encompass the abuse of the dominant position by a firm, which may use such position in a national market to limit the ability of foreign firms to enter this market.

140 This definition does not include export cartels, which are similar to hard-core cartels, agreements between firms that are authorised by states or exempted from national competition rules. See S.J. Evenett, M.C. Levenstein and V.Y. Suslow (2001), 'International Cartel Enforcement, Lessons from the 1990s' 24(9) *World Economy* 1221, at 1223. These types of cartels will be further explored in the context of the negotiations for a multilateral agreement at the WTO, in Chapter 6.

141 OECD (2002), *Fighting Hard-Core Cartels: Harm, Effective Sanctions and Leniency Programme* (Paris: OECD) 77.

142 J.I. Klein (1999), Luncheon Address delivered at the Anti-Cartel Enforcement Conference, Westin Grand Hotel, Washington, DC, 30 September 1999, available at www.usdoj.gov/atr/public/speeches/3727.htm (last visited on 2 December 2009).

that anti-cartel enforcement is active in a number of countries, such as the United States, Canada, the EU and its Member States, Australia, Israel, Japan and Korea.[143]

In parallel, the number of cartels which have an effect on the markets of multiple countries has substantially increased too. During the 1990s, over forty cartels with an international effect were prosecuted in the EU and the United States.[144] As far as the EU is concerned, among the twenty-eight cartels whose members were fined by the European Commission between the years 1986 and 2002, fifteen (accounting for 58 per cent) were caught in cooperation with the Antitrust Division of the US Department of Justice and the Canadian Bureau of Competition, and one of them was caught in cooperation with the Japanese authorities.[145]

International cartels also have detrimental effects on developing countries. As Levenstein, Suslow and Oswald have showed, in 1997, developing countries imported US$54.7 billion of goods from a subsample of nineteen industries that had seen a price-fixing conspiracy during the 1990s. These imports represented 5.2 per cent of total imports and 1.2 per cent of gross domestic product (GDP) in developing countries.[146] These cartels were active in the markets of steel, vitamins, fax paper, sugar, cement – therefore they were products used by a great proportion of the world population.

On the other hand, as another OECD report suggests, at least one in three (hard-core) international cartels remain undetected,[147] and various reasons may be playing a role here. One of them is that the more sophisticated the enforcement against cartels becomes, the more sophisticated these agreements between firms become too, making detection more difficult. OECD suggests that there have been cases where the parties to a cartel agreement have established mechanisms of prevention and punishment of cheating.[148]

143 OECD (2005), *Hard-Core Cartels: Third Report on the Implementation of the 1998 Recommendation* (Paris: OECD).

144 See Evenett, Levenstein and Suslow (2001), *supra* n. 140 at 1225.

145 European Commission (2006), 'The Fight Against Cartels', available at http://europa.eu.int/comm/competition/citizen/cartel_stats.html (last visited 21 March 2007). Such cooperation has been informal, while competition authorities have not yet been able to overcome problems relating to the exchange of confidential information, which would increase effectiveness. See Chapter 3.

146 M. Levenstein, V. Suslow and L. Oswald (2003), *International Price Fixing Cartels and Developing Countries: A Discussion of Effects and Policy Remedies*, William Davidson Working Paper No. 538, at 1.

147 Other estimations indicate that one in seven cartels remain undetected. See OECD (2002), *supra* n. 141 at 73.

148 *Ibid.* at 79; see also J.M. Griffin (2000), 'An Inside Look at a Cartel at Work: Common Characteristics of International Cartels', paper presented at the American Bar

It follows that some sort of coordination is needed between different states in order to address the problems caused by international cartels. In view of these observations, and as shown throughout the book, at least officially, enforcement of competition rules in cartel cases is probably the most important aim of any international agreement devoted to competition law and policy, and cartel deterrence is included in the agenda of any international organisation (such as the WTO, OECD and the ICN) which addresses competition law and policy.

(ii) Vertical restraints

Another business practice that could have an effect on the markets of more than one country is vertical restraint. Vertical restraints may be defined as agreements or concerted practices entered into between two or more undertakings each of which operates, for the purposes of the agreement, at a different level of the production or distribution chain, and relating to the conditions under which the parties may purchase, sell or resell certain goods or services.[149] In view of the expansion of multinational firms, the impact of such agreements may be significant on an international level.

An indicative example is the automobile industry. The automobile market is global, in the sense that a limited number of manufacturers dominate the sales of motor vehicles internationally. These manufacturers have organised dealership networks, which at least in industrialised nations is the only way of promoting and selling their products.[150] A consequence of the existence of global distribution systems is the fact that manufacturers have to face different rules relating to dealerships in different nations.[151] In addition, it can be observed that the planning and operation of its distribution network by a manufacturer may have an effect on all the countries where its product is finally sold.

A separate issue, with regard to the international effect of vertical restraints, may arise because of the existence of exclusive distribution agreements in the territory of one country, for instance between firms A

Association Section of Antitrust Law Forty-eighth Annual Spring Meeting, Washington, DC, 6 April 2000, available at www.usdoj.gov/atr/public/speeches/4489.htm (last visited on 2 December 2009).

149 European Commission (2002), 'Glossary of Terms Used in EU Competition Policy', available at http://ec.europa.eu/competition/publications/glossary_en.pdf (last visited on 2 December 2009).

150 G.P. Maxton and J. Wormald (2004), *Time for a Model Change: Re-engineering the Global Automotive Industry* (Cambridge University Press) 164.

151 As Maxton and Wormald have shown in the case of the automotive industry, the relevant laws vary considerably in the United States, the EU and Japan. See *ibid.* at 168.

and B, which may make it impossible for another foreign firm C to enter the market where A and B operate. A notable example here could be vertical Keiretsu in Japan, which according to US firms prevent foreign investors from entering the Japanese market.[152] In fact, a similar situation is also faced in the EU, where, for instance, exclusive distribution agreements between car manufacturers and dealers in various Member States make it difficult or even impossible for dealers from other Member States to penetrate the markets of the Member States where such agreements take place.[153]

(iii) Multijurisdictional mergers

A third business practice that may have an effect on the international marketplace is cross-border merger and acquisition. With the expansion of multinational firms, the number of such mergers has increased dramatically. As Gugler *et al.* have calculated, 21.7 per cent of all mergers and acquisitions with a value of at least US$1 million that were concluded internationally up to 1998 involved firms registered and operating in different countries.[154] It follows that these transactions had an effect on the economic environment of more than one jurisdiction and therefore in many instances more than one jurisdiction were interested in reviewing them. With regard to the operation of competition law, there are two sets of problems relating to this issue, one procedural and one substantive.

The procedural problem is related to the different notification procedures (in terms of deadlines to notify the merger and provide the required information) that apply in different states where the mergers have to be notified, which may cause both additional costs and legal unpredictability to the undertakings involved in the transaction. A notable example is the 1989 Gillette/Wilkinson transaction, which was notified in fourteen jurisdictions.[155] Another characteristic example is the one given by McDavid and Marshall regarding the attempt by a Canadian firm (Alcan

[152] Noted above, at 2.2.4 *supra*.

[153] See e.g., Case F-2/36.623/36.820/37.275 *SEP et al./Peugeot SA*, EC Commission Decision, 5 October 2005.

[154] K. Gugler, D.C. Muller, B.B. Yurtoglu and C. Zulehner (2003), 'The Effects of Mergers: An International Comparison' 21 *International Journal of Industrial Organisation* 625, at 632–3.

[155] See generally, OECD (1994), *Merger Cases in the Real World: A Study of Merger Control Procedures* (Paris: OECD). It has to be pointed out, though, that this merger occurred before the entrance into force of the EU Merger Regulation ((EC) 139/2004 of 20 January 2004 [2004] OJ L24/1), and thus the number of authorities that had to be notified is probably greater than it would be today where the 'one-stop-shop' principle of the Regulation greatly reduces the number of notifications.

Inc.) to merge with a rival firm. Alcan had to hire competition lawyers from thirty-five different firms and file sixteen competition notifications in eight different languages, all with different deadlines, information requirements and processes for approval.[156]

On the substantive side, the problem relates to the different standards that two jurisdictions may apply in the review of the same transaction. Notable examples regarding this issue include the conflict that occurred between the EU and the United States in relation to the mergers between Boeing/MDD and GE/Honeywell.

The Boeing/MDD case related to the attempt by two US companies (Boeing and McDonnell Douglas) to merge in December of 1996. This merger would have created the largest aerospace company in the world.[157] The US Federal Trade Commission (FTC) cleared the merger without conditions on 1 July 1997.[158] However, this was not the case with the European Commission. Basing its jurisdiction on the financial thresholds of the 'Community dimension' clause of the Merger Regulation, according to which no physical presence in the EC is required,[159] it made it clear that it would block the merger. At this point, the US government intervened and threatened the EU that, if the Commission blocked the merger, the United States would wage a commercial war against the EC by taking the case to the WTO or by imposing trade sanctions.[160] A more serious conflict was finally avoided, as the Commission decided to clear the merger on 30 July 1997 subject to some commitments that Boeing offered.[161]

On the other hand, the GE/Honeywell case concerned the merger between GE (the leading aircraft engine maker) and Honeywell (the leading avionics/non-avionics manufacturer). The merger would have created or strengthened a dominant position in different relevant markets where the two companies were involved. Despite the fact that during the merger review the US and EU agencies cooperated very closely, they did not arrive

[156] J.L. McDavid and L.K. Marshall (2001), 'Antitrust Law: Global Review Regimes' *National Law Journal*.

[157] For an analysis of the facts of the case see T.L. Boeder and G.J. Dorman (2000), 'The Boeing /McDonnell Douglas Merger: The Economics, Antitrust Law and Politics of the Aerospace Industry' XLV(1) *Antitrust Bulletin* 119.

[158] See 'Letter to Marc G. Schildkraut and Benjamin S. Sharp regarding the Proposed Acquisition of McDonnell Douglas Corporation by The Boeing Company' available at www.ftc.gov/os/caselist/9710051.htm (last visited on 2 December 2009).

[159] J.P. Griffin (1994), 'EC and US Extraterritoriality: Activism and Cooperation' 17 *Fordham International Law Journal* 353, at 360.

[160] A. Kaczorowska (2000), 'International Competition Law in the Context of Global Capitalism' 21(2) *European Competition Law Review* 117.

[161] *Boeing/McDonnell Douglas* [1997] OJ L336/16.

at the same decision. While the Antitrust Division of the US Department of Justice reached an agreement with GE and Honeywell regarding the Division's antitrust concerns related to the proposed merger,[162] the European Commission blocked the merger,[163] prompting strong reactions from the other side of the Atlantic.[164] The divergence with respect to this specific case is related to the correctness of the 'portfolio effect theory', a variety of different means by which a merger may allegedly create or strengthen a dominant position in non-overlap markets.[165]

These cases highlight two of the observations made in the previous section of the chapter: first, that the understanding of the operation of competition law and policy may vary in different countries; and secondly, that in cases where very crucial policy issues are involved (namely, in both cases, economic and employment policy in the very sensitive field of the aviation sector) and different national regulators claim jurisdiction, political considerations, such as the need to create and/or protect national champions, may have an obvious effect on the particular application of the rules by such regulators.

With the expansion of multinational enterprises, the opinion could be expressed that mergers have already been a problem for international trade, since the relevant market in the assessment of some mergers has already been identified as the 'global market', and furthermore, as we saw in the analysis of the Boeing/MDD case, considerations mostly related to the industrial policy of different countries in important sectors of their economies could lead to very serious conflicts between national governments.[166]

2.3.3 Governmental and hybrid practices

The discussion developed in the context of this section has highlighted the fact that a number of business practices that have traditionally been

[162] DoJ, 'Justice Department requires divestitures in merger between General Electric and Honeywell', Press Release of 2 May 2001.

[163] European Commission, 'The Commission prohibits GE's acquisition of Honeywell', Press Release IP/01/939 of 3 July 2001.

[164] DoJ, 'Statement by Assistant Attorney General Charles A. James on the EU's decision regarding the GE/Honeywell acquisition', Press Release of 3 July 2001.

[165] D. Giotakos, L. Petit, G. Garnier and P. De Luyck (2001), 'General Electric/Honeywell: An Insight into the Commission's Investigation and Decision' 3 *Competition Policy Newsletter* 5; D.E. Patterson and C. Shapiro (2001), 'Trans-Atlantic Divergence in GE/Honeywell, Causes and Lessons' *Antitrust* 18.

[166] This argument was also expressed at the first ICN conference. See ICN (2003), *A Report on the First Annual Conference of The International Competition Network, Naples, 28–29 September 2002*, at 4.

considered as falling under the realm of competition law may have a significant effect on multiple national markets. Apart from those practices, there are also competition-related governmental practices that may also have an influence on the operation of international trade. These may include industrial policy considerations, which may imply a lack of law, exemptions and exclusions from the application of competition rules or lack of enforcement or strategic enforcement of law, with the aim of strengthening particular firms, and creating national champions that would be able to compete at the international level.

This type of discretionary application of competition law in favour of particular firms is an aspect that has already been discussed in the context of the application of competition rules on a national level; nonetheless it may also have an effect on the ability of foreign firms to compete in national markets where such policies are applied.[167] This argument is relevant, for example, to the complaints raised by the United States that the entry or expansion of US firms into Japanese markets was hindered due to exclusionary anticompetitive practices conducted by Japanese firms, sometimes with the support of the Japanese government. It has been documented that such situations have occurred in the automobile industry, the flat glass market, the paper industry, the soda ash industry, the electronic equipment market and the film market.[168]

These policies may also be incorporated in the various regulations adopted by countries in particular sectors of their economies. On an international level, it has been argued that sector-specific regulation may have an effect both on the ability of foreign firms to enter a market and on consumer welfare.[169] As will be briefly outlined in Chapter 6, the relationship between competition law and sectoral regulation is an issue included in the agendas of both the WTO and the ICN. In addition, a number of sector-specific WTO agreements, such as the Reference Paper on Telecommunications and the Agreement on Services, include competition-related provisions.[170]

167 See International Competition Policy Advisory Committee (2000), *ICPAC Final Report to the Attorney General and the Assistant Attorney General for Antitrust*, at 206 available at www.usdoj.gov/atr/icpac/finalreport.htm (last visited on 2 December 2009).

168 *Ibid.* at 211–15.

169 See e.g., R.D. Anderson and P. Holmes (2002), 'Competition Policy and the Future of the Multilateral Trading System' 5(2) *Journal of International Economic Law* 531, at 539–40 and ICN (2005), *Report of the Working Group on Antitrust Enforcement in Regulated Sectors to the fourth ICN Annual Conference, Bonn, June 2005*, available at www.international-competitionnetwork.org/media/library/conference_4th_bonn_2005/Interrelations_Between_Antitrust_and_Regulation.pdf (last visited on 2 December 2009).

170 See 6.4 *infra*.

2.3.4 *Need for international cooperation on competition*

As observed in the second section, the variety of national policies which influence the particular application of national competition rules, along with the internationalisation of economic activity and the consequent appearance of business practices that have an effect on multiple markets, have a major impact on the international legal system. This assumption stems from the fact that, on the one hand, there are varied national competition laws and – more importantly – policies, and on the other, there are competition law-related international problems which have to be solved through cooperation of the affected states. As this book argues, in the field of competition, as in every field of international cooperation, such cooperation may take two main forms: formal cooperation through the adoption of international agreements, or informal cooperation, through the exchange of ideas and information between competition officials. This section discusses the elements which lead to this broad classification, and further introduces the theme that the book attempts to address, i.e. the international dimension of EU competition law and policy.

(i) Sovereignty and its implications for the internationalisation of competition law

International political order is based on the concept of state sovereignty.[171] State sovereignty emerged with the Peace of Westphalia in 1648, which marked the abandonment of the idea of the hierarchical structure of international society, at the top of which was the Pope and the Emperor, and was characterised by the co-existence of a variety of states, each sovereign within its territory and free from any external authority or organisation. It reflected a conception of the international political order that gradually extended itself from its European roots to encompass most of the world. It was a conception built around the central importance of a particular type of political actor: the territorial sovereign state.[172] The model mostly stems from the presumption that 'the coherence of society has to be provided through the unitary power of the state. Since the split of multitudes of individuals and the disorder of society cannot create collective reason, it

[171] A.-M. Burley (1992), 'Law Among Liberal States: Liberal Internationalism and the Act of State Doctrine' 92(8) *Columbia Law Review* 1907, at 1923–6; M. Dabbah (2003), *The Internationalisation of Antitrust Policy* (Cambridge University Press) 141–2.

[172] J.G. March and J.P. Olsen (1998), 'The Institutional Dynamics of International Political Orders' 52(4) *International Organisation* 943, at 944.

is the homogeneity and unity "of the state" and its sovereign power, which forges and represents the quasi-transcendental destiny of society'.[173]

From a legal perspective, the main consequence of such a system is that sovereign states are solely responsible for the regulation of any matter that arises within their territory,[174] and that they are the primary subjects of international law.[175] Both these assumptions have a major impact on the process of internationalisation of competition law, and in fact are the basis for the two sets of solutions put forward with regard to practices conducted by business firms, as well as hybrid practices that have an effect on the territories of multiple states.

When problems that affect multiple countries emerge, there are two possible options: the former assumption leads to unilateral solutions, which in the field of competition law and policy take the form of extraterritorial application of national competition laws. As argued in the following chapters, in the field of competition law, a number of countries – the United States being the prime example – have used their national laws to address problems caused by anticompetitive practices that have an international effect.[176] The latter assumption, the fact that sovereign states are the primary subjects of international law, is the basis for the conclusion of international agreements with which contracting parties state that they agree on particular competition law-related commitments;[177] such agreements are the focal point of subsequent discussion in the book.

(ii) Types of formal international cooperation: classification of international agreements and introduction of the working question

In the field of competition law, attempts to reach a multilateral agreement go back to the first half of the previous century; nevertheless, while they are still active, no consensus has been reached on a binding relevant agreement.[178] In this absence of a central international legislative and judicial

[173] U. Preub (1999), 'Political Order and Democracy: Carl Schmitt and his Influence' in Ch. Mouffe (ed.), *The Challenge of Carl Schmitt* (New York: Verso) 167. Cited by Jayasuriya (2001), *supra* n. 122 at 445.

[174] D. Philpott (1995), 'Sovereignty: An Introduction and Brief History' 48 *Journal of International Affairs* 353, at 356–7.

[175] M. Shaw (2004), *International Law* (5th edn, Cambridge University Press) 175–223.

[176] On the concept of extraterritoriality, see 3.2.4 *infra*.

[177] And in this regard, international agreements have been considered to be equivalent to a contract. A.T. Guzman (2005), 'The Design of International Agreements' 16(4) *European Journal of International Law* 579, at 585.

[178] See the discussion in Chapter 6.

body, alternative forms of formal cooperation have been developed. As the book argues, there are three distinct types of agreements which are devoted to or contain competition provisions, something that validates the argument that international law has been increasingly fragmented with the conclusion of various types of agreements, some of which also establish dispute settlement mechanisms.[179] These categories include bilateral enforcement cooperation agreements, bilateral trade agreements which include competition provisions, and plurilateral regional trade agreements which include competition rules. These agreements, along with the negotiations over the possible adoption of a multilateral competition agreement, are the focal point of further discussion.

In reviewing these agreements, the aim of the book is twofold. First, it attempts to identify the types of norms that have been included in the agreements, both substantive and procedural, and this exercise is mainly a textual one. In the same context nevertheless, the book also discusses the role of the particular categories of agreements in the creation of international competition norms.[180] Furthermore, the book examines the legal status of the agreements, i.e. whether the agreements oblige the signing parties to apply the agreed clauses (hard law) or whether the parties just express an intention to cooperate (soft law). Another issue addressed is the extent to which the provisions found in these agreements harmonise the competition laws of the contracting parties, or whether they simply provide mechanisms for enforcement cooperation. Finally, most of the agreements discussed in the book are trade agreements which include a chapter on competition law and policy, and therefore the role of competition law and policy in the broader group of issues addressed by these agreements is also discussed.

The second and main aim of the book is to evaluate the role of the EU in the formation of such agreements. Instead of reviewing the influence of the EU in the development of international competition norms as a whole, the book evaluates the policy of the EU with regard to the various distinct types of international agreements which are dedicated to competition, or include competition provisions. While the textual analysis

[179] M. Koskenniemi and P. Leino (2002), 'Fragmentation of International Law? Postmodern Anxieties' 15 *Leiden Journal of International Law* 553, at 556; see also UNCTAD (2006), *Fragmentation of International Law: Difficulties Arising from the Diversification and Expansion of International Law, Report of the Study Group of the International Law Commission*, A/CN.4/L.682, in particular at 10–17.

[180] The analysis of the various forms of cooperation shows that, at least to date, while competition law has been included in bilateral and plurilateral regional agreements, it has not survived the more complicated multilateral negotiations.

is of major relevance here too, since it can on certain occasions lead to the assessment of the extent to which the EU has succeeded in imposing its competition law on its co-signing countries by including competition provisions similar to EU law, this discussion is also political.

This assumption is based on the argument that the international system is based both on international law and the balance of power, which operate between, rather than above sovereign states.[181] To this end, various international relations theories have been developed with the aim of describing – and to a certain extent predicting – the way in, and extent to, which countries cooperate.[182] Some of these theories, such as policy networks, epistemic communities, isomorphism and realism, are employed in different parts of the study in the context of the discussion about the negotiations on or provisions of the agreements. Such policy considerations are more clearly taken into account in the context of the discussion about the role of the EU in the formation of multilateral competition rules, where, in the absence of a binding international agreement on competition, the relevant discussion is devoted to the analysis of the position taken by the EU and the relevant positions of a number of countries, and therefore the political factor is prevalent.

2.4 Conclusion

This chapter has attempted to outline some of the main features of competition law and policy both on a national and an international level. It did so by first introducing the historical origins of competition law, from the development of the relevant case law in England in the fifteenth century on restrictive trade practices to the proliferation of competition law in most of the countries of the world, in the last twenty years.

The chapter noted that economic theories may have a significant effect on the particular application of national competition rules, and argued that various sectors of national economies are exempted from the application of competition laws, and these sectors may vary depending on the particular country under examination. The socio-cultural factors that have an effect on the particular application of competition rules in different countries have also been briefly reviewed. It has been shown that such

[181] L. Gross (1948), 'The Peace of Westphalia, 1648–1948' 42(1) *American Journal of International Law* 20, at 28–9. In its extreme version, as Shaw notes, '[W]here survival is involved international law may take second place'. M. Shaw (2004), *supra* n. 179 at 8.

[182] See A.-M. Slaughter (1993), 'International Law and International Relations Theory: A Dual Agenda' 87 *American Journal of International Law* 205.

factors are used as a basis for case-specific exemptions from the application of competition rules. In this regard, it has been argued that a number of issues that are not related to competition policies are taken into account in the context of the examination of a particular anticompetitive practice. Finally, on a national level, the chapter has outlined some of the arguments that have been raised in the relevant literature for and against the adoption of competition rules by developing countries.

In identifying all of these particularities of competition law, the chapter has not questioned the validity of competition rules. In contrast, the statistics provided here reveal that a very large number of countries have adopted competition rules, and this, by itself, is a clear indication that competition law and policy is considered to be a key part of liberal political systems. The aim of the analysis of the variant and sometimes divergent aspects of national competition rules has been to highlight the fact that competition law is still a relatively new legal instrument and that there is a long way to go before consensus is reached as to its optimum application.

On the other hand, the chapter has also stressed that due to economic globalisation the number of multinational firms has been increased, and this in turn has increased the number of anticompetitive practices conducted by such firms that have an effect on multiple national markets. Three types of relevant practices have been briefly reviewed: hard-core cartels, vertical restraints and cross-border mergers and acquisitions. As also noted, a number of hybrid practices which include anticompetitive practices supported by governments or allowed by them through the exemptions from the application of competition rules may have an effect on international trade.

In view of the existence of such practices that should be dealt with by competition rules, it has been noted that there are two possible solutions. The first is unilateral, extraterritorial application of competition rules. Nonetheless, as argued, it is taken as an assumption in this book that international problems need international solutions and in this regard, international agreements, which provide for cooperation and/or harmonisation of competition rules, have been employed to address the anticompetitive practices by firms that have an international effect. These agreements will be the focal point of subsequent analysis in this study, and this analysis will be carried out from the perspective of the EU, in order to evaluate the role of the EU in the formation and application of these agreements.

3

Bilateral Enforcement Cooperation Agreements

3.1 Common characteristics of enforcement cooperation agreements

3.1.1 Enforcement cooperation as a substitute for harmonisation of competition laws

Bilateral (and trilateral) enforcement cooperation agreements are agreements that do not harmonise the competition laws of the contracting parties. These agreements provide for mechanisms of enforcement cooperation. In the field of competition law enforcement cooperation has been used as an alternative for the harmonisation of national competition laws. Since no agreement on a multilateral code on restrictive business practices could be achieved in the last century, a number of countries with active international trade (through multinational firms) and a developed competition law cooperated on enforcement of their competition laws in order to confront the consequences of the increasing number of restrictive business practices with an international effect.

Thus, as early as the late 1950s when a conflict arose between the governments of Canada and the United States in a case relating to a US investigation of a patent pool among Canadian radio and television makers designed to exclude US manufactured products from the Canadian market, the governments of the United States and Canada entered into negotiations in order to coordinate their enforcement activities and avoid similar conflicts. The outcome of this case and the subsequent negotiations was the Fulton-Rodgers understanding of 1959,[1] in which the two governments agreed to construct a channel of

An earlier version of this chapter has been published under the title 'Enforcement Cooperation Agreements' in P. Marsden (ed.) (2007), *Handbook of Research in Trans-Atlantic Antitrust* (Edward Elgar Publishing).

[1] Named after the Canadian Minister of Justice and the US Attorney General at that time. See K. von Finckenstein (2001), 'International Antitrust Cooperation: Bilateralism or

communication regarding antitrust matters, through notification and consultation.[2]

Furthermore, by 1967 enforcement cooperation between competition agencies had become an issue of interest at the OECD, which adopted its first Recommendation[3] encouraging its member countries to cooperate in enforcement on antitrust issues. This first Recommendation of 1967 has been modified several times, most recently in 1995.[4] Taking this most recent Recommendation (of 1995) as a model, member countries are encouraged to:

(i) notify other members when another member's 'important interests' are affected by an investigation or enforcement action;[5]
(ii) coordinate parallel investigations where appropriate and practicable;[6]
(iii) disclose information concerning an investigation or proceeding which is being conducted in one member country but that may affect important interests of another member, in order to permit the member country whose interests are affected to comment and consult with the member country in which proceedings are being conducted;[7]
(iv) exchange information which is related to anticompetitive practices in international trade (with the reservation of the rules concerning confidentiality and unless such a disclosure of information would be contrary to significant national interests of any member country);[8] and
(v) request the competition authorities of another member country to take action if the member considers that one or more undertakings situated in that country are or have been engaged in anticompetitive practices that are substantially and adversely affecting the member country's interests;[9]

Multilateralism?', speech delivered in Vancouver, 31 May 2001, available at www.apeccp.org.tw/doc/Canada/Policy/1a.htm (last visited on 2 December 2009).

2 C. Stark (2000), 'Improving Bilateral Antitrust Cooperation', speech delivered in Washington, DC, 23 June 2000, at 2, available at www.usdoj.gov/atr/public/speeches/5075.htm (last visited on 2 December 2009).

3 OECD, Recommendation of the Council concerning Cooperation between Member Countries on Restrictive Business Practices Affecting International Trade, 5 October 1967, C(567)53 final.

4 OECD, Recommendation of the Council, 27 and 28 July 1995, C(95)130 final.

5 *Ibid.* art. I.A.1. 6 *Ibid.* art. I.A.2.

7 *Ibid.* art. I.B.4.a. 8 *Ibid.* art. I.A.3.

9 *Ibid.* art. I.B.5.a in conjunction with art. I.B.5.c. The provision relating to positive comity was added to the Recommendation by the amendment of 1973.

Moreover, in the Preamble,[10] the member countries are required to take into consideration the principle of international comity ('traditional' or 'negative' comity).

As can be seen, the provisions of the OECD Recommendation are relatively vague, and the content of the agreements following the OECD Recommendations has been expanded; however, the basic structure of all these agreements follows to a greater or lesser extent the OECD Recommendation. The Recommendation is entirely voluntary; nevertheless, it is still an important step since the OECD was the first institution that encouraged its member states to be involved in mechanisms of cooperation on competition enforcement and consequently to create a framework of cooperation,[11] and to date it has been particularly active in this field.[12]

3.1.2 *Basic structure of the agreements*

As is clear from Table 3.1, enforcement cooperation agreements in the field of competition law follow the basic structure of the OECD Recommendations. Nonetheless, the level of cooperation provided varies. For instance, the Brazil–Russia agreement is modest, providing for a general undertaking by the parties to cooperate and consult with each other on cases of mutual interest. On the other hand, the United States–Australia agreement and the Denmark–Iceland–Norway trilateral agreement (also joined by Sweden) are the first to provide for exchange of confidential information and are the first legally binding enforcement cooperation agreements (the so-called second generation agreements, discussed at 3.4 below). All the other 'first generation' agreements are soft law agreements and therefore include limitations on the ability of the competition agencies to share confidential information (the so-called confidentiality clause and the limitation by the existing laws, both discussed below). Almost all of these agreements provide for a basic procedure of cooperation, that is to say notification of cases of mutual interest, exchange of information,

[10] *Ibid.* recital 7.

[11] M. Monti (2000), 'Cooperation Between Competition Authorities: A Vision for the Future', speech delivered at the Japan Foundation Conference, Washington, DC, 23 June 2000, speech/00/234.

[12] See ICN (2007), *Cooperation Between Competition Agencies in Cartel Investigations*, Cartels Working Group Report, presented at the ICN Annual Conference, Moscow, May 2007, at 5, available at www.icn-moscow.org/get_file.php?id=115 (last visited on 2 December 2009).

cooperation and coordination of enforcement activities and negative comity. These mechanisms are also analysed below.

3.1.3 *Bilateral agreements as a way to contextualise international cooperation in other fields of commercial law*

Bilateral agreements have also been extensively used in other fields of commercial law, namely investment and taxation. In particular, since the 1950s and until 2000, more than 1,300 bilateral investment treaties (BITs) were signed.[13] The main goal of these agreements is to encourage and create favourable conditions for investors from the signing party, such that some of them, for example the treaties signed by the United States and Canada, also include a most favoured nation (MFN) clause.[14] More than 1,500 double taxation treaties have also been signed between various states, with the aim of mitigating the effects of double taxation by allocating taxation rights between source and residence countries and providing for cooperation, exchange of information and dispute settlement.[15]

3.1.4 *Enforcement cooperation where there are trade flows*

Another observation to be made regarding enforcement cooperation agreements is that the vast majority of these agreements have been concluded between countries with significant trade flows. This justifies to an extent the fact that most of these agreements have been concluded among industrialised countries (such as the EU, the United States, Canada, Japan and Australia). In this regard, the EU has signed such agreements with its three most important partners, namely the United States, Canada and Japan, and it has recently concluded a relevant agreement with Korea.

Nonetheless, the fact that in the last five years or so a number of less developed countries have been involved in bilateral enforcement agreements should not be overlooked and considerable trade flows between the contracting parties is one of the main incentives for the conclusion of most of these agreements. For example, Papua New Guinea has signed an agreement with Australia, and this is justified by the fact that Australia is the country with which Papua New Guinea has the most developed trade relations. Statistically, in the year 2000, Australia was the destination of

[13] WTO Working Group on Trade and Investment (1998), *Bilateral, Regional, Plurilateral, and Multilateral Agreements*, WT/WGTI/W/22, at 4.

[14] *Ibid.* at 6. [15] *Ibid.* at 10.

Table 3.1 *Bilateral enforcement cooperation agreements*

Agreement	Notification	Exchange of information	Enforcement cooperation	Coordination
United States–Germany (1976)	√	√	√	
United States–Australia (1982)	√	√	√	
EU–United States (1991)	√	√	√	√
United States–Canada (1995)	√	√	√	√
Australia–Taipei (1996)	√	√	√	√
New Zealand–Taipei (1996)	√	√	√	√
EU–United States on positive comity (1998)			√	
United States–Australia (1999)		√	√	
EU–Canada (1999)	√	√	√	√
United States–Japan (1999)	√	√	√	√
United States–Brazil (1999)	√		√	√
Australia–Papua New Guinea (1999)	√	√	√	√
United States–Israel (1999)	√	√	√	√
United States–Mexico (2000)	√	√	√	√
Canada–Chile (2001)	√	√	√	√
Russia–Brazil (2001)			√	
Canada–Mexico (2001)	√	√	√	√
Australia–Fiji MOU (2002)		√	√	√
Australia–Korea (2002)	√	√	√	√
Canada–UK (2003)	√	√	√	√
EU–Japan (2003)	√	√	√	√
United States–Canada on positive comity (2004)			√	
Canada–Japan (2005)	√	√	√	√
Canada–Korea (2006)	√	√	√	√
Australia–New Zealand (2007)		√	√	√
Canada–Brazil (2008)	√	√	√	√
EU–Korea (2009)	√	√	√	√

Consultations	Meetings between officials	Technical assistance	Comity	Positive comity	Predominance of existing laws of the parties	Right to share confidential information
√			√		√	
√			√		√	
√	√		√	√	√	
√	√		√	√	√	
		√	√		√	
		√			√	
				√	√	
					√	√
√	√		√	√	√	
√	√		√		√	
	√	√	√	√	√	
√		√	√		√	
√	√		√	√	√	
√	√	√	√	√	√	
	√		√		√	
√	√				√	
√	√	√	√	√	√	
	√	√	√		√	
√	√	√	√		√	
	√		√		√	
√	√		√	√	√	
				√	√	
√	√		√	√	√	
	√		√		√	
√	√		√			√
	√		√		√	
√	√		√	√	√	

29.1 per cent of Papua New Guinea's exports and 21.2 per cent of Papua New Guinea's imports came from Australia. Moreover, according to the Australian Competition and Consumer Commission (ACCC) the agreement is a way to achieve greater access to Papua New Guinea's market for Australian exporters through proper utilisation of competition law in this market.[16] It is logical to assume that 'proper utilisation of competition law' aims for the creation of an environment of safe investment for Australian firms.

3.1.5 *Enforcement cooperation agreements (first generation) in the form of soft law*

A major characteristic of the first generation of agreements is that they are considered as soft law, which in turn has been seen as an alternative to hard law in the 'legalisation'[17] of international relations. Hard law refers to legally binding obligations that are precise (or can be made precise through adjudication or the issuance of detailed regulations) and that delegate authority for interpreting and implementing the law. Each of these characteristics of law (obligation, precision and delegation) may be present in varying degrees along a continuum, and each can vary independently of the others.[18] Accordingly, soft law is chosen once legal arrangements are weakened along one or more of the dimensions of obligation, precision and delegation. Put differently, soft law stands between hard law and purely political arrangements where legalisation is largely absent,[19] and includes elements from both these situations (that is, it includes legal provisions – an element of hard law – but these provisions are not legally enforceable – an element of purely political arrangements).

This difficulty in distinguishing between law and policy has led some international lawyers to condemn soft law as vague and inadequate to

[16] See the ACCC website, www.accc.gov.au/international/international.htm.

[17] By 'legalisation' is meant here the formalisation of international relations in the form of law (international agreements).

[18] K.W. Abbott, R. Keohane, A. Moravcsik, A.-M. Slaughter and D. Snidal (2000), 'The Concept of Legalisation' 54(3) *International Organisation* 401.

[19] K.W. Abbott and D. Snidal (2000), 'Hard and Soft Law in International Governance' 54(3) *International Organisation* 421, at 422. For a critique on this analysis, see M. Finnemore and S.J. Toope (2001), 'Alternatives to "Legalization": Richer Views of Law and Politics' 55(1) *International Organisation* 743, in which the authors hold that the distinction made by Abbott and Snidal has certain limitations, as it does not take into account other important ingredients of law, such as the features and effects of legitimacy, including the need for a certain link between law and underlying social practice.

regulate international economic relations. Weil, for instance, has argued that the increasing use of soft law can destabilise the whole international normative system into an instrument inadequate to serve its purpose.[20] In fact, these arguments to an extent can be applied in the case of this first generation of bilateral and trilateral competition enforcement cooperation agreements. The lack of legally binding obligations, along with the confidentiality clause, in reality give absolute discretion to the contracting parties to ignore the agreements in cases where they consider that their important interests would be impeded if they had to follow the agreements' provisions, and this is a significant drawback, in view of the discussion in Chapter 2 with regard to the different understandings about the nature and proper enforcement of competition law.

So what exactly are the factors that have led to the choice of soft law instead of hard law in the process of the legalisation of international economic relations? Soft law bilateral agreements have not only been used in the field of competition law but also in other areas of international law, such as taxation, investment and securities.[21] The reason for this choice, as a number of scholars have pointed out, is that soft law can overcome deadlocks in the relations between states that result from economic or political differences among them, when efforts at firmer solutions have been unsuccessful.[22] This general assumption can be applied to the process of internationalisation of competition law, where the lack of success in concluding a multilateral agreement has obviously led countries to opt for alternative solutions, including bilateral (and in fact voluntary) enforcement cooperation agreements. This form of cooperation is definitely more flexible than traditional international agreements with binding provisions and as Reismann puts it, 'thanks to soft law we still have people channeling efforts toward law and toward trying to achieve objectives through legal mechanism, rather than going ahead and doing it in other fashions'.[23]

Furthermore, a substantial amount of soft law can be attributed to differences in the economic structures and economic interests of different states.[24] This argument is also relevant in the case of competition law

[20] P. Weil (1983), 'Towards Relative Normativity in International Law?' 77 *American Journal of International Law* 413, at 423.

[21] A.-M. Slaughter (2000), 'Governing the Global Economy through Government Networks' in M. Byers (ed.), *The Role of Law in International Politics: Essays in International Relations and International Law* (Oxford University Press) 1077.

[22] M. Reismann (1991), 'A Hard Look at Soft Law: Panel Report' 82 *American Society of International Law* 371, at 377.

[23] Quoted in Reismann, *ibid.* at 377. [24] *Ibid.* at 375.

which, as argued in Chapter 2, may include different aims depending on the interests of different countries, with varied objectives and cultures. Supportive of this hypothesis are provisions regarding deceptive marketing practices included in the Canada–Australia–New Zealand[25] and the United States–Canada[26] agreements, which thus incorporate consumer protection law.[27] What soft law contributes to this situation is that it creates channels of communication. As the next section argues, cooperation between competition officials supports the development of common understandings among them in relation to the nature and proper operation of competition law. To this end, when such a common understanding has been achieved, it could be argued that cooperation through soft law instruments may lead to stronger forms of cooperation.[28]

3.1.6 Bilateral enforcement cooperation as a strategy of strong states

It is also clear from Table 3.1 that enforcement cooperation has taken the form of bilateral (and only lately trilateral) agreements. However, why bilateral and not, for example, multi- or plurilateral enforcement cooperation agreements? This question has to be answered especially in view of the fact that enforcement cooperation agreements have to a great extent been framed in accordance with the OECD Recommendation, which does not itself refer to bilateral cooperation.

A number of scholars and politicians attribute bilateralism in the field of competition enforcement cooperation to the US policy on international competition law in the post-Second World War period. The United States historically resisted participation in international institutional arrangements; they were perceived as jeopardising its political autonomy,[29] a phenomenon also illustrated in the process of internationalisation of competition law, in which the United States has consistently been the most prominent opponent of the development of the idea of a multilateral

25 See Canada–Australia–New Zealand agreement, art. I.2.

26 See United States–Canada agreement, art. VII.

27 According to Canadian officials the main aim of these provisions is to solve problems relating to deceptive telemarketing, i.e. person-to-person telephone calls used to make false or misleading representations in promoting the supply of a product or business interest. See G. Murphy (2001), 'Canada, Australia and New Zealand Competition Authorities Sign Cooperation Arrangement' 22(8) *European Competition Law Review* 322.

28 See 3.4.2 *infra* which discusses the cooperation between the United States and the United Kingdom, and United States and Canada, on criminal cases.

29 See Abbott *et al.* (2000), *supra* n. 18 at 401.

agreement on competition. Instead, US officials have advocated the application of US competition law as the most appropriate way to address problems created by restrictive business practices with an international effect, even in cases where US laws have to be applied in an extraterritorial manner.[30]

Furthermore, US officials have used bilateral agreements as a complementary strategy to unilateralism. As Braithwaite and Drahos claim, in international trade generally, the most fundamental US strategy is to 'act tough' on bilateral negotiations to set frameworks for subsequent multilateral negotiation.[31] This strategy has been observed in the area of intellectual property law, where it finally led to the adoption of the Agreement on Trade-Related Aspects of Intellectual Property Rights (TRIPS);[32] and can also be observed in the field of competition law, where the United States is the most frequent user of bilateral enforcement cooperation agreements, both in the form of soft law, through first generation agreements, and lately hard law, through the conclusion of a second generation agreement with Australia, and the use of mutual legal assistance treaties and extradition treaties with regard to the investigation of competition cases.[33]

Waller further argues that cooperation on enforcement agreements is currently in vogue because it increases national power.[34] It is definitely easier for politically and economically strong states to cope with negotiations and cooperation on a bilateral rather than on a multilateral basis. In the absence of a judicial body to decide on cases where a conflict arises, it is very much the political and economic power of the contracting parties that will decide the outcome of the conflict. Officials and academics of smaller countries have often expressed this concern. For instance, it has been argued that the possible conclusion of a multilateral competition agreement would be the best solution with respect to the problems stemming from restrictive business practices conducted by multinational enterprises, since 'parties with relatively little bargaining power will be able to join forces with similar countries to safeguard their interests, leading to a more balanced agreement',[35] an argument tested and validated in

30 See the discussion in 6.3.1 *infra*.

31 J. Braithwaite and P. Drahos (2000), *Global Business Regulation* (Cambridge University Press) 198.

32 *Ibid.* 33 See 3.4.2 *infra*.

34 S.W. Waller (1997), 'Internationalisation of Antitrust Enforcement' 77 *Boston University Law Review* 343, at 378.

35 R. Zach (1998), 'International Cooperation Between Antitrust Enforcement Agencies: A View from a Small Country' in H. Ulrich (ed.), *Comparative Competition*

practice in the context of the discussion regarding the negotiations over a possible WTO agreement.[36]

3.1.7 *Policy of the EU towards the adoption of first generation bilateral enforcement cooperation agreements*

All these arguments about bilateralism and the increase of national power have also been reflected in recent times in the EU, but not in the field of agreements on enforcement cooperation. Having concluded enforcement cooperation agreements only with the United States, Canada and Japan (and very recently Korea), the EU has not been as active as the United States in the adoption of this particular legal tool, despite the fact that the negotiation and application of such agreements are carried out solely by the Directorate-General on Competition, and this to a certain extent simplifies the procedure of negotiation of these agreements from an EU perspective.[37] Two main arguments may be put forward with regard to the observation that the EU has not been particularly active in this type of agreements. First, the EU throughout the 1990s and until the collapse of the WTO talks on competition formally supported the adoption of a possible WTO multilateral agreement, and therefore to a certain extent considered soft law bilateral agreements to be of secondary importance.[38] Secondly, given the voluntary nature of the agreements, it was considered by the European Commission that the use of such agreements was somewhat limited, since cooperation could be carried out in any event, irrespective of the existence of such agreements.[39] This second assumption is also supported by the fact that the EU has formally developed bilateral relations with Brazil and China, both important business partners, yet in the case of China no official agreement has been adopted, while in the case of Brazil, a Memorandum of Understanding (MOU) was signed

Law: Approaching an International System of Antitrust Law (Baden-Baden: Nomos Verlagsgesellschaft) 261.

[36] See 6.3.2 *infra* where it is noted that developing countries, which would normally be in a disadvantaged position in bilateral talks, have combined their forces and have had a major impact at the multilateral level.

[37] This observation is important in view of the fact that, e.g., in the case of the negotiations for a possible WTO competition agreement, there was divergence in the approaches taken by DG Competition and DG Trade, which as argued in Chapter 6, may have played a role in the overall position of the EU in the negotiations for such an agreement.

[38] See 6.2 *infra*.

[39] This position has been expressed by Stephen Ryan, of the European Commission, at a CEPR meeting in Paris, December 2005.

in 2009 and this MOU followed a coordinated 'dawn raid' carried out by EU, Brazilian and US authorities with regard to an investigation in the refrigeration compressor industry.[40] On the other hand, the EU in the context of its enlargement and its neighbourhood policy has been the most prominent user of bilateral trade agreements which include competition provisions, and (as will be argued in Chapter 4) to a certain extent it obliges its co-signing states to adopt legislation similar to that of the EU. In addition, as discussed in 3.4 below, the EU has more recently been interested in concluding second generation bilateral agreements, but these attempts have not been fruitful to date.

3.2 Content of first generation agreements

3.2.1 Early first generation agreements: reactive rather than proactive

The basic characteristic of the early first generation agreements is that their objective was to resolve conflicts that had already occurred and were relevant to the extraterritorial application of the US antitrust rules, rather than to avoid future conflicts. In this regard the agreements were reactive rather than proactive. For example, the exchange of information is dealt with in much more detail in the United States–Australia agreement and in the United States–Canada Memorandum of Understanding[41] due to the fact that they were concluded after the confrontation in the *Uranium Cartel* case. During the 1970s, a US court held in the *Uranium Cartel* case that it was justified in exercising jurisdiction against nine non-US uranium producers.[42] This decision created very serious friction and led a number of countries to adopt blocking statutes and/or claw-back statutes: the former were intended to prevent or limit the ability of the United States to obtain information located in countries with such statutes; the latter allowed citizens to seek compensatory damages from plaintiffs

[40] See N. Kroes (2009), 'Tackling Cartels: A Never-ending Task', speech delivered at the Anti-Cartel Enforcement Criminal and Administrative Policy Panel session, Brasilia, 8 October 2009, speech/09/454. It is noted that the content of the MOU has to date not been published. See also E.V. Legares (2010), 'International Agreements Regarding Cooperation in the Field of Competition: The New Strategy of the European Commission' *Journal of European Competition Law and Practice* 1.

[41] A.D. Ham (1993), 'International Cooperation in the Anti-trust Field and in Particular the Agreement between the United States of America and the Commission of the European Communities' 30 *Common Market Law Review* 571, at 576.

[42] W.K. Walker (1992), 'Extraterritorial Application of U.S. Antitrust Laws: The Effect of the European Community–United States Agreement' 33 *Harvard International Law Journal* 583, at 586.

who had prevailed in US litigation.[43] This confrontation was the reason for the adoption of the bilateral enforcement cooperation agreements between the United States and Australia in 1982, and Canada in 1985, respectively.

3.2.2 Agreement between the United States and the EU

The first proactive agreement was the agreement concluded between the EU and the United States in 1991.[44] In examining the content and impact of the first generation of bilateral enforcement cooperation agreements, this chapter will concentrate mainly on the agreement between the EU and the United States. Various arguments may be put forward for this approach. This agreement is arguably the most important for considering the impact of first generation agreements, as it relates to two major 'players' in international trade with mature competition systems; and, most importantly, it has been tested for almost twenty years and is in general the only agreement that can give us practical examples of situations where this kind of agreement has proved to be effective or ineffective. In addition, this agreement has also been the model for all the other similar agreements signed by the EU and the United States. Most relevantly to the theme that this book attempts to address, the analysis of the EU–United States agreement may provide insights into the way in which the EU has reacted with regard to the use of this type of international agreement.

3.2.3 Negative comity (avoidance of conflicts)

First generation agreements primarily aim at the avoidance of conflicts between the cooperating parties, and this aim is incorporated into the text of the agreements in the form of the principle of comity. Comity, or

[43] Pitofsky provides as an example the United Kingdom, which introduced such clauses in the Protection of Trading Interests Act 1980, as amended by the Civil Jurisdiction and Judgments Act 1982 and Statute Law (Repeals) Act 1993, Sch. 1, Pt XIV. He also notes that relevant laws have been adopted by Canada, France, Australia and South Africa. See R. Pitofski (1999), 'Competition Policy in a Global Economy: Today and Tomorrow' 2(3) *Journal of International Economic Law* 403, at 408.

[44] The agreement finally entered into force in 1995 following an action brought by the government of France against the European Commission successfully challenging the competence of the Commission to conclude this kind of agreement. The problem was finally solved with the approval of the agreement by the European Council. See A. Riley (1995), 'The Jellyfish Nailed? The Announcement of the EC/US Competition Co-operation Agreement' 16(3) *European Competition Law Review* 185.

more correctly negative comity (the term 'negative' is used in order to distinguish it from positive comity), developed in the Netherlands in the last quarter of the seventeenth century[45] and was especially influenced by the work of Ulrich Huber, who based his analysis on three axioms: (i) that each state had sovereignty in its territory (that is, the laws of each state bind all of its subjects within the boundaries of this state but not beyond); (ii) that every person who is found within each state is considered to be a subject of this state irrespective of whether he/she resides there permanently or temporarily; and (iii) that the rulers of each state should ensure (through the concept of comity) that the laws of other states are enforced within its boundaries in order to maintain the validity of other states' laws and impartiality towards other states' citizens. According to Huber, comity was based on the existence of a *jus gentium*, a form of common law which applied to conflicts of laws, since the general utility of nations gave rise to a common practice giving effect to foreign laws and judgments everywhere as laws. In contrast, other theorists claimed that comity was a matter of discretion for each sovereign state.[46]

This latter argument has prevailed in the literature on international law. Even though the notion of comity is not entirely clear in the field of public international law,[47] comity (as defined in general terms) is a concept under which extraterritorial determinations are often grounded in considerations of politeness or respect; it is 'a willingness to grant a privilege, not as a matter of right, but out of deference and good will'[48] in order to avoid conflicts relating to jurisdiction. Specifically with reference to competition law, the principle of comity encourages states parties to take into account, in the enforcement of their competition laws, the important interests of the other party so as to avoid the creation of conflicts during their enforcement activity. In considering the other party's important interests, the enforcing party applies the comity clause within the framework of its laws and to the extent compatible with its own important interests.[49]

[45] H. Yntema (1966), 'The Comity Doctrine' 65(1) *Michigan Law Review* 9.

[46] *Ibid*. at 26.

[47] Joel Paul gives sixteen alternative meanings of the principle, found in various scientific articles that deal with comity: J.R. Paul (1991), 'Comity in International Law' 32(1) *Harvard International Law Journal* 2, at 3–4.

[48] A.J. Himelfarb (1996), 'The International Language of Convergence: Reviving the Antitrust Dialogue between the United States of America and the European Union with a Uniform Understanding of Extraterritoriality' 17(3) *University of Pennsylvania Journal of International Economic Law* 909, at 914.

[49] C.-D. Ehlermann (1994), 'The International Dimension of Competition Policy' 17 *Fordham International Law Journal* 833, at 836.

Negative comity has been included in the OECD Recommendations (as described above) and has also formed part of almost every bilateral enforcement agreement. In the EU–United States agreement, the provision for comity is laid down in article VI: it is based on three principles. First, there is recognition that the important interests of one party would normally be reflected in laws, decisions or statements of policy by its competent authorities. A second principle is the recognition that, as a general matter, the potential for adverse impact on one party's important interests arising from enforcement activity by the other party is less at the investigative stage and greater at the stage at which conduct is prohibited or penalised, or at which other forms of remedial orders are imposed. The third principle (and actually the novelty introduced in this agreement) is a list of six situations where the important interests of one party may be affected. These include:

(a) the relative significance to the anticompetitive activities involved of conduct within the enforcing party's territory as compared to conduct within the other party's territory;
(b) the presence or absence of a purpose on the part of those engaged in the anticompetitive activities to affect consumers, suppliers or competitors within the enforcing party's territory;
(c) the relative significance of the effects of the anticompetitive activities on the enforcing party's interests as compared to the effects on the other party's interests;
(d) the existence or absence of reasonable expectations that would be furthered or defeated by the enforcement activities;
(e) the degree of conflict or consistency between the enforcement activities and the other party's laws or articulated economic policies; and
(f) the extent to which enforcement activities of the other party with respect to the same persons, including judgments or undertakings resulting from such activities, may be affected.

Clearly, the wording of the comity-related provisions of the agreement is quite detailed. This reflects the intention of the contracting parties to limit the possibilities of jurisdictional conflicts. Having said that, the following analysis shows that in both the United States and the EU, extraterritorial application of competition law is the guiding principle, and comity has been seen as a principle to be applied in exceptional circumstances.

3.2.4 *Extraterritorial application of competition rules*

In the last sixty years, the US courts have consistently applied US antitrust rules in an extraterritorial manner.[50] Nonetheless, the extent to which comity considerations may be taken into account in competition cases varies, depending on the particular case under examination.

The 'effects doctrine' was first introduced in the 1945 *Alcoa* case.[51] According to this doctrine, the US courts have the competence to apply US antitrust law to conduct that has occurred wholly or partly in a foreign state that is intended to affect the United States and has in fact such an effect. In its 1976 *Timberlane* decision,[52] the Ninth Circuit mitigated the effects test by taking into account a consideration of comity for foreign defendants, thus creating a rule of reason comity analysis, which was codified in the Foreign Trade Antitrust Improvements Act of 1982 (FTAIA).[53] The Act provided that the challenged conduct must have a 'direct, substantial and reasonably foreseeable effect' on US commerce or on the trade of a US citizen/company engaged in export commerce. The aim of the FTAIA was to provide clear guidance with regard to the extraterritorial application of US competition rules; nonetheless, it is widely acknowledged that it has failed to do so.[54]

In its 1993 *Hartford Fire* decision,[55] the US Supreme Court held, in justifying the extraterritorial application of the Sherman Act, that in terms of comity, the exercise of US jurisdiction would be limited to exceptional occasions and only if there were a 'true conflict', and it was therefore to be applied only in exceptional cases. This statement was confirmed by the Supreme Court in the *Nippon Paper* case, where it held that comity is 'more an aspiration' than an established rule, confirming in the process that the growth of comity in competition matters was stunted by *Hartford Fire*.[56]

[50] See generally S.E. Barnet (2004), 'Conflicts of Jurisdiction and International Comity in Extraterritorial Antitrust' 18 *Emory International Law Review* 555.

[51] *United States* v. *Aluminum Co. of America*, 148 F.2d 416 (2d Cir. 1945).

[52] *Timberlane Lumber Co.* v. *Bank of America*, 549 F.2d 597 (9th Cir. 1976).

[53] 15 U.S.C. s. 6a (1994).

[54] C. Springman (2005), 'Fix Prices Globally, Get Sued Locally? US Jurisdiction over International Cartels' 72 *University of Chicago Law Review* 265, at 271–3.

[55] *Hartford Fire Ins. Co.* v. *California*, 509 U.S. 764 (1993).

[56] *United States* v. *Nippon Paper Industries Co. Ltd et al.*, 109 F.3d 9 (1st Cir. 1997).

More recently, the Supreme Court once more examined the effects test in its *Empagran* decision,[57] where it held that foreign purchasers of vitamins based outside the United States did not have the right to bring a claim for treble damages in a US court for conduct that had taken place solely outside the US market, even where it was part of a wider cartel which did affect the US market. On remand from the Supreme Court,[58] the Court of Appeals held that, in order to obtain relief, the plaintiffs must show that there was a 'direct casual relationship' between the effect that the anticompetitive practices had in the US market and the injuries they suffered. The court found that the appellants could not show such a 'proximate causation' and thus they did not have the right to bring an action against the appellees.[59] Hence, even though US approach to comity has changed over time, comity considerations rarely apply in the US jurisprudence, while the extraterritorial application of US competition rules is the norm, and this assumption is also validated by the fact that, at least with regard to cartel enforcement, the United States has been very active in recent years in seeking extradition of foreign nationals who participate in cartels. [60]

Similarly, as far as the EU is concerned, there has been in the last twenty years or so a continuous effort from the European Commission to establish the effects doctrine in Europe, with the aim of extending the scope of extraterritorial application of EC competition law. In the *Wood Pulp* case,[61] the Commission found that thirty-six out of forty-two suppliers of wood pulp were violating European competition law (under then Article 81(1) of the EC Treaty). Forty of these forty-two undertakings were not resident within the EU. On appeal, the European Court of Justice (ECJ, now Court of Justice) ruled that an agreement concluded by undertakings that were not within the borders of the EU would be an infringement of European competition law, if the agreement was 'implemented' within the EU.[62] In taking

[57] *Hoffmann-La Roche* v. *Empagran S.A.*, 124 S. Ct. 2359 (2004). See K.S. Reinker (2004), 'Case Comment: Roche vs. Empagran' 28 *Harvard Journal of Law and Public Policy* 297.

[58] See *Empagran S.A.* v. *Hoffmann-La Roche Ltd et al.*, Opinion of the Court of Appeals, No. 01-7115c (2005).

[59] *Ibid.*

[60] As Watson-Doig notes, in the period between 2000 and 2005, of the eighty individuals serving jail sentences in the United States for cartel activity, eighteen were foreign nationals. See N. Watson-Doig (2007), 'Crime and Competition', *Competition Law Insight*, 10 April 2007, 8, at 9. See also the discussion on the Ian Norris case at 3.4.2 *infra*.

[61] Joined Cases C-89, C-104, C-114, C-116, C-117 and C-125–C-129/85 *Ahlstrom and others* v. *European Commission (Re Wood Pulp Cartel)* [1998] ECR 5193.

[62] The judgment reads: '[A]n infringement of Article 85 … [is] made up of two elements, the formation of the agreement, decision or concerted practice, and the implementation thereof'. See *ibid.* para. 16.

this decision, the ECJ refrained from relying on the effects doctrine despite the fact that the Commission had argued for the effects test. Instead, it used the implementation doctrine, according to which EU competition law can be applied whenever merely one sale occurs within the Community. Thus, the validity of the application of the effects doctrine in competition cases in Europe is still not clear, or at least not in the same way as in the United States.[63]

However, this is not the situation with regard to mergers. In the *Gencor* case,[64] the European Commission blocked a merger that was cleared by the South African competition authorities, despite the fact that both the companies involved in the merger were registered in South Africa, but which fell within the EU turnover thresholds which determine jurisdiction.[65] In its judgment, the Court of First Instance (CFI, now the General Court) declared that 'the application of the [Merger] Regulation is justified under public international law when it is foreseeable that a proposed concentration will have an immediate and substantial effect in the Community'.[66] Furthermore, commentating on this case, former Commissioner Mario Monti expressed his opinion that:

> I am confident, however, that this uncertainty is now behind us: the European Court of First Instance ... clearly states that the Community's exercise of jurisdiction over a merger taking place wholly outside of the Community is compatible with the principles of public international law, where the merger produces direct, substantial and foreseeable effects within the EU. [67]

It follows that despite the inclusion of a comity provision in the agreement, the main aim of competition officials in the EU is to establish the effects test (and the unilateral application of EU competition law) rather than take into account comity considerations.[68] Similarly, with the exception of the recent *Empagran* case, it has been observed that very little room for comity considerations has been left in the United States and, up to the present time, comity itself has not had any substantial impact on competition cases. Hence, we can observe that, at least in the case of EU–US

[63] J.D. Banks (1998), 'The Development of the Concept of Extraterritoriality under European Merger Law and its Effectiveness under the Merger Regulation following the Boeing/McDonnell Douglas Decision 1997' 19(5) *European Competition Law Review* 306, at 308.

[64] Case T-102/96 *Gencor Ltd* v. *Commission* [1999] ECR II-753.

[65] *Ibid.* paras. 78–88. [66] *Ibid.* para. 90.

[67] Monti (2000), *supra* n. 11.

[68] Nevertheless, it should be also pointed out that *Woodpulp* predates the conclusion of the agreement, and was probably among the factors that led to its adoption.

cooperation on competition, the principle of comity has had a minimal effect.

Finally, it should be noted that the tendency to apply national competition rules on an extraterritorial basis has in recent years found more supporters. For instance, in 2004, Korea for the first time applied its competition rules in an extraterritorial manner by imposing fines of US$8.5 million on six graphite electrode manufacturers, including four Japanese firms, one German company and one US company.[69]

3.2.5 Procedures of positive cooperation provided for by first generation agreements

Apart from the avoidance of conflicts, the first generation of enforcement cooperation agreements also provide for a mechanism of positive cooperation. This mechanism includes notification, exchange of information between officials, cooperation and coordination of enforcement activities, consultations, and finally, positive comity.

(i) Notification, cooperation and coordination

There is a provision for notification (i.e. the exchange of basic information) in every competition enforcement cooperation agreement that has been concluded so far. Notification is in fact the mechanism which triggers the process of cooperation between competition agencies. The basic content of a notification provision is that the parties have to notify one another whenever their competition authorities become aware that their enforcement activities *may affect important interests of the other party.* This provision has been included in cooperation agreements since the first agreement between the United States and Germany (1976). In the early agreements, there were no indications of when the important interests of a contracting party might be affected. Hence, the test appeared very general and it was in practice left to the absolute discretion of the parties when to notify the other contracting party.

However, this changed with the conclusion of the EU–United States agreement of 1991 (as revised), which was the first agreement to specify particular situations where the important interests of 'the other party' might be affected.[70] These included situations: that were relevant

[69] See OECD (2005), *Hard Core Cartels: Third Report on the Implementation of the 1998 Recommendation*, at 13.

[70] See EU–United States agreement, art. II.

to enforcement activities of the other party; that involved anticompetitive activities other than mergers and acquisitions which were carried out in significant part in the other party's territory; that involved mergers or acquisitions in which one or more parties to the transaction, or a company controlling one or more of the parties of the transactions, is a company incorporated or organised under the laws of the other party or its states; where the anticompetitive practice involved conduct that was encouraged or approved by the other party; or that involved remedies that would require or prohibit conduct in the other party's territory.

This list included almost any possible enforcement activity which could have an effect on the other party's important interests, and according to the European Commission the mechanism of notification was the clearest obligation stemming from the agreement.[71] The notification of the case to the other party should contain adequate information so that the other party's competition authority would be able to evaluate any effects on its interests. Moreover, the notification should be made to the other party far enough in advance in order to enable the other party's views to be taken into account before a final decision was adopted.[72] Hence, for example, in a merger case where the European Commission decides to scrutinise the transaction, and according to the above-mentioned provisions its involvement in the case may affect important interests of the United States, it must inform either the US Department of Justice (DoJ) or the US Federal Trade Commission (FTC) (depending on the case) as soon as it initiates proceedings.[73]

Furthermore, with regard to coordination, the agreement stipulates in article IV that where contracting parties have an interest in pursuing enforcement activities with regard to related situations, they agree that it is in their mutual interest to coordinate their enforcement activities. When considering if such coordination should be developed, the parties must take into account a number of factors.[74]

[71] European Commission (1998), *EC Commission Report to the Council and the European Parliament on the Application of the Agreement between the European Communities and the Government of the United States of America regarding the Application of their Competition Laws, 1 January to 31 December 1997* (Brussels, 11 May 1998) 3.

[72] See EU–United States agreement, art. II.3(a)(iii), (b)(iii).

[73] Successive notifications may occur in the same case. For example, in a merger case the Commission may notify at the outset of the case; then, as appropriate, when the Commission decides to initiate proceedings; and, eventually, 'far enough in advance … to enable the other party's views to be taken into account', before a final decision is adopted: European Commission (1998), *supra* n. 71 at 3.

[74] For instance, in the EU–United States agreement, these factors include the relative ability of the parties' competition authorities to obtain the information necessary to conduct

(ii) Exchange of information: meetings between officials

Exchange of information is the cornerstone of international cooperation and the main aim of these agreements. It is in fact *the* factor on which the effectiveness of these agreements depends. The exchange of information, according to the way that these agreements have been framed, has a dual function. First, it offers the chance for cooperating competition authorities to inform each other of, and on, cases of mutual interest. Notification, enforcement cooperation and coordination, consultation and positive comity are in one way or another based on exchange of information. However, the ability of competition authorities to exchange information is subject to the limitations imposed by the existing laws of the parties and the confidentiality clause, as discussed below.

Secondly, exchange of information can also be a process through which officials from different competition authorities can exchange their opinions on economic and political issues that are related to competition law enforcement. Perhaps the most important element of these agreements is that they provide for a mechanism through which officials of different national authorities are able to come into contact with one another and share their views on issues of mutual interest, thus developing a common understanding on the function of competition law and policy.[75] It has to be stressed here, again, that competition law is a relatively recent legal instrument, especially for countries which have only recently embarked on the process of creating an environment for competition in their internal markets; the existence of these agreements and the exchange of opinions and experience between officials regarding competition law and policy is a positive process towards the creation of a sound and effective framework for competition law.

The international relations and politics literature gives (at least) two alternative explanations for this phenomenon of the internationalisation of competition law through the exchange of views between officials. First, it is related to the literature that discusses *elite learning* and according to which decision-makers incorporate new values and interests through regular contact with decision-makers from other countries.[76]

enforcement activity, or the effect of such coordination on each party's ability to achieve its objectives.

[75] It is interesting to note that in recent times (since the conclusion of the United States–EU agreement) almost all of these agreements include a provision for meetings of officials, on an annual, semi-annual or periodic basis.

[76] See P. Kurzer (2001), *Markets and Moral Regulation: Cultural Change in the European Union* (Cambridge University Press).

An alternative explanation for this process is that given by the supporters of institutional isomorphism, who claim that diffusion of interests, values and norms occurs through the *homogenisation* of institutional structures.[77]

The result of this process is the creation of what political scientists call a policy, or government network. According to legal and political scholars, transgovernmentalism, which is the outcome of the creation of these networks, is a new vision of global governance. The idea of transgovernmentalism starts from the assumption that the primary state actors in the international realm are no longer foreign ministers or heads of states, but the same government institutions that dominate domestic policies, that is, administrative agencies, courts and legislators.[78] It then moves on to the conclusion that through different mechanisms of cooperation (among which are included bilateral enforcement cooperation agreements and MOAs) these groups of officials and domestic institutions are in fact the most important actors in the governance of the global economy. Hence, according to this theory, global governance is horizontal rather than vertical, decentralised rather that centralised, and composed of national government officials rather than a supranational bureaucracy.[79]

Bilateral enforcement cooperation agreements create mechanisms for diffusion of information about technical aspects of competition law and different state interests. The outcome of the creation of this web is twofold. First, the competition officials of one country will become familiar with the concerns of competition officials from other countries regarding the function of competition policy and the enforcement of competition law. Secondly, and with reference to the policy network idea, this web reinforces the role of competition officials in international governance.

Regarding specifically the EU–United States agreement, this exchange of information through meetings of competition officials happens through administrative 'arrangements of attendance', which include reciprocal attendance at a certain stage of individual cases involving the implementation of their respective competition rules.

(iii) Positive comity

Positive comity could be characterised as the most revolutionary form of cooperation that some of the first generation agreements provided for, even though it is not in fact a new practice. This mechanism of cooperation

[77] See J.W. Meyer, J. Boli, G.M. Thomas and F.O. Ramirez (1997), 'World Society and the Nation State' 103(1) *American Journal of Sociology* 144.

[78] Slaughter (2000), *supra* n. 21 at 1078–9.

[79] *Ibid.* at 1093.

was included in the United States-Germany Friendship, Commerce and Navigation Treaty of 1954[80] and subsequently in a number of bilateral treaties between the United States and Greece, Denmark, Japan, Italy and France.[81] It had been used between the United States and Japan as a mechanism of cooperation in the past, even before its inclusion in bilateral enforcement cooperation agreements.[82] Despite the fact that it has been included in the OECD Recommendations on cooperation since the amendment of 1973, positive comity has not yet been defined in a multilateral context.[83]

Nonetheless, since it was first included in the agreement between the United States and the EU, the provision for positive comity has been almost identical in every other agreement of this kind. According to the standard provision in bilateral agreements where positive comity is included, when a contracting party (A) believes that its important interests are affected by an anticompetitive practice that has been put into effect within the territory of the other contracting party (B) and in respect of which A does not have the competence to initiate enforcement proceedings, then A is able to request B to take action against this anticompetitive practice on behalf of A. Thus, rather than avoiding conflicts, positive comity requires the parties to conduct acts of positive cooperation.

The United States–EU Agreement on Positive Comity of 1998 The agreement between the United States and the EU on positive comity expands the notion of positive comity even further than the first agreement between the EU and the United States.[84] It provides that the competition authorities of a requesting party may petition the competition authorities of a requested party to investigate and, if warranted, to remedy anticompetitive activities in accordance with the requested party's competition laws. Such a request may be made even if the activities do not violate the requesting party's competition laws, and regardless of whether the competition authorities of the requesting party have commenced or contemplate taking enforcement activities under their own competition laws.

[80] K.E. Markert (1968), 'Recent Developments in International Antitrust Co-operation' 13 *Antitrust Bulletin* 355, at 359.

[81] See OECD (1999), *CLP Report on Positive Comity*, DAFFE/CLP (99).

[82] H. Iyori (1997), 'Japanese Cooperation in International Antitrust Law Enforcement' in H. Ulrich (ed.), *Comparative Competition Law: Approaching an International System of Antitrust Law* (Baden-Baden: Nomos Verlagsgesellschaft) 261.

[83] A.S. Grewlich (2001), 'Globalisation and Conflict in Competition Law: Elements and Possible Solutions' 24(3) *World Competition* 367, at 385.

[84] A similar agreement was signed between the United States and Canada in 2004.

It also provides for suspension of enforcement activities by the requesting party aimed at anticompetitive activities in the other party's territory (that is, the extraterritorial application of its competition law) in favour of a positive comity referral to the other party in two kinds of cases: (i) where the foreign anticompetitive activities do not directly harm the requesting party's consumers (for example, a cartel in one country that limits exports from the other); and (ii) where the foreign anticompetitive activities occur principally in and are directed principally towards the other party's territory, but incidentally harm the requesting party's consumers.

Nevertheless, the agreement excludes mergers[85] from its application (even though cross-border mergers are the most frequent object for cooperation) due to the different deadlines that the EU and the US laws contain for the adoption of decisions.[86] It was also due to the fact that, under the EC Merger Regulation, the European Commission has no discretionary power to examine mergers – in effect, it can only review mergers that have a 'Community dimension'. Hence, in the case of a request by the United States to the Commission to review a merger, the Commission would not have the competence to review the merger if it does not have a Community dimension.[87]

Positive comity: can it work? There are a number of factors that determine whether positive comity is applied upon a request of a contracting party. First, the anticompetitive conduct has to be prohibited not only by the competition law of the requesting party, but also by the competition law of the requested party: an example would be that an export activity permitted under the laws of the requested party will not be covered by the positive comity mechanism even if it adversely affects an important interest of the other party. Another example would be different theoretical approaches regarding the same practice.[88]

Secondly, and given the voluntary nature of these 'soft agreements', the application of positive comity as a tool for cooperation depends to a great extent upon the goodwill of the parties. It also requires great transparency during the enforcement procedures. It has been pointed out

[85] EU–United States agreement on Positive Comity, art. II(4).

[86] J.J. Parisi (1999), 'Enforcement Co-operation among Antitrust Authorities' 20(3) *European Competition Law Review* 133, at 136.

[87] J.P. Griffin (1998), 'Antitrust Aspects of Cross-border Mergers and Acquisitions' 19(1) *European Competition Law Review* 12, at 17.

[88] See the discussion in Chapter 2.

above (during the discussion on negative comity), that where important political and economic interests are involved, it would be unrealistic to expect such goodwill in order to provide radical solutions based on the positive comity provisions. In 1992, Atwood[89] predicted that, 'We are dealing here not just with the laws of competition but also with the laws of human nature … We should not expect the principle of positive comity … to impact dramatically on the proposition that laws are written and enforced to protect national interests'.

Atwood's assumption seems to have been proved correct. In fact, in the context of the US–EU agreement of 1998, this particular mechanism of cooperation has been used only a few times, and only once officially. Informally, positive comity is (at least publicly) known to have been used on three occasions. The first involved a referral by the US FTC to the Italian competition authority regarding anticompetitive practices by Italian ham exporters, which were harming US consumers with supra-competitive prices.[90] The second case involved a complaint by Marathon Oil to the European Commission in relation to anticompetitive practices conducted by European firms and which had significant negative effects on the US-based company.[91] Finally, the most publicised informal referral based on positive comity involved A.C. Nielsen, a company involved in the international market for retail tracking services (gathering of information regarding prices, sales, and relevant data sold by manufacturers and retailers in the form of market reports). Following complaints by IRI, a rival firm, both the European Commission and the US DoJ initiated investigations with respect to Nielsen's tying practices in countries where the company was in a dominant position, which were employed in order to achieve the conclusion of deals in countries where the company faced substantial competition. The US DoJ allowed the European Commission to lead the enforcement activities since most of the alleged conduct occurred in Europe. The outcome of this cooperation was an undertaking by A.C. Nielsen to change its practices, which satisfied both the European Commission and the US DoJ.[92]

[89] J.R. Atwood (1993), 'Positive Comity: Is It a Positive Step?' in Barry Hawk (ed.), *1992 Annual Proceedings of the Fordham Corporate Law Institute International Antitrust Law and Policy Conference* (New York: Fordham Corporate Law Institute) 79, at 86.

[90] M.E. Janow (2000), 'Transatlantic Cooperation on Competition Policy' in S.J. Evenett, A. Lehman and B. Steil (eds.), *Antitrust Goes Global: What Future for Transatlantic Cooperation?* (Brookings Institution Press) 29, at 38.

[91] *Ibid.*

[92] J.F. Rill and C.C. Wilson (2000), 'The A.C. Nielsen Case' in Evenett, Lehman and Steil, *supra* n. 91 at 193.

Furthermore, the only formal positive comity referral was made in the *Sabre/Amadeus* case, where the US authorities asked the European Commission to investigate specific allegations of discrimination in relation to a computerised system (Amadeus) set up by the airlines Lufthansa, Air France and Iberia. The Commission investigated the case in cooperation with the US DoJ, and the outcome was the Commission's decision to open a procedure against Air France for possible abuse of its dominant position.[93] The investigation was finally closed following a private settlement agreement between Sabre and Air France.[94]

These are the only occasions where positive comity was used as a cooperative mechanism. Since then it has been included in every agreement to which the EU and the United States have been contracting parties; however, it has failed to justify the enthusiasm that it generated in (mainly) US competition officials when it was first introduced. The International Competition Policy Advisory Committee (ICPAC)[95] admitted that 'after nine years and the experience derived from both formal and informal applications, the public officials appear to have tempered their enthusiasm'.

3.3 Limitations of first generation bilateral enforcement cooperation agreements

As mentioned above, all the previously discussed mechanisms for cooperation are weakened by the fact that most of these agreements are soft law instruments (that is, they do not create legally binding obligations for the contracting parties).[96] First generation agreements are not treaties. According to the European Commission they are 'administrative arrangements'; similarly, the US authorities regard the agreements as 'executive agreements'.[97] Therefore, the provisions of these agreements do

93 See European Commission, 'Commission opens procedure against Air France for favouring Amadeus Reservation System', Press Release IP/99/171 of 15 March 1999.

94 See European Commission, 'Commission acts to prevent discrimination between Airline computer reservation systems', Press Release IP/00/835 of 25 July 2000.

95 ICPAC Report, at 325.

96 Furthermore, they include a provision according to which contracting parties have the discretion to terminate the application of the agreement at any time (such a provision for discretionary termination of the agreement is included even in the two agreements that are not administrative arrangements but treaties).

97 This arises from the fact that: (i) under US law, in order to be a treaty, an international agreement has to be approved by the Senate; and (ii) in the EU, the European Commission lacks the competence to sign treaties on behalf of the EU as a whole.

not override the existing laws of the parties, and this has become a standard provision in every first generation agreement.

3.3.1 *The confidentiality clause*

The lack of legally binding obligations is reflected in the provision relating to the so-called 'confidentiality clause' contained in these agreements. Exchange of confidential information is one of the most sensitive issues relating to enforcement cooperation in the field of competition law. This is due to the fact that there are two groups of opposing interests underlying the exchange of confidential information. On the one hand, there is the interest of the competition authorities to receive as much information as possible regarding a practice under scrutiny. On the other side, there are important corporate interests that need to be taken into account. First, the information exchanged which relates to business goals and marketing strategy of the firms will not be made known to the competitors of the firm. Secondly, the information exchanged by the agencies in relation to a case will only be used for the particular reason that it is given to the other authority. This point is particularly sensitive in relation to cases where information could be used in relation to criminal liability of the firm's board.[98]

According to the 'confidentiality' provision, the parties can refuse disclosure of any information if the law of the party that possesses the information prohibits it or if this would be incompatible with the possessing party's important interests.[99] Put differently, and given the extent of discretion that the confidentiality clause leaves to the parties, in the case of these agreements it is more a matter of policy than a matter of law which finally determines the outcome of cooperation between competition authorities. Or, as Wood has pointed out, it is confirmation that nations believe that sovereignty privileges are much more important than any added benefits for competition law enforcement; in her own words, it also demonstrates that international companies 'are content to live in a world in which enforcement agencies must operate with one hand tied behind their back'.[100]

[98] See International Chamber of Commerce (1999), *ICC Recommendations to the International Competition Policy Advisory Committee (ICPAC) on Exchange of Confidential Information between Competition Authorities in the Merger Context*, Commission on Law and Practices relating to Competition Doc. 225/525 (21 May 1999).

[99] See e.g., EU–United States agreement, art. VIII; EU–Canada agreement, art. X; United States–Canada agreement, art. X; and the United States–Japan agreement, art. IX(5).

[100] D.P. Wood (1999), 'Is Cooperation Possible?' 34(1) *New England Law Review* 103, at 110.

With respect to the EU, a distinction is made between confidential agency information and confidential business information. The former relates to information gathered in the context of an investigation by the Commission, such as the identity of the undertakings being investigated and procedural aspects of the investigation. Such information may be given by Commission to the other authorities without the prior consent of the parties affected. The latter relates to business or trade secrets obtained as a result of the investigation. The Commission needs the consent of the affected parties in order to disclose such information to the US authorities.[101]

Provisions included in the Antitrust Civil Process Act (ACPA), the Federal Trade Commission Act (FTCA) and the Clayton Act, respectively, restrict the US authorities from sharing confidential information. The ACPA states that no documentary material, answers to interrogatories or oral testimony may be made available for examination without permission by the person who produced that material.[102] A similar provision can be found in the Clayton Act,[103] and in the FTCA[104] which in addition extends the protection of confidentiality by stating that the FTC does not have the authority to make public any confidential financial information or trade secret, except that which the FTC may pass on to any law enforcement agencies which can only be used for official law enforcement purposes.[105]

When these restrictions based on confidentiality apply, the competition authorities of the contracting parties can share information only if they receive a waiver of confidentiality from the party involved in the practice under examination. Such waivers mostly occur in merger cases, where the companies involved often allow the sharing of confidential information in order to gain a speedy clearance for their proposed merger, especially in cases where the competition agency has challenged the merger on the grounds of lack of sufficient information and the company is likely to abandon the transaction rather than to litigate the case (since the decision of the court may take up to two years or more).[106] Another incentive for parties to mergers to forego confidentiality may well be in order to have symmetrical remedies imposed by the antitrust authorities.

[101] G. Kiriazis (2001), 'Jurisdiction and Cooperation Issues in the Investigation of International Cartels', at 10–14, available at http://ec.europa.eu/competition/speeches/text/sp2001_010_en.pdf (last visited on 2 December 2009).

[102] 15 U.S.C. s. 1313 (c)(3). [103] 15 U.S.C. ss. 7A(h), 18(a).

[104] 15 U.S.C. s. 57-2(b). [105] 15 U.S.C. s. 46(f).

[106] See M. Monti (2001), 'The Future for Competition Policy in the European Union', speech delivered at Merchant Taylor Hall, London, 9 July 2001, speech/01/340.

Thus, it is hardly surprising that to date almost all instances where there has been successful cooperation between competition authorities have involved merger cases. According to US and EU officials, some notable examples of EU–US cooperation include the merger cases *WorldCom/MCI*,[107] *Guinness/Grand Metropolitan*, *Dresser/Halliburton*,[108] *Exxon/Mobil* and *Alcoa/Reynolds*.[109]

In contrast to mergers, parties involved in abuse of dominance or cartel cases are usually not eager to allow the competition authorities of different countries to exchange information which it would be impossible for them to share without a waiver of confidentiality from the parties involved. The experience of EU–US cooperation reveals that only in one case relating to abuse of a dominant position did a company offer a waiver of confidentiality, and this case was before the European Council approved the US–EU agreement. In the 1994 *Microsoft* case, the US DoJ and the European Commission cooperated closely in their investigations of Microsoft's activities following Microsoft's consent to the exchange of confidential information, which otherwise the authorities would not have been able to share.[110] The case was finally settled with trilateral negotiations between the two enforcement authorities together with Microsoft, and was undoubtedly an impetus for the final approval of the US–EU agreement.[111]

In the same period, there was not even one (publicly known) waiver of confidentiality with respect to a cartel case. This is not to say that there was no informal cooperation in such cases;[112] nevertheless, it has been suggested by competition officials that the effectiveness of cooperation in cartel cases depends greatly upon the ability of the agencies involved to share confidential information.[113] More importantly, the lack of binding

[107] US Department of Justice, 'Department of Justice clears WorldCom/MCI merger after MCI agrees to sell its Internet business', Press Release of 15 July 1998; having obtained the consent of the companies involved, the competition agencies were able to exchange confidential information.

[108] European Commission, 'Commission clears the merger of Halliburton and Dresser in the area of oilfield services', Press Release IP/98/643 of 8 July 1998.

[109] See Monti (2000), *supra* n. 11.

[110] Microsoft agreed to negotiate identical consent decrees with the Commission and the DoJ in order to resolve the allegations of anticompetitive practices made by Novell, Microsoft's main competitor in the software applications market. See Himelfarb (1996), *supra* n. 48 at 910–11.

[111] See European Commission, 'Following an undertaking by Microsoft to change its licensing practices, the European Commission suspends its action for breach of the competition rules', Press Release IP/94/653 of 17 July 1994.

[112] See ICN (2007), *supra* n. 12.

[113] Kiriazis (2001), *supra* n. 101 at 1.

provisions seems to be leading to a situation where actual cooperation occurs between agencies which have built up a working relationship of trust over time,[114] irrespective of whether these agencies have signed a first generation agreement. As noted above, this assumption is probably the most important reason behind the relatively limited activity of the EU, at least in comparison to the United States, in adopting such first generation agreements.

3.3.2 Inability of first generation agreements to address some important cases

Having discussed the mechanisms of cooperation and their impact, we can now return to the issue mentioned at the beginning of this section, that is, the inability of first generation agreements (i.e. soft law agreements) to deal with cases when important interests of both contracting parties are affected. The conflicts that arose between the US and the EU competition authorities (in particular in the *Boeing/MDD* and *GE/Honeywell* cases, reviewed in Chapter 2) made it clear that in cases such as these where both regulators claim jurisdiction[115] and very crucial policy issues are involved (namely, economic and employment policy in the very sensitive field of the aviation sector), bilateral competition agreements, at least in the form that they are concluded at present, seem to be incapable of offering viable solutions. Given the fast moving globalisation of the markets, on the one hand, and the attempts of states to create national champions in order to participate with strong 'players' in the world markets, on the other, it is not difficult to predict that such conflicts may occur in the future.

In fact, divergences have more recently arisen (although to a lesser extent) with regard to the Commission's decision to impose a fine of around US$497 million on Microsoft and to oblige the company to disclose particular source code and supply a version of its Windows

[114] See ICN (2007), *supra* n. 12 at 24.

[115] It should be noted that the decision of the EU to claim jurisdiction was disputed by some commentators. See e.g., A.F. Bavasso (1998), 'Boeing/McDonnell Douglas: Did the Commission Fly Too High?' 19(4) *European Competition Law Review* 243. However, see also K. Van Miert (1998), 'International Cooperation in the Field of Competition: A View from the EC' in Barry Hawk (ed.), *1997 Fordham Corporate Law Institute International Antitrust Law and Policy Conference* (New York: Fordham Corporate Law Institute) 13, at 18, where the former Commissioner claimed that in *Nippon Paper*, in terms of jurisdiction the US authorities went beyond what the Commission claimed in Boeing/MDD.

operating system without the company's Media Player, which clearly disappointed US officials, especially in view of the fact that in the United States Microsoft had reached a settlement with the US DoJ more than two years before the Commission issued its decision.[116]

In sum, since contracting states parties to these enforcement cooperation agreements are not bound by the provisions of these agreements, and furthermore such agreements do not provide a mechanism for resolving conflicts, for example provisions specifying the competent court or the dispute settlement body in the event that a conflict arises, it is inevitably the case that the political power of the contracting parties will determine the outcome of any such conflict.

This would not cause any major impact where such conflicts arise between two states of equal political and economic strength. Indeed, the conflicts between the United States and the EU regarding the two merger cases led to the negotiation and adoption of another soft law instrument, setting out best practice on cooperation in merger cases,[117] in which they expressed their commitment to effective cooperation. Its impact is limited nevertheless by the impossibility of exchanging confidential information in cases where there is no waiver of confidentiality by the parties involved in the transaction under investigation.

However, the controversies that may arise in the context of enforcement cooperation could have a major impact in cases where one of the states involved in the conflict is much stronger than the other. For instance, if we assume that such a conflict arose between the United States and a developing country, the latter's authorities would be extremely vulnerable to the threat of economic measures that the United States could impose. Bilateralism and, as shown above, soft law increase national power – or as an author from a developing country has put it, bilateral agreements, at least in the form of soft law, cannot overcome the test of hegemony and ethnocentricism.[118]

116 The decision of the European Commission was recently upheld by the CFI, see Case T-201/04 *Microsoft* v. *Commission*, Judgment of 17 September 2007. On the settlement between Microsoft and the US authorities, see US Department of Justice, 'Department of Justice and Microsoft Corporation reach effective settlement on antitrust lawsuit', Press Release of 2 November 2001. See also A. Burnside and H. Crossley (2005), 'Cooperation in Competition: A New Era' 30(2) *European Law Review* 234, at 254–5.

117 United States–EU (2002), Best Practices on Cooperation in Merger Investigations, available at http://ec.europa.eu/competition/mergers/legislation/eu_us.pdf (last visited on 2 December 2009).

118 D. De Noronha Goyos (1997), 'The Globalisation of Competition Law: A Latin American Perspective' 3(1) *International Trade Law Review* 20, at 21.

3.4 So what's next? Wider soft law cooperation and closer bilateral cooperation

Given the limitations of the agreements discussed above, alternative options of enforcement cooperation are discussed both at the bilateral and multilateral levels. As to the latter, discussions on enforcement cooperation focused on cartels have lately taken place at the International Competition Network (ICN), where a working subgroup has been devoted to the issue of cooperation on cartel cases.[119] In parallel, the OECD, in the context of its Recommendation on Hard Core Cartels[120] (which includes a definition of the term 'hard-core cartel' and provides that member states and non-member states should cooperate on cartel cases), is also working in this particular field, and has published reports on the application of the Recommendation.[121] The OECD has also issued guidance on best practice on the exchange of non-confidential information on cartel cases, which include provisions similar to the ones provided by the first generation agreements.[122] It seems, therefore, that in the context of soft law, enforcement cooperation has seen a shift in the last five years towards multilateral channels of communication (as discussed in Chapter 6).[123]

That said, there have also been developments in the field of enforcement cooperation at the bilateral level, and such developments are mainly concerned with the debate over the necessity for second generation agreements, i.e. binding agreements which would make possible the exchange of confidential information and provide for a compulsory process on behalf of the requesting party. Even though no such agreement has been signed by the EU to date, it seems that the Commission is looking in this direction. Former Commissioner Kroes stated that EU and US officials have explored the possibility of signing a second generation agreement which would allow for the exchange of confidential information.[124]

[119] See ICN (2007), *supra* n. 12, and the discussion in Chapter 6.

[120] See OECD, Recommendation of the Council concerning Effective Action against Hard Core Cartels, C(98)35 final (25 March 1998).

[121] See e.g., OECD (2005), *supra* n. 70.

[122] See OECD (2005), Best Practices for the Formal Exchange of Information between Competition Authorities in Hard Core Cartel Investigations, DAF/COMP(2005)25/FINAL.

[123] The issue has also been addressed by the WTO Working Group on the Relationship on Trade and Competition. See Chapter 6.

[124] N. Kroes (2005), 'The First Hundred Days', speech delivered at the Fortieth Anniversary of the Studienvereinigung Kartellrecht 1965–2005, International Forum on European Competition Law, Brussels, 7 April 2005, speech 05/205, at 5.

Nevertheless, it is questionable whether the adoption of such an agreement would be feasible, since on the basis of article 12(3) of Regulation 1/2003 any exchange of information between the Commission and the Member States cannot be used by the receiving authority to impose custodial sanctions. The Regulation therefore prevents particular Member States which have penalised cartels (such as the United Kingdom and Ireland) from using information received by the Commission or other Member States in order to impose custodial sanctions. In this regard, if the Commission entered into a second generation agreement which allowed for exchange of confidential information with the United States, where cartels are a criminal offence, it would in practice discriminate against certain other Member States which could only use such relevant information to a limited extent.

Hence, in order to achieve the conclusion of a second generation agreement, there are two options. The first is that the EU could sign an agreement which contains an express clause similar to article 12(3) of Regulation 1/2003, according to which the information exchanged may not be used with regard to custodial sanctions. While theoretically this would be possible, provided that the Commission obtained a mandate to negotiate such an agreement from the Council,[125] it would nevertheless be unrealistic in practice to expect the United States, which has had the imposition of custodial sanctions on members of cartels at the top of its enforcement agenda in recent years, to accept such a clause in a second generation bilateral enforcement cooperation agreement. The second option would entail an amendment of Regulation 1/2003, so that it would expressly allow for the exchange of information both between the Commission and Member States and between the Commission and third countries in cases which lead to custodial sanctions.

By contrast, as in the case of first generation agreements, the United States has become the first state to move towards the adoption of second generation enforcement cooperation agreements on competition, and has recently also used other types of bilateral hard law agreements, such as mutual legal assistance treaties (MLATs) and extradition treaties, for the purposes of antitrust enforcement.

[125] Something which may be difficult in itself, as even such a partial ability to exchange confidential information would definitely raise concerns for a number of Member States and business associations.

3.4.1 *Second generation agreements: the United States–Australia Agreement on Mutual Antitrust Enforcement Assistance and the Denmark–Norway–Ireland Agreement*

The United States adopted the International Antitrust Enforcement Assistance Act (IAEAA)[126] in 1994 to overcome constraints on the exchange of confidential information, by allowing the DoJ and FTC to share such information with cooperating states; however, the constraints were not in the event completely overcome. Due to pressure from business interests,[127] the materials obtained during the Hart-Scott-Rodino pre-merger notifications were protected by the IAEAA and could not be shared with other competition authorities.[128] Following the adoption of the IAEAA, the United States entered in 1999 into a mutual antitrust enforcement agreement with Australia, a state which had legislation in place which was similar to the IAEAA,[129] paving the way for the second generation of agreements. The United States–Australia agreement is not an executive agreement of a voluntary nature but a binding treaty. According to article II.G, the agreement complements the 1982 United States–Australia agreement on enforcement cooperation, and the combination of these agreements thus makes US–Australian cooperation on antitrust enforcement the most sophisticated of all, at least in terms of the capability to exchange official documents.

The parties have agreed to cooperate on a reciprocal basis in providing or obtaining evidence[130] related to enforcement of the other state's competition law. They have also agreed to disclose, provide, exchange or discuss antitrust evidence.[131] Moreover, the agreement provides that following a request (the form of which is described in great detail in article III of the agreement), a party may obtain antitrust evidence from the other party. This evidence may include taking the testimony or statements from persons; obtaining documents, or other forms of documentary evidence;

[126] International Antitrust Enforcement Assistance Act of 1994, 15 U.S.C. ss. 6201–6212.

[127] This was related to the fact that such materials included highly sensitive information regarding the business strategies of US firms. See L.N. Freeman (1995) 'U.S.–Canadian Information Sharing and the International Antitrust Enforcement Assistance Act of 1994' 84 *Georgetown Law Journal* 339, at 358–9.

[128] U.S.C. s. 6204(1).

[129] Mutual Assistance in Business Regulation Act 1992 and the Mutual Assistance in Criminal Matters Act 1987.

[130] See United States–Australia Mutual Antitrust Enforcement Treaty, art. I.A.

[131] *Ibid.* art II.1.

locating or identifying persons or things; executing searches and seizures; and disclosing, providing, exchanging or discussing such evidence.

The information exchanged under the provisions of this agreement must be used solely for enforcing antitrust laws.[132] The agreement does allow, however, for refusal to share information. Article IV of the agreement provides that a party may deny assistance in any case where such assistance would not be permitted by the law of the requested party (demonstrating that there are still laws that do not permit the sharing of information) or when sharing the information would be against the requested party's public interest. However, it is provided that a party refusing to provide the requested information must offer an explanation of the basis for denial.

Following a similar pattern, Denmark, Norway, and Iceland, which have adopted legislation which allows the exchange of such information,[133] signed in 2001 an agreement which provides for the exchange of confidential information. In 2003, Sweden also became party to the agreement.[134] The agreement follows the usual procedure of notification in cases where 'one authority becomes aware of the fact that its enforcement measures could have a bearing on significant competitive interests that come under the competence of another authority'.[135] The mechanism for cooperation in this process of sharing confidential information is not described in detail as it is in the United States–Australia agreement. Article IV of the Nordic agreement merely provides that the parties agree that it is in their common interest to exchange confidential information, subject to a duty of confidentiality on the authorities which receive the information, and a commitment that they will use the confidential information only for the purposes stipulated in the agreement.

Broadly speaking, it can be argued that these agreements are a positive step for enforcement cooperation since they provide clear legal obligations for the parties and they also provide competition agencies with the capability to exchange important information regarding enforcement

132 See art. VII.1 (with the exception of information that has become publicly known); art. VII.D; and art. VII.C (existence of written consent of the party which provided the information).

133 See Consolidated Danish Competition Act No. 687 of 12 July 2000, s. 18(a); Norwegian Competition Act No. 65 of 11 June 1993, ss. 1–8, as amended by Act No. 35 of 5 May 2000; Icelandic Competition Act No. 8 of 5 February 1993, s. 50a, as amended by the Act No. 107 of 2000.

134 See Danish Competition Authority (2004), 'Wider Nordic antitrust cooperation', Press Release of 2 March 2004, available at www.ks.dk/english/news/press-releases/2004/wider-nordic-antitrust-cooperation/ (last visited on 2 December 2009).

135 See agreement between Denmark, Iceland and Norway on cooperation in competition cases, art. II, para. 1.

against anticompetitive practices. Nonetheless, given the fact that reciprocal commitment from the contracting parties is needed in order for an agreement like this to be concluded, we cannot currently be optimistic about the prospects for the conclusion of many more agreements like the one between the United States and Australia, since there are very few countries with legislation similar to the IAEAA.[136] Burnside and Botteman argue that, in fact, the United States has been unsuccessful in its attempts to promote the adoption of agreements of this kind,[137] particularly in cases where competition law does not include criminal sanctions.

In addition, even though such agreements contain provisions that oblige the parties to exchange confidential information, the United States–Australia agreement contains exceptions to this obligation for reasons related to *public policy*. This may give the contracting parties significant leeway to avoid exchange of confidential information in specific cases, especially under the pressure that competition officials of the contracting parties may face from business organisations.

Finally, none of the competition agencies involved in the implementation of these agreements (the US DoJ and FTC and the ACCC in the case of the United States–Australia agreement, and the Danish, Icelandic, Norwegian and Swedish competition authorities in the case of the Nordic agreement) has issued any guidance on the implementation of second generation agreements. Hence, we cannot as yet safely draw any conclusions on their impact on international enforcement cooperation.

3.4.2 Use of MLATs and extradition treaties in competition cases

What nevertheless has become obvious in the last five years is that there is a trend, at least with regard to industrialised countries, towards closer

[136] In 2007, Australia signed an agreement with New Zealand which also provides for the exchange of confidential information.

[137] A. Burnside and Y. Botteman (2004), 'Networking amongst Competition Agencies' 10(1) *International Trade Law and Regulation*, 1, at 3. As expected, concerns with regard to the operation of such agreements have been expressed by business representatives, and despite the fact that the agreements include provisions which confirm that the information exchanged will be used only in relation to competition law, business organisations such as the International Chamber of Commerce and the Union of Industrial and Employers' Confederation of Europe (UNICE, now Business Europe) have already expressed their concerns about the United States–Australia agreement, especially that the shared information might be used for reasons other than competition, for example to impose criminal liability on the parties involved in the practice under scrutiny or to access the business strategy plans of the enterprises involved. See Parisi (1999), *supra* n. 86 at 139.

cooperation on competition matters, in the form, on the one hand, of exchange of confidential information and, on the other, of procedural cooperation, which may even include extradition of natural persons who have participated in cartels. As to the former, such exchange of information is provided under mutual legal antitrust treaties in criminal matters (MLATs). The United States is the most prominent user of such agreements, as it is a party to fifty of them. These agreements cover practices that constitute violations of criminal law in general and thus are useful in cases where both contracting parties include criminal sanctions in their competition rules. Examples of such MLATs that may be utilised in competition cases are the United States–Canada and United States–United Kingdom agreements;[138] as the OECD has noted, the United States–Canada MLAT has recently been used in a number of cartel cases.[139]

As to the latter form of cooperation – extradition of individuals on the basis of a competition infringement (cartel) – considerable debate has developed among competition experts in relation to the recent decision of the UK Home Secretary to order extradition to the United States of Ian Norris, a UK citizen and former CEO of a company that was found to be part of a price-fixing conspiracy for a period between 1999 and 2000 in the market for carbon products. In particular, Norris' extradition was ordered on the basis of his participation in a cartel and further attempts to obstruct justice in the context of the US grand jury investigation.[140] The decision was issued following a request of the US government on the basis of the UK Extradition Act 2003, which ratified the relevant extradition treaty between the two states,[141] under which the parties agreed to

[138] See P. Holmes, A. Papadopoulos, O. Kayali, and A. Sydorak (2005), 'Trade and Competition in Regional Trade Agreements: A Lost Opportunity?' in P. Brusick, A.M. Alvarez and L. Cernat (eds.), *Competition Provisions in Regional Trade Agreements: How to Assure Development Gains* (Geneva and New York: UNCTAD). That said, Zanettin argues that the United States–Italy and the United States–Spain MLATs may be used in competition cases, since they do not make dual criminality a prerequisite for assistance. B. Zanettin (2002), *Cooperation between Antitrust Agencies at the International Level* (Hart Publishing) 149.

[139] See OECD (2005), *supra* n. 69 at 38.

[140] See S. Hammond (2006), 'Charting New Waters in International Cartel Prosecution', speech delivered at the Twentieth Annual National Institute on White Collar Crime, 2 March 2006, at 12, available at www.justice.gov/atr/public/speeches/214861.htm (last visited on 2 December 2009).

[141] Extradition Treaty between the Government of the United Kingdom of Great Britain and Northern Ireland and the Government of the United States, available at www.fco.gov.uk/resources/en/pdf/pdf8/fco_pdf_cm5821_extraditiontreaty (last visited on 2 December 2009).

extradite natural persons in cases of criminal offences. While the initial aim of the treaty was to support the efforts of the states parties to fight terrorism, at least half of the extradition requests by US prosecutors relate to 'white collar' crimes, including price fixing, as in the case of Norris.[142]

This case has been highly controversial, in view of the fact that the extradition treaty requires dual criminality, while Norris was to be extradited on the basis of a practice (price fixing) which was criminalised in the United Kingdom in 2002, and therefore after the infringement came to an end.[143] The High Court rejected Norris' appeal and held that the price-fixing conspiracy should be regarded as dishonest and prejudicial to others, and therefore constituted a conspiracy to defraud, irrespective of the fact that price fixing had not been a criminal offence when the actions under examination took place.[144] Although Norris finally won the case, as the House of Lords upheld his appeal on the basis that price fixing was not a criminal offence at the time of the infringement, and therefore Norris was not in fact extradited to the United States, this case is still a very strong indication that where countries have reached a common understanding as to the proper treatment of an anticompetitive practice, in conjunction with the existence of a legal framework of cooperation, enforcement cooperation may be maximised. That said, at least at the present point in time, it seems that this will happen only on particular occasions – in fact only in cartel cases – and solely between countries that have criminalised this anticompetitive practice.[145]

3.5 Conclusion

The theme of this chapter is that first generation enforcement cooperation agreements have proved to be effective in relation to a number of problems concerning restrictive business practices with an international impact; however, they also have limitations.

Their most positive effect is that they create the mechanism through which officials of different national authorities are able to come into contact and have the opportunity to share their views on issues of mutual

[142] See B. Byrne, S. Goodman and E. Shapiro (2006), 'Extending the Long Arm of US Antitrust Law: The Ian Norris Extradition Battle', *Global Competition Review* (December 2005/January 2006) 2.

[143] *Ibid.* [144] See Watson-Doig (2007), *supra* n. 60 at 8.

[145] These countries include among others the United States, the United Kingdom, Ireland, Estonia, Germany, Canada, Australia, Japan and Israel. See Hammond (2006), *supra* n. 140 at 3.

interest. The provisions for meetings between competition officials and the provisions for technical assistance are evidence of this. Given that competition law, having only been adopted by most countries recently, is a relatively new legal tool, regular communication among competition authorities is definitely beneficial in terms of the creation of a competition culture around the world, and at a more advanced level, such cooperation may contribute to harmonisation of national competition laws, through the achievement of common understandings about the proper function of competition.

In addition, the experience primarily of the operation of the EU–US agreement highlights that on the whole the agreement has offered useful mechanisms for cooperation in a number of cases, particularly relating to mergers, where the parties will often give their consent to the waiver of confidentiality. The increase in the number of notifications also shows that everyday cooperation among competition officials is becoming stronger.

However, as mentioned above, it is indisputable that enforcement agreements have certain limitations. In the first place, most of these agreements include a 'confidentiality clause' making them ineffective in cartel cases and cases regarding abuse of dominant position. The two agreements between the United States and Australia, and the agreement between Denmark, Iceland, Norway (and Sweden) are undoubtedly very positive steps, since they provide the agencies of the contracting parties with the opportunity to exchange confidential information. However, we cannot as yet evaluate the effectiveness of these agreements given that there is no data available as to their application. On the other hand, recent developments have shown the possibility of far-reaching bilateral cooperation in cartel cases through the use of MLATs and extradition treaties; but such agreements can only be used by states which have criminalised cartels, and thus competition systems such as the EU cannot benefit from such cooperation.

Secondly, even in merger cases, where cooperation has proved to be effective, the United States–EU agreement failed to provide the authorities with adequate legal tools to deal with cases such as *Boeing/MDD* and *GE/Honeywell*, where very sensitive interests of the contracting parties were affected. This is a reflection of the voluntary nature of first generation agreements, and to a certain extent of the problems that may arise from the relationship between, and co-existence of, competition law and policy with other national policies.

Thirdly, bilateral and trilateral enforcement cooperation agreements are by definition insufficient to deal with situations where the interests of more than two or three nations are affected. A good illustration of this is the example of multiple notifications in cases of multijurisdictional mergers. For instance, the *Exxon/Mobil* transaction was notified in twenty jurisdictions.[146] Obviously, bilateral or trilateral agreements cannot provide any adequate mechanism of cooperation in such cases. The only possibility for resolving such problems, based on the provisions of bilateral or trilateral agreements, would be in a situation where all nations with a competition regime have concluded this kind of agreement. Such a solution, however, would be extremely complicated, since if we take into account only the OECD countries, we would need more than 400 bilateral agreements for the problems of international competition enforcement to be dealt with effectively.

All these considerations highlight the fact that, even though they are useful, enforcement cooperation agreements in the field of competition law are by no means adequate in themselves to provide radical solutions with respect to the problems caused by restrictive business practices with an international effect. It is also noteworthy that two of the most recent enforcement agreements discussed in this chapter are trilateral and this illustrates the need for expansion of the number of contracting parties. The substantial work that has been carried out by the ICN and the OECD further highlights the fact that, even in the field of voluntary enforcement cooperation, international problems need international solutions. Even US officials who (as illustrated above) have traditionally been opposed to a possible international harmonisation of competition law and have supported the proposition that bilateral cooperation will be adequate to solve problems relating to restrictive business practices with an international effect, seem to have changed their opinion. Characteristically, Charles James[147] admitted that:

> there have been days when we thought (or hoped) that such [bilateral] cooperation itself would eventually minimize or resolve even the most serious areas of antitrust divergence. More recently, however, we have come to understand that cooperation alone will not resolve some significant areas of divergence among antitrust regimes that must be addressed if we are to maintain the integrity of antitrust on a global stage.

[146] J.P. Griffin (1999), 'What Business People Want from a World Antitrust Code' 34(1) *New England Law Review* 39.

[147] C. James (2001), 'International Antitrust in the Bush Administration', Canadian Bar Association on Competition Law, Ottawa, Canada, 21 September 2001, available at www.usdoj.gov/atr/public/speeches/9100.pdf (last visited on 2 December 2009).

A reflection of this argument may be traced in the development of the policy of the EU with regard to the formation and application of soft law enforcement cooperation agreements. As the chapter has shown, the policy of the EU in the field of bilateral enforcement cooperation agreements has been somewhat neutral, in the sense that the EU has signed agreements only with its most important trade partners (the other members of the 'QUAD': the United States, Canada and Japan, and very recently with Korea), and has set up a more informal channel of cooperation with the agencies of another two important trade partners, Brazil and China. The agreement with the United States has probably been the most influential and important of the various agreements of this kind; however, in contrast to the United States, which has been the more extensive user of such agreements, the EU has shown no interest in offering such semi-formal cooperation to more commercial partners. It could therefore be argued that, to some extent, the formation of such agreements has not been at the top of the list of priorities in Brussels. On the other hand, while the EU in the last few years has demonstrated an interest in the possibility of adopting second generation agreements, these attempts have not as yet been successful, and therefore, no conclusions may safely be drawn at this point.

As the following chapters show, the efforts of the EU have instead been devoted to other forms of cooperation, such as bilateral trade agreements which include a chapter on competition, and the negotiations on a multilateral agreement on competition law and policy. In addition, the principal aim of the EU has been further development of its own competition policy, which as described in Chapter 5, is the most successful regime of a plurilateral regional agreement, and has been used as a model for the creation of various other relevant regional regimes around the world.

4

Bilateral Trade Agreements which Include Competition Provisions

4.1 Historical review of trade agreements

The formation of the first trade agreements goes back to the beginning of the eighteenth century, when the first trade agreements appeared in Europe. In 1707, England and Scotland signed the Act of Union, thus creating a bilateral customs union, i.e. an agreement which provides for elimination of internal tariffs and a unified external tariff. Similarly, in France the various internal tolls and tariffs in force since 1600 were abolished in 1790 after the French Revolution. Prussia also first considered an economic union in 1808, and this led to the establishment of the Zollverein in 1834, historically considered to be the first plurilateral regional trade agreement, under which most German states adopted the Prussian external tariff, thus operating as a fully-fledged customs union.[1]

In the mid-nineteenthth century England was the first nation to unilaterally open its national barriers to foreign trade, with the repeal of the Corn Laws in 1846, which was followed by a number of unilateral reductions or even removal of tariffs.[2] At the same time and until the end of the nineteenth century, a number of bilateral free trade agreements (FTAs) were signed between European countries, the most important of which was the Commercial Treaty signed between England and France in 1860.[3]

An earlier version of this chapter formed part of a paper written with P. Holmes, H. Muller and A. Sydorak (2005), 'A Taxonomy of International Competition Cooperation Provisions'. The paper was written in the context of a research project funded under the sixth framework programme, DG Research, European Commission, entitled Competition Policy Foundations for Trade Reform, Regulatory Reform and Sustainable Development and is available at www.cpftr.org/cpftr/deliverables/Deliverable13.pdf.

[1] D. Irwin (1993), 'Multilateral and Bilateral Trade Policies in the World Trading System: An Historical Perspective' in J. De Melo and A. Panagariya (eds.), *New Dimensions in Regional Integration* (New York: Cambridge University Press) 90, at 92.

[2] S.B. Clough and C.W. Cole (1941), *Economic History of Europe* (Boston, MA: DC Heath) 469–75.

[3] O. Accominotti and M. Flandreau (2005), *Does Bilateralism Promote Trade? Nineteenth Century Liberalisation Revisited*, CEPR Discussion Paper No. 5423, in which the authors

Under this treaty, France reduced its tariffs initially to 30 per cent and after 1865 to 20 per cent, and England decreased the number of dutiable goods from 419 to 48 and also reduced wine tariffs.

Following the adoption of this agreement a number of bilateral treaties were signed between European countries. These treaties were based on the most favoured nation (MFN) principle, according to which countries agreed that when a party to such agreements decided to negotiate and offer favourable trade concessions to a third country, it would have to offer the same concessions to the other party to the agreement.[4] By the 1860s, the MFN clause was applied to all British, German, Belgian and Dutch colonies, while the French colonies adopted the same tariff code as France, thus creating a customs union.[5]

A second period of proliferation of such agreements occurred between the two World Wars, when these agreements became the main strategy of the United States, which signed thirty-two of them with selected trade partners. In the aftermath of the Second World War, bilateral free trade agreements fell out of favour once more, as at the international level the creation of a multilateral trading system under the auspices of GATT, and subsequently the WTO, became the main focus.

Nonetheless, in the last twenty years or so, the conclusion of such agreements has once again been very much in vogue, and many of them include competition provisions. In particular, by the year 2005, 317 trade agreements had been notified to the WTO, and more than 80 per cent of these agreements had been concluded since 1990.[6] As Cernat has shown, recent trade agreements tend to encompass partners that are economically and geographically diverse.[7] He notes in particular that one-quarter of trade agreements are inter-continental (i.e. they are concluded by countries situated in different continents), and 65 per cent of the agreements are signed by countries which are at different stages of development.[8]

The EU has been a major user of this type of agreement. The United States has also concluded a number of bilateral trade agreements with

provide an examination of the actual increase in trade following the conclusion of the England-France agreement.

4 A.G. Kenwood and A.L. Lougheed (1971), *The Growth of International Economy* (London: Allen & Unwin) 75–8.

5 Irwin (1993), *supra* n. 1 at 98.

6 Estimation based on L. Cernat (2005), 'Eager to Ink but Ready to Act? RTA Proliferation and International Cooperation on Competition Policy' in P. Brusick, A.M. Alvarez and L. Cernat (eds.), *Competition Provisions in Regional Trade Agreements: How to Assure Development Gains* (Geneva and New York: UNCTAD) 7.

7 *Ibid.* at 2. 8 *Ibid.*

Australia, Bahrain, Chile, Colombia, Israel, Jordan, Korea,[9] Morocco, Oman, Panama, Peru and Singapore. Nonetheless, it is notable that most of the United States' bilateral FTAs do not include competition provisions (though some recent US bilateral agreements do so, namely United States–Singapore (2004), United States–Australia (2005), United States–Peru (2006), United States–Korea (2007)). Furthermore, Canada has also signed this type of agreement with Chile, Costa Rica and Israel, and within the last couple of years with Colombia, Jordan, Peru and the European Free Trade Area (EFTA). Australia has similar agreements with Singapore, Thailand, the United States, New Zealand and Chile.[10] In total, as noted above, more than 110 bilateral trade agreements include provisions relevant to competition law. The subsequent analysis in this chapter is based on the agreements signed by the EU.

4.1.1 *Bilateral agreements of the EU*

In the last fifteen years, bilateral trade agreements have been at the heart of the EU's external policy. As has been well documented, the EU is the most prominent example of a polity that has used bilateral trade agreements as a tool to export its trade policy, including competition policy, by using its negotiating power to export (or in certain cases impose) its *acquis communautaire*, the legal framework that regulates the relations between its Member States.[11] This strategy can be clearly discerned in the context of the accession process of the ten new Member States in 2004 and another two in 2007.[12] The relationship between the EU and the candidate countries was based on the relevant association agreements, the so-called Europe agreements. These agreements were bilateral agreements signed between the EU and the countries pursuing accession to the Union, and covered a wide range of regulatory measures. On the basis of these agreements, a set of accession criteria were adopted in 1993, which set the political, economic and legal preconditions, including competition law, that these states had to fulfil in order to achieve their goal of accession to the EU.[13] These criteria were set out in further detail in 1995 with the issuance

[9] Still pending Congressional approval.

[10] See P. Holmes, H. Muller, A. Papadopoulos and A. Sydorak (2005), 'A Taxonomy of International Competition Cooperation Provisions' at 68–9.

[11] See J.-M. Maur (2005), 'Exporting Europe's Trade Policy' 28(11) *World Economy* 1565.

[12] Cyprus, Czech Republic, Slovakia, Estonia, Hungary, Latvia, Lithuania, Malta, Poland and Slovenia. Romania and Bulgaria joined the EU in 2007.

[13] The so-called Copenhagen criteria, which were laid down at the European Council in Copenhagen, Denmark, June 1993.

of a White Paper by the European Commission,[14] which scrutinised very closely the process of adoption of the *acquis* by the candidate countries.[15] In the field of competition law in particular, this supervision was carried out primarily by the Directorate-General of Competition in cooperation with the Directorate-General of Enlargement (the Directorate of the Commission in charge of the enlargement process).

This policy of the EU has been criticised by various commentators, who have argued that the EU is not willing to cooperate, but only interested in imposing its competition laws on other states. In particular, it has been argued that in the context of their accession, candidate countries had to 'swallow all 80,000 pages of European laws and adapt their own legislation to accommodate them', with the entire process closely monitored by EU officials.[16] From this perspective, the assumption examined in Chapter 3 that bilateralism is a strategy used by economically strong states in order to increase their power over their weaker co-signing parties is of clear relevance here. On the other hand, one should not ignore the willingness of the EU's partners to accept the prerequisites of the EU in the context of their political and economic decision to join the regional bloc. In this regard, Trebilcock and Howse argue that 'deep economic integration among nation states is typically predicated either on the existence of a hegemonic power with the ability to impress its will on other smaller and

[14] European Commission White Paper (1995), *Preparation of the Associated Countries of Central and Eastern Europe for Integration into the Internal Market of the Union*, COM(95)163 final.

[15] Apart from the reference to the agreements with Romania and Bulgaria, the book does not further discuss Europe agreements, in view of the fact that following their accession, the development of the competition regimes of these Member States have become a part of the internal policy of the EU and therefore is no longer considered an element of the international dimension of EC competition law and policy. With regard to the process of accession from a competition law perspective, and the development of the national competition regimes of the new Member States thereafter, see Y. Devuyst, J. Kankanen, P. Lindberg, I. Orssich and G. Roebling (2002), 'EU Enlargement and Competition Policy: Where are We Now?' 1 *Competition Policy Newsletter* 3; D. Geradin (ed.) (2004), *Modernization and Enlargement: Two Major Challenges for EC Competition Law* (Intersentia) esp. chs. 13–17; J. Holscher and J. Stephan (2004), 'Competition Policy in Central Eastern Europe in the Light of EU Accession' 42(2) *Journal of Common Market Studies* 321; K. Sceres (2007), 'Multi-Jurisdictional Competition Law Enforcement: The Interface Between European Competition Law and the Competition Laws of the New Member States' 3(2) *European Competition Journal* 465.

[16] M. Leonard (2005), *Why Europe Will Run the 21st Century?* (Fourth Estate) 45. As to how the EU monitors the adoption and implementation of the *acquis*, see the European Commission website at http://ec.europa.eu/enlargement/enlargement_process/accession_process/how_does_a_country_join_the_eu/negotiations_croatia_turkey/index_en.htm#acquis (last visited on 2 December 2009).

weaker states … or on the willingness of member states to cede substantial aspects of their domestic political sovereignty'.[17]

The nexus of bilateral agreements of the EU substantiates this presumption, since, as the chapter shows, the EU has been involved in agreements with a large number of countries which surround it geographically. In particular, three broad categories of EU trade agreements, all of which include competition provisions, may be distinguished. First, there are the agreements with candidate (and more recently, potential candidate) countries, which have been the EU's main strategic and legal tool with regard to the process of enlargement. Secondly, there are the agreements with Southern Mediterranean and with former Soviet Union states, which the EU has adopted in an attempt to strengthen its overall cooperation with its neighbouring countries. Most of these countries have been included in the European Neighbourhood Policy (ENP). Finally, the EU has extended its network of bilateral agreements including competition provisions to certain selected trade partners around the world. Table 4.1 includes the relevant EU bilateral agreements.

(i) Agreements with candidate countries

The agreements with candidate and potential candidate countries are a group of agreements that the EU has concluded with countries pursuing EU accession. Following the accession of ten Member States in May 2004, and another two (Bulgaria and Romania) in 2007, the current official candidates to join the EU are Croatia, Turkey and Former Yugoslav Republic of Macedonia (FYROM).[18] The EU–Croatia Stabilisation and Association Agreement (SAA) was signed in 2001 and came into effect on 1 February 2005, but the trade provisions together with competition policy provisions were implemented in 2002.[19] The relationship between the EU and Turkey is governed by the customs union signed in 1995 and in operation since January 1996.[20] The SAA with FYROM was signed in 2001 and entered into

[17] See M. Trebilcock and R. Howse (1999), *The Regulation of International Trade* (2nd edn, Routledge) 129–34.

[18] While accession negotiations were launched with Croatia and Turkey in October 2005, accession negotiations have not yet started with FYROM. It is noted that Iceland is also a candidate to join the EU.

[19] On the developmental and political problems faced in the process of the negotiations with Croatia, see F. Schimmelfennig (2008), 'EU Political Accession Conditionality after the 2004 Enlargement: Consistency and Effectiveness' 15(6) *Journal of European Public Policy* 918, at 928–9.

[20] See the EC Commission website at http://ec.europa.eu/trade/issues/bilateral/countries/turkey/index_en.htm (last visited on 2 December 2009). See also Schimmelfennig (2008), *supra* n. 19 at 930–2.

Table 4.1 *Bilateral trade agreements*

EU	Title of agreement	Signed	Into force	Status of EU's co-signing partner
Albania	SAA and interim SAA	2006	1 April 2009 (interim SAA 12 June 2006)	potential candidate for accession
Bosnia and Herzegovina	SAA and interim SAA	2008	SAA not yet ratified (interim SAA 1 July 2008)	potential candidate for accession
Bulgaria	Europe agreement	1993	1993 (no longer in force)	EU Member State
Croatia	SAA	2001	2004	candidate for accession
FYROM	SAA	2001	2004	candidate for accession
Montenegro	SAA and interim SAA	2007	SAA not yet ratified (interim SAA 1 January 2008)	potential candidate for accession
Romania	EA	1993	1993 (no longer in force)	EU Member State
Serbia	SAA	2008		potential candidate for accession
Turkey	customs union	1995	1996	candidate for accession
Algeria	Euro-Mediterranean association agreement	2002	1 September 2005	ENP
Egypt	Euro-Mediterranean association agreement	2001	1 June 2004	ENP
Israel	Euro-Mediterranean association agreement	1995	1 June 2000	ENP
Jordan	Euro-Mediterranean association agreement	1997	1 May 2002	ENP
Lebanon	Euro-Mediterranean association agreement	2002	in ratification process	ENP
Morocco	Euro-Mediterranean association agreement	1996	1 March 2000	ENP
Palestinian Authority	interim Euro-Mediterranean association agreement	1997	1997	ENP
Tunisia	Euro-Mediterranean association agreement	1995	1 March 1998	ENP
Armenia	partnership and cooperation agreement	1996	1 July 1999	ENP

Table 4.1 (cont.)

EU	Title of agreement	Signed	Into force	Status of EU's co-signing partner
Azerbaijan	partnership and co-operation agreement	1996	1 July 1999	ENP
Georgia	partnership and co-operation agreement	1996	1 July 1999	ENP
Kazakhstan	partnership and co-operation agreement	1995	1 July 1999	—
Kyrgyzstan	partnership and co-operation agreement	1995	1 July 1999	—
Moldova	partnership and co-operation agreement	1994	1 July 1998	ENP
Russia	partnership and co-operation agreement	1994	1 December 1997	—
Ukraine	partnership and co-operation agreement	1994	1 March 1998	ENP
Uzbekistan	partnership and co-operation agreement	1996	1 July 1999	—
Chile	association agreement	2002	1 March 2005	—
Mexico	global agreement	1997	1 October 2000	—
South Africa	trade, development and cooperation agreement	1999	26 April 2004	—

force in 2004. As with the Europe agreements, the SAAs with Croatia and FYROM provide for political dialogue, cooperation in all areas of EU policies, approximation of the candidate countries' regulation to that of the EU, and the four freedoms of the internal market. The aim is entry of Croatia and FYROM into the EU. While accession negotiations with Croatia and Turkey started on 3 October 2005, FYROM became a candidate country in December 2005 but accession negotiations have not started as yet.[21]

In the last couple of years, the EU has furthermore signed SAAs, similar to the agreements concluded with Croatia and FYROM, with four Western Balkan states, Albania, Bosnia and Herzegovina, Montenegro and Serbia. These countries, along with Kosovo under UNSC Resolution 1244/99, are considered as potential candidate countries, in the sense that they have been promised by the EU the prospect of membership. While

[21] See the European Commission website at http://ec.europa.eu/enlargement/the-policy/countries-on-the-road-to-membership/index_en.htm (last visited on 2 December 2009).

of these SAAs, only the one with Albania has been ratified to date, the EU has also concluded interim SAAs on trade and trade-related matters with all four of the countries, and these interim agreements are already in force.[22] In the context of this study, these agreements are reviewed in this chapter. In addition, where relevant, the chapter also discusses the agreements that governed until accession the relationship between the EU and its two most recent Member States, Bulgaria and Romania.[23]

(ii) The European Neighbourhood Policy

Following the accession of ten Member States in 2004, the EU launched the so-called European Neighbourhood Policy which aims to establish closer cooperation with its neighbouring countries and to strengthen prosperity, stability and security in the neighbourhood.[24] The ENP is based on a number of bilateral partnership or association agreements signed with two groups of countries: Southern Mediterranean countries, with which the EU has signed the so-called Euro-Mediterranean agreements, and East European and Central Asian countries, with which the EU has concluded partnership and cooperation agreements. In addition, in the context of the ENP, the European Commission has already issued country-specific action plans for eleven of the countries included in the ENP, which set out specific measures for the fulfilment of the obligations under the relevant agreements.[25] As the Commission notes, there is significant disparity in the level of development of the countries that have

[22] *Ibid*. See also Schimmelfennig (2008), *supra* n. 19, for an evaluation of the overall EU enlargement strategy following the accession of the twelve new Member States. On the policy of the EU in this field, and a detailed review of the development of the negotiations with the Western Balkan countries, see European Commission (2008), *Communication to the Council, Western Balkans: Enhancing the European Perspective*, COM(2008)127 final.

[23] As with most of the countries which entered the EU in 2004, the relationship of Bulgaria and Romania with the EU was governed by the Europe agreements, signed in the 1990s. These agreements included provisions on all fields related to the EU internal market (trade liberalisation, free movement of services, payments and capital in respect of trade and investments, and the free movement of workers), according to which candidate countries committed themselves to approximating their legislation to the EU *acquis communautaire*.

[24] The ENP was first outlined in a 2003 Commission Communication. European Commission (2003), *Wider Europe – Neighbourhood: A New Framework for Relations with our Eastern and Southern Neighbours*, COM(2003)104 final (Brussels, 11 March 2003), which was followed by a more detailed Communication in 2004: European Commission (2004), *Communication from the Commission, European Neighbourhood Policy: Strategy Paper*, COM(2004)373 final (Brussels, 12 May 2004).

[25] See the European Commission website at http://ec.europa.eu/world/enp/documents_en.htm#2 (last visited on 2 December 2009).

been included in this single policy, and therefore, as the partnerships develop, the operation of the policy becomes increasingly differentiated, as there is a need to follow a country-specific approach which would take into account the particularities of each of these countries.[26] Over time, the implementation of these action plans, particularly in regulatory areas, will prepare the ground for the conclusion of a new generation of 'deep and comprehensive free trade agreements (FTAs)' with all ENP partners, such as the agreement which the EU is currently negotiating with Ukraine.[27]

1. The *Euro-Mediterranean agreements* are the group of agreements concluded between the EU and eight Mediterranean countries[28] in the context of the Barcelona declaration,[29] which provided for political dialogue, respect for human rights and democracy, establishment by 2010 of a (WTO compatible) free trade area, and economic, financial, social and cultural cooperation. The agreements also include provisions relating to intellectual property, services, public procurement, competition rules, state aids and monopolies, cooperation relating to social affairs and migration (including re-admission of illegal immigrants) and cultural cooperation between the EU and the countries of the Mediterranean. The Barcelona process was relaunched in 2008 as the Union for the Mediterranean at the Summit of Paris, with the aim of further activating the strategic relations between the EU and its southern neighbours.[30] All the Euro-Mediterranean countries are included in the ENP.

26 See European Commission (2007), *A Strong European Neighbourhood Policy*, COM(2007)774 final, at 3. In this communication, the Commission discussed the central issues of the development of partnerships with neighbouring countries. For a more detailed overview, see European Commission (2008), *Implementation of the European Neighbourhood Policy*, COM(2009)188(3), in which the Commission noted that due to the conflicts between Russia and Georgia, the Israeli intervention in Gaza, and the financial crisis, the implementation of the ENP has been difficult. Nevertheless, it also took the view that these difficulties should be an impetus for further cooperation between the EU and the ENP countries.

27 See European Commission (2006), *Communication to the Council and the Parliament on Strengthening the European Neighborhood Policy*, COM(2006)726 final, at 5.

28 Algeria, Egypt, Jordan, Israel, Lebanon, Morocco, Tunisia and the Palestinian Authority (with which an interim agreement has been concluded). See Table 4.1.

29 See the 'Barcelona Declaration' adopted at the Euro-Mediterranean Conference, 27 and 28 November 1995, available at http://ec.europa.eu/external_relations/euromed/index_en.htm (last visited on 2 December 2009).

30 In addition to the above-mentioned nine countries, the Union for the Mediterranean also includes Monaco, Croatia, Turkey, Albania, Bosnia and Herzegovina, Montenegro and Libya. This initiative is complementary to the agreements discussed in this chapter. See Joint Declaration of the Paris Summit for the Mediterranean, Paris, 13 July 2008, available at www.ue2008.fr/webdav/site/PFUE/shared/import/07/0713_declaration_de_paris/

2. *Partnership and cooperation agreements* were signed with a number of Eastern European and Central Asian countries.[31] These ten-year bilateral treaties provide the legal framework upon which the cooperation of the EU with these countries is built. They express the contracting parties' respect for democratic principles and human rights, and they further provide for political dialogue on issues relating to security and stability. The agreements also include provisions relating to the economic and trade relationship between the contracting parties; nonetheless, in contrast to the contractual relations with the EU's other neighbouring countries, the partnership and cooperation agreements grant neither preferential treatment for trade, nor a timetable for regulatory approximation.[32] On the other hand, with the exception of Russia (with which the EU cooperates independently of the ENP),[33] Kazakhstan, Kyrgyzstan and Uzbekistan, all of the other countries of the region that have concluded partnership agreements with the EU are included in the ENP.

(iii) Agreements with selected trade partners

Finally, three other agreements signed by the EU with selected trade partners are reviewed in this chapter. The first is the global agreement with Mexico,[34] which provides for political dialogue on a number of issues, such as democracy, human rights, poverty, terrorism, migration and regional development. The agreement further provides for the creation of a WTO compatible free trade area in goods and services, the liberalisation of capital movements and payments, mutual opening of the procurement markets, and adoption of disciplines in the fields of competition and intellectual property rights. Based on this agreement, the EU–Mexico Joint Council in 2000 adopted a decision which (among other matters) creates a legal framework for cooperation between the parties on competition-related issues.[35]

Joint_declaration_of_the_Paris_summit_for_the_Mediterranean-EN.pdf> (last visited on 2 December 2009).

[31] See Table 4.1. These partnership and cooperation agreements replaced the trade and cooperation agreement concluded between the European Community and the Soviet Union in 1989.

[32] See European Commission *Communication on Wider Europe* (2003), *supra* n. 24 at 5.

[33] In fact it has been documented that Russia excluded itself from the ENP, preferring to cooperate with the EU on an equal basis. See K.E. Smith (2005), 'The Outsiders: The European Neighbourhood Policy' 81(4) *International Affairs* 757, at 759.

[34] Signed in 1997 and entered into force on 1 October 2000.

[35] See EC–Mexico Joint Council, Decision No. 2/2000 of 23 March 2000, Annex XV [2000] OJ L157/10.

The second is the association agreement between the EU and Chile, signed in November 2002. The competition provisions of this agreement have been provisionally applied since 1 February 2003. The agreement replaced the earlier framework cooperation agreement (signed in 1996) which provided for political and economic association between Chile and the EU. This later agreement is very detailed[36] and provides for intensive cooperation on political and trade matters.

The third agreement is a trade, development and cooperation agreement (TDCA) signed by the EU with South Africa. The agreement includes provisions on trade-related issues, economic cooperation, social and cultural cooperation and political dialogue, financial assistance and development cooperation.[37]

4.1.2 Role of competition in trade agreements and the way that the EU has used such provisions

Competition provisions are included in bilateral trade agreements in the context of a much broader and diverse legal framework, which contains rules relating to political dialogue, trade liberalisation and commitment of the signing parties to respect human rights and democratic principles, and (in most of them) approximation of the contracting parties' laws.[38] Hence, commercial, political and cultural issues are all addressed by these agreements.

Nonetheless, the common denominator and starting point for further cooperation are rules relating to trade liberalisation. Tariff reduction and the gradual creation of a free trade area is the obvious goal of most of these agreements.[39] Accordingly, the main role for competition law is to reduce,

[36] The association agreement with Chile is probably the most detailed of all the bilateral free trade agreements signed by the EU. Former Commissioner for Trade, Pascal Lamy, has characterised the agreement as 'a twenty-first century model of trade relations'. See European Commission, 'EU–Chile Association Agreement to be signed today in Brussels', Press Release IP/02/1696 of 18 November 2002.

[37] The agreement was signed in 1999 and entered into force in 2004. Note also that the EU signed an agreement with Korea on 15 October 2009, chapter 11 of which is devoted to competition law and policy. However, as at the time of writing, the agreement had been concluded only a few weeks previously, it is not further assessed here.

[38] On the diversity of the reasons that have led to the conclusion of these agreements, see J. Pelkmans and P. Brenton (1999), 'Free Trade with the EU: Driving Forces and the Effects' in O. Memedovic, A. Kuyvenhoven and W. Molle (eds.), *Multilateralism and Regionalism in the Post-Uruguay Round Era: What Role for the EU?* (Boston: Kluwer).

[39] In particular, this goal is explicitly expressed in agreements with candidate and accession countries, in the Euro-Mediterranean agreements, and in the agreements signed with Chile, South Africa and Mexico.

and if possible to eliminate, practices carried out by private undertakings that may have an effect on trade between the contracting parties. This function of competition law as a tool to secure and strengthen market integration has been successfully tested in the context of the EU's own integration project, and the need for adoption and effective application of competition rules is most evident in the case of the agreements with candidate countries which aim at EU accession.

On the other hand, with its neighbourhood policy, the EU opted for the creation of closer political and economic relationships with the neighbouring countries. In this regard, the European Commission stated that 'the European Neighbourhood Policy's vision involves a ring of countries, sharing the EU's fundamental values and objectives, drawn into an increasingly close relationship, going beyond co-operation to involve a significant measure of economic and political integration',[40] and expressed the opinion that in the context of the proposed regulatory and legislative approximation, 'convergence towards comparable approaches and definitions, legislative approximation on antitrust as well as State aid regulations, will eventually be needed for partners to advance towards convergence with the Internal Market'.[41]

Convergence on competition rules is therefore, at least from the perspective of the EU, a way to achieve market integration with its co-signing parties, and in this regard its attempts, at least with regard to candidate countries and countries that have been included in the ENP, are dedicated to the approximation of the competition rules of these countries to the competition model of the EU. As indicated by an OECD study which compared the competition provisions found in forty-seven trade agreements, in terms of competition law and policy, one may distinguish two 'families' of trade agreements. The first, the EU-style agreements, mainly contain substantive competition provisions, i.e. provisions that aim to address anticompetitive behaviour. The second group of agreements, agreements where either the United States or Canada is a signing party, do not contain substantive competition law provisions, but provisions dedicated to cooperation and coordination of enforcement activities.[42]

As the chapter shows, this distinction cannot be an absolute one, since there are agreements signed by the EU which, apart from the substantive competition law provisions, also include provisions on cooperation with

[40] European Commission, *European Neighbourhood Policy: Strategy Paper* (2004), *supra* n. 24 at 5.

[41] *Ibid.* at 16.

[42] OECD (2005), *Competition Provisions in Regional Trade Agreements.*

the other contracting parties.[43] Nonetheless, the distinction used by the OECD offers some indication as to what distinguishes EU policy in this field when compared with the policies followed by the United States and Canada. Whereas the United States and Canada use both enforcement cooperation agreements on competition and bilateral trade agreements to put into context issues of cooperation on competition law, the EU through bilateral trade agreements imposes the application of EU compatible competition rules regarding practices that affect the common trade, and in certain cases it obliges contracting parties to adopt legislation identical to its competition law. The next two sections of the chapter will test this hypothesis by analytically reviewing the substantive competition provisions, as well as the rules providing for cooperation that are found in the EU bilateral agreements.

4.2 Substantive competition provisions in the EU bilateral agreements

In considering the substantive competition provisions found in these agreements, the first distinction to be made is the one between antitrust rules, i.e. rules that aim to regulate anticompetitive practices conducted by private firms, on the one hand, and state aid rules and rules regulating state monopolies of a commercial character and public undertakings granted exclusive rights, on the other, which refer to the regulation of state actions and fall within the realm of EU competition law.

It may be observed that, depending on the particular category of the agreements, the wording of the competition-related provisions is very similar, or even identical, and this may be attributed to two main reasons. First, by using identical provisions as a standard starting point of negotiations, such negotiations may be concluded more swiftly. One cannot overlook the fact that the resources of the European Commission, which negotiates bilateral trade agreements, are limited, while the number of agreements is increasing very rapidly. In addition, with regard to competition law, it is interesting to note that the chapters on competition of most of these agreements have been negotiated by officials who work for the Directorate-General for Trade (DG Trade) and not the Directorate-General for Competition (DG Competition). This is partly because DG Trade is responsible for the negotiation of these agreements and partly

[43] See 4.3 *infra*.

because DG Competition lacks adequate resources to become actively involved in the negotiations.[44]

4.2.1 *Provisions relating to private undertakings*

A further distinction should be made with regard to the antitrust provisions included in these agreements, as two groups of relevant provisions may be identified. The first includes provisions which require the EU's co-signing parties to approximate their competition laws to that of the EU. The second group of provisions includes provisions that prohibit particular anticompetitive practices conducted by private firms and have an effect on the common trade. This section reviews both groups of provisions relating to the regulation of anticompetitive practices of private firms.

(i) Agreements with candidate and potential candidate countries

A standard provision included in all the agreements concluded between the EU and candidate countries declares incompatible with their proper functioning, 'all agreements between undertakings, decisions by associations of undertakings and concerted practices between undertakings which have as their object or effect the prevention, restriction or distortion of competition';[45] similarly incompatible is abuse by one or more undertakings of a dominant position in the territories of the European Community or of the contracting party as a whole or in a substantial part thereof.[46] The agreements also state that the assessment of relevant cases will be on the basis of EU law.

[44] Fewer than ten officials work for the International Affairs Unit of DG Competition, which is the Unit responsible for all bilateral agreements and the work carried out in international organisations. This point was raised by an interviewee from the European Commission, Brussels, 15 November 2007.

[45] EU–Bulgaria agreement, art. 64.1.i; EU–Croatia agreement, art. 70.1.i; EU–FYROM agreement, 69.1.i; EU–Romania agreement, art. 64.1.i; EU–Turkey agreement, art. 32. The EU–Turkey customs union is the most comprehensive of all the agreements discussed in this section as it includes specific examples of agreements that fall within the scope of the relevant article. On potential candidate countries, see EU–Albania interim SAA, art. 37.1.i (SAA, art. 71.1.i); EU–Bosnia and Herzegovina interim SAA, art. 36.1.i (SAA, art. 71.1.i); EU–Montenegro interim SAA, art. 38.1.i (SAA, art. 73.1.i); EU–Serbia interim SAA, art. 38.1.i (SAA, art. 73.1.i).

[46] EU–Bulgaria agreement, art. 64.1.ii; EU–Croatia agreement, art. 70.1.ii; EU–FYROM agreement, art. 69.1.ii; EU–Romania agreement, art. 64.1.ii; and EU–Turkey agreement, art. 33. On potential candidate countries, see EU–Albania interim SAA, art. 37.1.ii (SAA,

Table 4.2 *Provisions relating to anticompetitive business practices*

EU	Obligation to harmonise national antitrust rules	Best efforts to approximate laws	General statement that approximation of competition law would strengthen parties' economic links	Prohibition of anti-competitive agreements affecting common trade	Prohibition of abuse of dominance affecting common trade
Albania	√			√	√
Bosnia and Herzegovina	√			√	√
Bulgaria	√			√	√
Croatia	√			√	√
FYROM	√			√	√
Montenegro	√			√	√
Romania	√			√	√
Serbia	√			√	√
Turkey	√			√	√
Algeria		√		√	√
Egypt		√		√	√
Israel		√		√	√
Jordan		√		√	√
Lebanon				√	√
Morocco		√		√	√
Palestinian Authority		√		√	√
Tunisia		√		√	√
Armenia			√		
Azerbaijan			√		
Georgia			√		
Kazakhstan			√		
Kyrgyzstan			√		
Moldova			√		
Russia			√		
Ukraine			√		
Uzbekistan			√		
Chile				√	√
Mexico				√	√
South Africa				√	√

It may be observed that the aforementioned provisions are copied from the EC Treaty (Articles 81 and 82 EC, now Articles 101 and 102 of the Treaty on the Functioning of the EU (TFEU)) and apply to cases where intraregional trade is affected. Being in the process of accession, candidate countries clearly have the obligation to approximate their existing and future competition legislation to that of the EU.[47] It follows that, while EU compatible law is to be applied when an anticompetitive practice affects the common trade, from the date of the adoption of the agreements, the EU co-signing countries also have to go a step further and align their legislation to that of the EU.

In practice, the process of the approximation of laws is closely scrutinised by the European Commission and, in terms of competition, DG Competition monitors this process. Once the accession negotiations are launched, the Commission works together with representatives of candidate countries and issues screening reports, with which it expresses its opinion as to the development of the adopted competition legislation and the enforcement of such legislation. In the case, for instance, of Bulgaria, such reports were annual until the accession of the country to the EU. Progress reports have also been published regarding the three current candidate countries, Croatia, FYROM and Turkey,[48] as well as regarding the potential candidate countries, Albania, Bosnia and Herzegovina, Kosovo, Montenegro and Serbia.[49]

On the other hand, this obligation on candidate countries to have and enforce EU compatible competition rules also includes an obligation to have in place institutions with the competence to apply the rules. This obligation is documented in the text of the EU bilateral trade agreements either

art. 71.1.ii); EU–Montenegro interim SAA, art. 73.1.ii (SAA, art. 73.1.ii); EU–Serbia interim SAA, art. 38.1.ii (SAA, art. 73.1.ii).

[47] EU–Bulgaria agreement, art. 69; EU–Romania agreement, art. 69; EU–Croatia agreement, art. 69. The EU–Turkey customs union provides that in areas of direct relevance to the operation of the customs union, Turkey will harmonise its legislation with that of the EU. Furthermore, approximation of laws is provided in the area of competition law and policy (arts. 32 and 39). With regard to FYROM, the SAA provides in art. 68 that approximation will take place in two stages and also states that approximation on competition law should be carried out in stage 1. See also EU–Serbia SAA, art. 72; EU–Montenegro SAA, art. 72; EU–Bosnia SAA, art. 70; and EU–Albania SAA, art. 70. In addition, all these agreements provide that anticompetitive practices will be assessed in the context of the EU's competition rules.

[48] On Croatia, see European Commission (2008), *Croatia 2008 Progress Report*, SEC(2008)2694; on FYROM, see European Commission (2008), *FYROM 2008 Progress Report*, SEC(2008)2695; on Turkey, see European Commission (2008), *Turkey 2008 Progress Report*, SEC(2008)2699.

[49] On Albania, see European Commission (2008), *Albania 2008 Progress Report*, SEC(2008)2692; on Bosnia and Herzegovina, see European Commission (2008),

directly, in the form of a clear obligation of the EU's co-signing parties to set up a competition authority, or indirectly, in two ways: by leaving this issue to be addressed by later decisions of the association or stabilisation councils, which are established by the agreements and consist of government representatives of the parties; or by including a general statement by the signing countries that they will have and enforce competition laws.

In particular, the customs union with Turkey[50] and SAA with Croatia[51] clearly provide that the parties should ensure that an operationally independent public body is entrusted with the powers necessary for the full application of the competition-related rules.[52] Europe agreements with Romania and Bulgaria state that the association council will adopt within three years the necessary rules for the implementation of the competition rules.[53] Even though the provision does not directly require the creation of an authority to apply the competition rules, in the case of both Bulgaria and Romania, these authorities were created before the adoption of the implementing rules.[54]

(ii) Euro-Mediterranean agreements

Two provisions similar to Articles 101 and 102 TFEU are also included in the agreements with Southern Mediterranean countries, and are to be applied in cases where the common trade is affected.[55]

Bosnia and Herzegovina 2008 Progress Report, SEC(2008)2693; on Kosovo, see European Commission (2008), *Kosovo (Under UNSCR 1244/99) 2008 Progress Report*, SEC(2008)2697; on Montenegro, see European Commission (2008), *Montenegro 2008 Progress Report*, SEC(2008)2696; and on Serbia, see European Commission (2008), *Serbia 2008 Progress Report*, SEC(2008)2698.

50 EU–Turkey customs union, art. 39.a.

51 EU–Croatia SAA, art. 70.3. Similarly, the SAAs with Albania (art. 71.3, 4), Bosnia and Herzegovina (art. 71.3, 4), Montenegro (art. 73.3, 4) and Serbia (art. 73.3, 4), include provisions under which the potential candidate countries undertake the commitment to set up operationally independent authorities to apply competition rules.

52 The agreement with FYROM does not include a similar provision, nevertheless, as noted *infra*, the obligation to have in place a competition authority is implied.

53 On the basis of this article, the EU–Bulgaria Association Council has adopted Decision No. 2/97 on the implementation of competition rules, and Decision No. 2/2001 of 23 May 2001 adopting the implementing rules for the application of the provisions on state aid. Similarly, the EU–Romania Joint Council has adopted Decision No. 2/1999 on the implementation of competition rules, and Decision No. 4/2000 of 10 April 2001 adopting the implementing rules for the application of the provisions on state aid.

54 Hence, the implementing rules refer to these authorities. As regards Romania, see art. 1(2) of the implementing rules, and as to Bulgaria, art. 1(2) of the implementing rules.

55 Regarding the prohibition of anticompetitive agreements that have an effect on the common trade, see EU–Algeria agreement, art. 41.1.a; EU–Egypt agreement, art. 34.1.i;

Some of the agreements[56] also provide that the aim of cooperation is to assist the Euro-Mediterranean countries to approximate their legislation to that of the EU, in the fields covered by the agreement (including competition). In agreements concluded with Egypt, Israel and Jordan, the wording is slightly different, as it is provided that the parties agree to make best efforts to approximate their laws in order to facilitate the application of the agreement.[57]

It is clear, therefore, that as opposed to the terms of the agreements signed with acceding and candidate countries, which include an obligation to adopt EU-style competition rules, in the case of the agreements with the Euro-Mediterranean partners, the commitments are less firm. Priority is given to the application of EU compatible rules on practices that affect intraregional trade, and, accordingly, in most of these agreements the parties agree that practices that have an intraregional effect contrary to the competition-related provisions will be assessed in accordance with Articles 81, 82 and 87 EC, including secondary legislation.[58]

The inclusion of such a clause highlights the fact that, despite there being no clear obligation on the co-signing countries regarding the adoption of competition rules, it is important for the EU, as far as intraregional trade is concerned, to impose the application of its own rules. The extent to which this goal has been achieved to date is a debatable issue, however. Geradin and Petit, for instance, note that the Euro-Mediterranean agreements are of limited value, and this is principally because, notwithstanding the provision found in most of the agreements stating that the association council will adopt the necessary rules implementing the

EU–Israel agreement, art. 36.1.i; EU–Jordan agreement, art. 53.1.a; EU–Lebanon interim agreement, art. 27.1.a; EU–Morocco agreement, art. 36.1.a; EU–Palestinian Authority interim agreement, art. 30.1; and EU–Tunisia agreement, art. 36.1.a. With regard to the prohibition of abuse of dominance, see EU–Algeria agreement, art. 41.1.b; EU–Egypt agreement, art. 34.1.ii; EU–Israel agreement, art. 36.1.ii; EU–Jordan agreement, art. 53.1.b; EU–Lebanon interim agreement, art. 27.1.b; EU–Morocco agreement, art. 36.1.b; EU–Palestinian Authority interim agreement, art. 30.1.b, and EU–Tunisia agreement, art. 36.1.b.

56 EU–Algeria agreement, art. 56, and similarly EU–Morocco agreement, art. 52; EU–Palestinian Authority interim agreement, art. 41; and EU–Tunisia agreement, art. 52.

57 EU–Egypt agreement, art. 48; EU–Israel agreement, art. 55; EU–Jordan agreement, art. 69.

58 EU–Jordan agreement, art. 53.2; EU–Morocco agreement, art. 36.2; EU–Palestinian Authority interim agreement, art. 30.2; EU–Tunisia agreement, art. 36.2. Furthermore, in the case of the EU–Egypt agreement, there is no similar joint statement by the contracting parties. Instead, the EU simply declared this position (EU–Egypt agreement, art. 34 and Declaration of the EU on art. 34). Finally, the agreements with Algeria and Israel, and the interim agreement with Lebanon, do not contain a similar provision.

competition provisions of the agreements, such rules have only been adopted in the case of the agreements with Algeria and Morocco.[59]

This claim has been partially confirmed by the European Commission in its reports on the Mediterranean countries, published in the context of the ENP. The Commission has observed that adoption and enforcement of competition rules in these countries is a slow process; nevertheless, some notable progress has been achieved in the last four years or so. In particular, the Commission noted that Egypt adopted competition rules in 2005, which were amended in 2008 so as to provide the Egyptian Competition Authority with some increased powers, and also introduced increased fines for infringements of the rules, and a leniency programme. In this context, the Commission further noted in its recent progress report that the Egyptian Competition Authority had continued to pursue violations of competition rules.[60]

The Commission has also recently reported some progress with regard to the application of competition rules in Morocco, where the President and the Members of the Competition Authority (which has a consultative function) were appointed.[61] Jordan adopted a competition law in 2004,[62] and the Commission noted that the relevant institutions have been set up, though nonetheless, further progress was needed in this field. Such progress could be achieved with the amendment of the existing competition law to provide for the establishment of an independent competition authority.[63]

59 See D. Geradin and N. Petit (2004), 'Competition Policy in South Mediterranean Countries' 3(1) *Review of Network Economics* 65, at 73 and 78. Most of the Euro-Mediterranean agreements also provide that in a period from three to five years (depending on each particular agreement) the association council will adopt the necessary rules for the application of the competition-related provisions. Nevertheless, as noted *supra*, such rules have only been adopted in the cases of Algeria and Morocco. In the case of Algeria, the rules have entered into force as part of Annex V to the agreement (a relevant annex, Annex VIII, is also included in the agreement with Syria, which nevertheless has not yet been ratified). With regard to Morocco, these rules were adopted in the form of a council decision. See EU–Morocco Association Council, Decision No. 1/2004 of 19 April 2004 adopting the necessary rules for the implementation of the competition rules [2005] OJ L165/10. The implementing rules include provisions relating to the cooperation of the competition authorities of the countries. These provisions are further discussed at 4.3 *infra*.

60 European Commission (2009), *Country Report: Egypt*, SEC(2009)523/2 (Brussels, 23 April 2009) 14–15.

61 European Commission (2009), *Rapport de Suivi Maroc*, SEC(2009)520/2 (Brussels, 23 April 2009) 13–14.

62 European Commission (2006), *ENP Progress Report: Jordan*, SEC(2006)1508/2 (Brussels, 4 December 2006) at 8.

63 European Commission (2009), *Progress Report: Jordan*, SEC(2009)517/2 (Brussels, 23 April 2009) 2 and 10–11.

Algeria has also adopted competition rules based on the EU model,[64] as has Tunisia. With regard to the latter, the Commission has taken the view that the country had achieved real development in the field of competition.[65] Finally, the Commission noted that Lebanon was in the process of drafting competition rules.[66]

(iii) Agreements with Eastern European and Central Asian countries

The agreements signed with Eastern European and Central Asian countries only include a general statement that the parties recognise that an important condition for strengthening the economic links between the EU and the co-signing party is the approximation of the co-signing party's existing and future legislation to that of the Community; and the agreements include competition in the extensive list of the relevant fields that have to be approximated.[67]

The agreements between the EU and Moldova, Russia and Ukraine further include a general commitment for the contracting parties to have and to enforce laws addressing restrictions of competition by enterprises within their jurisdiction. The term 'restriction of competition' is not further defined by these agreements.[68] The remaining agreements between the EU and Eastern European and Central Asian countries include a general commitment that the parties will examine ways to apply their respective competition laws on a concerted basis in any case where trade between them is affected by particular practices conducted by firms,[69] without any further specification of practices that are prohibited.

[64] See OECD Global Forum on Competition (2004), *Challenges/Obstacles Faced by Competition Authorities in Achieving Greater Economic Development through the Promotion of Competition: Contribution from Algeria*, CCNM/GF/COMP/WD(2004)21, at 4.

[65] European Commission (2006), *ENP Progress Report: Tunisia*, SEC(2006)1510 (Brussels, 4 December 2006) 6. See also European Commission (2009), *ENP Progress Report: Tunisia*, SEC(2009) 521/2 (Brussels, 23 April 2009) 11.

[66] European Commission (2009), *Country Report: Lebanon*, SEC(2009) 518/2 (Brussels, 23 April 2009) 10.

[67] EU–Azerbaijan agreement, art. 43.2; EU–Armenia agreement, art. 43.2; EU–Georgia agreement, art. 43.2; EU–Kazakhstan agreement, art. 43; EU–Kyrgyzstan agreement, art. 44.2; EU–Moldova agreement, art. 50.2; EU–Russia agreement, art. 55.2; EU–Ukraine agreement, art. 51.2; and EU–Uzbekistan agreement, art. 42.2.

[68] EU–Moldova agreement, art 48.2.1; EU–Russia agreement, art. 53.2.1; and EU–Ukraine agreement, art. 49.2.1.

[69] EU–Azerbaijan agreement, art. 43.4; EU–Armenia agreement, art. 43.4; EU–Georgia agreement, art. 44.2; EU–Kazakhstan agreement, art. 43.4; and EU–Uzbekistan agreement, art. 42.4. Only the EU–Georgia agreement further defines the term 'competition

Hence, the commitments undertaken by Eastern European and Central Asian countries are looser than those undertaken by candidate countries and by the Euro-Mediterranean states. That said, as in the case of the Mediterranean countries, the development of competition-related legislation in the former Soviet Union states included in the ENP is being followed by the European Commission. In Commission reports, it is noted that a competition law was adopted in Armenia in 2000, and an EU-financed project has provided support to the authority in developing implementing regulations to supplement the Competition Act adopted in 2000.[70] The relevant amendment came into force in 2007 and, as the Commission noted, overall the Armenian competition authority had been active in the detection of violations of the law.[71] Azerbaijan and Georgia both have competition laws in place that cover anticompetitive agreements, abuse of dominance and mergers.[72] In Georgia, progress with regard to competition law nevertheless remained limited, and there was an ongoing high level dialogue with the EU on the development of competition policy.[73] In Azerbaijan, a new competition law had been drafted (though not yet adopted) with the aim to approximate its law to that of the EU.[74] All these developments are clear indications of the significant influence that the EU has had in the process of adoption and development of competition rules in these countries.

In addition, much of the EU's attention naturally falls on Russia, which is the most important strategic partner of the EU in the region. Informally, the European Commission has been very interested in the development of competition rules in Russia,[75] which has adopted a competition law that

laws' and provides that the EU will provide Georgia with technical assistance on the formulation and implementation of competition law, and in particular in identifying and regulating agreements and associations between undertakings and concerted practices which may have the effect of preventing, restricting or distorting competition, abuse by undertakings of a dominant position in the market, state aids which have the effect of distorting competition, state monopolies of a commercial character, and public undertakings with special or exclusive rights.

70 European Commission (2005), *Country Report: Armenia*, SEC(2005)285/3 (Brussels, 2 March 2005) 17.

71 European Commission (2007), *Country Report: Armenia*, SEC(2008)92/3 (Brussels, 3 April 2008) 10.

72 See European Commission (2005), *Country Report: Azerbaijan*, SEC(2005)286/3 (Brussels, 2 March 2005) 19; European Commission (2005), *Country Report: Georgia*, SEC(2005)288/3 (Brussels, 2 March 2005) 19.

73 European Commission (2009), *Country Report: Georgia*, SEC(2009)513/2 (Brussels, 3 April 2009) 13.

74 European Commission (2008), *Country Report: Azerbaijan*, SEC(2008)391 (Brussels, 3 April 2008) 11.

75 Interview with EU official, Brussels, 15 November 2007.

includes prohibitions of anticompetitive agreements and abuse of dominance, as well as merger control. Nonetheless, as an OECD study notes, though relatively complete in terms of its areas of coverage, the competition law does not contain effective sanctions and fails to provide the Russian competition authority with sufficient investigative powers.[76]

(iv) Agreements with selected trade partners

Finally, the agreements concluded between the EU and Chile, and the EU and Mexico, require no substantive changes in co-signing partners' laws. The parties agree to apply their (already in place) competition regimes, in a manner consistent with the agreement. In contrast, even though South Africa had a competition law in place when the EU–South Africa agreement was signed, the agreement provided in article 36 that if, at the entry into force of the agreement, the contracting parties did not have the necessary laws and regulations for the implementation of the competition-related provisions of the agreement, they would have to put such laws in place within a period of three years.[77] In addition, EU compatible provisions on anticompetitive agreements[78] and abuse of dominance are included in the agreement with South Africa, and are to be applied in cases where the common trade is affected.

On the other hand, among the agreements explored here, only the agreement with Chile includes specific provisions relating to mergers. The parties declare that their merger regulations are included in the scope of competition law, as this is defined by the agreement.[79] That said, in view of the fact that the agreements with candidate countries and most of the Euro-Mediterranean agreements provide that anticompetitive practices

[76] OECD (2004), *Competition Law and Policy in Russia: An OECD Peer Review* (Paris: OECD).

[77] Note that Annex VIII of the agreement clearly states that anticompetitive practices will be assessed in the case of the EU on the basis of Articles 81 and 82 EC, while with regard to South Africa they will be assessed on the basis of South African competition law. Thus, there is no obligation created for South Africa to approximate its competition laws to those of the EU. See S. Szepesi (2004), *Comparing EU Free Trade Agreements: Competition Policy and State Aid*, ECDPM InBrief 6E (ECDPM, Maastricht). This differentiation in the case of the EU–South Africa agreement may be attributed to the fact that South Africa has special competition rules to deal with the apartheid legacy by supporting individuals who were traditionally victims of discrimination.

[78] EU–South Africa agreement, art. 35.a. Nonetheless, it has to be stressed that the agreement declares such practices incompatible with its proper functioning, 'unless the firms can demonstrate that the anti-competitive effects are outweighed by pro-competitive ones'.

[79] EU–Chile agreement, art. 172.2. With regard to the EU, the (later amended) Regulation (EC) 4064/89 is mentioned.

will be assessed in accordance with Articles 81, 82 and 87 EC, including secondary legislation, it could be argued that mergers are also covered by these agreements.

4.2.2 *Rules relating to state actions and public undertakings*

While the inclusion of competition provisions relating to private undertakings in the bilateral trade agreements of the EU to some extent reveals the attempt by the EU to export its competition law model, of equal or even greater importance are the rules relating to state aids and public undertakings. As noted in the context of the analysis carried out in Chapter 5,[80] state aid rules and rules on public undertakings, even though traditionally not considered to fall within the realm of competition law, have been treated as competition issues in the EU, as the relevant rules are enforced by the EU's central competition authority, the European Commission. Hence, the inclusion of such provisions is again an indication of the influence of the EU model on the development of international competition rules.

On the other hand, the inclusion of state aid rules and rules on public undertakings is of major importance, as most of the EU's associated states are countries which for decades were governed by communist regimes, and until the collapse of the Soviet Union, there was no market-based economy, and market activity was functioning in the context of a large administrative hierarchy.[81]

(i) Agreements with candidate and potential candidate countries

As in the case of rules relating to private undertakings, the provisions relating to state aids and public undertakings may be divided into two broad categories. First, in the context of their general obligation to align their legislation with the EU legislative framework, candidate and potential countries are obliged to adopt state aid rules and rules on public undertakings, compatible with those of the EU. Secondly, the agreements also include particular provisions on the application of state aid and public undertakings in cases that affect intraregional trade.

State aids: there is a common provision included in the agreements of the EU with candidate and potential candidate countries declaring

[80] See 5.2 *infra*.

[81] J.M. Litwack (1992), 'Legality and Market Reform in Soviet-Type Economies' 5(4) *Journal of Economic Perspectives* 77, at 79–83.

Table 4.3 *Provisions on state aids, state monopolies of a commercial character and public undertakings*

EU	Obligation to harmonise national state aid rules	Prohibition of state/ public aids	Abolition of countervailing duties insofar as signing countries have state aid rules in place	Obligation to apply state aid rules in a transparent way	Obligation to provide the other party with information on state aid	Obligation to harmon-ise national law on state monopolies and public undertakings with exclusive rights	Non-discrimination in the actions of state monopolies
Albania	√	√	√	√	√	√	√
Bosnia and Herzegovina	√	√	√	√	√	√	√
Bulgaria	√	√	√	√	√	√	√
Croatia	√	√	√	√	√	√	√
FYROM	√	√	√	√	√	√	√
Montenegro	√	√	√	√	√	√	√
Romania	√	√	√	√	√	√	√
Serbia	√	√	√	√	√	√	√
Turkey	√	√	√	√	√	√	√
Algeria		√					√
Egypt		√	√	√	√		√
Israel		√	√	√	√		√

Table 4.3 (*cont.*)

EU	Obligation to harmonise national state aid rules	Prohibition of state/ public aids	Abolition of countervailing duties insofar as signing countries have state aid rules in place	Obligation to apply state aid rules in a transparent way	Obligation to provide the other party with information on state aid	Obligation to harmon-ise national law on state monopolies and public undertakings with exclusive rights	Non-discrimination in the actions of state monopolies
Jordan		√	√	√	√		√
Lebanon		√					√
Morocco		√	√	√	√		√
Palestinian Authority		√	√	√	√		√
Tunisia		√	√	√	√		√
Armenia							
Azerbaijan							
Georgia							
Kazakhstan							
Kyrgyzstan							
Moldova		√			√		√
Russia		√			√		√
Ukraine		√			√		√
Uzbekistan							
Chile				√	√		
Mexico							
South Africa		√		√	√		

incompatible with their proper functioning, 'any public aid which distorts, or threatens to distort, competition by favouring certain undertakings or the production of certain goods'.[82] Similarly to the other competition provisions, it is provided that the assessment of relevant cases will be on the basis of EU law. The parties also guarantee transparency in the application of their state aid rules, and express their commitment to provide information on state aid schemes and individual state aids, upon request of the other party.[83]

A consequence of the inclusion of state aid rules in the context of competition legislation, and the subsequent obligation of the countries to have and enforce state aid rules, is that the agreements signed with candidate countries provide that subsidies are regulated by the provisions relating to state aids. That said, the right of the countries to apply countervailing measures[84] to the other contracting party is abolished in practice upon accession of the candidate countries to the EU.[85]

In addition, all the agreements provide that these countries will be considered, for a (renewable with a later agreement) period of five years, as areas identical to those areas of the EU where the standard of living is abnormally low or there is serious underemployment, as described in

[82] EU–Bulgaria agreement, art. 64.1.iii; EU–Croatia agreement, art. 70.1.iii; EU–Romania agreement, art. 64.1.iii. Similarly, see EU–Turkey agreement, art. 34; EU–Albania interim SAA, art. 38 (SAA, art. 71.1.iii); EU–Bosnia and Herzegovina interim SAA, art. 36.1.c (SAA, art. 71.1.c); EU–Montenegro interim SAA, art. 38.1.ii (SAA, art. 73.1.iii); EU–Serbia interim SAA, art. 38.1.iii (SAA, art. 73.1.iii). With regard to Euro-Mediterranean agreements, see EU–Egypt agreement, art. 34.2; EU–Israel agreement, art. 36.2; EU–Morocco agreement, art. 36.3; EU–Palestinian Authority interim agreement, art. 30.3; and EU–Tunisia agreement, art. 36.3.

[83] EU–Bulgaria agreement, art. 64.4.b; EU–Croatia agreement, art. 70.5; and EU–Romania agreement, art. 64.4.b. There is no such provision in the customs union with Turkey, and this is due to the fact that there is as yet no authority in Turkey to review state aids. EU–Albania interim SAA, art. 375 (SAA, art. 71.5); EU–Bosnia and Herzegovina interim SAA, art. 36.5 (SAA, art. 71.5); EU–Montenegro interim SAA, art. 38.5 (SAA, art. 73.5); EU–Serbia interim SAA, art. 38.5 (SAA, art. 73.5).

[84] Countervailing measures are extra duties ('countervailing duties') that may be charged by countries on subsidised imports that are found to be hurting domestic producers.

[85] In the case of the EU–Turkey customs union, it is provided in art. 44.1 that the association council is the competent body to suspend the application of trade defence measures; this has not yet been implemented, however. Furthermore, art. 70.9 of the Croatia agreement provides that 'Nothing in this Article shall prejudice or affect in any way the taking, by either Party, of antidumping or countervailing measures in accordance with the relevant Articles of GATT 1994 and WTO Agreement on Subsidies and Countervailing Measures or related internal legislation', and the same wording has been used in the case of the potential candidate countries. See EU–Albania interim SAA, art. 37.9 (SAA, art. 71.9); EU–Bosnia and Herzegovina agreement, art. 71.10; EU–Montenegro SAA, art. 73.10;

Article 92(3)(a) (now Article 107(3)(a)) TFEU,[86] in practice offering those countries the opportunity to be exempted from the application of the state aid rules for the given period.

Hence, the agreements with candidate and potential candidate countries include a provision that prohibits state aid which affects the common trade; they do not, however, include further clarification as to the way in which these provisions have to be applied. Cremona has identified a number of problems which arise in view of this generality of the state aid provisions. She notes that in the case of the Europe agreements with the current new Member States, more specific provisions were laid down in the rules implementing the state aid provisions of the agreements, and these rules provided that surveillance of state aid rules would be enforced by a national candidate country authority in cooperation with the European Commission.[87]

In contrast to the Europe agreements, the agreements with Croatia and with FYROM do not provide for the adoption of implementing rules, but have incorporated some of the implementing rules in the agreements themselves. In the case of Croatia and potential candidate countries, for instance, it is provided that they will set up an independent authority with the competence to review state aids in the country.[88] In the case of FYROM, no such obligation is explicitly stated in the agreement; nonetheless, the fact that FYROM undertakes the commitment to apply state aid rules within five years from the entry into force

EU–Serbia interim SAA, art. 38.10 (SAA, art. 73.10). The agreement with FYROM (art. 69.5) states that any measures regarding lack of application of the state aid rules have to be taken in accordance with the procedures and under the conditions laid down thereby or the relevant Community internal legislation.

[86] EU–Bulgaria agreement, art. 64.4.a; EU–Croatia agreement, art. 70.7.a; and EU–Romania agreement, art 64.4.a. In the case of Bulgaria and Romania, this period was extended by the association council for another five years. As regards Bulgaria, see EU–Bulgaria Association Council, Decision No. 1/2000. As to Romania, see EU–Romania Association Council, Decision No. 2/2000 of 17 July 2000 [2000] OJ L230/13. In the case of potential candidate countries the relevant period varies. It is ten years in the case of Albania (EU–Albania interim SAA, art. 37.7 (SAA, art. 71.7)); six years in the case of Bosnia (EU–Bosnia and Herzegovina SAA, art. 71.7); and five years for Montenegro and Serbia (EU–Montenegro interim SAA, art. 38.7 (SAA, art. 73.1.7) and EU–Serbia interim SAA, art. 38.7 (SAA, art. 73.7)).

[87] See M. Cremona (2003), 'State Aid Control: Substance and Procedure in the Europe Agreements and the Stabilisation Association Agreements' 9(3) *European Law Journal* 265, at 267–9.

[88] EU–Croatia SAA, art. 70(4); EU–Albania interim SAA, art. 37.4 (SAA, art. 71.4); EU–Bosnia and Herzegovina interim SAA, art. 36.4 (SAA, art. 71.4); EU–Montenegro

of the agreement, implies that the country has to establish a body to enforce the law.[89]

As with the provisions relating to private undertakings, in practice, as soon as accession negotiations are launched, the state aid schemes of the candidate countries are put under the microscope by the Commission, which reviews the type and amount of the aid granted by the governments of candidate countries.[90] For instance, in its recent progress report on Croatia, the Commission noted that some progress had been made recently in this field and in particular regarding state aid to the steel sector, as well as regarding the drawing up of a regional aid map and the alignment of fiscal aid schemes. Nevertheless, the Commission further stated that significant efforts were required regarding restructuring aid to the shipyards.[91] As opposed to Croatia, where some progress had been made, in relation to Turkey, the Commission noted that neither the legislative framework nor the enforcement level was satisfactory.[92] Similarly, the Commission noted in the relevant reports that no progress had been made in Bosnia and Herzegovina, or in Serbia, in the field of state aids.[93] By contrast, in its relevant 2008 report the Commission noted that in Albania there had been some progress with regard to state aids, since the relevant legislation had been adopted and the competent state aid commission had already reviewed state aid cases and issued an annual report.[94] Similarly, in the case of Montenegro, the relevant legislation had been adopted and the competent commission had been set up and issued an annual report in 2007; nevertheless, an effective and comprehensive system for *ex ante* control of state aids was not yet in place in this country.[95]

interim SAA, art. 38.4 (SAA, art. 73.4); EU–Serbia interim SAA, art. 38.4 (SAA, art. 73.4).

89 See Cremona (2003), *supra* n. 87 at 269.

90 This is secured in practice with the creation of inventories of state aid where the candidate and acceding countries notify any aid granted in their territory. See Cremona (2003), *supra* n. 87 at 280. In the case of potential candidate countries this obligation of the EU's partners to issue annual reports on state aids and establish comprehensive inventories of aid schemes on the basis of criteria set by EU law is included in the text of the relevant SAAs. See EU–Albania interim SAA, art. 37.5, 6 (SAA, art. 71.5, 6); EU–Bosnia and Herzegovina, art. 36.5, 6 (SAA, art. 71.5, 6); EU–Montenegro interim SAA, art. 38.5, 6 (SAA, art. 73.5, 6); EU–Serbia interim SAA, art. 38.5, 6 (SAA, art. 73.5, 6).

91 See European Commission (2008), *Progress Report on Croatia*, *supra* n. 48 at 34–5.

92 See European Commission (2008), *Progress Report on Turkey*, *supra* n. 48 at 47–8.

93 See European Commission (2008), *Progress Report on Bosnia and Herzegovina*, *supra* n. 49 at 38, and European Commission (2008), *Progress Report on Serbia*, *supra* n. 49 at 36.

94 See European Commission (2008), *Progress Report on Albania*, *supra* n. 49 at 30.

95 See European Commission (2008), *Progress Report on Montenegro*, *supra* n. 49.

State monopolies of a commercial character and public undertakings granted exclusive rights: the Europe agreements with Romania and Bulgaria, as well as the SAAs with Croatia and FYROM, and customs union with Turkey provide that the Member States and the candidate country undertake the commitment to progressively adjust any state monopolies of a commercial character so as to ensure that, by the end of the fifth year following the entry into force of the respective agreements, no discrimination regarding the conditions under which goods are procured and marketed exists between nationals of the Member States and of the candidate country.[96] It is therefore made clear in the agreements that upon entry into force, any state monopolies in the candidate countries have to compete on equal terms with firms registered in the EU.

In relation to public undertakings, or undertakings granted exclusive rights, the Europe agreements with Romania and Bulgaria[97] provided that with regard to such undertakings, the association council shall ensure that, as from the third year from the date of entry into force of the Agreement, the parties align their legislation to that of the EU (i.e. Article 86 EC),[98] and the principles adopted by the concluding document of the April 1990 Bonn meeting of the Conference on Security and Cooperation in Europe (notably entrepreneurs' freedom of decision). While a similar provision is included in the agreement with Turkey and FYROM,[99] in the case of the EU–Croatia SAA, the only reference in relation to public undertakings is made in article 70.3, in the context of the creation of an independent body to apply competition provisions, and this wording has also been followed in the case of the agreements with potential candidate countries.[100] On

[96] EU–Bulgaria agreement, art. 30; EU–Romania agreement, art. 30; EU–Croatia agreement, art. 40; EU–Turkey agreement, art. 42. The EU–Croatia agreement further provides that the stabilisation and association council will be informed of the measures adopted to implement this objective. A similar provision has been included in the agreements with the potential candidate countries; nevertheless, the period provided for adjustment varies. In particular, for Albania it is four years, and for Serbia three years (EU–Albania interim SAA, art. 27 (SAA, art. 40); EU–Serbia interim SAA, art. 28 (SAA, art. 43)). In the case of Bosnia and Herzegovina, and Montenegro, this clause is triggered as soon as the agreements enter into force (EU–Bosnia and Herzegovina SAA, art. 41; EU–Montenegro SAA, art. 43).

[97] See art. 66 in both agreements.

[98] Now Article 86 EC. A similar provision is included in the agreements of the candidate countries. See EU–Albania interim SAA, art. 38 (SAA, art. 72); EU–Bosnia and Herzegovina SAA, art. 72; EU–Montenegro interim SAA, art. 39 (SAA, art. 74); and EU–Serbia interim SAA, art. 39 (SAA, art. 74).

[99] EU–Turkey agreement, art. 41. The difference in the EU–Turkey agreement is that Turkey will ensure alignment of its legislation to that of the EU by the end of the first year following the entry into force of the agreement, EU–FYROM agreement, art. 70.

[100] In particular, the parties have to set up authorities to apply competition rules regarding private and public undertakings.

the basis of this provision, in conjunction with the country's obligation to align its competition rules to those of the EU, it may safely be assumed that the relevant rules applied by the Croatian institution have to be aligned with EU law. In any case, developments in the fields of state monopolies and public undertakings are also reviewed by the European Commission in the context of the accession negotiations of candidate countries, and accession can only be when these countries have reached satisfactory levels of approximation of their relevant regimes to EU law.

(ii) Euro-Mediterranean agreements and agreements with former Soviet Union states

State aids: With the exceptions of the EU–Algeria agreement and the interim agreement between the EU and Lebanon, all the Euro-Mediterranean agreements are identical to the agreements with candidate and acceding countries as they include a provision on state aids providing that public aids that distort or threaten to distort competition are incompatible with the proper functioning of the agreements.[101] The agreements also include a dual commitment by the signing parties to apply state aid rules in a transparent way and to submit any information required by the other party on state aid schemes and individual aids.[102] Some of them also state that the Mediterranean countries will be considered for a period of five years as areas where the standard of living is abnormally low as described in Article 87(3)(a) EC.[103] Some of the Euro-Mediterranean agreements contain provisions according to which the WTO rules on subsidies and countervailing measures will apply only for a period of three to five years (depending on each particular agreement) until the adoption of the relevant state (or public) aid rules.[104]

[101] EU–Egypt agreement, art. 34.2; EU–Israel agreement, art. 36.2; EU–Morocco agreement, art. 36.3; EU–Palestinian Authority interim agreement, art. 30.3; and EU–Tunisia agreement, art. 36.3.

[102] EU–Egypt agreement, art. 34.2; EU–Israel agreement, art. 36.3; EU–Jordan agreement, art. 53.4.b; EU–Morocco agreement, art. 36.4.b; EU–Palestinian Authority interim agreement, art. 30.5; and EU–Tunisia agreement, art. 36.4.b.

[103] EU–Jordan agreement, art. 53.4.a; EU–Morocco agreement, art. 36.4.a; EU–Tunisia agreement, art. 36.4.a; and EU–Palestinian Authority interim agreement, art. 30.4. The wording of the interim agreement between the EU and the Palestinian Authority is different. The parties agree that for a period of five years, the Palestinian Authority is permitted to grant public aid 'to undertakings as an instrument to tackle its specific development problems'.

[104] EU–Egypt agreement, art. 34.2; EU–Israel agreement, art. 36.2; EU–Jordan agreement, art. 53.3; EU–Palestinian Authority interim agreement, art. 30.3; and EU–Tunisia agreement, art. 36.3.

Hence, in terms of the legal text, the state aid-related provisions found in the Euro-Mediterranean agreements are very similar (or even identical) to the provisions included in the agreements with candidate countries. That said, the major difference between these two groups of agreements is that while candidate countries have undertaken the commitment to align their rules to those of the EU, and their regimes are scrutinised by the European Commission in the context of the accession process, the Southern Mediterranean countries only express that they will do their best to align their legislation with EU law. In view of this fact, in combination with the absence of rules implementing the state aid provisions, and the fact that the public policies of the Mediterranean countries involve more direct intervention, it comes as no surprise that, to date, none of these countries has adopted EU compatible state aid rules.[105]

In contrast to the agreements with Mediterranean countries, the agreements with former Soviet Union states do not include detailed state aid rules. In fact only three of them, namely the agreements that the EU has concluded with Moldova, Ukraine and Russia, state that the parties agree to refrain from granting state aids favouring certain undertakings or the production of products other than primary goods as defined in the GATT. They also agree to provide, upon request by the contracting party, information on their state aid schemes or individual state aids.[106]

On the other hand, all the agreements with former Soviet Union states include a 'best efforts' clause according to which the parties will cooperate in subsidies investigations and will do 'their utmost' to find a constructive solution to the problem. Furthermore, all these agreements clearly state that the provisions on competition law will not affect a party's right to apply countervailing measures.[107] Hence, the wording of the agreements with former Soviet Union states is largely based on the relevant WTO instruments, and not on the EU state aid model, an indication that at least

105 Interview with EU official, Brussels, 15 November 2007. This argument is also seconded by the European Commission in its recent ENP reports, where it is noted that there has been no progress with regard to the surveillance of state aid rules in Egypt, Jordan, Lebanon, Morocco and Tunisia.

106 EU–Ukraine agreement, art. 49.2.2, 3; EU–Moldova agreement, arts. 38.2.2 and 48.2.3. In the case of the EU–Russia agreement, the wording of the provision is a little different than in the other relevant provisions. Article 53.2.2 makes reference to 'export aid' (as opposed to state or public aid in the other agreements). The EU and Russia agree that for a transitional period of five years, Russia is permitted to adopt measures inconsistent with this provision (Annex IX).

107 EU–Armenia agreement, art. 14.6; EU–Azerbaijan agreement, art. 14.6; EU–Georgia agreement, art. 14.6; EU–Kazakhstan agreement, art. 13.6; EU–Kyrgyzstan agreement,

in terms of the text of the agreements, state aid rules are not included in the competition framework set out by the signing countries.

However, in at least two cases there have been developments in this field in this group of countries which might indicate that certain former Soviet Union states are moving towards the adoption of EU compatible state aid rules. In particular, in 2004 the Ukrainian Antimonopoly Committee submitted a draft state aid law which was closely modelled on the *acquis*; the law was, however, rejected by the Ukrainian Parliament. According to the European Commission, the Ukrainian agency intends to submit an amended version of the Ukrainian Competition Act to include elements of state aid.[108] Similarly, in the case of Armenia, even though there is no particular provision on state aids in its agreement with the EU, it has recently amended its competition law by the insertion of state aid rules.[109] In both countries, these developments have occurred in the context of projects of technical assistance provided by the EU,[110] something that highlights two issues: first, that these agreements are the starting point for cooperation and in practice the cooperation may go further than is provided in the articles; secondly, technical assistance offered by the EU may facilitate such closer cooperation. The various technical assistance tools used by the EU are discussed in more detail below.

State monopolies of a commercial character: with regard to state monopolies of a commercial character, the Euro-Mediterranean agreements, as well as the agreements with Moldova, Russia and Ukraine, include a standard provision, similar to the one included in the agreements with candidate countries, according to which the parties undertake a commitment to progressively adjust any state monopolies of a commercial

art. 13.6; EU–Moldova agreement, art. 18 in conjunction with art. 48.5; EU–Russia agreement, art. 18 in conjunction with art. 53.5; EU–Ukraine agreement, art. 19 in conjunction with art. 49.5; and EU–Uzbekistan agreement, art. 13.6.

108 See European Commission (2006), *ENP Progress Report: Ukraine*, SEC(2006)1505/2 (Brussels, 4 December 2006) 10–11.

109 See AEPLAC (2007), *Assessment of Institutional Standing in the Fields of Competition and State Aid*, report presented in the context of the EU-funded TACIS programme, at 25–28, available at http://old.aeplac.eu/pdf/2007/Compet/Compet.pdf (last visited on 2 December 2009). See also European Commission, *2007 Progress Report on Armenia*, *supra* n. 71 at 11.

110 On Armenia, see AEPLAC (2007), *supra* n. 109. The relevant project in Ukraine took place between 2001–2006, and the EU offered 2.5 million euros to assist the Ukrainian authority 'to facilitate improvement of the business climate in Ukraine through adjustment of competition rules and competition law enforcement in Ukraine, making it compatible with the international standards, and in particular, with the provisions of Partnership and Cooperation Agreement and requirements of the WTO'. See the

character so as to ensure that, by the end of the fifth year following the entry into force of the respective agreements, no discrimination regarding the conditions under which goods are procured and marketed exists between nationals of the Member States and of the candidate country.[111]

This provision could be of major importance in view of the fact that most of the EU's co-signing partners are economies in transition and the role of state monopolies is consequently considerable. Nevertheless, in the case of agreements where the obligations of the parties are limited to the expression of goodwill by the signing parties that they will do their best to approximate their legislation, the expected effects of this provision should not be over-estimated.

Public undertakings granted exclusive rights: with regard to public undertakings, and undertakings granted exclusive rights, in the Euro-Mediterranean agreements, and the agreements with Moldova, Russia and Ukraine, the parties agree that within five years from the adoption of the agreement, the association council will ensure that there is neither enacted nor maintained any measure distorting the parties' common trade to an extent contrary to their respective interests. The parties further declare that 'This provision shall not obstruct the performance, in law or fact, of the particular tasks assigned to such undertakings'.[112]

The wording of these agreements on public undertakings granted exclusive rights therefore differs from the wording of the agreements with candidate countries. On the one hand, the Mediterranean and former Soviet Union states do not have to align their legislation with the relevant EU rules; and on the other hand, they probably retain the discretion in

website of the EU delegation in Ukraine, http://ec.europa.eu/delegations/ukraine (last visited on 2 December 2009).

[111] With regard to the Euro-Mediterranean agreements, see EU–Algeria agreement, art. 42; EU–Egypt agreement, art. 35; EU–Israel agreement, art. 37; EU–Jordan agreement, art. 54; EU–Lebanon interim agreement, art. 28; EU–Morocco agreement, art. 37; EU–Palestinian Authority interim agreement, art. 31; EU–Tunisia agreement, art. 37. There is a transitional period of five years for the parties to adjust their legislation to this provision; this is, however, without prejudice to their commitments to GATT. See also EU–Moldova agreement, art. 48.2.4; EU–Russia agreement, art. 53.2.4; EU–Ukraine agreement, art. 49.2.4. Note that, depending on the terms of each particular agreement, the parties have to adjust their relevant legislation in a period between three and five years, which may be further extended by a new agreement between the parties (EU–Moldova agreement, art. 48.2.6; EU–Russia agreement, art. 53.2.5; and EU–Ukraine agreement, art. 49.2.6).

[112] EU–Algeria agreement, art. 43; EU–Egypt agreement, art. 36; EU–Israel agreement, art. 38; EU–Jordan agreement, art. 55; EU–Lebanon interim agreement, art. 29; EU–Morocco agreement, art. 38; EU–Palestinian Authority interim agreement, art. 32; EU–Tunisia agreement, art. 38. See also EU–Moldova agreement, art. 48.2.5; EU–Russia agreement, art.

practice to take measures which are incompatible with the EU competition rules, as the agreements state that only measures that are contrary to their respective interests are not allowed, without further indication as to how such interests may be determined.

(iii) Agreements with selected trade partners

State aids: Of the three agreements with selected partners (Mexico, Chile and South Africa), only the former does not make reference to public or state aids. The EU–Chile agreement does not define the term 'public' or 'state aid', nonetheless in article 177.3 the parties agree to provide the other party with information on state aids on an annual basis, including the overall amount of aids, if possible by sector. Each party may request information on individual cases affecting trade between the parties. The requested party will use its best efforts to provide non-confidential information. Despite the fact that the wording of the agreement on state aids resembles to a certain extent the wording of the agreements with candidate and Mediterranean states, in contrast to the agreements with these countries the Chile agreement makes it clear that the parties may take countervailing measures, in accordance with the WTO rules.[113]

The EU–South Africa agreement is the most comprehensive of the three on this particular issue. Section E of the EU–South Africa agreement is devoted to the regulation of public aid.[114] Article 41.1 of the agreement provides that public aid which favours certain firms or the production of certain goods, and which does not support a specific public policy objective or objectives of either party, is incompatible with the proper functioning of the agreement.[115] The parties also agree to ensure that public aid is granted in a fair, equitable and transparent manner,[116] and they express their commitment to transparency in the field of public aid.[117] In addition, the parties agree to provide, upon request of the other party, information

53.2.4; and EU–Ukraine agreement, art. 49.2.5. Note that the transitional period provided for by these agreements varies from three to four years from the adoption of the agreements. The parties have also agreed that they may extend this period with a new agreement.

113 EU–Chile agreement, art. 78.

114 Note that the provisions on public aid are included in a separate section of the agreement (section E) and not in the competition-related section (section D).

115 Annex IX of the agreement specifies a number of relevant public policy objectives: regional development, industrial restructuring and development, promotion of micro-enterprises and small- and medium-sized enterprises, advancement of previously disadvantaged persons, affirmative action programmes, employment, environmental protection, rescue and restructure of firms in difficulty, R&D, support to firms in deprived urban areas, training.

116 EU–South Africa agreement, art. 41.2.

117 *Ibid.* art. 43.

regarding their aid schemes, or individual cases of public aid. The parties also agree that exchange of information shall take into account the limitations imposed by laws relating to business or professional secrecy.[118] Similarly to the agreements with candidate and Mediterranean countries, the agreement with South Africa also provides in Annex IX that the WTO rules on subsidies and countervailing measures will be applied as long as rules on public aid are not adopted.

State monopolies of a commercial character: with regard to public monopolies of a commercial character, of the three agreements only the EU–Chile agreement includes relevant provisions.[119] Specifically, it is provided that nothing in the competition-related title prevents a party from designating or maintaining public or private monopolies according to their respective laws.

Undertakings granted exclusive rights: with regard to public undertakings or undertakings granted exclusive rights, the agreement between the EU and South Africa explicitly excludes public undertakings from the application of the rules relating to public aid[120] (Annex IX). There is no other specific reference to this matter. In contrast, the EU and Chile in their agreement (article 179.1) have included a similar provision to that in the Euro-Mediterranean agreements.[121]

4.3 Provisions on cooperation in competition

As mentioned earlier in the chapter, bilateral EU agreements primarily contain substantive competition law provisions. As this section observes, a number of these agreements also include provisions on cooperation on competition; the level of cooperation provided, however, varies considerably. For instance, supplementary agreements (rules implementing the competition provisions) have been signed with some candidate countries with the aim of strengthening and formalising cooperation on competition issues. Of the Euro-Mediterranean agreements, similar implementing rules have been adopted in the case of Algeria and Morocco, and include provisions on a number of cooperative instruments. In contrast to these agreements, the agreements signed with the former Soviet Union states include looser provisions on enforcement cooperation. On the other hand, the EU–Chile agreement and the EU–Mexico Joint Council

[118] *Ibid.* [119] EU–Chile agreement, art. 179.1.

[120] See EU–South Africa agreement, Annex IX.

[121] The difference in the case of this agreement is that no transitional period is provided. The provision applies as soon as the agreement enters into force.

Table 4.4 *Provisions on cooperation*

EU	Notification of cases	Consultation in the context of dispute settlement	Consultation as a cooperative instrument	Exchange of non-confidential information	Positive comity	Provision on technical assistance on competition	General provision in the context of approximation of laws
Albania	√	√		√			√
Bosnia and Herzegovina	√	√		√			√
Bulgaria	√	√	√	√	√	√	√
Croatia	√	√		√			√
FYROM	√	√		√			√
Montenegro	√	√		√			√
Serbia	√	√		√			√
Romania	√	√	√	√	√	√	√
Turkey	√	√		√			√
Algeria	√	√	√	√		√	
Egypt		√		√		√	
Israel		√		√			
Jordan		√		√			

Table 4.4 (*cont.*)

EU	Notification of cases	Consultation in the context of dispute settlement	Consultation as a cooperative instrument	Exchange of non-confidential information	Positive comity	Provision on technical assistance on competition	General provision in the context of approximation of laws
Lebanon		√					
Morocco	√	√	√	√		√	
Palestinian Authority		√		√			
Tunisia		√		√			
Armenia							√
Azerbaijan							√
Georgia							√
Kazakhstan							√
Kyrgyzstan							√
Moldova						√	
Russia							
Ukraine						√	
Uzbekistan							√
Chile	√		√	√		√	
Mexico	√		√	√			
South Africa	√	√	√	√	√	√	

Decision 2/2000, which supplements the agreement between the EU and Mexico, are the most detailed on cooperation issues, as they include (non-binding) provisions which are very similar to those included in competition enforcement cooperation agreements, discussed in Chapter 3.

More generally, it may be pointed out that in certain cases the actual level of cooperation depends on the political and economic closeness of the EU's co-signing party with the EU. In this regard, and irrespective of the content of the agreements, the level of cooperation with candidate countries is usually very high, in view of the scrutiny that these countries have to go through in the context of their aim to enter the EU. This section discusses in some more detail the relevant cooperative tools provided by the EU bilateral agreements.

4.3.1 *Notification of cases*

As noted in the context of the analysis carried out in Chapter 3, notification is the starting point for cooperation in cases where two countries have an interest in the same competition case. A number of the agreements reviewed in this chapter provide for notification of cases.

(i) Agreements with candidate and potential candidate countries

Such notification is obligatory in the case of the agreements with candidate countries, in view of the scrutiny the regimes of these countries have to undergo in the pre-accession process. Based on this information, the European Commission is able to review and express its opinion on the development of competition law and policy in these countries and on the extent to which they have aligned their rules to those of the EU. In the case of the EU agreements, the notification provision was included in the rules implementing the competition-related provisions of these agreements.

Hence, the relevant rules regarding Bulgaria and Romania made clear that the competition authorities of the contracting parties have to notify the authorities of the other contracting party of an enforcement activity, where such activity may have an effect to the other party's interests or relates to an anticompetitive practice that has been principally carried out in the territory of the other party.[122] Thus, these provisions lie between

[122] EU–Romania Association Council, Decision No. 2/1999 of 16 March 1999 on the implementation of competition rules, art. 2.1. [1999] OJ L96/22, and EU–Bulgaria Association Council, Decision No. 2/1999 of 7 October 1997 on the implementation of competition rules, art. 2.1.

negative and positive comity, as they describe cases which are not exactly negative comity (obligation to take into consideration the interest of the other party when enforcing competition law), nor positive comity (request of enforcement action by the other party with respect to practices that are conducted in the territory of the other party and have effects on the requesting party). While both negative and positive comity require some sort of action, or avoidance of action, the provisions discussed here only require notification of cases of mutual interest, and therefore may rather be a starting point for further cooperation on such cases.

A similar provision is included in the agreement between the EU and Turkey.[123] With regard to Croatia, and to FYROM, while no particular provision on case notification is included in the relevant agreements, the screening by the Commission of the development of the competition regimes of these countries indicates that these parties are in practice obliged to notify the Commission of any case of mutual interest. Even in a relatively looser way, this is also the case with the potential candidate countries, which have to fulfil certain criteria so as to proceed with the negotiations.

(ii) Euro-Mediterranean agreements and agreements with former Soviet Union states

As regards the Euro-Mediterranean agreements, provisions on notification are included only in the rules implementing the competition-related articles of the agreements with Algeria and Morocco. The rules provide that the parties have the obligation to notify the other party, in the initial stages of an investigation, of the following practices which: (a) the notifying party considers relevant to enforcement activities of the other party; (b) may significantly affect important interests of the other party; (c) relate to restrictions on competition which may directly and substantially affect the territory of the other party; (d) involve anticompetitive activities carried out mainly in the territory of the other party; or (e) condition or prohibit action in the territory of the other party. The provisions are similar to the provisions included in the bilateral enforcement cooperation agreements of the EU, and describe a broad group of activities. Nevertheless, their effect cannot be evaluated, since there have been no reports as to their implementation.

On the other hand, there are no particular notification provisions included in the agreements with former Soviet Union states.

[123] EU–Turkey agreement, art. 43.

(iii) Agreements with selected trade partners

In contrast to these agreements, a detailed provision on notification of cases is included in the agreements concluded with Chile and Mexico. The provision states that each party will notify the authorities of the other party of an enforcement activity, in cases similar to those described in the implementing decisions of the agreements with Bulgaria and Romania.[124] As with Algeria and Morocco, there are no publicly available documents regarding the implementation of these provisions.

4.3.2 Exchange of information

With the exception of the agreements with former Soviet Union states,[125] all the other agreements provide for some sort of information exchange on competition matters, which is subject to confidentiality clauses similar to those discussed in Chapter 3. For example, the agreements with candidate countries provide that the contracting parties will ensure administrative cooperation in the implementation of their respective competition legislations and exchange information taking into account the limitations imposed by the requirements of professional and business secrecy.[126] A similar provision is also included in the Euro-Mediterranean agreements,[127] and the agreement with South

[124] EU–Chile agreement, art. 174; EU–Mexico agreement, Annex XV, art. 3.

[125] Even though there are no formal documents explaining the non-inclusion of an information exchange provision, it may be suggested that this omission reflects to a certain extent a lack of confidence (at least on the part of the EU) regarding the prospect of the adoption, and more importantly the application, of competition rules by these countries. It may also be linked to the fact that only the agreements with Moldova, Russia and Ukraine include a clear commitment that the parties will have and enforce competition law, and even those agreements include no further clarifications as to the description of particular anticompetitive practices.

[126] EU–Bulgaria agreement, art. 64.7; and EU–Romania agreement, art. 64.7. Note that the parties further declare in the joint declaration concerning art. 64 that they 'shall not make an improper use of provisions on professional secrecy to prevent the disclosure of information in the field of competition'. The agreement with Croatia makes no specific reference to exchange of information on competition matters; nonetheless, extensive exchange of information is provided with regard to economic and political cooperation. The EU–Turkey customs union (art. 36) provides for exchange of information subject to the limitations imposed by laws relating to professional and business secrecy. Finally, the agreements with potential candidate countries explicitly provide for exchange of information in state aid cases (see *supra* n. 85); nevertheless, such exchange of information is also in practice provided on antitrust issues too, in the context of the supervision by the Commission of the development of the competition regimes of potential candidate countries.

[127] EU–Algeria agreement, art. 41.2; similarly, EU–Egypt agreement, art. 34.6; EU–Israel agreement, art. 36.6; EU–Jordan agreement, art. 53.7; EU–Lebanon interim agreement,

Africa.[128] Finally, the agreements with Chile and Mexico[129] contain a detailed provision on exchange of non-confidential information.

4.3.3 Consultations

Two distinct forms of consultations can be observed in the text of the agreements discussed in this section. The first is the consultation mechanism in the context of a party's decision to take action against a particular anticompetitive practice. The second is a part of the general cooperative framework provided by the agreements.

As to the former, the agreements with candidate, potential candidate, and Euro-Mediterranean countries provide for consultations within the association council, where one of the parties considers that a particular practice of a private firm is incompatible with the relevant provisions on competition. The parties may take action against this particular practice after consulting with the other party, or in any case after thirty working days following referral for such consultation.[130] A similar consultation process is provided by the EU–South Africa agreement in article 37. Hence, this form of consultation may be launched when the parties intend to take action against a practice which affects the common trade, and is applied in the context of the association council, i.e. at the intergovernmental level.

The second type of consultation refers to consultation as a cooperative instrument, in the sense that it is applied by the competition authorities of the parties. For instance, the EU–South Africa agreement also provides in article 38.4 that where a competition authority decides to conduct an investigation or intends to take any action which may have an effect on the interests of the other contracting party, the parties should consult at

art. 27.2; EU–Morocco agreement, art. 36.7; EU–Palestinian Authority interim agreement, art. 30.8; EU–Tunisia agreement, art. 36.7. Subject to the same limitations regarding professional and business secrecy, the EU–Algeria agreement further provides that the parties shall ensure administrative cooperation in the implementation of their respective competition legislations.

128 EU–South Africa agreement, art. 40.

129 EU–Chile agreement, art. 177; EU–Mexico agreement, Annex XV of the Joint Decision, art. 4.

130 EU–Bulgaria agreement, art. 64.6; EU–Croatia agreement, art. 70.9; EU–Romania agreement, art. 64.6. Similarly, EU–Turkey agreement, art. 38. With regard to potential candidate countries, see EU–Albania interim SAA, agreement art. 37.9 (SAA, art. 71.9); EU–Bosnia and Herzegovina SAA, art. 71.10; EU–Montenegro interim SAA, art. 38.10 (SAA, art. 73.10); and EU–Serbia interim SAA, art. 38.10 (SAA, art. 73.10). With regard to Euro-Mediterranean agreements, see EU–Algeria agreement, art. 41.3;

the request of either party and try to find a mutually acceptable solution in the light (among other matters) of comity considerations. A similar provision is included in article 176 of the EU–Chile agreement, as well as the rules implementing the agreements with Algeria and Morocco.[131]

4.3.4 *Positive comity*

Of the EU bilateral agreements, only the one with South Africa contains a provision regarding positive comity. In particular, Article 38.4 of the agreement provides that:

> The Parties agree that, whenever the Commission or the South African Competition Authority has reason to believe that anticompetitive practices, defined under Article 35, are taking place within the territory of the other authority and are substantially affecting important interests of the Parties, it may request the other Party's competition authority to take appropriate remedial action in terms of that authority's rules governing competition.[132]

4.3.5 *Technical assistance*

Almost all the agreements analysed in this section are concluded between the EU and developing or in-transition countries, and in this regard the offer of technical assistance is a very important condition for the adoption and application of competition rules in these countries.[133] A general (not specific to competition matters) provision on technical assistance is included in most of the EU bilateral agreements. On the other hand, some of the agreements also include provisions which require the grant of technical assistance specifically in the context of the cooperation of the signing countries on competition.

EU–Egypt agreement, art. 34.5; EU–Israel agreement, art. 36.5; EU–Jordan agreement, art. 53.3; EU–Lebanon interim agreement, art. 27.3; EU–Morocco agreement, art. 36.6; EU–Palestinian Authority interim agreement, art. 30.7; and EU–Tunisia agreement, art. 36.6.

[131] See EU–Algeria agreement, Annex V, art. 6.1 and EU–Morocco Association Council Decision implementing the competition provisions of the EU–Morocco agreement, *supra* n. 59, art. 6.1.

[132] Similar provisions are included in the EU–Bulgaria and EU–Romania Association Council decisions, *supra* n. 53.

[133] The importance of technical assistance with regard to the development of competition law in developing countries is discussed in some detail in Chapter 6, which looks at the development of the competition debate at the WTO. See particularly 6.3.2 *infra*.

(i) Agreements with candidate and potential candidate countries

In particular, in the framework of the obligation of Bulgaria and Romania to approximate their laws to those of the EU, the EU clearly took responsibility to provide these countries with technical assistance, which may include, among other things, the exchange of experts, the organisation of seminars, training activities and aid for the translation of Community legislation in the relevant sectors.[134] Similarly, the SAAs with Croatia and FYROM state that, in the context of regional cooperation, the EU will support projects having a regional or cross-border dimension through its technical assistance programmes.[135]

(ii) Euro-Mediterranean agreements and agreements with former Soviet Union states

Technical assistance provisions are also included in the rules implementing the competition provisions of the agreements with Algeria and Morocco. In particular, it is provided that technical cooperation will include training of officials, seminars for civil servants and studies of competition laws and policies.[136] Furthermore, in the case of the EU–Egypt agreement, there is a clear commitment (in article 72) undertaken by the EU to make a financial cooperation package available to Egypt, with the aim (among others) of establishing and implementing competition legislation.

Furthermore, in the context of legislative cooperation, the EU has undertaken a commitment to provide a number of the former Soviet Union states with technical assistance.[137] Some of these agreements specifically provide for technical assistance on competition matters. In particular, the agreements with Moldova and Ukraine provide that the Parties agree that they will provide, upon request of the other party and

[134] EU–Bulgaria agreement, art. 71; EU–Romania agreement, art. 71.

[135] EU–Croatia agreement, art. 11; EU–FYROM agreement, art. 11. See also EU–Albania SAA, art. 12; EU–Bosnia and Herzegovina agreement, art. 14; EU–Montenegro SAA, art. 14; and EU–Serbia SAA, art. 14. In addition, as regards potential candidate countries it is clearly provided in the relevant SAAs that the Commission will provide them with technical assistance in the context of their attempts to establish a functioning market-based economy. Such provisions are absent from the EU–Turkey customs union; nonetheless, substantial technical assistance has been and is being provided to this country too.

[136] See EU–Algeria agreement, Annex V, art. 7; and EU–Morocco implementing rules, art. 7.

[137] EU–Azerbaijan agreement, art. 43.3; EU–Armenia agreement, art. 43.3; EU–Georgia agreement, art. 43.3; EU–Kazakhstan agreement, art. 43.3; EU–Kyrgyzstan agreement, art. 44.3; EU–Uzbekistan agreement, art. 42.3.

within available resources, technical assistance for the development and operation of competition rules.[138]

(iii) Agreements with selected trade partners

Finally, the agreement with South Africa provides that the EU will provide South Africa with technical assistance in the context of the restructuring of its competition law and policy. The assistance will include the exchange of experts, training activities and the organisation of seminars. Article 178 of the EU–Chile agreement provides that 'the Parties may provide each other technical assistance in order to take advantage of their respective experience and to strengthen the implementation of their competition laws and policies'.

(iv) Application of technical assistance provisions

With regard to the application of technical assistance provisions, the EU has established different projects to provide its partners with such assistance in the various fields that are covered by the agreements.[139] It is not quite clear what part of these available funds is dedicated to competition law and policy, as there is no single database published by the European Commission which details the competition-related assistance.

It could be argued that the screening of competition policy in candidate and acceding countries during the process of accession definitely includes elements of sharing of expertise, in the sense that the Commission uses its expertise to supervise the process of alignment of these countries' competition law and policy to that of the EU. It could equally be argued, however,

[138] EU–Moldova agreement, art. 48.4; EU–Ukraine agreement, art. 49.4.

[139] For instance, the EU has offered extensive financial assistance to candidate and accession countries through the PHARE (in particular), SAPARD and ISPA programmes. The EU has also funded the Western Balkan States (Albania, Bosnia and Herzegovina, Croatia, FYROM, Serbia and Montenegro) through the CARDS programme. From 1 January 2007, the main instrument for technical assistance to candidate and potential candidate countries is the Instrument for Pre-Accession Assistance (IPA). It is notable that for the period 2007–2013, the total amount of funding will exceed 3.5 billion euros. See European Commission (2008), *Financial Assistance to the Western Balkans: Donor Cooperation*, Memo/08/144 of 5 March 2008. Until 2006, cooperation with Mediterranean countries was funded through the EU MEDA programme, and with Eastern European and Central Asian countries through the TACIS programme. See European Commission (2004), *European Neighbourhood Policy: Strategy Paper*, COM(2004)373 final, at 30. From 1 January 2007 onwards, these programmes were replaced by a single instrument, the European Neighbourhood and Partnership Instrument (ENPI). See Council Regulation (EC) 1638/2006 of 24 October 2006 laying down general provisions establishing a European Neighbourhood and Partnership Instrument [2006] OJ L310/1.

that given that candidate countries are obliged to approximate their competition laws and policies to the EU regime, this sort of supervision is mostly embedded assistance and less a voluntary form of cooperation.

That said, there are also projects which the EU's co-signing parties voluntarily accept. This is the case, for instance, with the so-called 'twinning' programmes, in which, by using EU funding, EU Member States' competition authorities assist governments of the EU's co-signing partners in their attempt to adopt EU compatible competition laws and establish the authorities that would apply the laws. For instance, the Romanian competition authority has been assisted by the Italian competition authority on issues of enforcement of competition law, in the context of such a twinning project financed by the EU.[140] A similar project has been carried out in Croatia, where the competition authority has been assisted by the relevant authorities of Germany and Croatia in the field of state aid.[141] In addition, such twinning projects have been carried out in Morocco (with the German competition authority),[142] Tunisia and Ukraine (both with the French competition authority).[143]

Another type of technical assistance provided by the EU involves the organisation of training programmes for officials of the EU's co-signing partners. Such training programmes are mainly financed by the Technical Assistance and Information Exchange programme (TAIEX), and take the form of short-term workshops. As has been well documented, such workshops have been organised on a number of issues, relating to both antitrust and state aids.[144] Finally, technical assistance may take the form of

[140] UNCTAD (2007), 'Criteria for Evaluating the Effectiveness of Competition Authorities', submission by Romania to the Inter-governmental Group of Experts, at 4–5, available at www.unctad.org/sections/wcmu/docs/c2clp_ige8p15Romania_en.pdf (last visited on 2 December 2009), where it was also noted that Romania received technical assistance from the United States in the drafting of its competition legislation.

[141] Croatian Competition Agency (2006), *Annual Report of the Croatian Competition Agency for 2005*, at 36, available at www.aztn.hr/eng/pdf/izvjesca/ANNUAL%20REPORT%20aztn%202005%20eng.pdf (last visited on 2 December 2009).

[142] See European Commission (2006), *ENP Progress Report: Morocco*, Commission Staff Working Paper accompanying the Communication from the Commission to the Council and the European Parliament on Strengthening the European Neighbourhood Policy, COM(2006)726 final, at 13.

[143] With regard to Tunisia, see UNCTAD (2006), *Voluntary Peer Review of Competition Policy: Tunisia*, UNCTAD/DITC/CLP/2006/2, at 26.

[144] UNCTAD (2005), Communication submitted by Turkey to the Fifth United Nations Conference to Review All Aspects of the Set of Multilaterally Agreed Equitable Principles and Rules for the Control of Restrictive Business Practices: Capacity Building and Technical Assistance in Competition Law and Policy', at 6, available at www.unctad.org/sections/wcmu/docs/tdrbpconf6p043_en.pdf (last visited on 2 December 2009).

internships of competition officials from one of the partner countries at the European Commission. Turkey has been a beneficiary of this form of technical assistance.[145]

4.4 Dispute settlement and the extent to which EU bilateral agreements are considered hard law

Having reviewed the substantive and cooperation provisions included in the EU bilateral agreements, a final issue to be examined is whether these agreements provide for the establishment of a decision body to review cases where a conflict has arisen relating to competition. The answer to this question is in the affirmative, as with the exception of Chile,[146] all the EU agreements include a provision relating to the creation of a dispute settlement mechanism to determine conflicts that may arise from their application.

Specifically, the agreements provide that the parties may refer to the association council[147] (which consists of government representatives) any dispute arising from the application of the agreement. The council will settle such disputes by means of decision, according to most of the agreements.[148] In the case of the agreements with Eastern European and Central Asian countries (where, as noted above, cooperation with the EU has been looser), the relevant council is entitled to settle disputes by issuing a recommendation. In addition, with the exception of the agreements with candidate countries and the one with the Palestinian Authority, the EU bilateral agreements provide for an arbitration procedure, if the council cannot reach a decision on the dispute.[149]

As noted in Chapter 3, the delegation of powers to interpret and implement the provisions is one of the elements that determine whether a norm may be considered as hard law. Thus, the inclusion of a dispute settlement procedure, not found in bilateral enforcement cooperation agreements, raises the issue as to whether such agreements may be classified as hard

[145] *Ibid.*

[146] Which explicitly excludes disputes relating to the competition provisions from the dispute settlement provision: EU–Chile agreement, art. 180.

[147] Or the stabilisation and cooperation council in the case of the EU–Croatia Agreement, and the cooperation council in the case of the agreement signed with Central Asian and Eastern European countries.

[148] According to all the agreements with candidate countries, the Euro-Mediterranean agreements and also the agreement with South Africa.

[149] Such an arbitration procedure is not applied in the agreement concluded between the EU and its candidate countries, nor in the EU–Palestinian Authority interim agreement.

law or soft law. In the case of candidate countries, where the operation of the conflict resolution procedure is definitely influenced by the commitment of these countries to approximate their laws to those of the EU, and consequently the fact that the EU has a substantially extended bargaining power over candidate countries, it could be expected that the decisions of the association council would be binding.

On the other hand, as Szepesi notes, even though the agreements with Euro-Mediterranean countries and those with Mexico and South Africa include similar dispute settlement provisions, the expected effect of such provisions varies.[150] The author notes that the agreements with Mexico and South Africa include much more detailed rules on dispute settlement than the agreements with Mediterranean countries, and in particular, as opposed to the latter, they include specific time limits within which a decision must be reached. In addition, neither the Euro-Mediterranean agreements nor the agreement with South Africa include any provisions as to the actions that a complaining party may take if the other party does not comply with the council's decision. These elements make the likely effects of these agreements of limited value. On the other hand, the agreement with Mexico is much more elaborate in terms of procedures, time limits and actions that the complaining party may take in case of non-compliance.

Apart from delegation of powers, two further components have to be taken into consideration in the attempt to evaluate whether the EU's bilateral agreements can be considered as hard law. These elements are the precision of the rules, and the obligations created by them.

With regard to the former, and at least in terms of substantive competition provisions, it may be argued that the extent of the activities covered by these agreements also varies. For instance, the Europe agreements with Romania and Bulgaria, the SAA with Croatia, the customs union with Turkey, as well as the Euro-Mediterranean agreements and the EU–Chile and EU–South Africa agreements include specific provisions prohibiting anticompetitive practices, i.e. agreement between undertakings and abuse of dominance, that have an effect on the trade between the signing countries. The agreements with candidate and Mediterranean countries also include provisions on state aids. It has been observed that Articles 101, 102 and 107 TFEU are copied into the text of these agreements, and from this perspective, the rules included in these agreements are quite precise. On the other hand, the obligation of the candidate countries to

[150] See Szepesi (2004), *supra* n. 77.

adopt EU compatible competition rules, an obligation not included in the other EU agreements, make the agreements signed with candidate countries far more precise than the rest.

In contrast to these agreements, the agreements with the former Soviet Union states include no particular substantive competition provisions other than general statements that the parties will make their best efforts to resolve problems that arise from anticompetitive practices that affect the common trade, and therefore the element of precision is entirely absent.

With regard to the obligations created by the agreements, it should be noted that every single agreement discussed in this section includes a 'catch-all' exemption clause, similar to Article 30 EC (now Article 36 TFEU), that reads:

> Nothing in this Agreement shall preclude prohibitions or restrictions on imports, exports or goods in transit justified on grounds of public morality, public policy or public security; the protection of health and life of humans, animals or plants; the protection of national treasures possessing artistic, historic or archaeological value; or the protection of intellectual, industrial and commercial property or regulations concerning gold and silver. Such prohibitions or restrictions shall not, however, constitute a means of arbitrary discrimination or a disguised restriction on trade between the Parties.[151]

Furthermore, all the agreements include a national security clause which exempts the application of competition rules to issues relating to the national security of the parties. Another sector exempted from the application of competition law in most of the agreements discussed in this section is agriculture. Finally, the parties may terminate these agreements any time subject to six months' prior notification.

Despite the wide list of exceptions and the ability to terminate the agreements at any time, as suggested above, the extent to which the EU's co-signing partners are obliged to apply the provisions of the agreement depends upon its economic and political closeness to the EU. In this respect, it has been noted that only candidate countries are in practice obliged to apply the rules contained in the agreements, since their application is a

[151] EU–Croatia agreement, art. 42; EU–Bulgaria agreement, art. 36; EU–Romania agreement, art. 36; EU–Turkey agreement, art. 7; EU–Algeria agreement, art. 27; EU–Egypt agreement, art. 26; EU–Israel agreement, art. 27; EU–Jordan agreement, art. 27; EU–Lebanon interim agreement, art. 23: EU–Morocco agreement, art. 28; EU–Palestinian Authority interim agreement, art. 24; EU–Tunisia agreement, art. 28; EU–Armenia agreement, art. 16; EU–Azerbaijan agreement, art. 16; EU–Georgia agreement, art. 16; EU–Kazakhstan agreement, art. 15; EU–Kyrgyzstan agreement, art. 15; EU–Moldova agreement, art. 19; EU–Russia agreement, art. 19; EU–Ukraine agreement, art. 20; and EU–Uzbekistan agreement, art. 15.

non-negotiable requirement for their accession to the EU. Neither the agreements with Mediterranean countries nor the agreements with former Soviet Union states and selected trade partners entail such a commitment, and therefore whether such agreements could be classified as hard law or soft law is a matter largely determined by the extent to which the signing states intend to cooperate. As observed above, the level of cooperation and commitment in the case of the Europe agreements is much higher than in the agreements signed with Mediterranean and former Soviet Union states, and in the agreements signed with South Africa, Chile and Mexico. This assumption also substantiates the argument that in the field of international law in general, and more particularly in that of trade agreements, one may observe a lack of a clear hierarchy between general international law and treaties, and more generally, between any two rules of international law, as the rights and obligations that arise from international agreements derive from the will or consent of states.[152]

4.5 Conclusion

This chapter has suggested that, as the strongest economic player in the region, the EU has used bilateral trade agreements to address its political and trade relations with a number of countries. The twenty-seven agreements reviewed here (in addition to twelve agreements no longer in force signed with the countries that joined the EU in 2004) make the EU the most extensive user of this particular instrument in the field of international relations.[153] Three broad categories of such agreements have been identified. The first includes candidates wishing to join the EU countries. The second encompasses countries that have been included in the ENP, a

[152] J. Pauwelyn (2001), 'The Role of Public International Law in the WTO: How Far Can We Go?' 95(3) *American Journal of International Law* 534, at 536.

[153] In fact this nexus of bilateral agreements will be further expanded soon with the conclusion of a number of economic partnership agreements between the EU and African, Caribbean and Pacific countries, in the context of the Cotonou Agreement. See S.R. Hurt (2003), 'Co-operation and Coercion? The Cotonou Agreement between the European Union and ACP States and the End of the Lomé Convention' 24(1) *Third World Quarterly* 161. It is noteworthy that this argument has recently been confirmed by a senior European Commission official who noted that 'we are just starting negotiations on a new generation of market access-driven Free Trade Agreements, which should have a strong competition dimension, ensuring that the positive changes induced by globalisation are not jeopardised by private anticompetitive practices or State induced distortions. Given that competition matters are off the agenda of the multilateral negotiations for now, we would try to move on competition issues bilaterally in the context of the new generation of market access-driven Free Trade Agreements'. See B. Galindo-Rodriguez

project launched by the EU after the completion of the 2004 enlargement, and is based on two groups of agreements: agreements with Southern Mediterranean countries and agreements with former Soviet Union states. Finally, the EU has also been involved in agreements with selected trade partners, the third category of EU agreements reviewed in this chapter.

All these agreements include competition law provisions. While it has been suggested that, depending on the particular category of the agreement, the wording of the agreements are similar or at times identical, the chapter has shown that there are variations not just across but within categories. This has made the attempt to review such a large number of agreements difficult; nevertheless, it is also a departure from the relevant literature on this issue, which tends to view EU bilateral agreements as homogenous in terms of their provisions on competition.

On the other hand, a common element of these agreements is that they include competition law provisions, in an attempt by the signing parties to secure that liberalisation of intraregional trade will not be distorted by anticompetitive practices. Hence, competition law, at least conceptually, is to be used in the way that the EU itself has used competition law and policy, i.e. both as a way to secure competitive conditions in the market, and as an additional tool for the achievement of market integration with its trade partners. This argument leads to a number of consequences, identified in the chapter.

First, the agreements include competition provisions to be applied to practices which have an effect on the intraregional market. In this respect, the agreements with candidate and Euro-Mediterranean countries, as well as those with Chile, Mexico and South Africa, provide that anticompetitive practices and abuse of dominance which have an effect on the common market are prohibited. Following the EU model, most of the agreements also provide for rules relating to state aids, state monopolies of a commercial character and public undertakings, and this is a clear indication that through these agreements the EU has (at least in terms of the text of the agreements) successfully exported its competition model to its trade partners.

Secondly, the agreements require that the signing countries have in place domestic competition rules and authorities to apply the rules, an assumption that is in certain cases explicitly referred to in the agreements, while in other agreements the parties leave this issue to be addressed with later decisions by the association or stabilisation councils, or the parties undertake a general commitment to have and enforce competition laws.

(2007), 'European Competition Policy: Development and Protectionism', speech delivered at the Sixth Annual ICN Conference, Moscow, 29 May 2007, available at www.icn-moscow.org/get_file.php?id=187 (last visited on 2 December 2009).

On the other hand, it has been argued that the actual application of the agreements to a major extent depends on the political and economic closeness of the EU to its co-signing partners. For example, the competition provisions found in the agreements with candidate countries have been most rigorously applied in the context of those countries' aim to accede to the EU, on the basis of which these countries undertook enormous non-negotiable, uniformly applied and closely enforced commitments.[154] Upon accession, candidate countries have to fully apply the competition rules of the EU, and therefore the European Commission closely reviews the development of their competition regimes. At the opposite end of the spectrum, as regards the provisions included in the agreements with former Soviet Union states, the competition provisions are much looser and include only general statements from the parties that they will have competition rules in place.

A further observation made in the chapter is that, while the EU bilateral agreements mostly include substantive competition provisions, some of them also provide for cooperation on competition law and policy, which includes notification of cases, exchange of information and consultations on cases of mutual interest. Given that most of the EU's co-signing partners are in-transition economies, and therefore have no experience of the operation of competition law and policy, probably the most important cooperation provision is the one relating to technical assistance. This chapter has argued that while the EU has established funding instruments for the different groups of countries with which it has adopted bilateral agreements, it is not really clear what part of these funds has been used to finance technical assistance projects on competition. However, it has also been pointed out that technical assistance has been granted to a number of countries, and has taken various forms, such as twinning projects, the organisation of seminars and internships at the European Commission.

On the other hand, it has been argued that the provisions on cooperation represent only a starting point for real cooperation, as the extent to which actual cooperation is carried out in the field of competition law and policy is mostly a matter of the parties' broader economic

154 M.A. Vachudova (2002), 'The Leverage of the European Union on the Reform in Post Communist Europe', paper presented at the workshop on Enlargement and European Governance, ECPR Joint Session Workshops, Turin, 22–27 March 2002, at 10, available at www.essex.ac.uk/ecpr/events/jointsessions/paperarchive/turin/ws4/Vachudova.pdf (last visited on 2 December 2009); J.K. Glenn (2004), 'From Nation-States to Member States: Accession Negotiations as an Instrument of Europeanization' 2 *Comparative European Politics* 3.

and political relations. This argument is not very different from the one made in the case of bilateral enforcement cooperation agreements, despite the fact that the bilateral EU trade agreements are much closer to hard law than enforcement cooperation agreements, as they are more precise than the latter and also provide for a dispute settlement procedure with the aim of resolving conflicts that arise from their application. However, even though bilateral trade agreements provide for a higher level of obligation on the part of the signing parties, the extent of such obligations varies in accordance with the group of countries under examination. In this respect, cooperation with candidate countries, which undertake the obligation to approximate their rules to those of the EU and aim to enter the EU, is intensive, while cooperation with the EU's other partners varies in intensity.

As a general observation, and based on the analysis carried out in this chapter, it could be argued that the EU has played a significant role in the development of international rules in the field of bilateral trade agreements. The EU has in practice used these agreements to export its competition model to a large number of neighbouring countries, some of which are already candidates for accession and selected trade partners. Irrespective of whether the EU model is appropriate for these countries, a difficult issue that the book will not touch upon further – the inclusion of competition elements in such a large number of international agreements – by itself makes the role of the EU in the formation of international competition rules significant. On the other hand, the extent to which these agreements have been implemented in practice varies. The closer the political and economic relations of the co-signing party with the EU, the more rigorous the implementation of the agreement. In addition, in view of the fact that most of these agreements have been adopted in the last five to ten years, and that, as noted in Chapter 2, it takes time for countries with little or no competition culture to develop competition regimes, it would be unrealistic to expect that such a large number of agreements could be applied equally effectively in so short a period. That said, the provisions found in these agreements may well prove a starting point for the adoption and, more importantly, the application of effective competition rules – an assumption that may only be tested in the future.

5

Plurilateral Regional Agreements which Include Competition Provisions

5.1 History of plurilateral regional agreements, reasons that led to their adoption and the role of competition law and policy

5.1.1 Historical development of plurilateral regional agreements

(i) Europe

While there can be discerned an overarching tendency in the last twenty years for states to become involved in plurilateral regional trade agreements, the origins of the creation of such agreements in various parts of the world date back to earlier centuries. For instance, in Europe, the continent where regionalism has developed further than anywhere else in the world, the ideas about unification of European countries originated in medieval times.[1] As seen in the previous chapter, a number of bilateral trade agreements were concluded between these countries in the nineteenth century, and the Prussian Zollverein established in 1834 was considered the first plurilateral regional agreement in the world. These agreements lost favour in the first half of the twentieth century, as nationalistic policies dominated the region and led to two destructive World Wars.[2] Nevertheless, following the Second World War, a wide network of agreements was created in Europe,[3] including the European Economic Community (which later became the European Union and which has been to date the most comprehensive and successful such initiative in

[1] See T.V. Kalijarvi (1963), 'Obstacles to European Unification' 348 *Annals of the American Academy of Political and Social Science: The New Europe: Implications for the United States* 46.

[2] That said, in the interwar period there were voices in many Western European countries that supported the creation of a federal state in the region. See D. Dinan (2004), *Europe Recast: A History of the European Union* (Lynne Rienner) 2–6.

[3] A. Sapir (2000), 'Trade Regionalism in Europe: Towards an Integrated Approach' 38 *Journal of Common Market Studies* 151.

history),[4] as well as the European Free Trade Association (EFTA) and the European Economic Area.[5]

(ii) Latin America

This tendency towards the creation of plurilateral regional agreements also appeared as early as the eighteenth and nineteenth centuries in certain other parts of the world, such as South America and Africa. In particular, in Latin America in the nineteenth century, Simon de Bolivar succeeded in uniting the territories of what are now Ecuador, Colombia, Venezuela and Panama into what he termed 'Nueva Granada'.[6] Following the Second World War, ideas concerning regionalisation were once more widespread in Latin America. With the EEC as the model, two major agreements were concluded in the 1960s, namely the Latin America Free Trade Association (LAFTA)[7] and the Central America Common Market (CACM),[8] with the aim of promoting economic cooperation between the signing states and (to a certain extent) of counter-balancing the hegemony of the United

[4] For a brief overview of the historical development of the EU, see Appendix 2.

[5] See Appendix 2 for an introduction to EFTA and the EEA.

[6] J.A.E. Vervaele (2005), 'MERCOSUR and Regional Integration in Latin America' 54 *International and Comparative Law Quarterly* 387, at 389.

[7] LAFTA included all South American countries plus Mexico. High barriers to external trade were maintained, and in general member states sought to regulate economic activity by legal agreements rather than by opening up the markets. Thus, in general it has been observed that the agreement served mostly political rather than economic purposes, and it was finally replaced in 1980 by the Latin American Integration Association, which consists of twelve countries (Argentina, Bolivia, Brazil, Chile, Colombia, Cuba, Ecuador, Mexico, Paraguay, Peru, Uruguay and Venezuela), and is mainly structured around bilateral trade preferences. For a brief review of this regional arrangement see the IMF Directory of Economic, Commodity and Development Organizations, available at www.imf.org/external/np/sec/decdo/contents.htm (last visited on 2 December 2009).

[8] CACM was established in 1960 by four countries, Guatemala, El Salvador, Honduras and Nicaragua, and in 1963 Costa Rica joined the agreement. The agreement included provisions related not only to commercial policy, but also to financial, fiscal, monetary and industrial policies. In the first years of its operation the agreement was a major success, however it collapsed in 1969, due to the war between Honduras and El Salvador. CACM was revived in 1991 when the five Central American countries plus Panama signed the Protocol of Tegucigalpa with the aim of facilitating economic and political integration in the region. Despite ambitious goals, such as the gradual creation of a customs union, a central customs authority and eventually the achievement of free movement of labour, capital and the establishment of a monetary union, the agreement has not been a success, as Panama has not ratified the agreement and Costa Rica has opposed the creation of a monetary union and more generally it has abstained from the attempts at political integration. See M.S. Wionczek (1970), 'The Rise and Decline of Latin American Economic Integration' 9(1) *Journal of Common Market Studies* 49, at 56–8.

States in the northern part of the continent.[9] In subsequent years, two other major plurilateral regional blocs were set up in the region, namely the Andean Community in 1969 and MERCOSUR in 1989, both presently in operation and whose competition systems are further discussed in this chapter.[10]

(iii) Africa

In Africa, the debate over regional integration and cooperation dates back to colonial times and became much more active following the Second World War, and especially following the independence of the majority of African countries in the late 1950s.[11] In 1963, the Organisation of African Union was established with the Treaty of Addis Ababa, which stressed the importance of the participating states' sovereignty, in the sense of non-interference with these states' internal affairs.[12] Accordingly, the organisation was in fact a plurilateral conference of heads of governments, and the organising principles were intergovernmental, as consensus was required to adopt decisions, while the role and powers of its supranational Secretariat were limited.[13] Despite some attempts to strengthen the political and economic cooperation and integration in the region,[14] a number of problems mainly relating to the political instability in the Member

[9] G.C. Hufbauer and B. Kotschwar (1998), 'The Future of Regional Trading Arrangements in the Western Hemisphere', paper prepared for the Michigan State University 10th Anniversary Conference, Institute of International Economics Paper, at 1, available at www.iie.com/publications/papers/paper.cfm?ResearchID=318 (last visited on 2 December 2009).

[10] On the main aims and institutional set-up of these two agreements, see Appendix 2. Note that the member states of these blocs recently signed in Brasilia the Treaty establishing the South American Union of Nations. See www.comunidadandina.org/ingles/csn/treaty.htm (last visited on 2 December 2009).

[11] See A. Adedeji (2002), 'History and Prospects for Regional Integration in Africa', speech delivered at the Third Meeting of the African Development Forum, Addis Ababa, 5 March 2002, available at www.uneca.org/eca_resources/Speeches/2002_speeches/030502adebayo.htm (last visited on 2 December 2009).

[12] See K. Gottschalk and S. Schmidt (2004), 'The African Union and the New Partnership for Africa's Development: Strong Institutions for Weak States?' 4 *Internationale Politik und Gesellschaft* 138.

[13] According to art. III of the Treaty, 'The Member States, in pursuit of the purposes stated in Article II solemnly affirm and declare their adherence to the following principles: 1. The sovereign equality of all Member States. 2. Non-interference in the internal affairs of States'.

[14] Mainly through the establishment of an economic community within thirty-four years (in accordance with art. 6(1) of the Abuja Treaty of 1991, which established the African Economic Community, see www.africa-union.org/root/au/Documents/Treaties/Text/AEC_Treaty_1991.pdf (last visited on 2 December 2009).

States, and most importantly the absence of sufficient institutions to carry out these demanding tasks, made the operation of the organisation problematic, and led to the adoption of the Treaty of Lomé in 2000, which created the new African Union.[15]

The African Union is the most inclusive regional organisation on the African continent, as fifty-three different African states participate in it. Under the umbrella of the Union,[16] there are currently fourteen plurilateral regional agreements in force in Africa, with overlapping membership[17] and varying structures, levels of integration and objectives.[18] According to an IMF study, these agreements first of all usually have ambitious goals; for example, the five major agreements in the region[19] aim to establish a customs union, and therefore require strong political commitment by the contracting parties. However, such strong commitment has not proved apparent in the past, as there have been long delays in the application of the agreements, and policy reversals by the member states' governments.[20] Secondly, these agreements are primarily focused on intraregional tariff reduction, and include varied and detailed rules of origin. Thirdly, despite the attempts to reduce intraregional tariffs, external trade barriers remain high.[21] Of these agreements, six are reviewed in this chapter: the West African Economic and Monetary Union (WAEMU); the Southern African Customs Union (SACU); the East African Cooperation (EAC); the Common Market for Eastern and Southern Africa (COMESA);

[15] See African Union (2007), 'African Union in a Nutshell', available at www.africa-union.org/root/AU/AboutAu/au_in_a_nutshell_en.htm (last visited on 2 December 2009).

[16] One of whose aims is to harmonise the rules provided by the various regional agreements in the continent. See *ibid.*

[17] This overlapping membership sometimes causes major problems with regard to the operation of particular agreements. For instance, Kenya and Uganda are members of both the EAC and COMESA. The EAC already operates as a customs union, applying an external tariff of of 0, 10 and 25 per cent (with the exemption of particularly sensitive products). On the other hand, COMESA was prepared to launch a common external tariff of 0, 5, 15 and 30 per cent. Given that Kenya and Uganda are bound by the EAC common external tariff, the initiation of the COMESA tariff, scheduled for November 2004, was postponed, and this problem has not yet been solved. See P. Khandelwal (2004), *COMESA and SADC: Prospects and Challenges for Regional Trade Integration*, IMF Working Paper No. WP/04/227, at 10.

[18] See M. Nyirabu (2004), 'Appraising Regional Integration in Southern Africa' 13(1) *African Security Review* 21.

[19] ECOWAS, WAEMU, COMESA, CEMAC and SADC.

[20] See Y. Yang and S. Gupta (2005), *Regional Trade Arrangements in Africa: Past Performance and the Way Forward*, IMF Working Paper No. WP/05/36, at 12–15.

[21] *Ibid.*

the Economic Community of West African States (ECOWAS); and the Southern African Development Community (SADC).[22]

(iv) North America and the Caribbean

In contrast to Europe, Latin America and Africa, in North America regionalism has occurred only in the last fifteen years, and this shift towards regionalisation is mostly a consequence of the decision by the US government in the mid-1980s to adopt a two-track approach regarding international trade liberalisation by adding the adoption of preferential trading agreements to its traditional encouragement of multilateral trade liberalisation.[23] The outcome of this policy was the adoption of the North American Free Trade Agreement (NAFTA) and the negotiations over a possible wide-ranging Free Trade Agreement of the Americas (FTAA). The competition provisions of these agreements, along with the relevant regimes of the Central America Free Trade Agreement plus Dominican Republic (CAFTA-DR), and the Caribbean Community (CARICOM), a plurilateral agreement formed by Caribbean countries, are briefly discussed in this chapter.

(v) Asia

Finally, among the regions discussed in this book, Asia has been the last to embark on the establishment of plurilateral regional trade agreements. Even to date, the major powers of the region, such as Japan, South Korea and China, prefer to enter into bilateral free trade agreements with selected trade partners, and not become involved in plurilateral trading schemes.[24] The main exception to this general observation is the Association of South East Asian Nations (ASEAN), which along with the Asia-Pacific Economic Cooperation (APEC), a cross-regional organisation that includes members from four continents, is further reviewed in this chapter.

[22] These agreements, along with the Economic Community for Central African States (ECCAS), are the agreements with the most significant economic impact in the region. See Yang and Gupta, *supra* n. 20 at 10.

[23] A.O. Krueger (2000), 'NAFTA's Effects: A Preliminary Assessment' 23(6) *The World Economy* 761, at 761–3, where the author further argues that with regard in particular to the creation of NAFTA, the decision of the Mexican government at the same time to liberalise Mexican external trade by removing quantitative restrictions and gradually eliminating tariffs was an equally important development leading to the conclusion of the agreement.

[24] See G.C. Hufbauer and Y. Wong (2005), *Prospects for Regional Free Trade in Asia*, IIE Working Paper No. WP 05–12.

Table 5.1 *Plurilateral agreements reviewed in Chapter 5**

Agreement	Formed (year)	Type of agreement	Current status of the bloc	Continent	Number of member/ negotiating states
Andean Community	1969	free trade area	free trade area	Latin America	4
APEC	1989	informal forum promoting economic liberalisation	-	cross-regional	21
ASEAN	1977 (amended 1995)	free trade area	proposed full free trade area for 5 members in 2010, for all members in 2015, economic union by 2020	Asia	9
CAFTA-DR	2005	free trade agreement	immediate free trade area on 80% of products and eventual full FTA in 10 years from adoption	North and Central America	7
CARICOM	1973	single market	partial single market	Caribbean	15
COMESA	1993	customs union	free trade area for 11 members, PTA for 8 members, proposed customs union by end of 2008	Africa	19
EAC	1967, collapsed in 1977, revived in 1999	customs union (to be completed in 2010) proposed common market and monetary union	customs union	Africa	5

Table 5.1 (*cont.*)

Agreement	Formed (year)	Type of agreement	Current status of the bloc	Continent	Number of member/ negotiating states
ECOWAS	1975 (amended 1993)	proposed economic and monetary union	economic integration very slow	Africa	15
EU	1957	customs union, common market, monetary union	customs union, common market, monetary union	Europe	27
FTAA	-	under negotiations (stagnant)	-	North and Latin America	34
MERCOSUR	1989	customs union	partial customs union (on 90% of products)	Latin America	4
NAFTA	1994	free trade area	free trade area	North America	3
SACU	1910 (amended 1969 and 2002)	customs union	customs union	Africa	5
SADC	1992	free trade area	free trade area for all members except Angola and DR Congo, proposed – customs union by 2010, common market by 2015 and monetary union by 2018	Africa	15
WAEMU	1994	Customs union, common market, monetary union	monetary union, partial customs union and common market	Africa	8

* For an overview of the structure and aims of the agreements, see Appendix 2.

5.1.2 *Factors that lead to the creation of plurilateral regional agreements*

In an attempt to review briefly the factors that lead to the establishment of plurilateral regional agreements, an initial observation is that, with the exception of APEC, all the agreements discussed in this chapter share a significant common characteristic: they are regional blocs, i.e. they are formed by neighbouring countries. The assumption that people living in geographically close countries develop a certain community of political and economic interests, and this leads to the creation of formal international norms, was tested as early as in 1943, when a paper published in the *American Political Science Review* attempted to identify the characteristics of regionalism and universalism.[25] Geographic proximity remains probably the most important factor that leads to the conclusion of such agreements, since it is believed that neighbouring countries are 'natural' trading partners,[26] and on the basis of this assumption a number of scholars have suggested that free trade agreements (FTAs) among regional groupings would usually have positive effects.[27]

Other factors that have been identified as significant in the decision of countries to establish regional agreements include the belief that the creation of larger (regional) markets would enable participating states to exploit economies of scale, increase domestic competition, and thus raise returns on investment and attract more foreign direct investment.[28] In addition, it has been argued that the formation of plurilateral regional blocs is linked to the attempt of certain neighbouring states to achieve peace and security in the region, as well as the attempts by particular groups of neighbouring countries to counter-balance the negotiating powers of other (existing) regional blocs. As to the former, it has been argued that the formation of the European Union was a way to ensure that France and Germany would not repeat the wars they fought during the preceding hundred years. The same arguments regarding democracy, peace and

[25] P.B. Potter (1943), 'Universalism Versus Regionalism in International Organisation' 37(5) *American Political Science Review* 850, at 852. See also 853 onwards for a critique on the arguments developed for and against regional integration.

[26] Despite the fact that in the last ten years or so, both the EU and the United States have concluded agreements with countries that are not geographically close to them. For instance, the EU has signed trade agreements with Mexico, Chile and South Africa, and the United States with Singapore and Jordan.

[27] P. Krugman (1991), 'The Move to Free Trade Zones' in *Policy Implications of Trade and Currency Zones* (Federal Reserve Bank of Kansas City) 7–42.

[28] Yang and Gupta (2005), *supra* n. 20 at 9.

economic stability were raised in the negotiations with three more recent Member States, that is Greece, Spain and Portugal, which suffered from dictatorships a few years before their accession to the Community.[29] As to the latter issue (counter-balancing of negotiating powers of other regional blocs),[30] it has been argued that both MERCOSUR and the Andean Community could be considered as a response to the establishment of NAFTA and the launch of negotiations for an FTAA.[31] Similarly, as Yang and Gupta argue, the creation of plurilateral trade agreements in Africa is, among other things, an expression of the assumption that regional trade agreements increase the bargaining power of the participating states in international trade negotiations, especially in Africa, which consists of a large number of poor states.[32] This debate directly refers to political realism, as it indicates that the main motive behind the conclusion of plurilateral trade agreements is the will of particular groups of countries to increase their power over other groupings.[33]

5.1.3 Role of competition law and policy in plurilateral regional agreements, and the role of plurilateral regional agreements in the development of international competition norms

As in the case of bilateral trade agreements, Appendix 2 shows that competition law is only one of the legal tools adopted in the context of these agreements, and at least in theory, its role is to ensure that trade liberalisation on the borders of these blocs' member states is not hampered by anticompetitive practices conducted by private firms. In this regard,

[29] See B. Eichengreen and J.A. Frankel (1995), 'Economic Regionalism: Evidence from Two 20th Century Episodes' 6(2) *North American Journal of Economics and Finance* 89, at 103, where the authors argue that the motives behind the negotiations with former members of the Soviet Union was also the promotion of peace, democracy and eventual stability in the region. Similarly, as noted in Appendix 2, among the main reasons that led to the creation of MERCOSUR was to avoid possible hostilities between the two strongest states in the region, i.e. Brazil and Argentina.

[30] See E.D. Mansfield and E. Reinhardt (2003), 'Multilateral Determinants of Regionalism: The Effects of GATT/WTO on the Formation of Preferential Trading Agreements' 57 *International Organization* 829.

[31] O. Brown, F. Haq Shaheen, S. Rafi Khan and M. Yusuf (2005), *Regional Trade Agreements: Promoting Conflict or Building Peace?*, International Institute for Sustainable Development Working Paper, at 6.

[32] Yang and Gupta, *supra* n. 20 at 25. The authors note that while Africa has 12 per cent of the world's population, it produces only 2 per cent of the world's output, because of low productivity.

[33] Chapter six examines the process of negotiations for a multilateral competition agreement and argues that various developing countries have coordinated their actions and

it could be argued that the more advanced the level of economic integration, the more vigorous the intraregional activity of private companies and, in consequence, the more demanding the need for effective competition regimes. This argument is substantiated by the fact that the EU has been the plurilateral regional agreement with both the deepest level of economic integration and the most developed competition regime in the world. On the opposite side, of equal significance is the role that competition law may play in the achievement of market integration, and this is a hypothesis also verified in the development of the EU, where, as was noted, competition law and policy have been used to facilitate market integration.

From a different perspective, it may also be argued that the inclusion of competition law and policy in such agreements is an important factor influencing the development of international competition norms. It could be argued, in particular, that the competition regimes provided by these agreements, some of which include a wide array of member states, may be considered as a miniature version of a possible future multilateral agreement on competition; and this hypothesis is based on the fact that as opposed to bilateral agreements, where in practice the stronger state on many occasions imposes the adoption of regulatory measures on weaker ones, plurilateral agreements are characterised by a more balanced distribution of national influence, and therefore they simulate to a certain extent the possible operation of competition law and policy at the multilateral level.

In addition, if all of these agreements have the success of the EU, the proliferation of such agreements may in the future lead to a situation where a handful of representatives from these regional blocs negotiate at the international level on behalf of the member states. Such a hypothesis, which could be of major significance with regard to competition law and policy, is to a certain extent validated in the next chapter, where it is observed that on particular trade issues under negotiation at the WTO, not only does the EU negotiate on behalf of its Member States, but in practice the members of other regional blocs, such as the African Union and CARICOM, have expressed a common unified approach at this level.[34]

On the basis of all these arguments, this chapter takes the approach that plurilateral regional blocs, and in particular their competition

through their regional blocs have consistently expressed their disagreement with the possible adoption of a multilateral agreement on competition under the auspices of the WTO.

[34] See 6.3.2 *infra*.

elements, should be examined as a distinct category of agreements. It is noted that, to date, relevant research which considers competition in regional agreements has tended to examine competition elements found in trade agreements collectively, i.e. both bilateral and plurilateral. While there is no doubt that, especially in terms of competition law, the parallel examination of bilateral and plurilateral trade agreements is very useful, as it offers the opportunity to observe and assess the development and impact of competition law in trade agreements, the position taken here, in view of the arguments made above, is that competition law in plurilateral regional agreements should be observed independently.

On the other hand, it also has to be noted that with the exception of the EU, whose competition regime has been widely researched, only very recently have the competition systems of plurilateral regional agreements been discussed in the relevant literature;[35] the motives behind the inclusion of competition rules in plurilateral regional agreements in general are equally under-researched. Besides, as shown below in the review of the competition regimes of various plurilateral regional agreements, with the exception of WAEMU, regional competition rules have not been applied to date for a number of reasons. In this regard, it is not possible to assess the actual effect of competition rules in these agreements, unless detailed analysis of the geopolitical factors that occur in the particular regions where these agreements operate is carried out, a task that cannot be undertaken in the context of this study. To this end, and in view of the theme of the book, i.e. the international dimension of competition law and policy of the EU, this chapter provides a brief review of the origins and competition regime of the EU, and then moves on to the presentation of the origins and competition regimes of a number of other regional blocs.

5.1.4 EU strategy regarding the formation and operation of plurilateral regional agreements

Before entering into the presentation of the competition regimes found in plurilateral regional agreements, a final (relevant) point concerning the broader issue under discussion is the overall strategy of the EU in the formation of other plurilateral agreements. As Bilal notes, the EU supports

[35] Exceptions to this general observation are papers written by Bellis and Hoekman in the late 1990s, and by Jenny and Horna, as well as Desta and Barnes more recently. See J.-F. Bellis (1997), 'The Treatment of Dumping, Subsidies and Anticompetitive Practices in Regional Trade Agreements' in P. Demaret, J.-F. Bellis and G. García Jiménez (eds.), *Regionalism and Multilateralism after the Uruguay Round: Convergence, Divergence and*

other regional initiatives in various forms.[36] First, the support is expressed by a general political support to these initiatives, which includes sharing of the EU's experience in the development of its own regional system. Such support for the operation of other regional agreements is evident, for instance, in the position taken by the European Commission with relation to the negotiation of economic partnership agreements (EPAs) with African, Caribbean and Pacific (ACP) countries. The Commission notes that regional integration in these regions is among the focal aims of the negotiations, along with partnership, development and compliance with the WTO provisions. As the Commission states:

> Regional integration is a powerful means of fostering integration into the world economy. The EU itself has built its strength on regional integration. The recent progress made in regional integration within the ACP reflects the political decision of the ACP States to base their own integration into the world economy on regional economic integration. EPAs will therefore be based on regional integration initiatives existing in the ACP. They will keep step with the integration process within the ACP, as provided for in the Constitutive Act of the African Union or as agreed among the ACP States as a whole.[37]

Besides providing political support and experience sharing, the EU has also committed a substantial share of its development aid and technical

Interaction (Brussels: European Interuniversity Press); B. Hoekman (1998), *Free Trade and Deep Integration. Anti-Dumping and Antitrust in Regional Agreements*, World Bank Policy Research Working Paper No. 1950; F. Jenny and P. Horna (2005), 'Modernization of the European System of Competition Law Enforcement: Lessons for Other Regional Groupings' in P. Brusick, A.M. Alvarez and L. Cernat (eds.), *Competition Provisions in Regional Trade Agreements: How to Assure Development Gains* (Geneva and New York: UNCTAD); M.G. Desta and N.J. Barnes (2006), 'Competition Law and Regional Trade Agreements' in Lorand Bartels and Federico Ortino (eds.), *Regional Trade Agreements and the WTO Legal System* (Oxford University Press) 239.

[36] S. Bilal (2004), 'Can the EU be a Model and a Driving Force for Regional Integration in Developing Countries?', paper presented at the Second Annual Conference of the Euro-Latin Study Network on Integration and Trade, Florence, Italy, 29–30 October 2004, at 9, available at www.ecdpm.org (last visited on 2 December 2009).

[37] See the website of the European Commission at http://ec.europa.eu/trade/wider-agenda/development/economic-partnerships/ (last visited on 2 December 2009). In a similar vein, the Commission has also on another occasion stated its opinion that regional integration can 'enhance efficiency, increase competition between peers in development, enable economies of scale, increase attractiveness to Foreign Direct Investment (FDI) and secure greater bargaining power … [and that] regional integration can contribute to the consolidation of peace and security'. In addition, the Commission noted that 'regional integration is enhanced when cooperation goes beyond border measures and is extended to deeper integration, including the convergence of domestic policies such as investment and competition policies'. See European Commission (2002), *Communication to the*

assistance to the support of regional initiatives, which is one of the six priority areas of its development assistance. In the framework of its partnership with the ACP states (the Cotonou Partnership Agreement), and as noted in Chapter 4 with respect to the Mediterranean countries, the EU has jointly carried out regional indicative programmes in parallel with aid granted to particular states.[38]

In the same political context, the EU has pursued and is still pursuing formalisation of its relationship with other regional blocs, through the adoption of interregional agreements with these blocs. The most characteristic and tested example is its participation in the European Economic Area (EEA), which has been set up by the relevant agreement signed between the EU and its Member States and three out of the four EFTA states. As noted in Appendix 2, the EEA extends the EU internal market to the participating member states of EFTA, thus creating strong links between itself and its Member States with the member states of EFTA. Competition law is one of the main tools of this internal market and the EEA agreement provides detailed substantive and procedural competition rules. In particular, both EFTA and the EEA have adopted substantive competition rules identical to those of the EU. In terms of delination of competences, it is provided that the EEA competition provisions are applicable whenever an anticompetitive practice has an influence on the territory of one or more EU Member State and one or more EFTA member state, and whenever a practice has an effect on the trade between EFTA member states. As to the former, concurrent jurisdiction is granted to the European Commission and its EFTA equivalent, the EFTA Surveillance Authority, to apply competition law. As to the latter, the EFTA Surveillance Authority has the competence to review the case, and its decision is subject to an appeal before the EFTA Court of Justice. In relation to mergers that fall within the realm of Regulation (EC) 139/2004 (Merger Regulation), the European Commission has the exclusive competence in the EEA to review mergers with a Community dimension.

In addition, the EU has recently concluded a comprehensive regional EPA with fifteen CARIFORUM countries.[39] While the agreement has been signed between the EU and the member states of the CARIFORUM[40] (and therefore not with CARICOM), it clearly states that regional integration

Council and the European Parliament on Trade and Development: Assisting Developing Countries to Benefit from Trade, COM(2002)513 final (18 September 2002) 13.

38 See Bilal (2004), *supra* n. 36 at 9.

39 See Economic Partnership Agreement between the CARIFORUM states and the EU [2008] OJ L289/I/3.

40 CARIFORUM includes CARICOM (and its members) and the Dominican Republic.

in the CARIFORUM area is among the most important objectives of the agreement.[41] Trade liberalisation, along with sustainable development of the contracting parties and political cooperation, are the broad goals of the agreement. In this context, the agreement includes detailed provisions on competition law, both in terms of substance and in terms of cooperation.[42] In particular, it covers anticompetitive agreements and abuse of dominance by firms that may have an effect on the trade between the parties.[43] It also provides that within five years from the entry into force of the agreement, the parties should have in place competition rules and also have the relevant institutions established to apply those rules.[44] Public undertakings and state monopolies are also covered by the agreements.[45] Finally, detailed provisions are included in the agreement that provide for exchange of non-confidential information and technical assistance.[46] The EU also negotiates similar agreements with regional blocs such as the Andean Community, MERCOSUR and ASEAN.[47] This strategy followed by the EU has been attributed to the fact that the EU sees itself as a role model for other regional agreements, and through the negotiation of such interregional agreements it aims to exploit economies of scale through market access.[48] It has been also argued that, through these agreements

[41] See e.g., art. 4 of the EPA, where it is provided (in para. 1) that 'The Parties recognise that regional integration is an integral element of their partnership and a powerful instrument to achieve the objectives of this Agreement'.

[42] In particular, see arts. 125–30 of the EPA.

[43] See arts. 125 and 126. The agreement notes that the relevant laws to be taken into consideration regarding the assessment of the legality of a practice are Arts. 81 and 82 of the EC Treaty (now Arts. 101 and 102 of the Treaty on the Functioning of the EU (TFEU)), as well as the relevant provisions of CARICOM (and the laws of the Dominican Republic in the case of that country).

[44] See art. 127 of the EPA.

[45] It is provided in particular that the parties are free to maintain state monopolies; nonetheless, they undertake the commitment that by the end of the fifth year following the entry into force of the agreement, no discrimination regarding the conditions under which goods and services are sold or purchased will exist between goods and services originating in the EU and those originating in the CARIFORUM states or between nationals of the EU Member States and those of the CARIFORUM states, unless such discrimination is inherent in the existence of the monopoly in question (see art. 129.1, 4 of the agreement). With regard to public enterprises, the agreement provides in art. 129.2 that these undertakings will be subject to competition law, insofar as the application of such rules does not obstruct the performance, in law or in fact, of the particular tasks assigned to them.

[46] See arts. 128 and 130 of the agreement.

[47] For detailed information, see the website of the European Commission at http://ec.europa.eu/external_relations/search/regions.htm (last visited on 2 December 2009).

[48] S. Meunier and K. Nicolaïdis (2006), 'The European Union as a Conflicted Trade Power' 13(6) *Journal of European Public Policy* 906, at 911 and 915. See also O. Elgstrom (2007),

(as in the case of bilateral agreements discussed in Chapter 4), the EU attempts to export its single market rules, and therefore includes in the agreements areas which include the environment, competition or intellectual property standards.[49] While it would be difficult to evaluate these arguments, given that, apart from the EEA agreements, only one interregional agreement has been concluded to date and this has not been yet tested, following the discussion below of the various regional competition regimes, these assumptions will be revisited in 5.5, in the context of the evaluation of the role of the EU and its laws in the formation of competition regimes in various other plurilateral regional agreements.[50]

5.2 Competition law and policy in the EU

Competition law and policy have been of primary importance in the development of the European Union. As early commentators on the political developments in the EU suggested:

> competition has been chosen as the motive force of the economic revolution that is to promote the interpretation of several national economies, prisoners for centuries of their different structures, different traditions and habits, and merge them in a new economic entity, the European Common Market.[51]

Against this background, competition provisions were inserted into the Treaty of Rome in order to ensure, according to Article 3(g) EC, that competition remains undistorted in the internal market.[52]

The Treaty further includes both substantive competition rules and general rules regarding the institutional structure of the regime. These provisions are found in Chapter 1 (Articles 81–9) of Title VI of the EC

'Outsiders' Perceptions of the European Union in International Trade Negotiations' 45 *Journal of Common Market Studies* 949, at 955–6.

[49] Meunier and K. Nicolaïdis (2006), *supra* n. 48 at 914.

[50] See 5.5 *infra*.

[51] F. Spaak and J.N. Jaeger (1961), 'The Rules of Competition Within the European Common Market' 26(3) *Law and Contemporary Problems* 485, at 487.

[52] Note that under the Lisbon Treaty the goal of achieving undistorted competition is withdrawn from Article 3 and has been moved into Protocol No. 27 annexed to the TFEU. Some authors have considered that with this amendment, competition law and policy have been downgraded, and that such treatment is inadequate to secure the effective development of competition law in the EU. See A. Heimler (2008), 'Competition Policy as a Tool of EU Foreign Policy: Multilateralism, Bilateralism and Soft Convergence', paper presented at the Latin American Competition Forum, Panama City, 10–11 September 2008; A. Riley (2007), 'The EU Reform Treaty and the Competition Protocol: Undermining EC

Treaty, relating to 'common rules on competition, taxation, and approximation of laws'. Following the entry into force of the Treaty on the Functioning of the EU (TFEU), competition rules are found in Articles 101–9 TFEU.

Given that it would be impossible in the context of this book to describe in detail the development of competition law in the EU, an issue that has been extensively researched,[53] the following section only attempts to highlight the main substantive provisions of the TFEU. In addition, it also makes reference to the institutional set-up of the EU relating to competition, and while probably too brief, this discussion is of significance for two reasons: first, because the EU is the only regional agreement (if not the only international agreement of any kind) where competition law has been applied in practice, and where competition policy has been developed; secondly, because this discussion may provide us with insights when we come to evaluate the institutional set-up of other plurilateral regional agreements.

5.2.1 Substantive provisions

(i) Articles 101 and 102 TFEU (ex Articles 81 and 82 EC)

The main antitrust provisions of the EU are found in Articles 101 and 102 TFEU. In particular, Article 101 TFEU declares as void any horizontal

Competition Law' 142 *CEPS Policy Brief* (September). These are obviously very important arguments; however, these arguments and the general implications of the amendment of the Treaty will not be further assessed in the context of this book since, as with any relevant change, it takes time before conclusions may safely be reached. It is further noted that competition and free markets are included in various other articles of the EC Treaty. For instance, Art. 10 provides that Member States shall take all appropriate measures, whether general or particular, to ensure fulfilment of the obligations arising out of the Treaty or resulting from action taken by the institutions of the Community. They must also facilitate the achievement of the Community's tasks and abstain from any measure which could jeopardise the attainment of the objectives of the Treaty, including competition law. This article, in conjunction with Arts. 101 and 102, has been applied by the ECJ on various occasions. See R. Whish (2003), *Competition Law* (4th edn, Butterworths) 184–9. Furthermore, Art. 27(c) provides that the Commission should take the measures appropriate to ensure undistorted competition with regard to finished goods, and Article 98 EC reiterates that 'The Member States and the Community shall act in accordance with the principle of an open market economy with free competition, favouring an efficient allocation of resources'.

[53] For an introduction to the competition law and policy of the EU, see Whish, *supra* n. 52; A. Jones and B. Sufrin (2004), *EC Competition Law: Text, Cases and Materials* (Oxford University Press); E.C. Goyder (2003), *EC Competition Law* (4th edn, Oxford University Press); B. Rodger and A. McCulloch (2004), *Competition Law and Policy in the EC and*

and vertical agreements and concerted practices by undertakings which have as an object or effect the prevention, restriction or distortion of competition in the common market, subject to certain exemptions that may be granted on the basis of the third paragraph of the Article.[54] On the other hand, Article 102 TFEU prohibits the abuse of a dominant position by one or more undertakings, where such practices have an effect on trade between Member States.[55]

As it has been noted in Chapter 2, on the basis of the market integration aim and the influence of ordoliberalism, the particular application of Articles 101 and 102 TFEU has been to a certain extent different from the way that the comparable sections 1 and 2 of the Sherman Act have been applied in the United States, although the extent of this divergence has been substantially reduced in recent years.

(ii) State aid and public undertakings

Apart from the provisions on anticompetitive agreements and abuse of dominance, of central importance in the development of the EU as a whole have been the rules relating to state aids and state monopolies or public undertakings offered exclusive rights. In fact, issues relating to subsidies and public undertakings have been traditionally considered to lie outside the realm of competition or antitrust rules, since these rules regulate the acts of states and not private undertakings. Nonetheless, in the EU, the existence of state dominated national markets prior to the creation of the EEC, and the fact the governments of these states were supporting particular public firms, made the inclusion of provisions to regulate particular aid schemes and public undertakings a very important tool for the achievement of undistorted competition.[56]

UK: An Introduction to Practice and Policy (3rd edn, Cavendish Publishing); G. Monti (2007), *EC Competition Law* (Cambridge University Press).

[54] The wording of the article has been extensively analysed both by academic commentators and the courts. On the development of Art. 101 TFEU, see O. Odudu (2006), *The Boundaries of EC Competition Law: The Scope of Article 81* (Oxford University Press); R. Nazzini (2006), 'Article 81 EC: Between Time Present and Time Past: A Normative Critique on "Restriction of Competition" in EU Law' 43(2) *Common Market Law Review* 497.

[55] See C.-D. Ehlermann and J. Rattlif (2005), *Mario Monti's Legacy for Competition Policy in Article 82*, Wilmer Cutler Pickering Hale and Dorr Antitrust Series Paper No. 50; J. Kallaugher and B. Sher (2004), 'Rebates Revisited: Anti-competitive Effects and Exclusionary Abuse under Article 82' 25(5) *European Competition Law Review* 263.

[56] See C. Cacciato (1996), *Subsidies, Competition Laws, and Politics: A Comparison of the EU and USA*, Centre for West European Studies, University of Pittsburgh Policy Paper No. 2, at 2.

In a more general context, the inclusion of state measures in the competition context was a clear statement of the states that formed the EEC in 1957 that their economies would be driven by free market principles, as opposed to the communist bloc, which was very powerful at the time, and where the economy was driven by governmental interventions in a system based on state monopolies. In its fifty-two years of existence, the EU experiment has shown that the inclusion of these provisions in the competition chapter, and most importantly the enforcement of these provisions by the institution in charge of the enforcement of competition law and policy, is a very successful initiative, and a very important factor for the establishment of the single market and the liberalisation process within the EU.

In particular, with regard to state aids,[57] Article 107(1) TFEU (ex Article 87(1) EC) states that 'any aid granted by a Member State or through State resources in any form whatsoever which distorts or threatens to distort competition by favouring certain undertakings or the production of certain goods shall, insofar as it affects trade between Member States, be incompatible with the common market', while in Article 107(2), (3), a number of occasions are identified where aid granted to specific undertakings, or relating to the production of particular goods, are[58] or may be[59] compatible with the Treaty. According to Article 108(3) TFEU, any plans of the Member States to grant or alter state aid must be notified to the European Commission, which decides as to whether such aid is compatible with EU law. Furthermore, Article 109 TFEU entitles the Council to adopt regulations on state aid, following a proposal by the Commission. On the basis of this article, the Council has adopted regulations relating to the procedure of review of state aid by Member States.[60]

[57] See in general A. Biondi, P. Eeckhout and J. Flynn (eds.) (2004), *The Law of State Aids in the European Union* (Oxford University Press).

[58] These include aid given to recover the damage caused by natural disasters or exceptional occurrences, and aid having a social character.

[59] These include, among others, aid that promotes economic development in poor regions and promotes culture and heritage conservation. In a recent paper, EU competition officials have pointed out that, with regard to Art. 107(3) EC, more economic analysis should be used by the Commission. See H.W. Friederiszick, L.-H. Roller and V. Verouden (2006), 'European State Aid Control: An Economic Framework' in Paolo Buccirossi (ed.), *Advances in the Economics of Competition Law* (MIT Press); see also European Commission (2005), *State Aid Action Plan: Less and Better Targeted State Aid – A Roadmap for State Aid Reform 2005–2009*, COM(2005)107 final (Brussels, 7 June 2005).

[60] Council Regulation (EC) 659/1999 of 22 March 1999 laying down detailed rules for the application of Art. 93 (now Art. 88) EC [1999] OJ L83/1; Commission Regulation (EC)

With regard to state monopolies, Article 106(1) TFEU provides that in the case of public undertakings or undertakings to which the Member States have granted special or exclusive rights, the Member States shall not adopt or maintain measures which are in conflict with the Treaty provisions, and in particular with the competition-related provisions. Article 106(2) provides that undertakings entrusted with the operation of services of economic interest or having the character of revenue-producing monopoly are also governed by competition rules, 'insofar as the application of such rules does not obstruct the performance, in law or in fact, of the particular tasks assigned to them'. According to Article 106(3), the Commission is the competent body to ensure that the provisions of Article 106 are respected by Member States and address appropriate directives and decisions to them. The importance of this provision is highlighted by the fact that Article 106(3) has been the main legal basis for the liberalisation project which has transformed public undertakings across the EU in fields such as telecommunications and energy.[61]

(iii) Control of mergers

As opposed to anticompetitive agreements and unilateral conduct, the Treaty of Rome includes no provisions with regard to mergers, despite the fact that provisions on mergers had been included in the Treaty establishing the ECSC (in Article 66). In fact, it took thirty-two years before the EU first introduced merger-related legislation with the adoption of its original Merger Regulation.[62] A number of factors played a role in this delay,[63] the most important of which was the hesitation of Member States

794/2004 of 21 April 2004 implementing Council Regulation 659/1999 [2004] OJ L140/1. The Council has also adopted Regulation (EC) 994/98 of 7 May 1998 on the application of Arts. 92 and 93 (now 87 and 88) EC to certain categories of horizontal state aid [1998] OJ L142/1, which gives the European Commission competence to adopt block exemption Regulations. On the basis of this, the Commission adopted a block exemption Regulation in 1998 and also adopted Regulations regarding *de minimis* aid, training aid, employment aid and aid offered to small and medium size enterprises. If the criteria of these Regulations are met, then the Member States are not obliged to notify the aid in advance. See European Commission (2008), 'Vademecum Community Rules on State Aid', available at http://ec.europa.eu/competition/state_aid/studies_reports/vademecum_on_rules_09_2008_en.pdf (last visited on 2 December 2009).

61 See the website of the European Commission at http://ec.europa.eu/comm/competition/liberalisation/legislation/legislation.html (last visited on 21 May 2007). See also J.L.B. Sierra (2000), *Exclusive Rights and State Monopolies under EC Law: Article 86 (former Article 90) of the EC Treaty* (Oxford University Press).

62 Council Regulation (EC) 4064/89 of 21 December 1989 [1989] OJ L395/1.

63 L. McGowan, and M. Cini (1999), 'Discretion and Politization in EU Competition Policy: The Case of Merger Control' 12(2) *Governance* 175, at 178–80.

to expand the competence of the European Commission to the examination of mergers, which by definition encompasses important economic and political interests of the Member States.[64] Until the adoption of the Regulation in 1989, the problem of anticompetitive effect that mergers could create to the common market was being resolved mainly by the application of Article 102 TFEU (then Article 86 EC).[65]

In 2004, a new Merger Regulation was adopted[66] in order to address a number of problems that appeared in the application of the merger control system. The most significant amendments were the change in the substantive test,[67] the extension of the one-stop-shop review mechanism,[68] and the right of the merging parties to notify the merger before a binding agreement between them was reached.[69]

5.2.2 *Institutional set-up: role of the European courts and the European Commission*

What differentiates the EU competition regime in relation to any relevant national regime is the fact that competition policy in the EU has been applied in a transnational rather than a national environment, since to a

64 See F.G.A. Van Kraay (1977), 'Proposed EEC Regulation on the Control of Mergers' 26(2) *International and Comparative Law Quarterly* 468.

65 The first major case examined under Art. 86 was Case 6/72 *Europemballage Corp. and Continental Can Co. Inc.* v. *European Commission* [1973] ECR 215. In its 1986 judgment in the 'Phillip Morris' case, the ECJ ruled that Art. 101 (then Art. 85) could also be used for the control of concentrations. See Joined Cases 142 and 156/84 *British American Tobacco Co. Ltd and R.J. Reynolds Industries Inc.* v. *European Commission* [1986] ECR 1899.

66 Council Regulation (EC) 139/2004 of 20 January 2004 on the control of concentrations between undertakings [2004] OJ L24/1.

67 Whereas according to Regulation 4064/1989, art. 2(3), a concentration should be prohibited where it 'creates or strengthens a dominant position as a result of which effective competition would be significantly impeded in the common market or a substantial part of it', under new Regulation 139/2004, a concentration should be prohibited where it 'would significantly impede effective competition, in the common market or a substantial part of it, in particular as a result of the creation or strengthening of a dominant position'.

68 Regulation 139/2004 gives (in art. 4(5)) the merging parties the right to provide the Commission with a 'reasoned submission' requesting it to assert jurisdiction over a case where the turnover thresholds are not satisfied but which would otherwise require to be notified in three or more Member States.

69 See Regulation 139/2004, art. 4(1)(b). For an analysis of the main innovations of the new Merger Regulation, see N. Levy (2005), 'Mario Monti's Legacy in EC Merger Control' 1(1) *Competition Policy International* 99; W. Berg (2004), 'The New EC Merger Regulation: A First Assessment of its Practical Impact' 24 *Northwestern Journal of International Law and Business* 683.

great extent EU Member States retain their sovereignty. That said, in terms of competition, the fact that the EU is considered as one single polity is by itself an indication of the success this agreement has had in the fifty-three years of its application. Such uniform development is attributed to the institutional set-up of the EU with regard to competition law. In particular, it may be argued that two supranational bodies have played the most significant role in the development of competition law in the EU: the European Court of Justice (ECJ, now Court of Justice) and the Commission.

(i) Role of the ECJ

The ECJ has played a significant role in the development of the competition system of the EU in three main ways.[70] First, by developing in the 1960s three legal doctrines which put into context the relationship between the European institutions, on the one hand (most notably the European Commission) and the Member States, on the other, the Court facilitated the operation of the EU. These principles include the doctrine of direct effect of EU law, the doctrine of supremacy of EU law and the doctrine of implied powers.[71] According to the doctrine of direct effect, EU law creates legally enforceable rights for individuals, who can rely on those rights before the courts of the Member States.[72] The doctrine of the supremacy of EU law is based on the presumption that EU norms are superior to national norms of the Member States, irrespective of whether these national norms have been adopted before or after the adoption of the EU norms.[73] Finally, according to the principle of implied powers, in areas where the European Commission had internal competence it was implied by the Treaty of Rome that the European Commission also had the competence to negotiate and conclude international agreements.[74]

[70] K.J. Alter (1998), 'Who are the "Masters of the Treaty"? European Governments and the European Court of Justice' 52(1) *International Organisation* 121, at 128.

[71] J.H.H. Weiler (1991), 'The Transformation of Europe' 100(8) *Yale Law Journal* 2403, at 2412–17. The author identifies a fourth equally important doctrine, that of human rights.

[72] See Case 26/62 *Van Gend en Loos* v. *Nederlandse Administratie Belastingen* [1963] ECR 1. On the development of the doctrine, see P. Craig and G. De Burca (2003), *EU Law: Text, Cases, and Materials* (Oxford University Press) ch. 5, at 179–229.

[73] See R. Schutze (2006), 'Supremacy Without Pre-emption? The Very Slowly Emergent Doctrine of Community Pre-Emption' 43 *Common Market Law Review* 1023. In relation to competition law, the doctrine of supremacy of EU law over national laws of the Member States was confirmed by the ECJ in Joined Cases 14–16/69 *Walt Wilhelm and others* v. *Bundeskartellamt* [1969] ECR 1.

[74] See Case 22/70 *European Commission* v. *Council (ERTA)* [1971] ECR 263; Joined Cases 3, 4 and 6/76 *Kramer* [1976] ECR 1279; and Opinion 1/76 on the Draft Agreement Establishing

The 'intellectual leadership'[75] of the ECJ in the early years of competition law in the EU was further highlighted by two decisions. With the first decision, the ECJ supported the argument of the Commission that an agreement which segments markets of the Member States has as its object the restriction of competition and that therefore no further analysis was needed as to its effects, thus highlighting the importance of market integration in the development of competition law in the EU.[76] The second related to the expansion of the scope of Article 101 TFEU, which was applicable to agreements that 'may affect trade between Member States'. The Court, in its *Société Technique Minière* judgment, which was issued on the basis of the preliminary ruling system,[77] opined that Article 101 could be applicable not only to agreements between undertakings in different Member States, but also to agreements operating in a single Member State that could have a wider effect on the regional trade, such as elimination of imports in or exports from a Member State.[78]

In the following years, as also seen in the following section, the Commission took the lead in the development of competition law and policy in the EU, the courts (the ECJ and, from 1989, the Court of First Instance (CFI), now the General Court) developed extensive jurisprudence in the field of competition law,[79] and in this way they contributed greatly to the development of the competition-related rules, but also to the convergence of

a Laying-up Fund for Inland Waterway Vessels [1977] ECR 741. Nonetheless, note that the principle is not applicable in the field of commercial policy, where the EU has been given by Art. 133 (ex Art. 113) EC external competence. The same applies with regard to association agreements with third parties which the EU has the power to negotiate and conclude, on the basis of Art. 310 (ex Art. 238) EC.

[75] See D. Gerber (2000), *Law and Competition in the Twentieth Century: Protecting Prometheus* (Oxford University Press) 352–3.

[76] See Joined Cases 56 and 58/64 *Etablissements Consten SA and Grundig-Verkaufs-GmbH* v. *European Commission* [1966] ECR 299.

[77] According to Art. 234 EC, the ECJ has jurisdiction to give preliminary rulings on issues addressed to it by courts or tribunals of the Member States relating to the interpretation of the EC Treaty, the validity and interpretation of acts of the institutions of the Community and the European Central Bank, or the interpretation of the statutes of bodies established by an act of the Council where those statutes so provide. Given the lack of direct competence of the Court to decide upon the extent to which a measure of a Member State is compatible with EU law, it encourages national courts to use the preliminary rulings mechanism, under which the ECJ reviews such issues of compliance. The Treaty of Nice (Art. 225(3)) gives also to the CFI the competence to give such rulings in specific areas under the Statute of the Court of Justice. The CFI may refer the case to the ECJ where it considers that the issue under consideration could affect the consistency of EU law.

[78] See Case 56/65 *Société Technique Minière* v. *Maschinenbau Ulm GmbH* [1966] ECR 235.

[79] See generally the material cited *supra* n. 53.

competition laws of the Member States.[80] In addition, the courts on specific occasions have questioned the policy followed by the Commission, and have thus caused modifications not only in the way that the Commission applies the rules, but also in the internal structure of the Commission itself.[81]

(ii) Role of the European Commission and the modernisation of enforcement

While the role of the ECJ has been of major significance in the development of competition law and policy in the EU, the most distinctive feature of EU competition law and policy has been the wide competence granted to the European Commission, a supranational regional body, to apply competition rules. The TFEU itself does not contain detailed rules as to the competences of the Commission in the field of competition. Article 105 TFEU only contains a general statement that the Commission is the competent body to ensure the application of Articles 101 and 102 TFEU. Furthermore, Article 103 TFEU provides that the Council is empowered to adopt, on the proposal of the Commission with a qualified majority and having consulted the European Parliament, the appropriate regulations and directives for the implementation of Articles 101 and 102. These two provisions set out the general rules on the enforcement of competition law in the bloc; nevertheless, the particular institutional set-up of the competition system was detailed in Regulation (EC) 17/62,[82] which was adopted by the Council in 1962, following lively debate between the Member States.[83]

Regulation 17/62 offered the Commission the competence to remove the authority from the jurisdiction of the Member States, by initiating its own proceedings, since according to article 9(3), the Member States could apply Articles 101(1) and 102 only if the Commission had not initiated any procedure in the case under consideration. The competence of the Commission was further strengthened by article 9(1) of Regulation 17/62,

[80] See F. Van Waarden and M. Drahos (2002), 'Courts and (Epistemic) Communities in the Convergence of Competition Policies' 9(6) *Journal of European Public Policy* 913.

[81] A recent example is the effect of the CFI's decisions to annul three Commission merger decisions in 2002: Case T-310 *Schneider Electric SA* v. *European Commission* [2002] ECR II-4071; Case T-342/99 *Airtours plc* v. *European Commission* [2002] ECR II-2585; Case T-5/02 *Tetra Laval BV* v. *European Commission* [2002] ECR II-4381. Following these developments, new legislation was put in place (the new Merger Regulation), a Chief Economist was appointed by the Commission and the Merger Task Force was abolished.

[82] Council Regulation (EC) 17/62 implementing Arts. 85 and 86 (now Arts. 101 and 102) EC [1962] OJ 13/204.

[83] See Goyder (2003), *supra* n. 53 at 30–4.

according to which the Commission (subject to judicial review by the ECJ) had the sole right to apply Article 101(3) TFEU and thus declare inapplicable the provision of Article 101(1) for agreements that met certain requirements. Furthermore, under articles 2, 3 and 6 of the Regulation, the examination of such cases could be carried out by the Commission, following a notification either by the Member States, or by the parties involved in the agreement. Thus, the system of examination of business agreements that could have an anticompetitive effect on the common market was centralised, and until the entrance into force of Regulation 1/2003, which replaced Regulation 17/62, the Commission had been offered in practice a jurisdictional monopoly to enforce the competition rules of the EC Treaty.[84]

These extensive jurisdictional powers of the Commission were further strengthened in two ways. First, according to Regulation 17/62, the Commission could issue decisions and impose fines which were binding upon the firms that were found to be infringing the competition rules of the Treaty. These decisions were subject to judicial review by the ECJ and, after 1989, by the CFI. Secondly, with the issuance of Regulation 19/65, the Commission was granted the competence to issue block exemptions, on the basis of Article 101(3) TFEU, without approval by the Council.[85]

While a number of experts, including Members of the European Parliament and high profile judges of the European courts, have extensively criticised the broad powers granted to the Commission,[86] it has been also argued that such centralisation of enforcement has been the secret

[84] This model of enforcement is called the 'authorisation system', and was borrowed from German law. The model was based on the assumption that all such agreements were considered unlawful until they obtained negative clearance from the Commission (under Regulation 17/62, art. 2). Despite the fact that notification was not obligatory, the companies involved in such agreements had to notify them to the Commission for purposes of legal certainty. Note also that when the Regulation was under discussion, an alternative option, backed by the French government, was the 'directly applicable exemption system', under which each firm itself was required to consider the legality of its agreements, and thus no prior notification to the Commission was needed. However, it was the authorisation system which finally prevailed in Regulation 17/62. See Goyder, *supra* n. 53 at 41. Nevertheless, the competition authorities of the Member States were given the competence to apply Arts. 101 and 102 in cases where their national legislation allowed them to do so, while at the same time Arts. 101(1) and 102 had direct effect, and therefore national courts could apply these provisions.

[85] Council Regulation (EC) 19/65 on the application of Art. 85(3) (now Art. 101(3)) EC to certain categories of agreements and concerted practices [1965] OJ 36/53.

[86] I.S. Forrester and A.P. Komninos (2006), *EU Administrative Law: Competition Law Adjudication*, Sectoral Report on Adjudication in the Competition Field, American Bar Association, European Union Administrative Law Project, at 6.

behind the success of the EU competition system, as the broad competence granted to the Commission has ensured the uniform development of competition law in the EU, and the appropriate use of competition-related rules for the facilitation of the most important goal of the Treaty, i.e. market integration.[87] This same argument applies to the authorisation model applied to Article 101(3), especially in view of the fact that at the time when Regulation 17/62 came into force and for a long period after its adoption, there were Member States without a competition law in place,[88] or with a competition law that was in practice inactive.[89]

Nevertheless, this centralised system gradually created a number of problems, the most serious of which was the fact that the Commission had to review an enormous number of applications for exemption in the context of Article 101(3), despite the fact that since the 1960s the Commission had: (i) adopted a number of block exemptions, which applied in various fields;[90] (ii) developed procedures to review notifications informally through the so-called 'comfort letters'; and (iii) attempted (in the 1990s) to involve the competition authorities of the Member States in the examination of notifications.[91]

[87] See C.-D. Ehlermann (1992), 'The Contribution of EC Competition Rules to the Single Market' 29 *Common Market Law Review* 257.

[88] Jenny and Horna (2005), *supra* n. 35 at 327 n. 2.

[89] For instance, the competition law in Greece, Law No. 703/1977 for the Protection of Free Competition, was first adopted in 1977 but for at least twenty years it was rarely applied by the competent national enforcing institutions.

[90] Under these block exemption Regulations, agreements which met their requirements were automatically exempted from the application of Art. 101(1), and therefore did not have to be notified. See e.g., Commission Regulation (EC) 1983/83 of 22 June 1983 on the application of Art. 85(3) EC (now Art. 101(3) TFEU) to categories of exclusive distribution agreements [1983] OJ L173/1, as amended by Commission Regulation (EC) 1582/97 of 30 July 1997 [1997] OJ L214/2. Relevant block exemption Regulations were also adopted by the Council in the 1980s relating to exclusive purchasing agreements and franchising agreements. All these Regulations were replaced in 1999 by Commission Regulation (EC) 2790/1999 of 22 December 1999 on the application of Art. 81(3) EC (now Art. 101(3) TFEU) to categories of vertical agreements and concerted practices [1999] OJ L336/21. Currently, there are also block exemptions on agreements in the motor vehicle sector (Commission Regulation (EC) 1400/2002 of 31 July 2002 on the application of Article 81(3) EC (now Art. 101(3) TFEU) to categories of vertical agreements and concerted practices in the motor vehicle sector [2002] OJ L203/30); in the insurance sector (Commission Regulation (EC) 358/2003 of 27 February 2003 on the application of Article 81(3) EC (now Art. 101(3) TFEU) to certain categories of agreements, decisions and concerted practices in the insurance sector [2003] OJ L53/8); and on the transfer of technology (Commission Regulation (EC) 772/2004 of 27 April 2004 on the application of Article 81(3) (now Art. 101(3)) EC to categories of technology transfer agreements [2004] OJ L123/11).

[91] See Monti (2007), *supra* n. 53 at 398, 399.

Apart from these practical problems, and according to commentators on EU law, by the late 1990s it was obvious that this centralised system had become out-dated. This was so for three main reasons. First, it was inadequate to meet the requirements of vigorous proactive enforcement, given that a large amount of resources were dedicated to the examination of agreements that were not really significant from a competition viewpoint. Secondly, the system failed to provide companies with legal certainty, in view of the fact that it provided no clarification as to the type of agreements that should be notified to the Commission.[92] Thirdly, as Giorgio Monti notes, in the mid-1990s particular Member States expressed their concern about the lack of transparency in the Commission's decisions concerning mergers. In this regard, German commentators started demanding institutional restructuring and the establishment of an independent central competition agency.[93]

It should be taken into account that Regulation 17/62 was adopted to regulate competition enforcement in a Community of six Member States. By the end of the 1990s, the Member States had become fifteen and were to be further increased to twenty-five by 2004. This led the Commission in 1999 to publish a White Paper on the modernisation of the competition enforcement system.[94] It is also notable, however, that when the Treaty of Rome was adopted, only Germany had a competition law in place, but that by 1999, all of the Member States except Germany had competition law rules which were compatible with the EC rules,[95] and that by 2004, the ten new Member States had adopted EC compatible competition law rules on the basis of the Europe agreements referred to in Chapter 4.

As noted above, convergence of national laws has been attributed to the regional courts that have developed detailed jurisprudence. That said, such convergence has also been attributed to the development of a community of legal experts or 'epistemic community' which developed a common understanding as to the proper function of competition law; such common understanding was built on the basis of EU competition

[92] J. Venit (2003), 'Brave New World: The Modernisation and Decentralisation of Enforcement under Articles 81 and 82 of the EC Treaty' 40 *Common Market Law Review* 545, at 550.

[93] A proposal which nonetheless found no further support. See Monti (2007), *supra* n. 53 at 400.

[94] See European Commission (1999), *White Paper on the Modernisation of the Rules Implementing Articles 85 and 86 of the EC Treaty*, Commission Programme 99/027 (Brussels, 28 April 1999). See C.-D. Ehlermann (2000), 'The Modernisation of EC Antitrust Policy: A Legal and Cultural Revolution' 37 *Common Market Law Review* 537.

[95] See Monti (2007), *supra* n. 53 at 401.

law, which was transposed into national legal systems.[96] In this regard, it may be argued that the centralised application of competition law has had as a side-effect the development of harmonised rules, even in those Member States which were not obliged to adopt relevant rules in order to enter the EU.

The public debate triggered by the White Paper finally led to the adoption of Regulation 1/2003, which entered into force on 1 May 2004 (which, incidentally, was also the date of accession of the ten new Member States).[97] The new Regulation introduced two major changes. First, it replaced the authorisation system with a directly applicable exemption system. Unlike under Regulation 17/62, if the agreements met the criteria of Article 101(3) EC, no negative clearance was required.[98] The second major change was that the competent institutions (national competition authorities and national courts) of the Member States had to apply Articles 101 and 102 TFEU when they reviewed cases that might have an effect on trade between Member States.[99]

These provisions did not preclude the Member States from having and applying stricter national rules on unilateral conduct, nor from applying provisions of national law that predominantly pursued an objective different from the objectives pursued by Articles 101 and 102 EC,[100] thus leaving room for governmental intervention and industrial policy in national markets, as long as trade within the EU was not affected. Nevertheless, in cases where intrastate trade might be affected, then the competent national bodies were bound by Articles 101 and 102, and by the jurisprudence of the EU Courts and the decisional practice of the Commission.[101]

Furthermore, the European Competition Network (ECN) was launched in 2002. The ECN is not an administrative body, but a mechanism for cooperation and coordination as regards the competition agencies of the Member States.[102] The aim of the network is twofold: it attempts to ensure,

[96] See Van Waarden and Drahos (2002), *supra* n. 80, in particular at 931–2.

[97] Council Regulation (EC) 1/2003 of 16 December 2002 on the implementation of the rules on competition laid down in Articles 81 and 82 (now Arts. 101 and 102) EC [2003] OJ L1/1.

[98] Regulation 1/2003, art. 1(2).

[99] *Ibid.* arts. 3, 5 and 6.

[100] *Ibid.* art. 3(2), (3). [101] *Ibid.* art. 16.

[102] European Council and European Commission (2002), 'Joint Statement of the Council and the Commission on the Function of the Network of Competition Authorities', available at http://ec.europa.eu/comm/competition/ecn/joint_statement_en.pdf (last visited on 2 December 2009).

first, the efficient allocation of cases,[103] and, secondly, the uniform application of the competition law rules.[104] These important issues were also further addressed by Regulation 1/2003 itself.

As to the former objective, i.e. overcoming overlaps in the application of Articles 101 and 102, Regulation 1/2003 also included provisions on the cooperation of the Commission with national competition authorities. Specifically, the Commission still has the competence to remove a case that is being reviewed by a national authority where it believes that the case might have an effect on the common market, subject to the obligation to consult with the Member State.[105] It is also competent to refer to the national authorities a complaint submitted to it on the basis of Articles 101 and 102 where it considers that the case under examination is not of major interest and it has previously made its policy clear through other relevant cases.[106]

As to the latter objective, i.e. the uniform application of law, Regulation 1/2003 in articles 11(3) and (4) provides that whenever the national authorities decides to initiate proceedings relating to a case in which Articles 101 and 102 were to be applied, they had to notify the Commission. They are also obliged to notify the Commission at least thirty days before the adoption of the decision. In practice, when the Commission receives the draft decision of the national authority it examines the way that the law is interpreted and applied; in those cases where it disagrees with their application of the Treaty Articles, it returns the case to the authorities with comments. A database has been created in order to ensure the efficient supervision of the network. This provides a mechanism, to which all the Member States have access, for the Commission and the national authorities to notify relevant cases.

The relationship between the Commission and national authorities and courts, and important features relating to the application of Community rules, have been further clarified by a number of Notices, which are soft law instruments[107] that the Commission published on the date of adoption of

[103] *Ibid.* paras. 11–19. [104] *Ibid.* paras. 20–6.

[105] Regulation 1/2003, art. 11(6).

[106] There is no particular provision on this procedure, apart from the general statement in art. 11(1) of Regulation 1/2003 which provides that 'The Commission and the competition authorities of the Member States shall apply the Community competition rules in close cooperation'. Nonetheless, based on this general provision and the non-binding European Commission (2004), Notice on Cooperation within the Network of Competition Authorities [2004] OJ C101/43, which sets out jurisdictional criteria, in practice the Commission refers cases to the national authorities.

[107] On the use of soft law instruments, such as notices, recommendations and guidelines in the field of EU competition policy, see H.A. Cosma and R. Whish (2003), 'Soft Law in the Field of EU Competition Policy' 14(1) *European Business Law Review* 25.

Regulation 1/2003. In particular, the Commission has published Notices on cooperation within the ECN,[108] cooperation with the courts,[109] the handling of complaints,[110] the effect on trade,[111] the application of Article 101(3),[112] and on access to the file.[113]

5.2.3 *Some points on the EU competition regime*

While, to a certain extent, it would be premature to evaluate the effect of Regulation 1/2003, given the short period of time that has passed since its adoption,[114] from this brief analysis of the EC competition law regime, it would be useful to keep some elements in mind, particularly in view of the subsequent presentation of competition regimes of a number of plurilateral agreements. The first such element is that it takes time until a competition regime may be developed at a regional level, and this is an argument that is not much different from the one made in Chapter 2 with regard to developing countries. That said, the extra factor that has to be taken into account when discussing a regional regime is that the diverse political preferences of the various member states of a bloc may delay the adoption of certain regional substantive rules. This is a problem evident in the fact that merger rules were adopted in the EU thirty-two years after the adoption of the Treaty of Rome.

[108] Commission Notice on Cooperation within the Network of Competition Authorities, *supra* n. 106.

[109] European Commission (2004), Notice on the Cooperation between the Commission and the Courts of the EU Member States in the application of Arts. 81 and 82 (now Arts. 101 and 102) EC [2004] OJ C101/54.

[110] European Commission (2004), Notice on the Handling of Complaints by the Commission under Arts. 81 and 82 (now Arts. 101 and 102) EC [2004] OJ C101/65.

[111] European Commission (2004), Notice: Guidelines on the Effect on Trade Concept contained in Arts. 81 and 82 (now Arts. 101 and 102) EC [2004] OJ C101/81.

[112] European Commission (2004), Notice: Guidelines on the Application of Art. 81(3) (now Art. 101(3)) EC [2004] OJ C101/97.

[113] European Commission (2004), Notice on the Rules for Access to the Commission File in Cases pursuant to Arts. 81 and 82 (now Arts. 101 and 102) EC, Arts. 53, 54 and 57 of the EEA Agreement and Council Regulation (EC) 139/2004 [2005] OJ C325/7.

[114] The assessment of the effect of Regulation 1/2003 is an ongoing process, following the first evaluation by the Commission of the application of Regulation 1/2003, in which the Commission noted that while the application of the Regulation had been a success overall, there were a number of issues that merited further examination, relating to (i) the extent of the investigative powers of the Commission; (ii) the assessment of complaints that do not raise major issues and therefore whose examination is not prioritised; (iii) the divergence in standards regarding unilateral conduct among the Member States; (iv) the inability of Member States to use information gathered under the procedure in Regulation 1/2003, art. 12(3) for the imposition of custodial sanctions;

On the other hand, at the enforcement level, and irrespective of the fact that the EU competition system is far from perfect,[115] the European project has demonstrated that a centralised enforcement system, where a supranational body and a well established regional court have the competence to apply the regional rules, may be adequate for the development of an efficient competition regime, even in cases where competition law is scarce or non-existent in the member states. The EU experience has also shown that it was only when (i) the supranational body (i.e. the Commission) had gained enough experience in the application of the regional rules; (ii) the Member States have adopted EU compatible competition laws and established competition authorities; and (iii) even more importantly, a certain level of common understanding has been developed among their competition agencies that the Commission was ready to decentralise the enforcement of the regional rules. These arguments will be revisited in 5.4, which provides us with a comparative reading of competition provisions found in the various regional agreements, including the EU.

5.3 Competition provisions in other plurilateral regional agreements

Having briefly reviewed the competition regime of the EU, which is characterised by the existence of detailed substantive competition provisions which are to be applied at the regional level and by the fact that such regional rules are enforced by supranational and national institutions, in the attempt to evaluate the role of the EU on the formation of other plurilateral regional agreements, this section provides a presentation of the competition regimes established by a number of other agreements. In contrast to the analysis of bilateral enforcement cooperation agreements and bilateral trade agreements, the comparative reading of the competition regimes of the various plurilateral regional agreements is a more complex task, due to the fact that the competition-related provisions of

(v) the convergence of leniency programmes of the Member States; (vi) the observed divergence in various aspects of the enforcement systems of the Member States; (vii) the need for more active participation of the Commission as *amicus curae*, in the context of art. 15(3); (viii) the notification of national court decisions relating to Arts. 101 and 102 EC to the Commission; and (ix) issues relating to the exchange of information between the Commission and the Member States and the Commission and third parties. See European Commission (2009), *Report on the Functioning of Regulation 1/2003*, COM(2009)206 final; European Commission (2009), *Staff Working Paper on the Functioning of Regulation 1/2003*, SEC(2009)574 final.

[115] Something that is proved by the fact that it has been recently amended.

these regimes are far less homogenous than the relevant provisions found in bilateral enforcement cooperation agreements and the bilateral trade agreements of the EU. To this end, the chapter first presents separately the competition provisions found in the various plurilateral regional agreements reviewed, and then attempts to provide generalisations as to the competition-related content of those agreements, as well as comparisons with the EU regime.

5.3.1 Andean Community

Article 93 of the Cartagena Agreement, which is the Treaty establishing the Andean Community,[116] contains a mandate that 'before 31 December 1971, the Commission shall adopt, at the General Secretariat's proposal, the rules which are needed to guard against or correct practices which may distort competition within the Subregion'. It took more than twenty years, however, before the first regional legislation was enacted with the aim of establishing a competition law and policy system largely based on the EU model: Decision No. 285 of 1991.[117] Thus, rules prohibiting anticompetitive practices and abuse of dominance which could have a regional effect were introduced.[118] These rules would be enforced by a centralised transnational body, the Board of the Commission, which had investigatory and decision-making powers as well as the competence to launch investigations following a petition submitted either by a member state or an undertaking.[119]

The competition system of the Andean Community has not been a successful one for a number of reasons relating both to the internal political dynamics of the member states and to the institutional set-up of the regional enforcing body, i.e. the Board of the Commission. As regards the former, a lack of political will to apply competition laws by some participating countries, such as Bolivia and Ecuador, has been observed.[120] As

[116] Andean Subregional Integration Agreement, the 'Cartagena Agreement', available at www.comunidadandina.org/INGLES/normativa/ande_trie1.htm (last visited on 2 December 2009).

[117] Andean Community, Decision No. 285, Rules and regulations for preventing or correcting distortions in competition caused by practices that restrict free competition, available at www.comunidadandina.org/INGLES/normativa/d285e.htm (last visited on 2 December 2009).

[118] See Decision No. 285, arts. 3–5.

[119] For detailed provision, see *ibid.* arts. 6–15.

[120] In addition, it should be pointed out with regard to the other three participating countries, that even though they have adopted competition laws, they have applied the laws on an inconsistent basis. See Jenny and Horna (2005), *supra* n. 35 at 306.

regards the latter, the Board did not have punitive powers that could force firms to implement its decisions; furthermore, the fact that it did not have the power to initiate investigations *ex officio* substantially decreased the effectiveness of the institution's work.[121]

It was against this background, in 2005, that Decision No. 608 was introduced, amending the competition rules with the aim of improving the operation of the competition regime in the bloc. A number of reforms were introduced, which to a certain extent show the influence of the EU competition model, while it also has to be noted that the EU provided the Andean Community with funding in order to harmonise competition rules in the Andean region.[122] First, further competences were granted to the Board: it may now initiate its own investigations and can also impose fines and, in cases where it finds it appropriate, order interim measures. The Board has also been granted the competence to request the cooperation of national competition authorities. Furthermore, the Decision provides for the creation of an advisory committee (the Andean Committee for the Protection of Competition) which consists of members of the national authorities. In addition, national competition authorities, consumer organisations, and legal entities and individuals may lodge complaints to the Board.[123]

According to article 49 of Decision No. 608, national competition authorities may apply regional competition rules to cases which have an

[121] See A.J. Jatar and L. Tineo (1998), 'Competition Policy in the Andean Countries: Ups and Downs of a Policy in Search of its Place' in M. Rodriguez Mendoza, P. Correa and B. Kotschwar (eds.), *The Andean Community and the United States: Trade and Investment Relations in the 1990s* (Organization of American States) 169, at 183–4; and Decision No. 285, arts. 16–17.

[122] See Andean Community, 'European cooperation for harmonizing rules on free competition in the Andean region', Press Release of 8 June 2001, available at www.comunidadandina.org/ingles/press/press/np8-6-01.htm (last visited on 2 December 2009), according to which: 'The project aim will be pursued through two lines of measures: 1. Definition and implementation of a harmonized regional legislative, administrative, and judicial framework; and 2. Support for national and regional institutions responsible for overseeing enforcement of the rules of free competition. These objectives are expected to be accomplished through technical assistance, training and information activities, including visits by Andean technicians to European institutions. These measures will make it possible for Europe's experience and know-how in this area to be made available to the CAN'. It is also noteworthy that a US-funded project was carried out in parallel. See R. Moss Ferreira (2005), 'Regional Cooperation Agreement and Competition Policy: the Case of Andean Community' in M. Mashayekhi, and T. Ito (eds.), *Multilateralism and Regionalism: The New Interface* (Geneva and New York: UNCTAD).

[123] R. Galindo Sanchez (2005), 'New Antitrust ANDEAN Regulation', available at www.brigardurrutia.com.co, at 4 (last visited on 2 December 2009).

effect on the regional trade. In this way, countries with no national competition law, such as Bolivia and Ecuador, can apply the regional rules in such cases.[124] Finally, article 5 of the Decision includes an extended notion of 'community effect' as it provides that such an effect may be produced by a practice conducted in the territory of one or more member states and have an effect on the territory of another member state, or by a practice that takes place in the territory of a non-member state and whose real effects are felt in one or more member states. Room is therefore left for the application of the regional rules in an extraterritorial manner. In view of these developments and despite the lack of efficient enforcement of a competition regime in the Andean region, the amendments provided by Decision No. 608 may be a starting point for improvements in the application of competition law and policy in this particular region. It is noted, furthermore, that Ecuador adopted competition law in 2009, while Bolivia adopted competition legislation in 2008, and these developments may be indications of the development of competition law in the region.[125]

5.3.2 MERCOSUR

Competition-related issues are addressed in MERCOSUR by the Fortaleza Protocol for the Defence of Competition, which was signed in December 1996, seven years after the establishment of the bloc.[126] The similarity to the EU model can be seen in the substantive provisions of the Protocol, although less so in relation to enforcement.[127] In particular, article 4 of the Protocol prohibits agreements and concerted practices whose purpose

[124] See UNCTAD (2006), *COMPAL Global Annual Report 2005*, UNCTAD/DITC/CLP/2006/1, at 10.

[125] That said, note that in the case of Bolivia, the legislation was passed in the form of an executive decree and not a law since it failed to gain approval from the parliament. See P. Marcos (2007), *Downloading Competition Law from a Regional Trade Agreement: A New Strategy to Introduce Competition Law to Bolivia and Ecuador*, Berkeley Program in Law and Economics, Latin American and Caribbean Law and Economics Association (ALACDE) Annual Paper No. 050107'8 (University of California, Berkeley), in which the author also discusses the problems that Bolivia and Ecuador have faced in the process of adopting regional-compatible competition rules and agencies.

[126] Common Market of the Southern Cone (MERCOSUR), Protocol on the Defence of Competition, the 'Fortaleza Protocol', available at www.ftaa-alca.org/Wgroups/WGCP/English/cpa/cpa3_e.asp (last visited on 2 December 2009). For a more detailed analysis of MERCOSUR's competition provisions, see A.F.Z. De Azevedo and M. Tavares De Araujo (2006), 'MERCOSUR Competition Law: Developments and Perspectives' (mimeo, on file with the author).

[127] As noted in Appendix 2, this is also the case in general regarding MERCOSUR, the initial aim of which was to create a customs union and a common market based on four

or final effect is to restrict, limit, falsify or distort competition or access to the market, as well as abuse of dominance that affects intraregional trade.[128] State monopolies fall within the realm of the competition provisions, insofar as the rules of this Protocol do not prevent the regular exercise of their legal attributions,[129] while article 32 requires member states, within two years from the adoption of the Protocol, to have in place the legislation and mechanisms for the control of state aids which may have an effect on the common trade. The relevant legislation should be in accordance with the WTO rules on subsidies.[130]

As for the institutional set-up, the Protocol is to be enforced by two intergovernmental bodies, the MERCOSUR Trade Commission (MTC), which performs adjudicative functions, and the Committee for the Defence of Competition (MCDC), which consists of representatives of signing countries' national competition authorities, and is responsible for the investigation of cases in cooperation with the national authorities of the state in which the defendant is domiciled.[131] According to the Fortaleza Protocol, proceedings are initiated by the competition authorities of the member states either *ex officio* or following a complaint by an interested party.[132] The national authorities, after a preliminary determination of whether the practice has MERCOSUR implications, may submit the case to the MCDC for a second determination, and both evaluations must be based on a rule-of-reason analysis in which a definition of the relevant market and evidence of the conduct and the economic effects of the practice must be provided.[133]

When the investigation is completed, the national agency provides the MCDC with a conclusive ruling, and the MCDC, taking into account the view of the national competition agency, and subject to approval by the MTC, decides upon the possible infringement found, the sanctions to be applied to the infringing parties, and any other appropriate measure.[134]

freedoms (free movement of goods, persons, services and capital). Despite the obvious similarities with the EU, the institutional set-up of the bloc differs from that of the EU. For more detail, see Appendix 2.

[128] Article 6 of the Protocol further specifies the types of practices (agreements and abuses of dominance) that are incompatible with the Protocol, on the basis of art. 4.

[129] Fortaleza Protocol, art. 2(2). [130] *Ibid.* art. 32(2).

[131] *Ibid.* arts. 8, 9 and 15. See J. Tavares de Araujo, Jr (2000), 'Competition Policy and the EU–MERCOSUR Trade Negotiations', paper presented at the Working Group on EU–MERCOSUR Trade Negotiations, Paris, 12–13 May 2000, at 12, available at www.sice.oas.org/compol/Articles/cpeumerc.doc (last visited on 2 December 2009).

[132] Fortaleza Protocol, art. 10.

[133] *Ibid.* art. 14, and Tavares de Araujo Jr (2000), *supra* n. 131 at 12.

[134] *Ibid.* arts. 18, 19 and 20(1). Under art. 20(2), the measures taken have to be applied by the national authority of the state which conducted the investigation, while art. 20(3)

On the basis of the Protocol, the MERCOSUR member states have also signed a Complementary to the Protocol Regulation (not yet ratified) in 2002, and in 2003 a cooperation agreement, similar to the first generation agreements discussed in Chapter 3, which focuses on cooperation issues and technical assistance programmes.[135]

In sum, more than ten years after its adoption, and despite the relatively detailed substantive and institutional rules that it contains, the Protocol has not been successful. This is for a number of reasons. First, as noted in Appendix 2 with regard to the general operation of MERCOSUR, unlike under the EU system, there is no strong supranational administrative body in place to enforce the Protocol's provisions. Secondly, even though article 7 of the Protocol provides that the signing countries have to adopt (Protocol-compatible) competition legislation and ratify the Protocol within two years of its adoption, Paraguay does not have competition legislation in place, and the Protocol has been ratified only by Brazil and Paraguay.[136] Thirdly, there has been strong resistance by the member states, especially with regard to provisions on the regulation of state aids.[137] In addition, as De Azevedo and Tavares De Araujo note, there is no clear delineation of the cases that fall within the realm of the regional rules and those that do not have a regional impact, and furthermore there is a lack of clarity in relation to provisions regulating the competences and function of the MCDC as the body competent for the application of the regional competition rules.[138] In view of all these difficulties faced in MERCOSUR, there are ongoing negotiations over the possible amendment that would enhance the effectiveness of the regional competition system.

provides that in case of disagreement between the competent bodies as to the final decision, the MTC must refer the case to the Common Market Group, which is the main executive body of MERCOSUR (see Appendix 2).

135 See UNCTAD (2004), 'Cooperation and Dispute Mediation Mechanism in MERCOSUR related to Competition Law and Policy', Communication submitted by Brazil Ministry of Justice, available at http://r0.unctad.org/en/subsites/cpolicy/docs/IGE1104/Brazil_cooperation.pdf (last visited on 21 May 2007). MERCOSUR member states have also signed an Understanding on Cooperation for Merger Review in 2004, however the approval of this agreement is still pending before the Council of the Common Market. See De Azevedo and Tavares De Araujo (2006), *supra* n. 126 at 14.

136 See C.A.J. Schmidt (2002), 'The Defence of Competition in the MERCOSUR', available at www.seae.fazenda.gov.br/central_documentos/textos_artigos/2002-1/3-pdfwin32 (last visited on 2 December 2009). See in more detail, De Azevedo and Tavares De Araujo, *supra* n. 126 at 15.

137 See Jenny and Horna (2005), *supra* n. 35 at 312.

138 See De Azevedo and Tavares De Araujo, *supra* n. 126 at 16–19.

5.3.3 NAFTA

Competition policy issues are addressed in Chapter 15 of the NAFTA. In particular, article 1501 of the agreement provides (without providing any further specifications as to the required content of such rules) that the signing parties should have and enforce competition rules. The agreement also includes provisions on state enterprises and monopolies. Articles 1502 and 1503 stipulate that the signing parties are allowed to establish public enterprises and monopolies, as long as they have notified them to the other parties and have a minimum set of rules in place to ensure that the other provisions of the agreement are not infringed by their operation. In addition, article 1501(2) of the agreement includes a general statement according to which the signing parties recognise the importance of cooperation and coordination in the enforcement of competition cases, and further states that such cooperation should be based on mutual legal assistance, notification, consultation and exchange of information relating to the enforcement of laws in the free trade area. On this basis, detailed bilateral enforcement cooperation agreements, already reviewed in Chapter 3, have been signed between the signing parties.

In general, with regard to competition law and policy, NAFTA includes modest substantive rules and excludes the application of competition-related provisions from the dispute settlement mechanism.[139] The agreement further operates as a basis for cooperation of the signing countries in the enforcement of competition rules.[140] Hence, the operation of competition in the context of NAFTA resembles the US model of bilateral trade agreements referred to in Chapter 4, and differs substantially from the EU model.

5.3.4 CAFTA-DR

CAFTA-DR, which was adopted in 2004,[141] includes no provisions on competition.

5.3.5 FTAA

As noted in more detail in Appendix 2, the FTAA has been the most ambitious of all the regional initiatives carried out in North and South

[139] NAFTA, art. 1501(3).

[140] See OECD (2008), *Note by the United States to the Latin America Competition Forum*, DAF/COMP/LACF/WD(2008)1.

[141] For a brief review of CAFTA-DR, see Appendix 2.

America.[142] In terms of competition law and policy, the draft Chapter 19 of the proposed FTAA includes very detailed provisions. The provisions of the draft chapter, like the FTAA in general, include a combination of rules of other plurilateral trade agreements which operate in the region. Hence, like NAFTA, the draft chapter includes a provision according to which the signing parties should have and enforce competition provisions. The draft chapter also includes provisions which are similar to NAFTA on public enterprises and state monopolies,[143] and provides for enforcement cooperation on competition issues between the signing parties.[144]

On the other hand, unlike NAFTA, the draft chapter also includes substantive provisions. In particular, it includes a prohibition of anticompetitive agreements and abuse of dominance by business firms; it also includes provisions on state aids, and therefore follows the precedent set by the EU.[145] The Committee on Competition, an intergovernmental body which would consist of representatives of the member states, would be the enforcing institution of the agreement.[146]

5.3.6 CARICOM

A chapter of the revised Treaty establishing CARICOM[147] is devoted to the regulation of anticompetitive practices. Article 169 sets out the objectives of the CARICOM competition regime: (i) to ensure that the benefits expected from the establishment of the CARICOM single market economy (CSME) are not frustrated by anticompetitive business conduct; (ii) to promote competition and the enhancement of efficiency; and (iii) to promote consumer welfare and consumer interests. With regard to substantive provisions, article 177(2) contains an extensive list of agreements that would constitute an infringement of competition law, while article 177(4) exempts the above-mentioned agreements from the application of competition rules provided certain conditions are met. Finally,

142 Negotiations for a possible FTAA started in 1994. However, due to a number of reasons identified in Appendix 2, negotiations have been stagnant in the last four years.

143 See draft FTAA, ch. 15, art. 9.

144 In particular, art. 8 of the draft FTAA provides for exchange of information, which is subject to a confidentiality clause (under art. 4). Article 14 provides for consultations and art. 16 for technical assistance in the field of competition law and policy.

145 See draft FTAA, ch. 15, arts. 6(2) and 10.

146 *Ibid.* art. 12.

147 Revised Treaty of Chaguaramas establishing the Caribbean Community including the CARICOM Single Market and Economy, available at www.caricom.org/jsp/community/revised_treaty-text.pdf (last visited on 2 December 2009).

articles 178 and 179 of the revised Treaty refer to the abuse of dominant position.

Furthermore, article 170(1)(b)(i) requires member states to adopt competition legislation consistent with the revised Treaty. Article 170(1)(b) (iii) and (iv) require member states to establish and maintain institutional arrangements and administrative procedures to enforce competition laws and to take effective measures to ensure access by nationals of other member states to competent competition authorities, including the courts, on a transparent and non-discriminatory basis. Nonetheless, only Jamaica, Barbados, and Trinidad and Tobago of the CARICOM member states have adopted competition rules to date.[148]

Competition law is to be applied mainly by a CARICOM Competition Commission[149] and by the Court of Justice. In addition, based on article 182 of the revised Treaty, the Council for Trade and Economic Development (COTED) published a comprehensive CARICOM model law in 2003, which includes not only substantive competition law provisions but also addresses procedural issues regarding the application of competition at the regional level.

In sum, CARICOM has developed a comprehensive competition framework similar to the one developed by the EU. The EU authorities have informally shown interest in the development of the bloc's competition regime, by considering possible ways of financial assistance, a project that has not been fruitful to date.[150] In addition, there are still a number of problems regarding the application of competition law in the region. As already noted, only three of CARICOM's members currently have a competition law in place. Moreover, further research should be undertaken in order to evaluate whether competition laws are needed in the micro-economies of CARICOM's member states. In any case, technical assistance is needed so as to educate competition officials who would be asked to apply the competition rules and also for businesses operating in the region.[151] On the other hand, it should be noted that the fact that such a comprehensive framework has been developed, not to mention the fact that the Court of Justice, which has the competence to apply CARICOM's

[148] Antigua and Barbuda also passed a Bill on the Protection of Unfair Competition in 2001.

[149] See revised Treaty, arts. 171–6.

[150] Interview with European Commission official, Brussels, 15 November 2007. As also noted in 5.1.4 *supra*, the EU has signed an agreement with the CARIFORUM states.

[151] See T. Stewart (2001), 'Challenges of Developing a Competition Regime in CARICOM', available at www.iadb.org/sds/doc/IFM-Taimoon_Stewart-E.pdf (last visited on 2 December 2009).

competition rules, has started operating, and that the Competition Commission was established in 2008, may indicate that competition law and policy could evolve rapidly in this particular region.[152]

5.3.7 *WAEMU*

WAEMU is probably the regional agreement in Africa with the most comprehensive set of competition rules. The region's competition regime is also influenced by the EU competition framework.[153] In particular, article 88 of the Treaty establishing WAEMU declares as void anticompetitive agreements and abuse of dominance that may affect intraregional trade. Article 88(c) also declares void state aid which would limit competition by favouring particular companies. According to article 90, the institution responsible for the application of the WAEMU competition rules is the Commission, while the Council of Ministers, with a two-thirds majority, has the competence to adopt further competition rules (article 89 of the Treaty).

On the basis of this provision, the Council of Ministers, following a study that was financed by the European Commission,[154] adopted in 2002 three Regulations and two Directives which comprise the competition law of WAEMU.[155] This secondary legislation regulates anticompetitive agreements, abuse of dominance, state aids, transparency of the financial

[152] For a recent review of the challenges that have to be faced with regard to the application of competition rules in the region, see D.S. Beckford (2009), 'CARICOM: Perspectives on Challenges to Meeting Regional and Multilateral Obligations', paper presented at UNCTAD Regional Seminar on Trade and Competition, Prospects and Future Challenges for Latin America and the Caribbean, 20–21 April 2009, SP/SRCC–PFDALC Di No. 18–09.

[153] As noted in Appendix 2, WAEMU follows the EU model in general.

[154] The study was carried out by a Belgian law firm, which was responsible for the legal aspects, and a US consultancy firm, which dealt with the economic aspects. According to officials of WAEMU, 'It should be stressed at the outset that, among the several dozen technical assistance projects financed by the European Union since 1996, the study on the development of community competition law is regarded as one of the most satisfactory to the WAEMU Commission'. See OECD Global Forum on Competition (2002), *Contribution by UEMOA*, CCNM/GF/COMP/WD(2002)30, at 3–4.

[155] Règlement 02/2002/CM/UEMOA relatif aux pratiques anticoncurrentielles à l'intérieur de l'UEMOA; Règlement 03/2002/CM/UEMOA relatif aux procédures applicables aux ententes et abus de positions dominantes à l'intérieur de l'UEMOA; Règlement 04/2002/CM/UEMOA relatif aux aides d'Etat à l'intérieur de l'UEMOA et aux modalités d'applications de l'article 88(c) du traité; Directive 01/2002/CM/UEMOA relative à la transparence des relations financieres d'une part entre les etats membres et les entreprises publiques, et d'autre part entre les Etats membres et les organisations internationales ou étrangères; and Directive 02/2002/CM/UEMOA relative à la coopération

relationship between members states and public enterprises and between public enterprises and international organisations, and cooperation between WAEMU's Commission and national competition authorities.

The institutional set-up of the regional competition system also resembles the EU model. The WAEMU Commission (in which two officials from every member state participate) has the sole responsibility to apply regional competition law,[156] and there is cooperation between national competition authorities on cases investigated by the Commission. In addition, Directive 02/2002/CM/UEMOA further provides for the creation of a network that links national competition authorities with the regional body, the Commission. According to the Directive, national competition authorities are required to collaborate with the Commission and to assist it in the investigation of competition cases. Nevertheless, to date, in practice most of the member states do not have the human and financial resources to set up functional national competition authorities able to cooperate with the Commission.

Of the agreements discussed in this chapter which contain substantive regional competition rules, WAEMU is the only bloc (with of course the exception of the EU) that has applied these rules in practice. In particular, the Commission has issued three decisions based on the regional competition rules. In two cases in 2004 and 2005, the Commission granted a comfort letter to firms in the framework of the West African Gas Pipeline Project between Benin and Togo, and also issued a comfort letter to Benin and Togo regarding harmonised tax law provisions adopted in the framework of this Project. Also in 2005, the Commission issued a decision imposing an injunction which ordered Senegal to stop the state aid it provided to a firm.[157]

entre la commission et les structures nationals de concurrence des Etats membres pour l'application des articles 88, 89 et 90 du traité de l'UEMOA.

[156] See WAEMU Treaty, art. 90. The most notable difference between the EU and WAEMU in terms of institutional structure is that, in contrast to the EU where national competition authorities may apply both the national competition rules and the regional rules, in the case of WAEMU, the regional institution (the Commission) has exclusive competence regarding the application of the regional rules. The Regional Court of Justice in its opinion 003/2000/CJ/UEMOA further delineated the distribution of competences regarding the substantive competition rules, agreements and abuse of dominant position between the Union and the member states. It was made clear that the Union held exclusive competence to enact competition rules in the areas of agreements, abuse of dominant position and state aid. I am grateful to Dr Mor Bakhoum for these suggestions.

[157] M. Bakhoum (2006), 'Delimitation and Exercise of Competence between the West African Economic and Monetary Union (WAEMU) and its Member States in Competition Policy' 29(4) *World Competition* 653, at 665. See in more detail, UNCTAD

While a number of issues with regard to the operation of the competition regime in this bloc remain unaddressed,[158] the fact that the regional body has already applied the regional competition rules is a significant development in the context of the discussion about the development of competition regimes in plurilateral regional agreements, as it demonstrates that competition law can be applied in the context of a relevant agreement. This assumption remains to be fully tested in practice, since the EU has been the only relevant bloc which has effectively developed and applied regional competition legislation over a sustained period of time.

5.3.8 ECOWAS

In contrast to WAEMU, ECOWAS has not yet adopted competition laws. That said, there has recently been an initiative regarding the adoption of a competition framework in this regional bloc. In particular, a report has been issued by ECOWAS, which discussed the advantages that a possible competition regime would offer to the bloc, and proposed that the following four steps should be taken towards operation of an effective competition regime. First, substantive competition rules should be adopted. Secondly, rules relating to the implementation of the rules, including the procedures to be followed in the case of merger notifications, the fines that may be imposed on companies that violate the rules and the procedures for the filing of complaints and initiation of investigations, should be adopted. Thirdly, the regional competition authority which would enforce the rules should be set up. Fourthly, an advisory board should be established, with a dual competence: to assist in the development of the internal rules of procedure to be followed by the competition authority, and to assist the competition authority and any other regional institution with the implementation of competition-related rules.[159]

(2008), *Voluntary Peer Review of Competition Policies of WAEMU, Benin and Senegal* (New York and Geneva: United Nations) 62–3.

[158] For instance, the fact that there is lack of a competition culture in the region and that the Commission is understaffed as it currently employs only two competition experts (interview with EC competition official, Brussels, 15 November 2007). For a recent detailed review of the application of competition law and policy in the region, see UNCTAD (2008), *supra* n. 157.

[159] See ECOWAS, Regional Competition Policy Framework, available at www.ecowas.int/publications/en/actes_add_commerce/1.Regional_Competition_Policy_Framework-final-P.pdf (last visited on 2 December 2009).

5.3.9 EAC

The Treaty establishing the EAC provides[160] that competition law provisions should be included in the Protocol establishing the EAC customs union. In parallel, in the Development Strategy of the EAC, a common competition policy is envisaged to promote free competition; it should be enforced by a central autonomous institution.[161] The Customs Union Protocol, signed in 2004, includes a provision similar to Article 101 TFEU, according to which the partner states must prohibit any practices that adversely affect free trade including any agreement, understanding or concerted practices which has as its objective or effect the prevention, restriction or distortion of competition within the Community.[162]

2004 also saw the drafting of the EAC Competition Act which was enacted in September 2006. The Act is a comprehensive piece of legislation, since it includes provisions on anticompetitive agreements, abuse of dominance and mergers, as well as subsidies.[163] In other words, it follows the EU model.[164] The Act also provides for the establishment of the EAC Competition Committee, an intergovernmental institution composed of the representatives of the member states,[165] which is proposed to be the

160 See EAC Treaty, art. 75, available at www.eac.int.

161 See EAC (2001), *The Second East African Community Strategy Paper.*

162 See EAC, Protocol on the Establishment of the East African Customs Union, art. 21, available at www.eac.int/EAC_CustomsUnionProtocol.pdf (last visited on 2 December 2009). The article also includes a paragraph similar to Art. 101(3) EC, which exempts a number of agreements that have other positive effects.

163 It also includes provisions on public procurement and consumer protection. See EAC Competition Act, arts. 18–20 and 28–36, respectively.

164 The influence of the EU model in the drafting of competition rules in the EAC is also documented by a recent submission of the EAC to UNCTAD, where it stated that 'the European Union is arguably the most successful regional integration organisation in terms of effectiveness in the enforcement of competition law and policy. *A priori*, if one were to consider best international practices, the EU cannot be ignored'. See 'Contribution by Kenya to the UNCTAD Group of Experts' in EAC (2006), 'Regional Cooperation on Competition Policy and Law: The Experience of the East African Community', available at www.unctad.org/sections/wcmu/docs/c2clp_ige7p25_en.pdf (last visited on 2 December 2009).

165 WTO (2006), *Trade Policy Review, Report by the Secretariat: East African Community,* WT/TPR/S/171, at 25. This has been one of the reasons which have delayed its final approval by the Assembly, in view of the fact that a number of countries have argued that the Committee should be a supranational body with a separate budget and capable of undertaking competition advocacy through the promotion of public awareness and understanding of competition in the EAC.

institution with the competence to enforce the competition provisions of the Competition Act.[166]

5.3.10 COMESA

Competition rules were first introduced in the region with the COMESA Treaty of 1993. It is to be noted that up until the early 1990s, most COMESA countries followed an economic system which involved the state in nearly all aspects of production, distribution and marketing, leaving the private sector to play a minor economic role. This system promoted import substitution and subsidised consumption. The inefficiencies inherent in this system contributed significantly to the economic decline of the COMESA region, and probably this was one of the reasons that led to the need for the enactment of a regional competition regime.[167]

The COMESA Treaty[168] includes a number of provisions that regulate anticompetitive practices. In particular, article 55 prohibits anticompetitive agreements that may have an effect on the common market, and further states that: 'The Council shall make regulations to regulate competition within the Member States'. A Regulation on competition was published,[169] and was approved by the Council in 2005.[170] It contains extensive provisions on anticompetitive business practices. The Regulation 'applies to all economic activity whether conducted by private or public entities within, or having effect within the common market'.[171] It also contains provisions on restrictive business practices,[172] abuse of dominance by firms,[173] mergers[174] and consumer protection.[175] Based on this Regulation, the draft COMESA Competition Rules have been published.[176] The Rules contain

[166] The Commission has not yet been established. See EAC (2009), 'The EAC Competition Act', available at http://trade.eac.int/index.php?option=com_content&view=article&id=116&Itemid=81 (last visited on 2 December 2009).

[167] I am grateful to Dr Heba Shahein for raising this argument regarding COMESA.

[168] COMESA Treaty, available at http://about.comesa.int/attachments/comesa_treaty_en.pdf (last visited on 2 December 2009).

[169] Draft COMESA Competition Regulations, available at www.tralac.org/unique/tralac/pdf/Comesa_competition_regulations_feb2003.pdf (last visited on 2 December 2009).

[170] L. Muhara (2007), 'Brief on Progress and Challenges of the Competition and Fair Trading Commission in Malawi', paper presented at the eighth Session of the Intergovernmental Group of Experts, UNCTAD, Geneva, 17–19 July 2007, at 9.

[171] Draft COMESA Competition Regulations, art. 3, subject to the exemptions in art. 4.

[172] *Ibid.* arts. 16 and 20. [173] *Ibid.* arts. 17 and 18.

[174] *Ibid.* arts. 23–6. [175] *Ibid.* arts. 27–39.

[176] Draft COMESA Competition Rules, available at www.tralac.org/pdf/COMESA_Competition_Rules_-_21.10.2002.rtf (last visited on 2 December 2009).

more specific provisions on the function of the Competition Commission, a supranational body established in 2008 which has broad competences relating to the application of the regional rules.[177] According to the Treaty, conflicts that may arise between COMESA's member states regarding the application of regional competition rules should be resolved by the Court of Justice.[178]

Hence, COMESA is another example of a plurilateral regional bloc with a comprehensive competition regime on paper, which is similar to the competition regime of the EU. Indeed, the EU has financially supported the establishment of the competition rules in COMESA.[179] Nevertheless, the regional competition regime has not to date been applied in practice. Of the nineteen member states of COMESA, only six have adopted competition rules, and the regional enforcement institution, the Competition Commission, was only very recently established.[180] As Lipimile and Gachuiri observe, this absence of a regional competition system has already had major consequences in the region, in the light of a number of global mergers which have been individually notified to and reviewed by the competition authorities of the member states.[181]

5.3.11 SACU

With regard to competition law and policy, even though the promotion of conditions of fair competition in the common customs area is a stated objective of SACU,[182] the agreement only includes a general provision according to which the member countries shall cooperate on competition

[177] On the competences of the Commission, see in detail P. Muchoki Njoroge (2008), 'Capacity Building and Technical Assistance Activities on Competition Law and Policy: COMESA's Case', paper presented at the UNCTAD Intergovernmental Group of Experts on Competition Law and Policy, Geneva, 16–18 July 2008.

[178] See Khandelwal (2004), *supra* n. 17 at 10.

[179] See European Commission (2003), *Technical Assistance Programmes and Projects Provided by the European Community and its Member States in the Field of Trade and Competition Policy*, WT/WGTCP/W/223.

[180] See 'COMESA Competition Commission Launched', available at www.comesa.int/lang-en/component/content/article/060_Nairobi%20_DECLARATION_november2008.pdf (last visited on 2 December 2009).

[181] G.K. Lipimile and E. Gachuiri (2005), 'Allocation of Cases Between National and Regional Competition Authorities: The Case of COMESA' in Brusick, Alvarez and Cernat, *supra* n. 35 at 377–85.

[182] Southern African Customs Union (SACU) agreement, art. 2(c), available at www.sacu.int/main.php?include=docs/legislation/2002-agreement/main.html (last visited on 2 December 2009).

issues while developing their own national competition policies.[183] To this end, the agreement follows the US (NAFTA) model of agreements, which provides for cooperation on, and not harmonisation of, the competition rules of the parties. On the other hand, it should be pointed out that, of the five SACU member states, currently only South Africa and Namibia have adopted competition laws and therefore no particular conclusions may be drawn with regard to the actual application of the competition-related provisions of the SACU agreement.[184]

5.3.12 SADC

Similarly to SACU, article 25 of the SADC Protocol on Trade[185] includes a general statement, according to which 'Member States shall implement measures within the Community that prohibit unfair business practices and promote competition'. On this basis, a group of experts has been convened and has re-expressed the commitment of SADC members to strengthen cooperation on competition matters in the region. The SADC Secretariat should play an important role in this regard, both by facilitating such cooperation and by providing the member states with assistance in their attempt to establish national competition regimes.[186]

5.3.13 ASEAN

No competition provisions have been adopted in the context of ASEAN, and the discussion over the usefulness of competition law for the strengthening of regional integration is ongoing. In particular, the Hanoi Action Plan of 1999 referred to the need for cooperation in order to 'explore

183 SACU agreement, art. 40; for an analysis of possible options with regard to the development of competition policy in the region, see J. Mathis (2005), *The Southern African Customs Union (SACU) Regional Cooperation Framework on Competition Policy and Unfair Trade Practices* (Geneva and New York: UNCTAD).

184 See P.M. Horna and B.O. Kayali (2007), 'National Implementation of Competition-related Provisions in Bilateral and Regional Trade Agreements' in A.-M. Alvarez and L. Wilse-Samson (eds.), *Implementing Competition-related Provisions in Regional Trade Agreements: Is It Possible to Obtain Development Gains*? (Geneva and New York: UNCTAD) 21, at 46.

185 Adopted on the basis of art. 22 of the amended Treaty.

186 SADC Secretariat (2007), 'SADC Expert Group Meeting on Competition Law and Policy', app. II, available at www.sadc.int/attachments/calendar/251/1892_Expert%20Group%20Meeting%20on%20Competition%20Law%20&%20Policy%20Record%20(Draft).pdf (last visited on 21 May 2007). Note further that in the context of its technical assistance agenda, the EU has recently financed a competition-related project in

the merits of a common competition policy'.[187] Furthermore, in 2003, Indonesia recommended the setting up of the ASEAN Consultative Forum for Competition (ACFC) with the aim of serving as a forum for exchange of opinions among officials of the participating countries (members of ASEAN) on competition-related issues of common interest, as well as to exchange such ideas with other international organisations.[188] The ACFC was finally established in 2004.

5.3.14 APEC

In the context of APEC, a Competition Policy and Deregulation Group (CPDG) was established and has been in operation since 1996. It has the task of discussing competition issues in the member states and possible influence that competition policy has on investment in the region. The CPDG convenes on an annual basis and has been particularly active after 1999, when the APEC Principles to Enhance Competition and Regulatory Reform were endorsed by the ministers of the member states.[189] These Principles expressed a number of competition-related aims, including the promotion of advocacy of competition policy and regulatory reform, the building of expertise in competition and regulatory authorities, the courts and the private sector, and the attainment of adequate resources for regulatory institutions, including competition institutions.[190] On this basis, the CPDG has set up a series of training courses and framed a four-year action plan (2005–2009) with the aims, among others, of gathering information on the development of competition law and policy in the member states, encouraging cooperation among national authorities,

the SADC. In this regard, a four-day EU-funded seminar entitled 'Competition Law and Policy Seminar for SADC Members' took place in August 2009 in Botswana.

[187] P.J. Lloyd (2002), 'Competition Policy in the Asia-Pacific Region' 14(2) *Asian-Pacific Economic Literature* 1, at 8.

[188] There is no Secretariat established in the context of the ACFC, and in this regard the network resembles the ICN. From 2005, the members of the ACFC have met once a year. See O.K. Yong (2006), 'Opening Remarks at the Second ASEAN Conference on Competition Policy and Law, Bali, Indonesia, 14–16 June 2006', available at www.aseansec.org/18507.htm (last visited on 2 December 2009), in which the speaker also noted that, to date, Indonesia, Singapore, Thailand and Viet Nam have enacted specific competition laws, and Malaysia and the Philippines are considering the enactment of a competition law.

[189] The submissions of the participating countries in the annual meetings may be found on APEC's Competition Policy and Law Database at www.apeccp.org.tw/ (last visited on 2 December 2009).

[190] See APEC (1999), APEC Principles to Enhance Competition and Regulatory Reform, Implementation, para. 6, available at www.oecd.org/dataoecd/48/52/2371601.doc (last visited on 2 December 2009).

Table 5.2 *Substantive provisions of regional agreements*

Agreement	Prohibition of anti-competitive practices	Prohibition of abuse of dominance	Mergers	State aid rules included in the competition context	Rules on public /state monopolies
EU	√	√	√	√	√
Andean Community	√	√			
APEC					
ASEAN					
CAFTA-DR					
CARICOM	√	√			
COMESA	√	√	√		√
EAC	√	√	√	√	
ECOWAS					
FTAA	√	√		√	√
MERCOSUR	√	√		√	√
NAFTA					√
SACU					
SADC					
WAEMU	√	√		√	√

and undertaking capacity-building programmes to assist members' economies in implementing Principles.[191]

5.4 Competition provisions in plurilateral agreements: a comparative reading

The brief presentation of the competition regimes of the various agreements to a certain extent validates what has been argued above, i.e. that there is wide acceptance by regional blocs that some sort of competition rules are needed, since most of the regional blocs discussed here have adopted relevant provisions. Only four of these agreements, namely CAFTA-DR, ECOWAS, ASEAN and APEC, contain no competition provisions at all. Nonetheless, of those four agreements only in one (CAFTA-DR) have there been no attempts to date to adopt competition rules.[192]

[191] See APEC Committee on Trade and Development (2006), *Annual Report to the Ministers*, APEC#206-CT-01.6, at 110, app. VII.

[192] It should, however, be pointed out that the CAFTA-DR is an agreement that has only been adopted very recently and in this regard it is probably too early to judge whether regional competition has been totally overlooked by the participating countries.

In contrast to CAFTA-DR, in ECOWAS, there has recently been an initiative towards the adoption of competition rules in the region, while both ASEAN and APEC have established mechanisms for the exchange of ideas and experiences of the member states on competition matters, and this is a process referred to in various parts of the book as a mechanism for the development of common understandings and the final formation of rules.

On the other hand, the presentation of these blocs' competition regimes show that while the content of these regimes varies, there are also certain common characteristics among the agreements. This section attempts to expose such common characteristics in two broad areas: substantive competition provisions provided by the agreements, and the institutional set-up of these agreements.

5.4.1 Substantive competition provisions in plurilateral regional agreements

In a broad context, in terms of substantive competition law provisions, with regard to the agreements that have included competition rules in their framework, as in the case of bilateral free trade agreements, there are two main competition-related models followed. The first model is the one first adopted by NAFTA, according to which countries undertake a general obligation to have an operational domestic competition regime and a commitment to cooperate on competition matters of common interest. This model is also followed by SACU and SADC. SADC has only adopted a single provision that requires the member states to have and promote domestic competition rules; SACU also includes a provision according to which the member states must cooperate with each other on competition matters. Hence, no particular substantive regional competition rules are provided by these agreements.[193]

The second model includes a number of substantive competition provisions and is the one followed by the EU. This model has been followed by most of the regional blocs discussed here. A common characteristic of these agreements is that they prohibit specific anticompetitive business practices and, in particular, they include provisions that aim to address anticompetitive agreements and the abuse of a dominant position which have an effect on the regional market. Nonetheless, the extent to which

[193] A similar set of provisions are found in the proposed FTAA, which also contains substantive competition provisions that are to be applied to cases where the regional market is affected.

the EU model is further followed varies considerably among the different regional blocs, as only some of the blocs include substantive rules on mergers, public undertakings and state aids.

This variation may be attributed to the fact that the more extended the scope of competition rules, the more direct the intervention in the sovereign national systems of the member states. An indicative example may be found in the field of mergers. As noted in the context of the analysis of the EU competition regime, merger rules were introduced in the EU thirty-two years after the adoption of the founding Treaty, and this has been primarily attributed to the hesitance of the Member States to grant authority to a regional body to apply rules that relate to the performance of the most important companies of the Member States (and therefore rules that indirectly impact upon some of the most important economic and political interests of these states). Hence, it comes as no surprise that only two of the agreements discussed in this chapter, namely EAC and COMESA, have adopted rules for the control of mergers, and such rules have yet to be applied.

Similarly, only EAC and WAEMU have included the examination of aid granted to undertakings by the state within the realm of competition law, while three of the agreements discussed in this chapter, namely MERCOSUR, WAEMU and COMESA, have also included competition law provisions that regulate practices conducted by public enterprises and/or state monopolies, thus following the EU model.[194] Nevertheless, the relevant provisions also vary. While COMESA's competition provisions clearly apply (or are to be applied) equally to private and public firms, WAEMU's competition regime includes provisions which aim at securing transparency of the financial relationship between member states and public enterprises. MERCOSUR's competition law includes state monopolies within the realm of the regional competition rules only in those cases where these rules do not prevent the regular exercise of their legal rights; it is similar therefore to the relevant EU provision of Article 106(2) TFEU.

At least in terms of drafted rules, the inclusion of state aid rules and rules relating to public undertakings are indications of the tendency to include the public sector within the scope of the competition rules contained in particular regional agreements. As mentioned in the context of the presentation of the EU competition regime, such rules have been viewed as being essential in view of the fact that prior to their existence, national markets

[194] See Table 5.2.

of the EU Member States were state dominated, and these rules to a certain extent ensured that the regional markets would be framed on principles of free markets. In this regard, these rules can help protect private initiative against the actions of the state. However it should also be pointed out that, with the exception of WAEMU (where at least two cases on state aid have been decided by the WAEMU Commission) and the EU (in which the competent institutions, the European Commission and the ECJ (Court of Justice), have developed detailed jurisprudence), in none of the other agreements discussed in this chapter have these rules been operational.

5.4.2 Institutional set-up and implementation of the rules

As noted in the context of the discussion of the EU competition regime, of equal or even major importance to the substantive rules included in the plurilateral regional agreements are the provisions which organise the institutional structure of these blocs. Of the regional blocs examined here, no such provisions are adopted by ECOWAS and CAFTA-DR, which have in place no competition rules at all. As also noted, ASEAN and APEC have set up group of experts and officials with the task to discuss the issues relating to the optimum operation of competition law, both in the national and in the regional context.

On the other hand, with regard to the agreements that have adopted competition rules, as a general observation it could be noted that there are also two broad types of institutional structures provided. The first is the one adopted by NAFTA, and followed by SACU and SADC, in which no regional institution is provided and all the competition-related issues are to be resolved by the national competition authorities of the participating countries. In this regard, both NAFTA and SACU specifically provide that the participating states should cooperate in competition matters, and as has been seen in Chapter 3, in the case of NAFTA the signing parties have also concluded non-binding bilateral enforcement cooperation agreements.

The second type of institutional structure follows the EU approach and provides for the creation of a centralised body that has the competence to enforce competition law in the region. With this model, however, the type of the regional body established to apply the rules varies. In particular, the Andean Community, CARICOM, WAEMU and COMESA are blocs that have opted for the creation of a supranational body equivalent of the European Commission. That said, of these institutions, only the WAEMU Competition Commission has recently begun to operate by issuing its first decisions.

Table 5.3 *Institutional set-up of regional agreements*

Agreement	Obligation of members to harmonise their rules to those of the regional agreement	General obligation of members to have a national competition law	Number of members with national competition laws in place (as of 2008)	Type of regional institution competent to apply competition rules*	Court competent to review the decisions of the regional authority	Provisions on co-operation between members' national authorities
Andean Community			4/4	S	√	
APEC			17/21			
ASEAN			6/10			
CAFTA-DR			5/7			
CARICOM	√		4/15	S	√	
COMESA			6/19	S	√	
EAC			2/5	I	√	
ECOWAS			5/15			
EU	√		27/27	S	√	√
FTAA		√	–	I		√
MERCOSUR	√		3/4	I		
NAFTA		√	3/3			√
SACU		√	2/5			
SADC		√	7/15			
WAEMU	√		5/8	S	√	√

* S = supranational; I = intergovernmental

In contrast to the EU precedent, two of the regional blocs, EAC and MERCOSUR, have opted for the establishment of an intergovernmental institution competent to apply the regional rules. In EAC, competition law is to be applied by an intergovernmental body; and in MERCOSUR, the competence to apply regional competition rules has been granted to two relevant bodies. In these cases, it is obvious that the contracting parties were not ready to offer the competence to a non-national institution to review cases that may have an effect on their national markets.

In a broader context, what also becomes obvious from this data is that even with regard to the agreements which have opted for the adoption of substantive regional competition laws, i.e. those that by-and-large follow the EU model, there is no agreement as to what type of centralised enforcement body is appropriate to enforce the competition rules and, more particularly, whether such a body should be supranational or intergovernmental. This debate over the positive and negative features of supranationalism vis-à-vis intergovernmentalism is a lively one, in the context of the EU's institutional set-up itself,[195] and the extent to which either of these institutional designs is appropriate for a regional competition regime can only be examined by conducting research on every particular agreement, a task that cannot possibly be undertaken in the context of this study; with the exception of the EU and lately WAEMU,[196] it is an issue that is under-researched in the relevant literature. On the other hand, as noted above, the EU experiment has shown that in terms of competition law and policy, where to date the EU regime has been the only successful and operative regional regime in the world, the delegation of powers to a supranational institution (the Commission) is of major importance if a credible regional regime is to be achieved.[197]

As also argued in this chapter, in the case of the EU, the regional courts have been of equal significance in the development of competition; they have extensively interpreted and applied the regional competition rules, and have also developed principles which delineate the relationship between the supranational body and the national authorities. To this end, the fact that some of the agreements (namely the Andean Community, CARICOM, WAEMU, EAC, COMESA and SADC) also provide for the establishment of regional courts which have the competence to review cases relating to the regional competition rules may be considered as a choice that should normally lead to the more efficient application of competition rules. Nevertheless, this hypothesis cannot yet be tested as, with the exception of the WAEMU Court of Justice, none of these courts have to date applied the competition rules: in practice the competition regimes have not been operational in these other blocs.

Furthermore, the brief presentation of the EU competition system has also shown that the system is a dynamic one, in the sense that it changes over time. For instance, with regard to the institutional set-up of the EU, it has been noted that while until recently the European Commission had sole competence to apply the competition-related provisions, Regulation 1/2003 has provided for decentralisation of enforcement, requiring

[195] See G. Tsebelis and G. Garrett (2001), 'The Institutional Foundations of Intergovernmentalism and Supranationalism in the European Union' 55(2) *International Organization* 357; J. Tallberg (2002), 'Delegation to Supranational Institutions: Why, How, and with What Consequences?' 25(1) *West European Politics* 23.

[196] See Bakhoum (2006), *supra* n. 157 at 125.

[197] See L. McGowan (2007), 'Theorising European Integration: Revisiting Neofunctionalism and Testing its Suitability for Explaining the Development of EC Competition Policy' 11(3) *European Integration Online Papers* 1, at 4–5.

Member States to apply regional rules in cases that have an effect on intra-regional trade. In this regard, and while the adoption of competition rules is not a clear legal prerequisite for the EU Member States,[198] this development in the competition system in practice requires Member States to have national competition institutions in place, and apply the regional rules in particular instances.

From a broader viewpoint, the EU experience has shown that in the longer term, the development of an effective regional competition regime may lead to the adoption and development of national competition regimes which are equivalent to the regional one.[199] If the EU hypothesis is to be applicable to these other agreements, then it should be expected that the development of the regional regime should precede the relevant development of national competition regimes, particularly with regard to regional agreements which include developing countries, where the adoption, and more importantly the development, of effective competition regimes is a very difficult task.[200]

To this end, and in view of the fact that to date almost none of the reviewed competition regimes have been operational, it comes as no surprise that despite the fact that certain agreements require their member states to have competition laws in place,[201] while others go a step further and require adoption of national competition rules compatible with the substantive regional rules,[202] in most of these blocs a number of member states have not as yet even adopted a competition law.[203]

5.4.3 *Some final thoughts on the comparative reading of competition provisions in regional blocs*

The previous section has attempted to highlight some of the common characteristics of the competition regimes that have been set up, or that are in the process of being set up, by various regional blocs. Given the fact

[198] This argument does not apply to the Member States which joined the EU from 2004 onwards, where the adoption of a competition law compatible with the EU was among the obligations that these Member States had to fulfil in order to secure EU accession. See Chapter 4.

[199] This argument has been already made with regard to competition law and policy in Greece. It should not be overlooked, however, that certain Member States have only relatively recently adopted national competition rules, e.g., the Netherlands in 1994.

[200] On the problems faced by developing countries in the process of adoption and application of competition rules, see Chapter 6.

[201] These agreements include NAFTA, FTAA, SADC and SACU.

[202] Including MERCOSUR, CARICOM and WAEMU.

[203] See Table 5.3.

that comparative research on the competition elements of these agreements has been very limited to date, this discussion's main observation is that it provides us with a clear indication that there is wide recognition that some sort of regional competition law is important for the effective operation of the regional blocs.

As indicated earlier in the chapter, the role of competition law and policy in these arrangements is to ensure that regional trade liberalisation, a goal pursued by all the agreements discussed, is not hampered by anticompetitive business practices with an effect on the regional markets. Thus, most of these blocs have adopted or are in the process of adopting competition rules, and some further provide for the enforcement of competition rules in their region.

Some very basic common norms and procedures of these groups of countries on competition may also be identified. In particular, of the agreements that already have a competition regime in place, two broad categories may be distinguished. The first includes the agreements which encompass both substantive competition rules that are to be applied at the regional level, and provisions on the establishment and operation of the institutions that are to apply the rules. In particular, a number of the agreements reviewed here have included in their regional legislation provisions that prohibit anticompetitive agreements and abuse of dominance that have an effect on intraregional trade. Some of the agreements have gone further and have included rules relating to merger control and the regulation of state monopolies and public undertakings. In addition, all the agreements that have adopted substantive rules also provide for some form of institutional mechanisms for the application of the rules. Despite the fact that there is variation in the rules and procedures provided by these agreements, as also analysed in the next section, in terms of structure, these agreements are inspired by the precedent of the EU.

The second model of a regional competition regime has been introduced by NAFTA and to a certain extent this model has been followed by another two regional agreements, namely SACU and SADC. As mentioned in Chapter 4 and earlier in this chapter, the NAFTA model provides no substantive competition rules, and is based on the commitment undertaken by the participating countries to have in place and apply competition rules, and to cooperate on competition matters.Nevertheless, these assumptions should be further tested by future research, since in practice competition law on a regional level has only been applied in the EU.

As noted in the chapter, this lack of application of the competition rules may be attributed to various factors, including the fact that, as the EU experiment has shown, it takes time for a regional competition regime to develop. The hesitation of particular member states to accept a regional body to apply rules that may have an effect on companies supported by the governments of these states is another factor, as is the lack of sufficient resources regarding the enforcement of competition rules, particularly in regional blocs that have to address much more basic issues such as the poverty of their populations before they would seriously look at the development of effective competition regimes.[204]

Thus, further research has to be undertaken to analyse the competition framework of individual plurilateral regional agreements before further conclusions may safely be drawn with regard to the actual development of competition law and policy in the various regions discussed here. Such research should (i) focus on the examination of the particular regional markets created by these agreements; (ii) evaluate the particular needs of these markets; and (iii) propose substantive rules appropriate for their effective operation, as well as rules that would better support the effective enforcement of such rules. To this end, major international organisations such as UNCTAD, OECD and the IMF have recently started looking at this issue.

5.5 Role of the EU in the formation and application of competition rules in regional blocs

Returning to the main issue that this book attempts to address, i.e. the international dimension of EU competition law and policy, and more particularly in the context of this chapter, the impact of the EU in the formation of competition regimes in other plurilateral regional agreements, a first observation to be made is that the use of regional competition rules as a concept complementary to trade liberalisation was first introduced and applied by the EU. This model seems to be broadly followed by a number of other similar regional blocs, both in terms of substance and in terms of institutional set-up.

Indeed, the EU model has been followed by many more agreements of this kind than the NAFTA model. While it has also been suggested above that the extent to which the EU model of competition has been followed varies considerably among the various blocs which have opted for this model, this observation is still of some significance, as it suggests that a

[204] On this last argument regarding availability of resources, see the discussion developed in Chapter 6 with regard to competition law in developing countries.

model of sorts for a regional competition regime may be arising in the field of international competition. This model encompasses substantive competition provisions, at least regarding the prohibition of anticompetitive agreements and abuses of dominance which have an effect on the common regional market, and is also based on the creation of regional institutions, either supranational or intergovernmental, that will apply these rules.

In an attempt to evaluate this phenomenon, and on the basis of the analysis carried out in this chapter, two main possible reasons may be put forward as to why the EU competition model was chosen by a number of other blocs. First, it might be argued that the EU itself has encouraged other regional blocs to adopt competition rules similar to those of the EU. The second, more conceptual hypothesis is that a number of regional blocs have followed the EU model because of its success.

As to the former, as noted above, the EU in a broader context has supported the creation and operation of regional blocs, and has expressed its position in this regard through policy statements, aid granted to regional agreements and the negotiation of trade agreements with other regional organisations. The negotiation and conclusion of the first (EEA excluded) interregional agreement between the EU and its Member States with the CARIFORUM states, which includes competition rules, is a clear indication that the EU supports regional integration and further pursues cooperation with regional blocs in every part of the world.

It has also became clear from the chapter's analysis that, nevertheless, in encouraging the adoption of competition rules by other plurilateral regional agreements, the EU has not been as active as in the case of bilateral free trade agreements with neighbouring countries and selected trade partners, which most of the technical assistance resources of the European Commission have been devoted to. It should also be noted that at least up to six years ago, as demonstrated in Chapter 6, in the field of international competition, much of the resources of the Commission (at least as far as DG Competition and DG Trade are concerned) have been devoted to the talks on competition at the WTO.[205]

[205] It is interesting to note that neither of the last two Commissioners for Competition (former Commissioner Monti and Commissioner Kroes) has publicly expressed the position that the EU actively supports the formation of competition rules in other regional blocs. This should not lead us to the opposite view that the European Commission has not been eager to support such initiatives; nevertheless, it is indicative of the fact that such support has not been of primary importance, at least as far as DG Competition is concerned.

Furthermore, no proof has been offered in the chapter regarding possible attempts by the EU to impose its own competition rules on other regional blocs through the adoption of interregional agreements, a practice that, as exposed in Chapter 4, has been the main strategic tool of the EU in the field of bilateral trade agreements. That said, the chapter has shown that on several occasions support for regional initiatives, and in particular for the establishment of regional competition regimes, has been expressed by the EU through the funding of competition-related projects in regional blocs, such as the Andean Community, COMESA and WAEMU. While the exact conditions upon which such assistance has been granted have not been made publicly available, it is noted in the context of the discussion that the general aim of the financial aid was to assist these regional blocs in their attempts to adopt competition law, and therefore it could safely be argued that such assistance has been based on the experience gained through the application of the EU competition regime. Thus, in view of the fact that the assistance has been offered to other regional blocs which are comparable with the EU, it might be argued that such projects have been a vehicle through which the EU has attempted to export its own competition model.

As to the second possible reason leading to the adoption of competition regimes broadly following the EU model, it may be argued that the EU model of competition has to a certain extent been followed by a number of other regional blocs due to the fact that it has been considered by these blocs as a benchmark and a tool for the achievement of regional integration. This phenomenon – a country or group of countries copying the legal regime of another country or group of countries – has been explained by economic theory, which suggests that competitors imitate strategies which are successful over a given period of time.[206] This assumption may be applied by analogy to the field of plurilateral regional agreements, where the successful application of the EU regime in general, and its competition regime in particular, has been imitated (at least on paper) by a number of other plurilateral agreements.

Similarly, in the international relations literature, the concepts of mimetic and normative isomorphism have been advanced in order to explain the reasons that lead to the adoption of similar competition

[206] D.D. Sokol (2007), *Why is This Chapter Different from All the Others? An Examination of Why Countries Enter into Non-Enforceable Competition Policy Chapters in Free Trade Agreements*, Legal Studies Research Paper Series Paper No. 2007–13, at 50.

regimes by different regional agreements.[207] According to mimetic isomorphism, certain organisations mimic other organisations due to uncertainty. The more frequent the practice, the more likely it is that other organisations imitate such a practice. On the other hand, according to normative isomorphism, an organisation imitates another organisation in cases where the approaches and procedures of the latter on a given issue are considered to be superior and based on prevailing thought. While mimetic and normative isomorphism are based on different causal grounds (mimetic on uncertainty and lack of information, and normative on the assumption of superiority), the outcome of both is the imitation of the most successful approaches. To this end, the adoption by a number of agreements of the EU competition model is a consequence of the fact that the EU model is a tried and tested one, and moreover is considered to be a very successful one, and superior to other (underdeveloped) competition regimes. These arguments may justify the observation in this chapter that the EU model has been used as a template to be followed by other competition regimes (WAEMU, CARICOM and COMESA being the prime examples) which, having accepted the argument that the operation of an effective competition law could have a positive effect on the bloc, have followed, at least to a certain extent, the EU competition regime.

5.6 Conclusion

This chapter has reviewed the competition regimes of a number of plurilateral regional agreements around the world. It first presented the historical development of regional agreements, and identified the factors that led to the establishment of the various regional blocs. Geographic proximity, the aim of the signing states to achieve peace and increased welfare in the region, and their aim of counter-balancing the bargaining powers of other regional blocs and strong states at the international level are all important factors.

The chapter also referred to the role of competition law and policy in the operation of the various regional blocs. It was noted that, since most of the agreements discussed have adopted some sort of regional competition law, it may safely be argued that competition law has been considered, at

[207] *Ibid.*, in which the author refers to the work of DiMaggio and Powell who first developed the concept of institutional isomorphism, a concept mentioned previously in the context of the analysis of bilateral enforcement cooperation agreements (see Chapter 3). See P.J. DiMaggio and W.W. Powell (1983), 'The Iron Cage Revisited: Institutional Isomorphism and Collective Rationality in Organizational Fields' 48 *American Society Review* 147.

least conceptually, as an important tool for the achievement of operationally effective and competitive regional markets. In the context of a brief examination of the competition regime of the EU (the focal point of study in this book), it was argued that EU competition law and policy has been built around two main elements: detailed substantive competition rules and effective enforcement of these rules, carried out by two supranational institutions, the European Commission and the courts. Hence, the EU model requires the adoption of detailed substantive regional rules and centralised enforcement of such rules. This is in contrast to the NAFTA model which is limited to a commitment undertaken by the member states to have national rules in place and provides mechanisms for voluntary cooperation..

The EU model has been broadly followed by a number of other regional blocs, and certainly these agreements outnumber the agreements that follow the NAFTA model. That said, as noted above, while all the agreements that follow the EU model include provisions on the prohibition of anticompetitive practices and abuse of dominance, there is great variation both as to the remaining substantive provisions included in the other agreements and as to the institutional set-up they provide for. In particular, it has been noted that only some of the agreements include provisions relating to mergers, state aids and abuse of dominance. In terms of institutional set-up, of the agreements that have granted the competence to enforce the competition rules to regional bodies, two of them, namely EAC and MERCOSUR, have granted it to intergovernmental bodies, thus departing from the EU model which is based on a supranational body, i.e. the Commission.

Some further indications regarding the influence of the EU in the formation of competition regimes by other plurilateral regional agreements have been pointed out in the chapter. In particular, while the EU administration has not been as active in this field as in the case of bilateral trade agreements (at least until six years ago, with the negotiations over a possible competition agreement at the WTO), it has nevertheless been suggested that the EU has supported the development of organisations similar to itself (i.e. the formation of regional blocs), and has pursued cooperation with such organisations. Furthermore, there have been particular instances where the EU has financed small-scale projects relating to the adoption of competition rules by regional blocs. Finally, the chapter has argued that the reason that a number of plurilateral regional agreements have followed the competition regime of the EU (even partially) may be mainly attributed to the fact that the EU model is to a certain extent considered as a benchmark, and has therefore been followed by a number of other agreements which have adopted substantive competition rules and have granted the competence for the application of the rules to centralised enforcement bodies. As pointed out in the chapter, the theoretical basis of this phenomenon is a tendency among organisations to imitate tested and successful strategies and practices of other organisations. Given that the EU in general, and the EU competition regime in particular, have been major successes, it comes as no surprise that other regional blocs have imitated the EU precedent.

Nevertheless, and despite the number of issues discussed here which provide strong indications that the EU has had a significant impact on the adoption of competition rules by other regional blocs, it would not at this point be possible to quantify this impact further, since this could be clarified only by further research. Such research would involve individually examining the regional settings, considering the positions taken in the context of the negotiations for the adoption of the regional competition regimes, observing the needs of the particular regional markets, and proposing an optimum framework for the application of the rules. Ideally, this research would also observe the process from the drafting of the rules up until their application. Given the importance of the various socio-political and economic factors that are taken into account in the context of the application of competition rules at any level (national or regional), one would need to look at the way in which competition law has been applied in the various regional agreements, in order to identify the extent to which these settings follow the EU model of competition. This latter exercise, however, could not be undertaken at the present time, since the WAEMU is the only non-EU agreement that has applied the regional rules to date.

6

The Role of Competition Law and Policy of the EU in Multilateral Negotiations on Competition

6.1 Historical development of the negotiations on the adoption of a multilateral agreement on competition

6.1.1 Attempts under the aegis of the League of Nations and the proposed International Trade Organization

The history of the attempts to adopt a multilateral agreement on competition law goes back to 1925 when the first international competition code was proposed in a study conducted under the aegis of the League of Nations.[1] The proposal was finally rejected by the League on the basis of arguments not much different than those developed to explain the lack of success of subsequent attempts at the adoption of a multilateral competition agreement: that divergent national attitudes towards restrictive business practices precluded the creation of an international code; and that an international regime would heavily infringe upon state sovereignty.[2]

Almost twenty years later, a second significant attempt to include competition law in the international trading system was made. In particular, Chapter V[3] of the proposed Havana Charter was dedicated to the regulation of restrictive business practices. According to the provisions of this charter, the member states of the proposed International Trade Organization (ITO) would have been obliged to adopt appropriate legislation and to cooperate with the ITO in order to prevent private and public commercial enterprises from engaging in practices that would restrain competition, limit access to markets, or foster monopolistic control, whenever such practices would have harmful effects on the expansion of production or trade and would interfere with the achievement of any of

[1] A. Furnish (1970), 'A Transnational Approach to Restrictive Business Practices' 4 *International Lawyer* 317, at 317–19.

[2] *Ibid.*

[3] See Havana Charter, Chapter V, arts. 46–54.

the other objectives listed in article 1 of the Charter.[4] An extensive list of such practices was included in the proposed code.[5]

Member states would have been entitled to complain about prohibited restraints of competition to the ITO,[6] which according to the proposed Charter would have been empowered to investigate and demand information during its investigation.[7] If the ITO were to find that the alleged practice would have a restrictive effect on competition, it would have been empowered to request each member involved to 'take every possible remedial action'.[8] Moreover, article 48(8) would have entitled the ITO to request from the offending member state full reports in relation to the progress of its remedial measures.

Although most of the countries that participated in the discussions favoured the adoption of the Havana Charter, the proposed Charter failed to find favour in the US Congress which, as well documented, was essentially motivated by the traditional concerns over international incursions into US domestic political sovereignty and by the feeling that the competition rules of Chapter V were not adequate for the United States.[9] Thus, the US Congress withdrew its support for the Charter and the negotiations failed to produce an agreement.

6.1.2 *UNCTAD: the Restrictive Business Practices Code*

No significant initiative for a multilateral competition agreement was then taken until the 1970s.[10] At that time, the desire for discussions

[4] *Ibid.* art. 46(1).

[5] *Ibid.* art. 46(3). The list included price-fixing, sales or purchase quotas, excluding enterprises from business activities, dividing territorial markets or fields of business, and limiting production or fixing production quotas.

[6] *Ibid.* art. 48(1).

[7] *Ibid.* arts. 46(2) and 48(3).

[8] *Ibid.* art. 48(7).

[9] See S. Timberg (1973), 'An International Antitrust Convention: A Proposal to Harmonise Conflicting National Policies Towards the Multinational Corporation' 8 *Journal of International Law and Economics* 157.

[10] In the period between 1950 and 1970, two initiatives are noteworthy: first, the UNESCO committee's endorsement of a second draft of the Havana Charter's Competition Principles, which failed due to the withdrawal of US support (see Furnish (1970), *supra* n. 1 at 323); secondly, the work of a group of experts that was appointed in 1958 to discuss the possible inclusion of competition provisions in GATT. The decision was again in the negative, notwithstanding that the contracting parties recognised the problems that restrictive business practices create in international trade. See M.-C. Malaguti (1998), 'Restrictive Business Practices in International Trade and the Role of the World Trade Organisation' 32(3) *Journal of World Trade* 117, at 120.

concerning a multinational agreement came from less developed countries. These countries were concerned about the increasing expansion of multinational enterprises, which from their point of view were powerful and abusive.[11] Under pressure from the developing countries, the issue of negotiating a multilateral competition agreement was once again raised. The discussions were held under the aegis of the United Nations Conference on Trade and Development (UNCTAD), and the result of these negotiations was the adoption of a Restrictive Business Practices Code (RBP Code)[12] which, contrary to the initial proposal of the developing countries, was a recommendation and thus not legally binding.[13]

In terms of substance, the Code includes provisions addressing horizontal restraints of competition (price-fixing, boycotts and market and consumer allocation).[14] In relation to vertical restraints, the Code declares that such restraints should be condemned only when they are conducted by a dominant firm and they are abusive in character.[15] Concerning abuse of a dominant position by a firm, the Code states that each practice should be examined on its own merits (purpose and effect).[16]

Generally, it could be said that the RBP Code has been noteworthy since it is the only multinational competition agreement that has been adopted, and it represents the only time that the United States has supported the adoption of such an agreement. It probably comes as no surprise that, in the relatively long story of multilateral negotiations concerning a competition agreement, the only time when consensus was reached on substantive competition provisions it was for a non-binding agreement. However, on the basis of the analysis of soft law instruments in earlier chapters, this may be considered as a first step towards further and more formal (in the form of a binding agreement) multilateral cooperation on competition.[17] Such a position is also revisited in the context of the discussion on

[11] E.M. Fox (1995), 'Competition Law and the Agenda for the WTO: Forging the Links of Competition and Trade' 4 *Pacific Rim and Law Policy* 1, at 4.

[12] Set of Multilaterally Agreed Equitable Principles and Rules for the Control of Restrictive Business Practices, UN Doc. TD/RBP/CONF 10/Rev.1 (1980), endorsed by GA Res. 63, UN Doc. A/RES/35/63 (1980), reprinted in (1980) 19 ILM 813.

[13] The Code is not a treaty but a Resolution of the General Assembly. Article 10 of the UN Charter defines such Resolutions as 'Recommendations to States'.

[14] RBP Code, *supra* n. 12 para. D-3.

[15] *Ibid.* para. D-4.

[16] *Ibid.* para. D-4 and note accompanying the word 'abuse'.

[17] See I. Lianos (2007), 'The Contribution of the United Nations to the Emergence of Global Antitrust Law' 15(2) *Tulane Journal of International and Comparative Law* 2, esp. 34–41, where the author argues that the RBP Code may contribute to the creation of customary international competition rules.

the work of the International Competition Network (ICN),[18] itself a body that has also issued a number of soft law instruments. In view of the fact that no binding agreement has been reached to date on this issue, it may also be an indication that with regard to an issue such as competition law, where there is no common approach as to its optimum operation, semi-formal arrangements in the form of soft law are a second best, but yet the only, solution as regards the treatment of anticompetitive business practices with an international effect.

On the other hand, it has been pointed out that as the RBP Code is a soft law instrument, many of its provisions are vague, and many of the rules that developing countries wished to be included in the Code did not survive the negotiation process (due to the opposition of the developed countries participating in the negotiations).[19] Both of these points render the Code a legislative text of relatively limited value. That said, as discussed in the following section, the work of UNCTAD in this field has been very important, as it is the organisation that most actively supports the interests of developing countries.

6.1.3 Re-opening of the debate on a multilateral agreement on competition in the 1990s

The debate over the adoption of a multilateral agreement on competition law and policy was revived in the mid-1990s under the auspices of the WTO, which was established in Marrakech in 1994.[20] The WTO was the product of the Eighth Round of Multilateral Trade Negotiations (the Uruguay Round) which was held between 1986 and 1994 under the General Agreement on Tariffs and Trade (GATT), and integrates approximately thirty Uruguay Round agreements and 200 previous GATT agreements into one single legal framework.[21]

As already noted, when the WTO was established no binding multilateral agreement on competition had yet been adopted. Nonetheless, at that time, especially in Europe, there were voices that enthusiastically

[18] See 6.3 *infra*.

[19] D.L. Miller and J. Davidow (1982), 'Antitrust in the United Nations: A Tale of Two Codes' 18(2) *Stanford Journal of International Law* 347, at 354–5.

[20] Agreement Establishing the World Trade Organisation, Final Act Embodying the Results of the Uruguay Round of Negotiations, Marrakech, 15 April 1994 (hereinafter 'WTO Agreement').

[21] E.-U. Petersmann (1994), 'Proposals for Negotiating International Competition Rules in the GATT-WTO World Trade and Legal System' 49 *Swiss Review of International Economic Relations* 231, at 264.

supported the adoption of such a multilateral agreement. With the European Union being at the forefront of a group of WTO members which promoted the issue before the Singapore Ministerial Conference in 1996, the possible inclusion of competition within the WTO was finally discussed in that Conference. The Ministerial Declaration provided no consensus among the state representatives on possible substantive action that should be taken;[22] nonetheless, Member States agreed on the creation of a working group to study the interaction between trade and competition policy, including anticompetitive practices, and to identify the areas that may merit further consideration in the WTO framework.[23] Thus, competition was included on the WTO agenda, along with another three topics: investment, transparency in government procurement and trade facilitation. These four new topics are referred to at the WTO as the 'Singapore issues'.

The establishment of the working group on trade and competition at the WTO triggered a lively debate over the usefulness of competition law and policy in the international trade system. Hundreds of papers from member states were submitted to the working group, expressing the states' positions on the issue.[24] In this regard, the consultations at WTO level have proved to be a reality check regarding the status of competition law and policy from an international trade perspective.

Most of the issues raised in the context of this study were discussed at the WTO. These included the optimum operation of competition law at the national level; the optimum operation of competition law at the international level, and more particularly the types of anticompetitive practices that should be dealt with by international competition rules; the relationship between competition law and WTO law, including the application of general principles of WTO law, such as transparency, non-discrimination and the principle of the most favoured nation in competition; the examination of restrictive business practices that have an effect

[22] C. Cocuzza and M. Montini (1998), 'International Antitrust Co-operation in a Global Economy' 19 *European Competition Law Review* 156, at 161.

[23] WTO (1996), 1996 Singapore Ministerial Conference of the Parties to the WTO, Singapore Ministerial Declaration WT/MIN(96)/DEC.

[24] Specifically, 246 communications (papers) were submitted to the working group by WTO members, as well as by international organisations such as the OECD. Twenty of these communications were submitted by the EU. In relation to the other Singapore issues, the number of communications is high. For instance, 146 relevant communications were submitted in the context of the discussions in the working group on trade and investment, 41 to the Working Group on transparency in government procurement practices. See the WTO website, www.wto.org.

on the markets of multiple states; and the analysis of methods of co-operation between Member States on competition issues, including issues of technical assistance and capacity building.

On the basis of these consultations, in Doha in November 2001 the WTO members decided to include competition law and policy in the next round of the WTO negotiations. According to paragraph 25 of the Ministerial Declaration:

> In the period until the Fifth Session, further work in the Working Group on the Interaction between Trade and Competition Policy will focus on the clarification of: core principles, including transparency, non-discrimination and procedural fairness, and provisions on hard-core cartels; modalities for voluntary cooperation; and support for progressive reinforcement of competition institutions in developing countries through capacity building. Full account shall be taken of the needs of developing and least developed country participants and appropriate flexibility provided to address them.[25]

Once again, however, as in Havana in 1947, the Ministerial Conference in Cancun in 2003 failed to produce any results, and the negotiations on competition were wound up.[26] The Singapore issues were finally withdrawn from the agenda in the so-called 'July package', i.e. the decision adopted by the WTO General Council a few months after the Cancun Conference that aimed to reactivate the negotiations, with the exception of trade facilitation. The Council noted that it:

> agrees that these issues, mentioned in the Doha Ministerial Declaration ..., will not form part of the Work Programme set out in that Declaration and therefore no work towards negotiations on any of these issues will take place within the WTO during the Doha Round.[27]

The following sections attempt to understand the debate about the possible inclusion of competition law within the WTO framework as it developed during the negotiations in the context of the working group on trade and competition. In view of the central question that the book tries to address, the focus of subsequent analysis is the policy followed by the EU in this field. Accordingly, the next section will discuss the reasons that led

[25] WTO (2001), 2001 Doha Ministerial Declaration, WT/MIN(01)/DEC/1, paras. 23–5.

[26] WTO Ministerial Statement, WT/(MIN)03/20, where it is stated that further work should be carried out in the context of the Doha Declaration without any reference to particular tasks and deadlines.

[27] WTO (2004), Decision Adopted by the General Council on 1 August 2004, WT/L/579, at 3.

the EU to the initial proposal for adoption of a WTO competition agreement, consider how the United States and developing countries received and reacted to this proposal, and attempt to identify the factors that led to the final collapse of negotiations at Cancun.

6.2 Factors that led to the EU proposal for inclusion of competition within the WTO framework

As noted above, the EU was the most enthusiastic supporter of the inclusion of competition law in the WTO framework. This section attempts to identify the reasons that initially led to EU support for the idea of concluding a binding agreement on competition, and the reasons that led to the withdrawal of the EU proposal in 2004.

6.2.1 Leadership of Lord Brittan and creation of a network of academics and politicians who supported the adoption of a multilateral agreement at the WTO

One of the most significant factors that played a role in the relaunch of discussions over a possible WTO agreement on competition was the development in Europe in the early 1990s of a network of academics and officials who supported the adoption of such an agreement. As most of the experts interviewed in the context of this study have stressed, Lord Brittan was the leader of this group and the most influential individual in the development of the EU position.[28] In fact, he was the first to launch the issue within the European Commission, and the first to express the belief that competition law and policy should find a place in the WTO nexus of agreements.

Brittan was the Commissioner for Competition from 1989 until 1993, when he undertook the position of Commissioner for the EU's external affairs and became the EU's chief negotiator at the Uruguay Round. He was a major supporter of free trade in general and a strong opponent of the use of antidumping measures. According to one of the interviewees,

[28] These interviewees include four officials from the European Commission, as well as an EU and a US competition practitioner (interviews conducted in Brussels, 20 and 21 July 2003). The importance of the role of particular individuals in the development of new policies in the international arena has been extensively discussed in the political science literature. See e.g., O.R. Young (1991), 'Political Leadership and Regime Formation: On the Development of Institutions in International Society' 45 *International Organisation* 281.

he once stated that 'anti-dumping is chemotherapy which kills the patient'.[29]

He first publicly expressed his belief that competition rules should be included in the GATT/WTO framework in 1992, when he was still the Commissioner for Competition.[30] When he became the EU chief negotiator at the WTO, he found in Karel Van Miert, the new Commissioner for Competition, a strong ally in his attempt to incorporate competition within the WTO framework. For both Commissioners, the issue became a priority and being in leading positions at the Commission they had a major impact in the process of the negotiations.

In parallel, a network of academics was being developed in Europe who supported the idea of a binding multilateral agreement on competition. In particular, in 1993 a group of competition and trade experts, the so-called 'Munich Group' (which consisted of nine German, one Japanese and two US academics, all lawyers),[31] proposed a Draft International Antitrust Code (DIAC),[32] which would be introduced in the GATT-MTO (Agreement establishing the Multilateral Trade Organisation, as the Munich Group called the WTO) as a plurilateral competition agreement.[33]

These experts proposed the adoption of a detailed competition code[34] which would include provisions for horizontal restraints,[35] vertical restraints,[36] concentrations,[37] abuses of a dominant position,[38] and a regime for public undertakings and state authorisation[39] similar to Article 86 (now Article 102) of the EC Treaty for public undertakings. Moreover, the DIAC provided for the establishment of an international competition agency which would operate within the institutional framework of the MTO (WTO)[40] and which would have the right to bring individual

[29] Interview with EU competition practitioner (Brussels, 21 July 2003).

[30] See L. Brittan (1992), *Competition Policy and International Relations* (Brussels: Centre for European Policy Studies).

[31] The private international antitrust code working group was composed of W. Fikentscher, E. Fox, J. Drexl, A. Fuchs, A. Heinemann, U. Immenga, H.P. Kunz-Hallstein, E.-U. Petersmann, W.R. Schluep, A. Shoda, L.A. Sullivan and S. Soltysinski.

[32] Draft International Antitrust Code, a GATT-MTO Plurilateral Trade Agreement: Antitrust and Trade Regulation Report (BNA) at 126 (Special Supplement No. 1628, 19 August 1993) (hereinafter DIAC).

[33] See DIAC, art. 1.

[34] For an analysis of the Munich Code see W. Fikentscher (1994), 'Competition Rules for Private Agents in the GATT/WTO System' 49 *Swiss Review of International Economic Relations* 281.

[35] DIAC, art. 4. [36] *Ibid.* art. 5.

[37] *Ibid.* arts. 8–13. [38] *Ibid.* art. 14.

[39] *Ibid.* art. 16. [40] *Ibid.* art. 19.

cases to the national courts, or to the International Antitrust Panel which would be established.[41]

As is obvious, the DIAC had many similarities with Chapter V of the Havana Charter, and since it included proposed provisions on almost every aspect of competition law, was a very ambitious plan for the creation of a multilateral code. Nonetheless, it was almost immediately felt that such a proposal was too optimistic, and to a certain extent unrealistic, being a very detailed piece of legislation proposed at a time when no more than thirty states had competition laws in place.[42]

Two years after the publication of the proposal, another group of academics and EU officials[43] (convened by Commissioner Karel Van Miert) produced a report,[44] in which they argued that a plurilateral agreement under Annex IV of the WTO would be the most realistic option with regard to the possible adoption of a multilateral agreement on competition.[45] According to the report, the agreement would be adopted as a first stage by countries with a mature competition system.[46] It would include elements that were included in bilateral enforcement cooperation agreements such as procedural notification, cooperation, negative and positive comity obligations, and some minimum substantive principles for cross-border cases, such as the prohibition of horizontal agreements (cartels, including export cartels), vertical restraints (for which a rule-of-reason test was provided), abuse of a dominant position, and national monopolies with exclusive or special privileges.[47] These principles would be incorporated into the national laws of the member countries in much the same way as EU Directives: each country would have to incorporate

[41] *Ibid.* art. 20.

[42] In it is noteworthy that even some members of the Munich Group had expressed their concerns in relation to a detailed competition code and supported a more limited approach with a code embodying only fifteen principles. See E.M. Fox (1997), 'Towards World Antitrust and Market Access' 91(1) *American Journal of International Law* 1, at 10.

[43] The group of experts was composed of the Commission officials Claus-Dieter Ehlermann, Roderick Abbott, Jean-Francois Marchipont, Francois Lamoureux, Alexis Jacquemin and Francois Pons, with external experts, Frederic Jenny, Ulrich Immenga and Ernst-Ulrich Petersmann.

[44] See European Commission (1995), *Report of the Group of Experts, Competition Policy in the New Trade Order: Strengthening International Competition and Rules*, COM(95)359 final (hereinafter *Report of EU Experts*).

[45] This approach has been named 'the building block approach' or the 'instalments approach'.

[46] *Report of EU Experts, supra* n. 44 at 16–17. At the initial stage, the report suggested that the signatories should be all the member countries of the OECD, the Central and Eastern European countries, and Hong Kong, Korea, Singapore, Taiwan.

[47] See *Report of the EU Experts, supra* n. 44 at 17.

the principles in its national legislation, but would not be obliged to amend its legislation in cases where the legislation already contained the principles or was open to similar interpretation.[48]

In terms of enforcement, the report proposed that the WTO dispute settlement mechanism should review competition cases, envisaging four distinct types of possible disputes: disputes over international procedural obligations, disputes over per-se prohibitions, disputes over rule-of-reason violations, and disputes over impediments to market access.[49] Such a plurilateral agreement would develop and expand its coverage progressively through a 'domino effect', both in terms of its geographic scope, substantive coverage and surveillance.[50]

It is clear that by advocating an 'instalment approach', the proposal of this group of experts was far more realistic than the one proposed by the Munich Group. Irrespective of the substance of the proposal, what is of importance is the fact that in the mid-1990s a network of academics and EU officials had emerged and clearly expressed the belief that competition law should be included in a binding international agreement. It should be noted that Professors Petersmann and Immenga both participated in the Munich Group and the group of experts appointed by Commissioner Van Miert, an indication of the intellectual links between the two groups.[51] It is also important to note that no business representatives participated in the preparation of these reports. On the contrary, major business confederations, such as UNICE (now Business Europe), repeatedly expressed their concerns over a possible binding agreement within the WTO framework. For instance, in 1999, UNICE expressed concern:

> about a binding multilateral agreement on specific competition rules concluded in the WTO as opposed to clear objectives or guidance for a voluntary set of rules. WTO is not intended or equipped to operate at the private-to-private level. UNICE fears that a binding agreement cannot

[48] *Ibid.* at 17; see also E.-U. Petersmann (1996), 'International Competition Rules for Governments and for Private Business: The Case for Linking Future WTO Negotiations on Investment, Competition and Environmental Rules to Reforms of Anti-Dumping Laws' 30(3) *Journal of World Trade* 5, at 26.

[49] See *Report of EU Experts*, *supra* n. 44 at 18–19.

[50] *Ibid.* at 20.

[51] Note that in the second half of the 1990s, a number of alternative proposals emerged with regard to the inclusion of competition policy in the WTO. Such proposals included the setting of minimum substantive standards of competition law, the expansion of the scope of current WTO agreements in order to bring non-violation complaints, the introduction of competition criteria in antidumping measures, the prohibition of export cartels and the adoption of procedural and due process norms. For a review of these proposals from a developing country perspective, see B. Hoekman and P. Holmes (1999), 'Competition Policy, Developing Countries and the WTO' 22(6) *The World Economy* 875.

> but result in binding review of specific essentially private cases by bodies that are inappropriate and ill-equipped for that task. This will greatly slow down commerce and escalate private disputes to international problems.[52]

Given the reluctance of EU business to support a competition agreement in the WTO, it follows that the network that re-activated the debate over an international binding agreement on competition included academics and, more importantly, EU officials, primarily from the Directorate-General for Competition. The issue was a creature of the EU bureaucracy, and it was initially put forward for two main reasons: (i) due to the belief that the EU model for the regulation of competition should be expanded and applied on a global basis; and (ii) so as to open up international markets for EU companies (market access goal). Another two possible driving forces behind the persistence of the EU as regards the adoption of a WTO competition agreement may be put forward: the attempt of the EU at the time to limit the expansion of the application of competition rules by the United States in an extraterritorial manner; and the desire of the EU bureaucracy to slow down agricultural reform at the WTO, an issue of major importance for developing countries. All these arguments are further discussed in the remaining part of this section.

6.2.2 *Expansion of the EU model on a global scale*

The most profound reason behind EU support for the adoption of an international binding agreement on competition was the fact that the EU itself had successfully met the challenge of creating an effective competition framework that was applied in all its Member States. In the context of the EU, competition law and policy had been used to facilitate the development of intraregional trade. Thus, given this experience it is no surprise that the EU was the leading proponent of the idea to adopt a multilateral competition agreement.[53]

The aim of expanding the EU approach to multilateral agreements on competition is also reflected in the Communication that the former Commissioners Brittan and Van Miert addressed to the Council in

[52] See UNICE (1999), *Preliminary UNICE Comments on the Commission Discussion Paper: Trade and Competition: WTO Framework on Competition Rules*, UNICE Paper No. 1/30/1.

[53] See Fox (1997), *supra* n. 42 at 4–10, where the author discusses the analogy between the EU experience in the use of competition rules in a wider trade context and the possible operation of competition rules in an international context.

1996, in the context of the negotiations on the issue at the WTO. The Commissioners noted that 'enhanced commitment to competition policy enforcement would strengthen the trading system along the lines of our legal systems and market economies, of which competition law is a basic feature'.[54] Along the same lines, it has been argued in the political science literature that, in view of its own experience with the successful development of a common market composed of a number of sovereign states, the EU has been far more pro-multilateralist than other countries, and especially than the United States. According to Higgott, 'Europe, in theory if not always in practice, exhibits a stronger normative, some would say "post-modern" attitude towards multilateral governance structures developing constitutional and regulatory frameworks that increasingly transcend the nation state'.[55]

6.2.3 EU pursued inclusion of competition agreement within the WTO in order to secure market access for its firms to other national markets

Apart from the ideal of a single universal market where competition would be used as a way of avoiding distortions in the market caused by private firms, another clear motive behind the EU's persistence in the mid-1990s in attempts to include competition provisions in a multilateral agreement was its desire to secure market access for European businesses in third countries. Market access was a priority for the Commission at the time and this is clearly expressed in a Memorandum issued by the Commission in 1996:

> Much of the prosperity and job creation in Europe depends on foreign trade and investment. The European Commission is therefore determined to pursue a more active market opening strategy for the benefit of the European exporters, who face a huge number of trade barriers in foreign markets. We are entitled to demand that our trading partners respect their international commitments: a deal is a deal. Our market is open and we expect others to open theirs also.[56]

[54] See European Commission (1996), *Communication to the Council on an International Framework of Competition Rules*, COM(96)284.

[55] R. Higgott (2005), *The Theory and Practice of Global and Regional Governance: Accommodating American Exceptionalism and European Pluralism*, GARNET Working Paper No. 01/05, at 10.

[56] See European Commission (1996), *How a Unified Strategy Can Help European Business: Background Note on the Market Access Strategy*, MEMO/96/108. In order to implement this goal, the Commission created a database which lists the trade barriers in

Lack of competition law in general, or lack of effective enforcement of competition law in national markets where European firms wanted to do business, was considered to be one of the trade barriers that could obstruct EU firms. Hence, the attempts to adopt a multilateral agreement on competition was part of the Community's strategy on market access: 'anti-competitive practices are keeping our firms out of third country markets but they cannot, in the absence of proper enforcement measures in those third markets, be tackled effectively without international rules'.[57]

It follows that, behind the apparently 'romantic' motivation of the EU to expand its successful EU model on a global level, lay a major strategic goal of the EU bureaucracy, namely offering EU businesses the opportunity to expand their operation into new markets.[58]

6.2.4 *Multilateral agreement in order to avoid conflicts in the enforcement of competition law and weaken the effect of extraterritorial application of US laws*

Another reason put forward by the Commission in support of the inclusion of competition within the WTO framework was the avoidance of conflicts in the enforcement of competition rules by multiple states. According to the Commission, 'convergence and conflict avoidance would also increase the legal security of firms operating in different jurisdictions, as well as reduce their costs of compliance with competition laws'.[59]

This is obviously a rational argument, particularly when one considers the discussion developed in earlier chapters concerning the multijurisdictional review of mergers and, most importantly, the extraterritorial application of competition rules (by the United States). It should be pointed out that from the beginning of the Clinton Presidency, the United States was much more aggressive in the pursuit of antitrust violations in comparison to the Reagan and Bush administrations.[60] This was an issue of major concern among EU officials, who felt that it could lead to extensive extraterritorial application by the US antitrust authorities.

different regions and states of the world, available at http://mkaccdb.eu.int/ (last visited on 2 December 2009).

57 See European Commission (1996), *supra* n. 54.

58 This argument was mentioned by two interviewees, a European Commission official and an EU practitioner (Brussels, 20 and 21 July 2003, respectively).

59 See European Commission (1996), *supra* n. 54.

60 See R.E. Litan and C. Shapiro (2001), *Antitrust Policy during the Clinton Administration*, Competition Policy Centre, University of California Working Paper No. CPC01–22, at 19.

In fact, the intentions of US officials to expand the scope of extraterritorial application of antitrust rules became apparent with the *Pilkington* case in 1994, where the basis of US intervention was harm to US exporters rather than to US consumers.[61] According to an EU official who participated in the WTO negotiations on competition, by proposing a WTO agreement on competition, the EU attempted to limit the extraterritorial enforcement of the competition rules by the United States.[62] Officially, this concern was also expressed in the Communication of the Commission to the Council, in which the Commission stated that 'enhanced international cooperation would limit competition authorities' need to resort to extraterritorial action. There are compelling advantages to solving problems through cooperation, especially if such cooperation improves the likelihood that the anticompetitive behaviour can be eliminated'.[63]

It follows that the EU at the time preferred cooperation over extraterritoriality. One should remember, however, that in contrast to the United States where extraterritorial application of competition rules was already established in the 1940s, and despite the attempts of the European Commission since the 1980s to apply the effects doctrine, the EU's ability to apply competition rules extraterritorially was relatively limited by the decisions of the ECJ.[64]

6.2.5 Proposal for an agreement on competition as a way of avoiding reforms on agriculture

A final correlated scenario worth mentioning is that the EU sought to add the Singapore issues, and consequently competition, to the WTO agenda in order to slow down agricultural reform at the WTO.[65] This argument is based on the assumption that the EU, being aware that developing countries would not agree to the inclusion of these issues in the WTO framework, would have an extra bargaining chip in order to satisfy the very

[61] The case related to allegations that Pilkington Plc established a network of restrictive distribution agreements impeding the market access of US companies to the UK and other national glassware markets. See *United States* v. *Pilkington plc*, 1994–2 Trade Cas. (CCH) 70842.

[62] 'At the time, Joel Klein would have enforced section 1 of Sherman Act all over the world'. Interview with European Commission official (Brussels, 21 July 2003).

[63] See European Commission (1996), *supra* n. 54 at 5.

[64] See the discussion on extraterritoriality in Chapter 3.

[65] See S. Woolcock (2004), *The Singapore Issues in Cancun: A Failed Negotiation Ploy or a Litmus Test for Global Governance?*, LSE Working Paper, available at www2.lse.ac.uk/internationalRelations/centresandunits/ITPU/docs/woolcocksingaporeissues.pdf (last

strong lobby of agricultural producers in several EU states, on the one hand,[66] and resist the pressure of developing countries for extensive liberalisation of the agricultural sector, on the other.[67]

6.2.6 Development of the EU proposal in the context of the work of the working group on trade and competition

Initially, the position of the EU reflected the ideas contained in the report of the group of experts and the subsequent Communication of the Commission to the Council. Thus, in its first submission, the EU proposed that the working group on trade and competition should focus on the following issues:

(i) examination of anticompetitive practices that may have an effect on international trade;
(ii) examination of the feasibility of a commitment by all WTO members to adopt competition rules;
(iii) examination of the way that the WTO could contribute to the strengthening of cooperation among its member states;
(iv) examination of possible core principles that could be adopted at the international level; and
(v) examination, in a second stage, of the extent to which the WTO dispute settlement rules could be applied in order to ensure compliance with the contemplated agreement on competition.[68]

In subsequent submissions, the EU elaborated on these proposals. In particular, with regard to substantive provisions, the EU noted that priority should be given to the examination of business practices which have a foreclosure effect (and which would therefore negatively affect consumer welfare in the country where the practice is being implemented),

visited on 2 December 2009). This point was also raised by an EU practitioner interviewee (Brussels, 21 July 2003). A similar point has been raised by De Bievre, who claims that through its demands on regulatory issues, including competition, the EU attempted to balance future market access concessions on agriculture. D. De Bievre (2006), 'The EU Regulatory Trade Agenda and the Quest for WTO Enforcement' 13(6) *Journal of European Public Policy* 851, at 852.

[66] See e.g., C. Daugbjerg (1999), 'Reforming the CAP: Policy Networks and Broader Institutional Structures' 37(3) *Journal of Common Market Studies* 407.

[67] See S. Laird, R. Peters and D. Vanzetti (2004), *Southern Discomfort: Agricultural Policies, Trade and Poverty*, Centre for Research in Economic Development and International Trade, University of Nottingham Working Paper No. 04/02.

[68] See Communication from the European Community and its Member States of 11 June 2007, WT/WTGTCP/W/1, at 4–6.

and which, at the same time, affect the legitimate interests of the country whose producers are being denied equality of competitive opportunities. According to the EU these practices included horizontal agreements, certain abuses of dominant position, vertical restraints and mergers.[69]

By 1999, and in view of the resistance by both the United States and developing countries to the possible adoption of a comprehensive competition agreement,[70] the EU representatives narrowed the scope of their proposal. This is reflected in their acceptance that the use of the dispute settlement mechanism in competition cases would not be appropriate, at least for the examination of individual cases.[71] At this point, it seems that the EU representatives began to depart from the views of Sir Leon Brittan, who at an OECD conference in the same year had stated that:

> A WTO Agreement on competition would have no added value unless it was binding on governments. Even if there was consensus on a list of substantive rules, these would have no teeth or credibility if they remained purely 'paper' obligations. I am therefore convinced that the commitments to be included in a multilateral competition agreement should be subject to WTO dispute settlement.[72]

In 1999 the EU further proposed that a possible WTO agreement on competition should include three main elements: [73]

[69] See Communication from the European Community and its Member States of 5 March 1998, WT/WTGTCP/W/62.

[70] See 6.3.1 and 6.3.2 *infra*.

[71] According to the EU's submission, 'Dispute settlement modalities will need to be further considered once there is greater clarity about the scope of the commitments to be assumed under a WTO agreement so that they are well adapted to the specifics of competition law. In any event, there should be no dispute settlement review of individual decisions'. See Communication from the European Community and its Member States of 12 July 1999, WT/WTGTCP/W/130, at 6, which was submitted one month after the speech of Brittan. See also Communication from the European Community and its Member States of 29 May 1999, WT/WTGTCP/W/115, at 11, where the EU notes that 'A WTO agreement could therefore establish a basic framework of rules, relating to the adoption and enforcement of domestic competition law, and provisions on cooperation among WTO Members. It would not at all be envisaged that the WTO should develop any powers of investigation or enforcement on anticompetitive practices. The commitments assumed under the multilateral framework will be incorporated in the domestic competition law of WTO Members'.

[72] See L. Brittan (1999), 'The Need for a Multilateral Framework of Competition Rules', paper presented at the OECD Conference on Trade and Competition, Paris, 29–30 June 1999, in OECD (1999), *Trade and Competition Policies: Exploring the Ways Forward* (Paris: OECD) 32, at 36.

[73] See Communication WT/130, *supra* n. 71.

(1) Core principles and rules on competition law and its enforcement which would be incorporated in the domestic legislation of WTO members. With regard to the core principles, the EU proposed that the WTO principles of non-discrimination and transparency should be applied to competition law.[74]

(2) A specific focus on anticompetitive practices with a significant impact on international trade and investment.[75] According to the EU, priority should be given to hard-core cartels. It was also accepted that in cases concerning vertical restraints and abuses of a dominant position there was a need for a case-specific evaluation, and thus the adoption of general rules on competition in the context of the WTO would be too rigid. The EU took the view that with regard to such practices, further cooperation and exchange of experiences between the WTO members would be needed. Such cooperation was also considered important for the review of multijurisdictional mergers and export cartels.[76] Even though the EU never pursued officially at the WTO the inclusion of vertical restraints, abuse of dominance and mergers in a possible WTO competition agreement, the inclusion of such practices had been proposed by the group of experts back in 1995, but by 1999 it was clear that inclusion of such practices[77] could not survive the WTO negotiations.

(3) Modalities of international cooperation. Such cooperation should have, according to the EU, a dual aim. The first was to provide technical assistance to countries that had recently enacted competition laws or were in the process of enacting such laws. This position reflected to a certain extent the concerns expressed by a number of developing countries about the viability of competition law at the national as well as international level when no technical assistance was provided by rich industrialised countries. In this context the EU took the view that this could include a framework to facilitate the exchange of experiences and information on competition law and its enforcement, voluntary peer reviews, and the possibility of periodic reports on global trends in competition law and policy. Secondly, the EU proposed that cooperation modalities utilised under enforcement cooperation agreements should also be included in a WTO competition agreement.

[74] See Communication WT/115, *supra* n. 71 at 11.

[75] See Communication WT/130, *supra* n. 71 at 4. [76] *Ibid.*

[77] See European Commission (1996), *supra* n. 54, Annex, and Communication WT/62 *supra* n. 69, in which the EU proposes the examination of the impact of such agreements.

These modalities, examined in some detail in Chapter 3, include the notification of cases, consultations and exchanges of non-confidential information. The EU also proposed that positive comity could be included in a possible agreement, but noted that on such an occasion the provision on positive comity would be applied in a discretionary manner by the member countries and thus would not be binding.[78]

Hence, by 1999, the EU had submitted a minimal proposal for a competition agreement within the WTO framework. However, the reception of this proposal was never tested, as the talks at the Seattle Ministerial Conference were suspended amidst very serious street protests.[79] Following this development, the EU continued to work on the competition agenda; however, it also acknowledged the difficulties concerning the adoption of an agreement due to the widespread concerns expressed by a number of industrialised and developing countries. In its submission to the working group in 2000, the EU clearly expressed these uncertainties:

> the decision on whether to launch negotiations on competition is essentially political in nature, and as such, does not correspond to this Working Group, whose mandate is exploratory and analytical; …the elements of a possible future WTO agreement on competition could only be determined as a result of multilateral negotiations and on the basis of input from all WTO Members. The elements mentioned in this paper are, therefore, no more than our current ideas about the possible architecture of a WTO competition agreement. We wish moreover to acknowledge that our thinking on many of these issues is influenced by the contributions made by many countries – both developed and developing – to substantive discussions in this Working Group.[80]

In this submission, the EU repeated its support for the adoption of an agreement on competition and its position that such an agreement should include the three main elements discussed prior to the Seattle Conference: core principles on domestic competition law and policy, modalities for international cooperation, and support for the progressive reinforcement of competition law and institutions in developing countries.[81]

[78] Communication WT/62 *supra* n. 69.

[79] See 'The new trade war', *Economist*, 2 December 1999.

[80] See Communication from the European Community and its Member States of 25 September 2000, WT/WTGTCP/W/152, at 10–12, in which the EU expresses its support for the establishment of enforcement institutions in developing countries and relevant technical assistance for capacity building.

[81] *Ibid*. For a synopsis of the EU proposals, see also I.G. Bercero and S. Amarasinha (2001), 'Moving the Trade and Competition Debate Forward' 4(3) *Journal of International Economic Law* 481.

In another submission in 2000, the EU attempted to highlight the development benefits of competition law and policy.[82] It was clear by now that developing countries had to be persuaded that competition law and policy in general, and competition provisions in the WTO context in particular, would benefit or at least would not harm these countries. Thus, the concepts of flexibility and progressivity were further discussed.[83] It seems that by these concepts the EU returned to the building-block approach that was first recommended by the group of experts in 1995: it noted in this submission that it had not proposed that a prospective agreement should be applied equally and instantly to all WTO members. Instead, the EU suggested that, in particular with regard to developing and least developed countries, the adoption and enforcement of competition rules and the subsequent participation in a future agreement 'should be of a progressive and flexible nature'.[84]

6.2.7 *From Doha to Cancun*

The Doha Declaration, issued at the conclusion of the Doha Ministerial Conference in 2001, put the discussions into context. According to the Declaration, member states 'agree that negotiations will take place … on the basis of a decision to be taken, by explicit consensus, at that Session on modalities of negotiations'.[85] Hence, despite the contrary opinion of the EU representatives, it was agreed that the issue was not mature enough to be negotiated immediately. On the other hand, it left the issue open to be discussed after the next Ministerial Conference in Cancun, if all the members would agree on that, and set out the particular issues that the working group should further discuss.

According to paragraph 23 of the Doha Declaration, the working group should focus its work on four main issues: (i) the examination of core principles, with an emphasis on non-discrimination, transparency and procedural fairness; (ii) further examination of the types of discretionary cooperation between the member states (which is linked to the

[82] See Communication from the European Community and its Member States of 8 June 2000, WT/WTGTCP/W/140, esp. at 2–4.

[83] The EU first referred to these concepts in 1997. See Communication from the European Community and its Member States of 24 November 1997, WT/WTGTCP/W/45.

[84] See Communication WT/140, *supra* n. 82 at 7. On this matter, see also OECD Joint Group on Trade and Competition (2001), *The Role of 'Special and Differential Treatment' at the Trade, Competition and Development Interface*, OECD COM/TD/DAFFE/CLP(2001)21 final.

[85] See Doha Declaration, *supra* n. 25 para. 23.

practice of the enforcement cooperation agreements); (iii) further work should be carried out in the field of hard-core cartels, which was the only anticompetitive practice discussed by the working group that was put forward to be part of a possible agreement; and most importantly, (iv) special consideration should be given to developing countries. The notion of flexibility was included in the text to make it clear that developing countries would be given the time to develop their own competition policies, something that was in compliance with the Doha Round, which was the Development Round.

The Doha Declaration[86] also stressed the need for technical assistance to be offered to developing countries in order to evaluate the implications of closer cooperation at the multilateral level for their own development policies and objectives, and to establish institutions that could effectively enforce competition law. It was also noted that, on the basis of this commitment, the working group should cooperate with other international institutions, with particular reference to UNCTAD, as the international organisation most closely associated with developing countries. Finally, the Declaration recognised the importance of regional and bilateral agreements, through which technical assistance to developing and least developed states would be provided.

Thus, the Doha Declaration asserted in a more formal manner that some kind of minimal agreement on competition could be negotiated. It came as a surprise that the United States, which had traditionally opposed the adoption of any binding agreement at the multilateral level, gave its consent to the possible inclusion of competition in the agenda of the next round of negotiations. On the other hand, the Declaration also reflected the serious concerns that had been expressed by developing countries over the possible adoption of an agreement on competition.[87]

These concerns were confirmed during the negotiations that took place on the way to and during the Cancun Ministerial Conference. Through its submissions to the working group, the EU continued to support the inclusion of competition in the WTO agreement and elaborated on the topics provided by the Doha Declaration.[88] A major disagreement arose in Cancun, however, and the inclusion of the Singapore issues, along with

[86] *Ibid.* para. 24. [87] See 6.3.2 *infra*.

[88] See Communications from the European Community and its Member States of 22 April 2002, WT/WTGTCP/W/184 on international cooperation; of 1 July 2002, WT/WTGTCP/W/193 on hard-core cartels; of 19 November 2002, WT/WTGTCP/W/222 on core principles; and of 26 June 2003, WT/WTGTCP/W/234 on progressiveness and flexibility.

the elimination of export agricultural subsidies, were the main concerns of developing countries. As reported at the time, 'the European Union ... denied it had ever promised to get rid of export subsidies. Led by India, many poor countries denied that they ever signed up for talks on new rules [on the Singapore issues]'.[89]

Thus, no agreement was reached and finally, as already noted, discussions on competition were withdrawn from the agenda in July 2004. Since then, the issue of competition law and policy has not been (formally) discussed at the WTO.

6.3 Reasons that led to the failure of the EU proposal

The main reason behind the failure of the EU proposal for the adoption of a competition agreement within the WTO context was the opposition of the United States and a number of developing countries on this issue.

6.3.1 Resistance by the United States

The first major reason for the failure of the EU's proposal for a WTO agreement on competition was the traditional opposition of the United States to the adoption of a multilateral competition agreement. As noted above, both the talks in 1925 at the League of Nations and in 1947 on the Havana Charter failed, in the final analysis, as a result of US opposition, and this was to a certain extent repeated in the context of the WTO talks in the mid-1990s and early 2000s. As stated in the first submission of the United States to the WTO working group:

> although the United States has stated on other occasions, and continues to believe, that there is not the degree of consensus today that would support negotiation in the WTO of constructive competition policy disciplines, the proposed work programme is intended to foster among Member countries a common understanding of the relationship of competition matters to the WTO framework and to be neutral regarding any conclusions that may be reached.[90]

The reasons behind this position were restated a couple of years later by Joel Klein. During a speech at the OECD, Klein made it clear that a WTO agreement on competition could not be concluded, since there was

[89] 'New rules' relate to the Singapore issues, including competition. See 'The WTO under fire', *Economist*, 18 September 2003.

[90] See Communication of the United States of 19 June 1997, WT/WGTCP/W/6, at 4.

still a lack of experience on the part of developing countries concerning competition law and policy. He also re-emphasised the US concern that using the WTO dispute settlement mechanism to review competition cases would entail the danger of politicising the application of competition rules, as it 'would necessarily involve the WTO in second-guessing prosecutorial decision-making in complex evidentiary contexts – a task in which the WTO has no experience and for which it is not suited'.[91] Instead, the United States would support the adoption of bilateral enforcement cooperation agreements (a strategy discussed in Chapter 3), while attempting to provide developing countries with technical assistance in this field.[92]

The US approach was to a large extent realistic, at least in view of the fact that a competition culture has not emerged at the international level. In fact, as noted in earlier chapters, there are still a number of elements that may have an influence on the particular application of competition law at the domestic level and such elements may vary considerably from state to state. It has also been pointed out that many countries only enacted a competition law in the last fifteen years or so, and this obviously means that there is little experience in the application of the rules in these countries.

That said, it should also be pointed out that the main reason behind the US opposition to the possibility of adopting a binding multilateral agreement on competition is the so-called 'hegemonic' stance that has characterised the country's external policy in various fields of international law, competition law included.[93] As has been shown in earlier chapters, the United States has been the most regular promoter of extraterritoriality in the enforcement of its antitrust laws. Such extraterritorial application of US law is complemented by the application of section 301 of the 1994 Trade Act, according to which the United States has the right to retaliate in cases where foreign countries follow policies which, among other things, lead to 'toleration of systematic anticompetitive practices' by a firm in the market of the foreign country, and which result in the inability of US firms to enter this

[91] See J.I. Klein (1999), 'A Reality Check on Antitrust Rules in the World Trade Organization, and a Practical Way Forward on International Antitrust', speech delivered at OECD Conference on Trade and Competition, Paris, 29–30 June 1999, in OECD, *Trade and Competition Rules: Exploring the Ways Forward* (Paris: OECD) 37, at 41–2.

[92] *Ibid.* See also Communication from the United States of 25 May 1999, WT/WGTCP/W/116, in which cooperation through regional settings such as the NAFTA and non-binding multilateral cooperation through the OECD are also mentioned.

[93] See M. Byers and G. Nolte (2003), *United States Hegemony and the Foundations of International Law* (Cambridge University Press).

particular market.[94] Put differently and with regard to the current debate, this position reflects the traditional perception in the United States that US antitrust law is superior to other national laws, and thus, until other countries reach the US level of competition enforcement, national US competition law should be applied to resolve situations where US firms are harmed due to inefficient enforcement of national competition laws by other countries. This hypothesis is further examined in the next section.

(i) Establishment of ICPAC and the introduction of a 'new global initiative'

It was against this background that the International Competition Policy Advisory Committee (ICPAC) was set up in November 1997 by the (then) Attorney General Janet Reno and Joel Klein. The Committee consisted of politicians, academics and business representatives with legal and economic backgrounds.[95] In comparison to the composition of the relevant group of experts that emerged in Europe in the 1990s, which introduced the idea of a multilateral regime, the Committee was more inclusive as it included business representatives and economists. The aim of the Committee was threefold: to review the effect of multijurisdictional mergers; to examine the relationship between trade law and competition law; and to evaluate the prospects of further international cooperation on competition.[96]

ICPAC produced a very comprehensive report in 2000 that contributed significantly to the current debate on multilateralism in the field of competition; indeed, it was an important factor leading to the establishment of the International Competition Network.[97] With regard to the possible inclusion of competition within the WTO context, the report simply repeated the traditional US concerns on the necessity of such an

[94] For an analysis of s. 301, see M. Dabbah (2003), *The Internationalisation of Antitrust Policy* (Cambridge University Press) 225–7. The author notes nonetheless that, in the United States, s. 301 has never been used in competition cases, and points out that the United States uses this legal instrument as a medium to negotiate the removal of unfair trade practices with the authorities of other countries. See *ibid.* at 226.

[95] International Competition Policy Advisory Committee (2000), *ICPAC Final Report to the Attorney General and the Assistant Attorney General for Antitrust* (hereinafter 'ICPAC Report'), Annex 1-B, available at www.usdoj.gov/atr/icpac/finalreport.htm (last visited on 2 December 2009).

[96] See M.E. Janow and C.R. Lewis (2001), 'International Antitrust and the Global Economy: Perspectives on the Final Report and Recommendations of the International Competition Policy Advisory Committee to the Attorney General and the Assistant Attorney General for Antitrust' 24(1) *World Competition* 3.

[97] See 6.4 *infra*.

agreement. It expressed the opinion that the WTO should not develop competition rules under its umbrella, and concluded that:

> while recognizing that in some instances it may not be a fully satisfactory result, the Advisory Committee believes that national authorities are best suited to address anticompetitive practices of private firms that are occurring on their territory. If anticompetitive and market blocking practices are occurring in a jurisdiction that does not have a competition authority or that authority is unable or unwilling to remedy the problem, then the harmed nation may be able to apply its own laws in an extraterritorial fashion.[98]

The report also summarised the reasons which lead to the US rejection of the proposal for a competition agreement at the WTO. According to its drafters, such an agreement would lead to the potential intrusion of WTO dispute settlement panels into domestic regulatory practices, a concern regularly asserted by US officials. It nonetheless went on to note that a WTO competition agreement would be inappropriate for another two reasons: first, because of the inappropriateness of obliging countries to adopt competition laws; and secondly, because such an agreement could also lead to the distortion of competition standards due to the *quid pro quo* nature of the WTO negotiations.[99]

As to the former, it could be argued that such an argument is, at first sight, rather puzzling since the United States has been the leader in the development of international economic laws in the GATT and WTO system and the subsequent obligations created for the participating countries. In addition, it has been noted in the context of the discussion on bilateral trade agreements that some of the US agreements include a commitment undertaken by the signing countries that they will have a competition law in place. On the other hand, it has to be noted that this position of the United States also reflects the position of a number of developing countries, which by the end of the 1990s questioned not only the value of such an agreement, but also the necessity of domestic competition rules.[100] Thus, for different reasons, both the United States and developing countries seemed to be pursuing the same aim.[101]

[98] See ICPAC Report, *supra* n. 95 at 278–9.

[99] 'Various concerns animate the Advisory Committee's scepticism toward competition rules at the WTO, including the possible distortion of competition standards through the *quid pro quo* nature of WTO negotiations; the potential intrusion of WTO dispute settlement panels into domestic regulatory practices; and the inappropriateness of obliging countries to adopt competition laws.' See ICPAC Report, *supra* n. 95 at 278.

[100] See 6.3.1 *infra*.

[101] It is noteworthy that a European Commission officialinterviewee (Brussels, 15 November 2007) argued that in the process of the negotiations the United States 'was hiding behind the position of the developing countries'.

As to the latter, it could be argued that along with concerns over the operation of the dispute settlement mechanism, the assertion that a possible WTO agreement could lead to the distortion of antitrust standards lies at the heart of the debate on competition in the WTO context. As seen in Chapter 2, an operational US competition regime has been in place for more than 110 years. This regime is probably the most comprehensive in the world. US competition analysis is predominantly based on efficiency concerns and still differs to a certain degree from competition enforcement within the EU.[102] In relation to developing countries which have just embarked on the adoption and application of competition law and policy, such differences are chaotic.

In this connection, Calvani notes that the reluctance of the United States to accept the inclusion of competition law in a binding multilateral agreement, also expressed in the ICPAC Report, reflects the concern of politicians and certain academics in the United States that compromises at the WTO could lead to 'populist antitrust divorced from economic underpinnings',[103] in the sense that the *quid pro quo* nature of the negotiations at the WTO entailed the risk of accepting principles not directly related to the 'proper function' of competition law, in the sense in which the United States understands the notion of 'proper function'.

To this end, the ICPAC proposed the creation of 'a new global initiative' to act as a forum where developed and developing countries, as well as non-governmental organisations and business representatives, could exchange their views and experiences on anti-cartel enforcement, merger review, analytical tools, enforcement cooperation, technical assistance, and any other relevant issue.[104] This proposal was instrumental in the establishment of the ICN, discussed below.

(ii) Paradox in Doha

US policy has been consistent in its opposition to the inclusion of competition law within the WTO framework. It has also been observed that towards the end of the 1990s, this position remained unchanged among competition officials in the United States. That said, in Doha, the US trade representatives signed the Conference Declaration, which provided for

[102] For a recent review of the current debate on the remaining differences between the US and EU competition laws, see also W. Kolasky (2004), 'What is Competition? A Comparison of US and Europe Perspectives' 49 (1/2) *Antitrust Bulletin* 29.

[103] See T. Calvani (2005), 'Conflict, Cooperation, and Convergence in International Competition' 72 *Antitrust Law Journal* 1127, at 1133.

[104] See ICPAC Report, *supra* n. 95 at 224.

negotiations on particular competition issues, and this decision has been one of the most fascinating and at the same time unexpected incidents in the development of the negotiations on competition at the WTO.

In fact, the first signs of a shift of the US trade administration on this issue became apparent in July 2001 when Robert Zoellick, the US chief negotiator, suggested that the United States would be ready to support the application of core principles of transparency, non-discrimination and procedural fairness to competition; he also emphasised that the United States supported further technical assistance and capacity building projects in developing countries.[105] He also noted that the United States was working to understand more clearly the EU proposal and was in discussions with the EU about possible ways in which the EU could accommodate the concerns of the United States and other WTO members.[106] Zoellick went on to express his concerns about the way that obligations stemming from the application of core principles of competition law would be addressed, and noted that it was not clear whether the EU was also proposing the use of the dispute settlement mechanism in antitrust cases.[107]

Four months later in Doha, the United States gave its consent not only to the inclusion of the core principles in the final Declaration, but also to the inclusion of the issue of hard-core cartels. The US community of experts was considerably surprised by this development, as reflected in the comments that the Antitrust Division of the American Bar Association (ABA) submitted to the US trade representatives, in which, on the basis of the reasons already expressed by Klein and the ICPAC Report, the ABA urged the US trade representatives to express strong reservations regarding the proposals for a WTO competition framework.[108]

It is difficult to interpret the reasons that led the United States to accept competition policy as a possible issue for negotiations in Doha. Following the Doha Declaration, Zoellick made clear in a letter to the US Congress that the aim of US strategy in this field was only to develop, through the working group on trade and competition, a common culture on

[105] See 'Statement of US Trade Representative Robert B. Zoellick on US–EU efforts to launch a global round of trade negotiations', Press Release of 17 July 2001, available at http://ustraderep.gov/Document_Library/Press_Releases/2001/July/Statement_of_US_Trade_Representative_Robert_B_Zoellick_on_US-EU_Efforts_to_Launch_a_Global_Round_of_Trade_Negotiations.html (last visited on 2 December 2009).

[106] *Ibid.* [107] *Ibid.*

[108] See ABA Antitrust Division (2003), 'Comments and Recommendations on the Competition Elements of the Doha Declaration', at 16, available at www.abanet.org/antitrust/at-comments/2003/05–03/doha.pdf (last visited on 2 December 2009).

competition among WTO members, for instance through a peer review mechanism. He further stated that the United States intended to ensure that the work at the WTO would not undermine US antitrust laws and enforcement, and that the decisions of the US authorities would not be subject to the WTO dispute settlement mechanism.[109] However, this does not explain why and how paragraphs 23–5 of the Doha Declaration were accepted by the US representatives.

Various suggestions may be put forward in relation to this development. It may be argued, for instance, that the United States accepted the competition-related part of the Declaration in the context of the broader negotiations at the WTO, in view of the fact that by this time it had become obvious that developing countries would not support the inclusion of competition in the list of WTO agreements. In particular, it could be suggested that the United States supported the prospect of a minimal agreement on competition in order to be able to withdraw such support later on in the context of negotiations on issues of more importance to the United States. If accurate, this line of argument would demonstrate the correctness of the concern of competition experts in the United States that the WTO is not the right forum for competition policy, as competition is only one of the many 'bargaining chips' on the table of discussions.[110]

On the other hand, it should be kept in mind that the Doha Round took place only two months after September 11, 2001, and as has been well documented, Robert Zoellick used the occasion to propose further trade liberalisation at the WTO, with the inclusion of new issues on the agenda of negotiations, and thus went on even to accept the prospect of a possible minimal agreement on competition.[111]

In any event, the fact that competition was included in the Doha Declaration is an indication that in the United States, the trade administration is more sympathetic to the possibility of adopting competition rules in the WTO than the antitrust administration (which has consistently opposed it). Nonetheless, there have been no tensions as yet apparent from this divergence, since competition policy was finally withdrawn from the negotiations after the collapse of the talks in Cancun.

[109] See 'Zoellick notifies Congress of progress on global trade talks', Press Release of 5 November 2002, available at www.ustr.gov.

[110] This was also expressed during an interview with a US competition practitioner (Brussels, 21 July 2003).

[111] E. Zedillo (2006), 'The WTO's Biggest Problem at 10: Surviving the Doha Round', speech delivered at the conference WTO at 10: Governance, Dispute Settlement and Developing Countries, Columbia University, 7 April 2006, at 3, available at www.ycsg.

6.3.2 *Coordinated resistance by developing countries*

When Lord Brittan introduced his proposal for inclusion of competition law and policy in the global trading system, the position of developing countries was not much of a concern. In fact, as described by Peter Carl Mogens, former Director-General of the Directorate-General for Trade, during the Punta Del Este Conference of 1986, which launched the Uruguay Round, it was the (participating) developing countries that suggested multilateral negotiations on competition – proposal was rejected by the industrialised countries.[112]

This position was reversed ten years later at the Singapore Ministerial Conference, when the first signs of opposition from developing countries to the possible adoption of a competition agreement became apparent. Since then, developing countries have successfully maintained a common front on a number of issues on the trade agenda, including competition policy, and resisted negotiating on these issues not only in Seattle but also during the Ministerial Conferences in Doha and Cancun.[113]

In fact, until the late 1990s only a handful of developing countries had actively participated in the GATT and WTO talks, with the more delicate negotiations largely dominated by the 'QUAD'.[114] This situation began to change at the Singapore Ministerial Conference in 1996, and the change became apparent in a dramatic way in the 1999 WTO Ministerial Conference in Seattle, where developing countries demonstrated coordinated and concerted negotiating leverage through the formation of a number of groups of countries that dealt with particular policy issues.

yale.edu/center/forms/doha.pdf (last visited on 2 December 2009), where the author notes that following the 9/11 events, Zoellick reiterated that 'The international market economy – of which trade and the WTO are vital parts – offers an antidote to this violent rejectionism. Trade is about more than economic efficiency; it reflects a system of values: openness, peaceful exchange, opportunity, inclusiveness and integration, mutual gains through interchange, freedom of choice, appreciation of differences, governance through agreed rules, and a hope for betterment for all peoples and lands'.

112 See P.C. Mogens (2001), 'Towards Basic Rules on Trade Related Competition Policy', speech delivered in Brussels, 2 March 2001, available at http://trade.ec.europa.eu/doclib/docs/2004/november/tradoc_120130.pdf (last visited on 2 December 2009).

113 A.R. Young and J. Peterson (2006), 'The EU and the New Trade Politics' 13(6) *Journal of European Public Policy* 795, at 803.

114 The QUAD states are the EU, United States, Canada and Japan. See J.-M. Metzer (2000), 'Seattle: Failure or New Departure?', *OECD Observer*, July 2000, where the author notes that 'Countries such as India, Brazil, Egypt and Morocco, as well as Bangladesh, El Salvador, Tanzania and Jamaica, to name a few, have always participated actively in the work of the GATT and its successor, the WTO'.

One such example is the so-called 'Like Minded Group', initially consisting of eight countries, that aimed to block the inclusion of the Singapore issues in the WTO agenda.[115] Other examples include a number of coalition groups that appeared in Doha and Cancun, such as the African Group, the African, Caribbean and Pacific (ACP) Group, the Least Developed Countries (LDCs) Group, and the Small and Vulnerable Economies Group.[116] These groups pursued a variety of aims at the negotiations, on issues such as agriculture, special and differential treatment, development, and opposition to the inclusion of the Singapore issues on the table of negotiations.[117] Another such example is a coalition called the 'Core Group', which consisted of Latin American and African countries which emerged during the period between Doha and Cancun[118] with the aim of blocking negotiations on the Singapore issues.

With regard to competition in particular, the groups of developing countries which opposed the adoption of a competition law agreement at the WTO was led by India, which expressed its disagreement regarding the adoption of a multilateral competition agreement on various occasions.[119] For instance, in Doha, where competition was included in the final Declaration which provided that negotiations on these issues would start in the next round of negotiations only if all the WTO members consented, Yussuf Hussain Kamal, the Conference chair, issued at the request of India a statement where he clarified that 'in my view, this would give each Member the right to take a position on modalities that would prevent negotiations

[115] The initial members of the coalition were Cuba, Egypt, India, Indonesia, Malaysia, Pakistan, Tanzania and Uganda. These countries were later joined by Dominican Republic, Honduras, Sri Lanka and Zimbabwe, while Jamaica and Kenya also attended the meetings of the Group. For an analysis of the way that the Group operated in the context of the WTO negotiations from 1998 until the Doha Ministerial Conference, see A. Narlikar and J. Odell (2003), 'The Strict Distributive Strategy for a Bargaining Coalition: The Like Minded Group in the World Trade Organization', paper presented at the Conference on Developing Countries and the Trade Negotiation Process, UNCTAD, Geneva, 6–7 November 2003.

[116] See A. Narlikar and D. Tussie (2004), 'The G20 at the Cancun Ministerial: Developing Countries and their Evolving Coalitions in the WTO' 27(7) *The World Economy* 947, at 948–51.

[117] *Ibid.*

[118] The countries which joined this group were Bangladesh, Cuba, Egypt, India, Indonesia, Kenya, Malaysia, Nigeria, Pakistan, Venezuela, Zambia and Zimbabwe.

[119] For an extensive review of the position of India on this matter in relation to the relevant EU position, see P. Holmes, J. Mathis, T.C.A. Anant and S. J. Evenett (2003), 'The EU and India on Competition Policy at the WTO: Is there a Common Ground?' in L.A. Winters and P.S. Mehta (eds.), *Bridging the Differences:Analyses of Five Issues of the WTO Agenda* (Jaipur: CUTS).

from proceeding after the fifth Session of the Ministerial Conference until that Member is prepared to join in an explicit consensus'.[120]

In Cancun, once again developing countries opposed the possible inclusion of competition in the negotiations, and this could be considered the main reason for the collapse of the talks. The Core Group gained support from a number of countries and, on the last day of the meeting, a group of twenty-nine developing countries, including India and China, and with Bangladesh signing on behalf of the LDCs, sent a letter to Pierre Pettigrew, the Facilitator for the Singapore Issues at the Cancun Ministerial Conference, in which they insisted that the Singapore issues should not proceed to negotiation.[121] As described by Narlikar and Tussie, on the final day of the Cancun conference, Botswana, speaking on behalf of the African Union, stated that the Union would not agree to any deal regarding the Singapore issues. Following this statement, South Korea retaliated and stated that it would not accept any deal without an agreement on all four of the Singapore issues, and this therefore became the main reason behind the failure of the talks.[122]

It is thus obvious that developing countries used their bargaining power[123] to block the adoption of even a minimal agreement on competition at the WTO; they did this against the wishes of (in particular) the EU. In this regard, it has been suggested in the political science literature that agreements which are adopted on the basis of the principle of sovereign equality of states enjoy the highest degree of legitimacy.[124] The logic of the GATT/WTO is that, in the negotiations, each member is a sovereign state able to determine for itself whether a proposed agreement is to its advantage, to decide the criteria by which to identify the relevant advantages and disadvantages, and to apply those criteria by the formula that the member considers appropriate.[125]

120 Cited in A. Singh (2003), *Competition and Competition Policy Development in Emerging Markets: International and Developmental Dimensions*, ESRC Working Paper No. 246, at 2.

121 See www.ictsd.org/ministerial/cancun/docs/developing_country_%20letter_SI.pdf (last visited on 2 December 2009).

122 See Narlikar and Tussie (2004), *supra* n. 116 at 950.

123 On discussion of the 'veto power' of the developing countries, which comprise more than 50 per cent of the WTO, see A. Matoo and A. Subramanian (2004), 'The WTO and the Poorest Countries: The Stark Reality' 3(3) *World Trade Review* 385, at 391–2.

124 See R.H. Steinberg (2002), 'In the Shadow of Law or Power? Consensus-based Bargaining and Outcomes in the GATT/WTO' 56(2) *International Organisation* 339, at 361. At the other end of the spectrum, it has also been suggested that powerful states have preferred sovereign equality rules to weighted voting at the GATT/WTO, because they provide incentives and opportunities for collecting the information necessary for a successful agenda-setting process. See Steinberg (2002) *ibid.*

125 See M. Finger and A. Winters (2002), 'Reciprocity in the WTO' in B. Hoekman, A. Mattoo and P. English (eds.), *Development, Trade and the WTO* (World Bank) 50, at 51.

The more balanced allocation of power in international organisations has been already asserted in earlier chapters, in the context of the tendency of bilateral agreements to increase the power of strong industrialised states. As seen in this section, it has been to a certain extent this balance of powers at the WTO which has led to the failure of talks on competition, in view of the opposition of a number of developing countries on the issue. What is more important at this stage, however, is to identify the reasons that led to the opposition by most of the developing countries to the EU proposal for a multilateral agreement on competition under the auspices of the WTO.

As already noted in Chapter 2, developing countries have taken divergent positions as to the necessity of adopting competition rules, and this is despite the fact that international organisations such as the IMF and the World Bank, and states with mature competition regimes such as the United States and the EU, have encouraged developing countries to adopt such laws. Similarly, there are various and divergent approaches as to the usefulness of an international agreement on competition for developing countries, as well as the desirable content of such an agreement from a developing country perspective.[126] Among the various arguments developed in relation to this debate, this section focuses on four main factors that led to the rejection by developing countries of the EU proposal to include a competition agreement within the WTO context.

(i) Developing countries, competition law and industrial policy

The first relevant argument put forward by developing countries against a WTO competition agreement is based on the assumption that competition law and policy in developing countries should include broad industrial policy exceptions. This point was raised by India in the context of the discussions in the working group on trade and competition. In one of its communications, India noted that:

[126] See e.g., Singh (2003), *supra* n. 120; A. Bhattacharjee (2006), 'The Case for a Multilateral Agreement on Competition Policy: A Developing Country Perspective' 9(2) *Journal of International Economic Law* 293; C. Aubert (2003), 'Competition Policy for Countries with Different Development Levels', paper presented at the CEPR Competition Policy in International Markets Workshop, 17–18 October 2003, available at www.cepr.org/meets/wkcn/6/6613/papers/Aubert.pdf (last visited on 2 December 2009); T.W. Hertel, B.M. Hoekman and W. Martin (2002), 'Developing Countries and a New Round of WTO Negotiations' 17(1) *World Bank Research Observer* 113; Hoekman and Holmes (1999), *supra* n. 51.

> developing countries do not yet have the kind of well-developed safety nets that exist in industrial countries to provide for those displaced by import competition. There is thus a greater need to cushion its impact by suitable industrial restructuring measures ..., which would also enable developing countries to embrace greater trade liberalization.[127]

This concern has also been expressed by various scholars. For instance, Singh, looking at the development of East Asian countries, China, as well as Italy and other European countries, has suggested that a combination of competition with cooperation between firms is more likely to increase societal welfare rather than competition alone.[128] Along the same lines, Bhattacharjee notes that with the exception of the United States, all other industrialised countries have for long periods utilised extensive exemptions from the application of competition rules in order to promote social and political objectives, and have moved only progressively towards more efficiency-related objectives.[129]

In fact, the Doha Declaration took these arguments into account by including the notion of flexibility, and the EU would have accepted exemptions as long as such exemptions were clearly set out. However, this line of argument was never developed in a more specific context, due to the withdrawal of the issue from the agenda in 2004. Given the importance of the issue for developing countries, more work would be needed on this issue in the context of any future multilateral talks on competition, as the recent experience of the negotiations has highlighted that certain developing countries have still not come to terms with the concept of competition law or more particularly with the optimal application of competition law.

Along the same lines, the representative of Kenya stressed at Cancun:

> [We] believe that this Ministerial Conference should therefore focus on how to expand the space of understanding of the Singapore Issues and launch a process of improving that understanding. Kenya cannot accept the launching of negotiations on issues that we do not clearly understand and whose implications for our economies have not been assessed. Moreover, although Kenya attaches a lot of importance to technical assistance and capacity building, we are fully convinced this should be provided to enhance understanding of issues involved before negotiations are launched.[130]

[127] See Communication from India of 26 September 2002, WT/WGTCP/W/216.

[128] See Singh (2003), *supra* n. 120 at 14.

[129] See Bhattacharjee (2006), *supra* n. 126 at 316–18.

[130] See Comments by Kenya on the Second Revision of the Draft Cancun Ministerial Text of 14 September 2003, WT/MIN(03)/W/21; see also Declaration of the Group of 77 and China on the Fifth WTO Ministerial Conference, Cancun, Mexico, 10–14 September 2003, at 15, available at www.g77.org/main/docs/FinalG77Decl-22aug-5thWTO.pdf (last visited on 2 December 2009).

(ii) Implementation issues: lack of institutional capacity and need for technical assistance

The above statement by the Kenyan representative, i.e. concerning the need for technical assistance, is another issue raised by a number of developing countries, and relates to the costs that they would have to bear in order to develop efficient enforcement of competition law. This is an issue that has been raised with regard to a number of agreements adopted in the context of the Uruguay Round, such as the agreements on customs valuation, technical standards, sanitary and phytosanitary measures and intellectual property rights. Implementation of all these norms by developing countries requires the purchasing of equipment, the training of people, the establishment of systems of checks and balances, etc.[131]

Finger and Winters have pointed out that, even though these agreements do not go so far as to regulate domestically the issues they regulate at the international level, their content is binding and thus they have significant influence on the behaviour of the contracting parties, which have to frame their national legislation in accordance with the international rules included in the agreements.[132] On the other hand, all these agreements contain technical assistance clauses,[133] according to which industrialised countries should help developing countries with the institutional set-up needed in order to apply the rules that arise from the agreements. Nonetheless, these provisions are not binding, something that has caused complaints by developing countries that industrialised countries have not done much to assist them.[134] In fact, in the field of competition law a number of developing countries have raised concerns that industrialised countries have not in practice offered enough technical assistance, and therefore they are not able to establish institutions that would efficiently enforce competition rules.[135]

In the same context, Hertel *et al.* make reference to similar issues raised with regard to intellectual property rights discussed during the Uruguay Round of negotiations. The authors note that even though there was a

[131] For an evaluation of the costs that developing countries have to bear in order to set up domestic institutions that would apply the measures adopted under the various agreements, see J.M. Finger and Ph. Schuler (2000), 'Implementation of Uruguay Round Commitments: The Development Challenge' 23(4) *The World Economy* 511.

[132] See Finger and Winters (2002), *supra* n. 125 at 51.

[133] See e.g., art. 9 of the WTO Agreement on the Application of Sanitary and Phytosanitary Measures, art. 67 of the TRIPS Agreement, and art. 20(3) of the Agreement on Implementation of Article VII (Customs Valuation).

[134] See Finger and Winters (2002), *supra* n. 125 at 51–2.

[135] Interview with European Commission official (Brussels, 20 July 2003).

final agreement on the issue (the TRIPS Agreement), poor countries have not yet created intellectual property regimes, and most importantly they have not identified the alternative options that could be used to upgrade and enforce their national products, health and safety standards, or to regulate sectors which are subject to market failure.[136] The authors conclude that on such issues, the WTO rules should allow for experimentation and learning and must be coupled with technical assistance to help these countries establish efficient enforcement bodies.[137]

Given that there are still unaddressed issues with regard to the enforcement of rules arising under agreements that have already been adopted in the context of the WTO, further commitments by developing countries on competition enforcement would create more extensive financial costs for them. Moreover, competition law is not a major priority for a number of developing countries which suffer from poverty and significant co-related financial and social problems. Thus, it comes as no surprise that the governments of many of these countries have not been eager to spend part of their limited budget on the enforcement of competition law, and have therefore been extremely reluctant to accept binding WTO provisions on competition.

(iii) Export cartels

Apart from the institutional difficulties faced by these countries and the need for technical assistance, of major concern among the representatives of developing countries has been the fact that export cartels are very often exempted from the application of competition laws of industrialised countries. In a recent study, Levenstein and Suslow found that, of the fifty-five countries that they examined, thirty-four had explicit export cartel exemptions, seventeen had implicit exemptions, while only four of them had no statutory exemptions.[138]

In an export cartel, producers from a country agree to cooperate in order to fix prices or allocate market shares only in a foreign market and not in the market in which they are based. From an economic perspective, there may be instances where export cartels increase the total domestic welfare of the exporting country; nevertheless, at the same time they also decrease total international welfare.[139] This happens because, due to the

[136] Hertel, Hoekman and Martin (2002), *supra* n. 126 at 129. [137] *Ibid.*

[138] See M.C. Levenstein and V. Suslow (2005), 'The Changing International Status of Export Cartel Exemptions' 20 *American University International Law Review* 785, at 806.

[139] See P.S. Crampton and C.L. Witterick (1997), 'Trade Distorting Private Restraints and Market Access: Learning to Walk Before We Run' 24 *Empirica* 53, at 56.

existence of an export cartel, domestic firms become more efficient than they would be if the operation of the cartel had not been exempted from the application of competition law. At the same time, the creation of the cartel may increase prices at an international level, and thus decrease total welfare internationally.

As Fox and Ordover have pointed out, export cartels and the negative impact they have on international trade could easily be nullified if nations would agree to prohibit this practice.[140] This is recognised in a 1996 Commission Communication, in which Brittan and Van Miert noted that 'although such cartels are covered by the legislation of most importing countries, they are hard to tackle due to a lack of information in the importing country. An international agreement to outlaw export cartels would put an end to these "beggar thy neighbour" policies'.[141]

At the WTO, the issue of export cartels arose as one of the most contentious ones. Several developing countries expressed their concern with regard to the negative effects that cartels originating from other (industrialised) countries had on their economies, while other developing countries argued that export cartels should be exempted from the competition rules of developing countries in the context of flexibility and progressiveness that should be offered to them.[142]

The opposition to the possible inclusion of export cartels in a WTO agreement came mainly from the United States, which has been the oldest and most prominent supporter of this type of business practice.[143] In its submissions to the working group, the United States argued that the 'laws of most countries do not reach outbound joint export activities that do not have anticompetitive spillover effects in their home markets, i.e., the

[140] See E.M. Fox and J.A. Ordover (1995), 'The Harmonisation of Trade Law and Competition Law: The Case for Modest Linkages of Law and Limits to Parochial State Action' 19(2) *World Competition Law and Economics* 5, at 18–19. Eleanor Fox has also argued in a later paper that export cartels could be also prohibited under art. 11.1(b) of the Safeguard Agreement, under which states 'shall not seek, take or maintain any voluntary export restraints, orderly marketing arrangements or any other similar measures on the export or the import side', and in art. 11.3 this prohibition is extended to the 'adoption or maintenance by public and private enterprises of non-governmental measures equivalent to those referred to in paragraph 1'. See E. Fox (1999), 'Competition Law and the Millennium Round' 2(4) *Journal of International Economic Law* 665, at 675.

[141] See European Commission (1996), *supra* n. 54.

[142] For a review of the relevant positions taken at the working group on trade and competition, see A. Bhattacharjee (2004), 'Export Cartels: A Developing Country Perspective' 38(2) *Journal of World Trade* 331, at 334–6.

[143] Export cartels have been exempted in the United States from the application of competition rules since 1918 when the Webb-Pomerene Act was enacted. In 2003, there were 153

kind of effects at which antitrust laws are aimed', and went on to suggest that the OECD Recommendation on Hard-Core Cartels should exclude export cartels from its application, as far as such exclusions are transparent and no broader than necessary to achieve their overriding policy objectives.[144]

In view of its earlier commitment to include export cartels in a possible WTO agreement on competition, the EU did not deny that some sort of international mechanism was needed in order to address these practices. Nevertheless, given the consistent US opposition to such a prospect and the fact that, in the EU, export cartels are in practice excluded from the application of competition rules as EU competition rules apply only to practices that have an effect on the trade between the Member States, the EU offered only voluntary international cooperation with regard to export cartels.[145]

As expected, these positions were not welcomed by developing countries. India again, through a submission at the WTO working group on trade and competition, noted that:

> until such time as developed countries are willing to consider the impact of mergers on consumers in foreign countries, to rescind the exemption of export cartels in their competition laws, to give serious consideration to enforcing the UNCTAD set of measures to control RBPs [restrictive business practices], and to extend the benefits of 'positive comity' in competition law enforcement to developing countries, the latter will have to retain the right to challenge foreign mergers and RBPs that have an effect on domestic consumers.[146]

This position, especially with regard to export cartels, was confirmed by an EU official who was interviewed in the context of this study, who noted that 'it has been made clear that developing countries would not accept a WTO agreement on competition if such an agreement would not include a clear ban on export cartels. On the other hand, the EU as well as the United States and a number of other countries are not ready to accept such a commitment'.[147]

It is quite a paradox that neither the United States nor the EU, with arguably the most mature competition systems, major enthusiasm for

registered export cartels there. See Levenstein and Suslow (2005), *supra* n. 138, at 790 and 792.

144 See Communication from the United States of 15 August 2002, WT/WGTCP/W/203, paras. 7–8.

145 See Communication WT/184, *supra* n. 88, para. III.B.

146 See Communication from India of 26 September 2002, WT/WTGTCP/W/1, para. 3.

147 Interview with European Commission official (Brussels, 20 July 2003).

competition law and expressed antipathy towards cartels, were ready to accept a commitment on the prohibition of export cartels. On the other hand, this is a clear indication that what is of utmost importance in the context of the negotiations of competition at the international level is the reassurance that national interests are satisfied before any sort of mutual commitments may be made.

(iv) Developing countries and concerns relating to agriculture

All the issues so far discussed that led developing countries to oppose a WTO competition agreement are directly related to competition law and policy. However, it was also mentioned in the context of the discussion about the possible inclusion of competition rules in the WTO, that the negotiations at the WTO include a number of other co-related issues. One of them is the regulation of agriculture, which has been an issue of major concern among developing countries, and is linked to the debate on competition.

A considerable amount of academic opinion has been dedicated to the discussions on agriculture at the WTO, and estimations of the effects of further liberalisation of agriculture on developing countries vary.[148] What is beyond doubt is that developing countries have repeatedly expressed their disapproval of the agricultural policies followed primarily by the EU, but also by other rich countries such as the United States and Japan. For instance, at Cancun, in a letter to the WTO regarding the draft Ministerial Declaration, Mauritius, on behalf of the African Union, the ACP Group, and the LDCs, made it clear that these countries were not satisfied with the progress made during the discussions on agricultural reform at the WTO level, and requested a number of amendments of the draft Declaration.[149] These changes were not accepted by developed countries and thus the talks reached a dead-end.

[148] On the complex issue of agriculture in the WTO and its effects on developing countries, see K. Anderson and W. Martin (eds.) (2005), *Agricultural Trade Reform and the Doha Development Agenda* (World Bank and Palgrave Macmillan); K. Anderson (2003), *How Can Agricultural Reform Reduce Poverty?*,Centre for International Economic Studies Discussion Paper No. 0321; J.C. Beghin and A. Aksoy (2003), *Agricultural Trade and the Doha Round: Lessons from Commodity Studies*, Centre for Agricultural and Rural Development, Iowa State University Briefing Paper No. 03-BP 42; J. Fabiosam, J. Beghin, S. de Cara, A. Elobeid, C. Fang, M. Isik, H. Matthey, A. Saak, P. Westhoff, D. Scott Brown, B. Willot, D. Madison, S. Meyer and J. Kruse (2005), 'The Doha Round of the World Trade Organisation and Agricultural Markets Liberalisation: Impacts on Developing Economies' 27(3) *Review of Agricultural Economics* 317.

[149] See Communication from Mauritius of 12 September 2003, WT/MIN(03)/W/17. The fact that the Communication was sent on behalf of two regional organisations, i.e. the

Two general observations may be made with regard to the indirect importance of agriculture to the development of the talks on competition. The first is that the WTO is a forum where differentiated and conflicting aims are pursued by the member states. It is also an indication that at the multilateral level, progress on one issue may depend upon relevant progress in another not directly related issue. Thus, apart from analysis on the extent to which competition law is important to developing countries, any future attempts to include competition law in the WTO should take into serious consideration these related policies.

The second observation is similar but relates to the EU. As mentioned above, it has been suggested in the literature that the EU initially proposed the inclusion of competition policy in the WTO framework in order to slow down agricultural reform. This argument cannot be substantiated here; nonetheless, the persistent efforts of the EU on the Singapore issues had profound effects on the development of the negotiations on agriculture.

6.3.3 Back to the European Commission: did everybody in the Commission really want an agreement at the WTO?

As already shown, only hard-core cartels qualified for possible further negotiations at the WTO in Doha. In contrast, the inclusion of vertical restraints and of types of abuse of dominance by firms within a competition agreement, something that was initially proposed by the European Commission, did not find favour at the WTO. Furthermore, the Commission, even though it initially insisted that the WTO dispute settlement mechanism should be included in a possible agreement on competition, had by this time limited this proposal by accepting the much softer peer review system, due to the opposition expressed by the United States.

On the other hand, it became clear at Cancun that not even the minimal proposal of the EU, which included core principles such as non-discrimination, transparency and due process, a provision on hard-core cartels and modalities for cooperation and technical assistance, could survive the negotiations, due mainly to the opposition expressed by developing countries.

African Union and CARICOM, is a clear indication of the coordinated action of developing countries at the WTO. In addition, this may further strengthen the argument made in Chapter 5 that the proliferation of plurilateral regional agreements may lead to a situation in which international negotiations are conducted by the representatives of those organisations.

The additional argument made in this section is that, in parallel with the realisation that exogenous factors (i.e. the opposition expressed by the United States and developing countries) blocked the EU proposal for the adoption of a competition agreement at the WTO, there were also endogenous factors that had an effect on the development of the EU position. In particular, it is argued that the EU proposal for a competition agreement at the WTO was mainly a product of DG Trade, while DG Competition, which is responsible for competition law and policy, was much more hesitant about the inclusion of competition in the WTO.

In fact, this argument has been raised by Chad Damro, who in discussing the theory of venue shopping, according to which 'actors will choose the venue, depending on its institutional features, through which it may expect to achieve the best results',[150] notes that DG Trade may have different interests in the field of competition law and policy than those of DG Competition. He further argues that 'it should be noted that Brittan and DG Trade were the primary advocates of this position. DG Competition had little interest in promoting such a competition measure in the WTO'.[151] He also notes that DG Trade promoted the inclusion of competition within the WTO in the context of the broader attempt to pursue non-trade goals within the organisation. On the other hand, DG Competition preferred to avoid linking issues such as trade and non-trade goals, and consequently trade and competition, since such issue linkages increase the likelihood of political intervention in the performance of its mandate, which is the optimal application of the EU competition rules.[152] The research undertaken in the context of this book builds upon Damro's argument by analysing the position of the European Commission, which represents the EU at the WTO.[153]

As an EU official noted when interviewed, the idea of proposing a binding agreement at the WTO was entirely a project of DG Trade, and from the beginning of the talks at the WTO there were voices within DG Competition opposing such a prospect.[154] Such voices became more persistent as the negotiations proceeded. As already noted, the proposal for a competition WTO agreement came from Sir Leon Brittan, who was at the

[150] C. Damro (2006), 'The New Trade Politics and EU Competition Policy: Shopping for Convergence and Co-operation' 13(6) *Journal of European Public Policy* 867, at 868.

[151] *Ibid.* at 878. [152] *Ibid.* at 873.

[153] In particular, the Commission negotiates in consultation with the so-called 133 Committee, which consists of representatives from the twenty-seven EU Member States on the basis of Art. 133(3) EC.

[154] Interview with European Commission official (Brussels, 20 July 2003).

time the Commissioner in charge of external trade. It has also been noted that Karel Van Miert, at least officially, supported the promotion of the issue at the WTO. Nonetheless, during the next four to five years or so the dynamics changed, in any event with regard to DG Competition. In 1999, both Commissioners Brittan and Van Miert had to resign because of the resignation of the entire Santer Commission. In the same year, Pascal Lamy became the Commissioner for Trade and Mario Monti became the Commissioner for Competition.

Throughout his tenure, the main objective of Mario Monti, an economist, was to introduce more efficiency-centred economic analysis on the cases reviewed by the Commission, therefore bringing the EU competition regime closer to the one developed in the United States. It did not appear that Monti was against the inclusion of competition in the WTO, but he expressed the view that the Commission should be realistic as to what could be achieved at this level. In 2002, he expressed this position clearly by stating that 'we have to be pragmatic and focus initially on what can be achieved'.[155] As noted by an interviewee, from a strategic point of view, and in view of the continuous opposition both by the United States and a large number of developing countries, at a certain point in the negotiations, Monti and his staff realised that by insisting on the inclusion of competition in the WTO the Commission was 'betting its money on a losing horse'.[156] Thus, following the resignation of Brittan and Van Miert from the Commission, it seems that DG Competition began to take the position that competition law and policy should be pursued in every possible forum (international organisation), and not only at the WTO.

On the opposite side of the spectrum, DG Trade remained committed to the WTO. It should be pointed out that, in terms of competence, the possibility of including competition in a WTO agreement was an 'all or nothing' situation for DG Trade, as the WTO is the only international organisation in which the EU is represented on competition matters exclusively by this Directorate-General. On the other hand, and in line with Damro's arguments, DG Trade considered the WTO as an expanded version of the EU model. This argument has recently been confirmed by an EU trade official, who has noted that the:

[155] See M. Monti (2002), 'A Global Competition Policy?', speech delivered at European Competition Day, Copenhagen, 17 September 2002, speech 02/399, in which former Commissioner Monti expressed his belief that a WTO agreement should be adopted by 2005.

[156] Two European Commission officials confirmed this suggestion (Brussels, 20 and 21 July 2003).

> WTO 'feels European' in its mission and even its politics: starting from the opening of trade between members on a largely voluntary basis, arriving at binding rules (with consequences), and the pooling of sovereignty, but this time on a global scale.[157]

This divergence of approaches has been described by an EU official interviewee who noted that:

> International organisations in a sense lead their own life. They try to develop their own arguments in order to justify their own existence, and this is the case with the EC Commission as well. WTO would be good for the Commissioner for Trade, while if the ICN will take the lead then the merit goes to Monti.[158]

6.4 Future of competition at the WTO and alternative options

As the chapter has argued, both external and internal factors have played a major role in the way that the EU, which put the issue on the table of negotiations, first had to limit its proposal, and then withdraw the proposal altogether. Despite these developments, it would be far from accurate to assume that competition law in the WTO is a finished story, and a number of factors lead to this conclusion.

First, the WTO as an institution has developed its own dynamics with regard to the possible inclusion of competition law and policy. At the moment, the talks in general at the WTO have slowed down dramatically, but in view of the globalisation of markets (and the ongoing aim of more developed countries to further liberalise world markets), it would be realistic to expect that at some time in the near future the negotiations will be launched again.

Secondly, there is no doubt that, even in the absence of a WTO competition agreement, the organisation will still deal with competition issues since a number of WTO agreements contain competition-related provisions. Such provisions are found in GATT, as well as in TRIPS, the General Agreement on Trade in Services (GATS) and the 'Reference Paper' which complements the WTO Telecommunications Agreement.[159] The existence

[157] See M. Baldwin (2006), 'EU Trade Politics: Heaven or Hell?' 13(6) *Journal of European Public Policy* 526, at 533.

[158] Interview with European Commission official (Brussels, 20 July 2003).

[159] See OECD (1999), *Trade and Competition Policies for Tomorrow* (Paris: OECD) 59–75 (see Chapter 4).

of these provisions may lead to the examination of particular cases on the basis of competition law. In fact, the WTO dispute settlement mechanism has already reviewed two cases on this basis, first the *Kodak/Fuji* case,[160] and secondly the *Telmex* case.[161] Quite surprisingly, in view of the consistent opposition of the United States regarding the adoption of a multilateral agreement on competition, both cases were examined on the basis of complaints submitted by the US government.

The *Kodak/Fuji* case related to a complaint by the US government that the Japanese Fuji Film company, with (according to the United States) the assistance of the Japanese government in not properly enforcing the relevant antitrust legislation, had prevented all the major Japanese distributors from distributing the products of foreign competitor firms, and thus had excluded Eastman Kodak, a US company, from the Japanese market.[162] The complaint was based on article XXIII.1(b) of GATT, which could be invoked:

> if any contracting party should consider that any benefit accruing to it directly or indirectly under this Agreement is being nullified or impaired or that the attainment of any objective of the Agreement is being impeded as the result of ...(b) the application by another contracting party of any measure, whether or not it conflicts with the provisions of this Agreement.

The WTO panel which examined the case found that there was no infringement by the Japanese government, mainly due to the fact that there was no proof that Japanese law was applied in a discriminatory manner to US firms, on the basis of the historical existence of 'Keiretsu' in the Japanese markets.[163]

The *Telmex* case related to the privilege granted by Mexican legislation to the dominant telecommunications company, Telmex, to fix the rate to be paid by all foreign carriers terminating calls in Mexico. In this case,

160 See WTO Panel Report, *Japan – Measure Affecting Consumer Photographic Film and Paper*, WT/DS44/R.

161 See WTO Panel Report, *Mexico – Measures Affecting Telecommunications Services*, WT/DS204/R.

162 Note that when the dispute arose, Sir Leon Brittan expressed the view that 'Europe has important export interests in this area. The European market of photographic film and paper is open to competition. Our industry would like the same conditions to prevail in other markets as well. We therefore welcome the critical analysis of market conditions in Japan, which this panel will conduct'. See European Commission, '*Kodak-Fuji* case: EU to join the WTO/GATT Panel: statement by the European Commission', Press Release IP/96/931.

163 Keiretsu refers to long-term closely interconnected relationships among Japanese companies through formal and/or informal relations. See M. Furse (1999), 'Competition

the WTO panel found that Mexico infringed its obligations under the Reference Paper as it failed to maintain appropriate measures to prevent anticompetitive practices by a firm that was a 'major supplier', it failed to ensure interconnection at cost-oriented rates, and it also failed to ensure reasonable and non-discriminatory access and use of telecommunications networks.[164]

Thus, irrespective of whether competition law and policy as such will return to the WTO agenda of negotiations, it is quite logical to suggest that more competition-related cases will reach the WTO dispute settlement mechanism in the future, in view of the fact that competition provisions are found in a number of WTO agreements. Nevertheless, as has been argued above, this case-specific analysis based on sector-specific competition provisions cannot replace a multilateral competition agreement, as such an application of the law might lead to an inconsistent competition policy across sectors.[165] In parallel, the problems identified in Chapter 2 with regard to the international aspects of competition law and policy still exist, which means that international solutions are still needed in order to resolve these international problems. Bilateral and plurilateral agreements may provide solutions, but such solutions are by definition limited.

In any event, both of the major international institutions which carried out work in this field before the launch of competition talks at the WTO, UNCTAD and the OECD, have continued their work. In particular, as noted earlier in this chapter, UNCTAD is the only organisation that has issued a (non-binding) multilateral set of rules. Furthermore, it has been and still is the main institution which deals with the relevant problems faced by developing countries. To this end, UNCTAD has been very active in carrying out peer reviews of competition regimes of developing countries, as well as in providing developing countries with

Law and the WTO Report: "Japan – Measures Affecting Consumer Photographic Film and Paper"' 20(1) *European Competition Law Review* 9.

164 The legal basis of the decision was arts. 1.1 and 2.2(b) of the Reference Paper, and 5(a) and (b) of the GATS Annex on Telecommunications. For an analysis of the Panel Report, see E.M. Fox (2006), 'The WTO's First Antitrust Case – Mexican Telecom: A Sleeping Victory for Trade and Competition' 9 *Journal of International Economic Law* 271; K.Y. Lee (2005), *The WTO Dispute Settlement and Anti-competitive Practices: Lessons Learnt from Trade Disputes*, University of Oxford Centre for Competition Law and Policy Working Paper No. (L)10/05; P. Marsden (2004), 'WTO Decides First Competition Case with Disappointing Results' *Competition Law Insight* (May) 3.

165 J.R. Shelton (1999), 'Competition Policy: What Chance for International Rules?' 1(2) *OECD Journal of Competition Law and Policy* 51, at 56.

technical assistance on competition.[166] The OECD, which is regarded as a group dominated by rich industrialised countries, has issued a number of recommendations and best practices already referred to above,[167] and has carried out considerable work in the field through its Competition Committee and the Global Forum on Competition. In addition, in 2001 the ICN was launched, and has become probably the most important forum for discussions on the multilateral aspects of competition law and policy. The next section attempts to expose the main features of this 'virtual' institution, and evaluate the reaction of the EU as regards its operation.

6.4.1 Genesis and operation of the ICN

As noted above, the establishment of the ICN was first proposed by the ICPAC Report in 2000, and was clearly the US response to the EU proposal for a binding competition agreement under the auspices of the WTO. This type of behaviour by powerful states, i.e. proposing the creation of new organisations in cases where they do not intend to support the adoption of binding international rules, or where they feel that the negotiations under the auspices of an international organisation have reached a dead-end, has been analysed in the political science literature. In particular, as Steinberg notes:

> when aimed at a group of states – and in its most potent form – coercion takes the form of a threat to exit the organization that is unable to achieve consensus … In other cases, the exit tactic may involve simply ignoring the deadlocked organization and creating a new organization that will become a source of future legal benefits in the issue area.[168]

Similarly, Krisch, discussing the relationship between hegemony and international law, notes that dominant states have two major options with regard to their position towards international law. The first is to support the adoption of international agreements where there is the belief that

[166] For instance, in the context of the COMPAL Project (Competition and Consumer Policies for Latin America), UNCTAD currently provides technical assistance on competition matters to Nicaragua, Costa Rica, El Salvador, Peru and Bolivia.

[167] In particular, on enforcement cooperation and cartels. In addition, the OECD has issued recommendations on merger review and on competition assessment, providing guidance on the assessment of public policies that distort competition; and guiding principles for regulatory quality and performance, which provide guidance on the proper functioning of sector-specific regulations from a competition perspective.

[168] See Steinberg (2002), *supra* n. 124 at 349.

international commitments would have a positive effect on the domestic markets, as in the case of the WTO where the United States has pushed for increased legalisation. The second alternative is to withdraw from international law and to turn to other strategies which do not necessarily involve violations of existing law; but will certainly include shifts away from legal mechanisms in areas central to the dominant state's interests, and in particular attempts to reduce the legal constraints on the tools of dominance, such as those on the use of force.[169]

Amidst the various problems identified and objections raised with regard to the possible inclusion of competition law in the WTO, the US proposal found considerable support within the community of competition experts. In September 2000, Joel Klein reaffirmed the ICPAC's proposal for the creation of a Global Competition Initiative, comparable to the work carried out by the OECD Competition Law and Policy (CLP) Committee, and in particular by the OECD Global Forum on Competition, but which would encompass a larger number of participating countries (since the OECD's membership was too limited and consequently it could not serve as the organisation to address competition issues on a global scale).[170] Commissioner Monti, who has been considered as one of the strongest proponents of the work undertaken by the ICN,[171] welcomed the proposal of Joel Klein.[172]

A few months later, in February 2001, forty representatives of competition authorities and experts met in Ditchley Park in the United Kingdom and examined the possible way forward with regard to the establishment and operation of this new organisation. The ICN was finally launched only eighteen months after the ICPAC proposal at the Fordham Corporate

[169] N. Krisch (2005), 'International Law in Times of Hegemony: Unequal Power and the Shaping of the International Legal Order' 16(3) *European Journal of International Law* 369, at 379.

[170] See J. Klein (2000), 'Time for a Global Competition Initiative?', speech delivered at the EC Merger Control 10th Anniversary Conference, Brussels, 14–15 September 2000, at 7, available at www.usdoj.gov/atr/public/speeches/6486.pdf (last visited on 2 December 2009). As noted in Chapter 3, the OECD comprises thirty members. The CLP includes representatives from these states as well as particular observers from other non-OECD countries. In addition, in the context of the Global Forum on Competition (GFC), which was created in parallel with the ICN in 2001, business and consumer representatives participate in some of the CLP and GCF meetings.

[171] See W. Kolasky (2005), 'Mario Monti's Legacy: A US Perspective' 1(1) *Wilmer Cutler Hale and Dorr LLP* 159, at 176.

[172] See M. Monti (2000), 'The Main Challenges of a New Decade of EC Merger Control', speech delivered at the EC Merger Control 10th Anniversary Conference, Brussels, 14–15 September 2000, speech 00/311.

Law Institute's annual international antitrust conference by officials from fourteen jurisdictions.[173] Since then, the development and work of the ICN has been significant. More than ninety states participate in the Network, which, according to its website, is the 'only international body devoted exclusively to competition law enforcement'.[174]

The ICN is a virtual organisation without a permanent Secretariat. It is led by a steering group of fifteen expert representatives of competition authorities, and holds an annual conference in which representatives of all its member states, along with a limited number of invited business representatives and academics, participate. Most of its work is carried out by the various working groups set up to examine particular issues,[175] and in particular issues relating to merger notifications and procedures, capacity building, technical assistance, cooperation on cartels, the relationship between sectoral regulation and competition, the role of competition in the telecommunications sector, and recently the analysis of unilateral conduct. Thus, it may be argued that the issues covered by the ICN working groups are to a certain extent similar to the topics discussed at the WTO. The major differences with regard to the operation of these two institutions are the following.

First, no trade officials are invited to the ICN conferences, despite the fact that for a decade or so, the negotiations for a multilateral agreement at the WTO were carried out by trade and not competition officials.[176] With regard to EU participation in the ICN, based on the arguments raised above regarding the different preferences of the European Commission's trade and competition officials at the WTO, it comes as no surprise that EU competition officials have expressed satisfaction with this development, as the work of the ICN is carried out by competition experts, while trade experts are actually excluded. As Janow has noted, the informal but often repeated motto for the ICN has become 'all competition all of the time'.[177]

[173] See US Department of Justice, 'US and foreign antitrust officials launch International Competition Network: new international venue will assist in global convergence on important antitrust enforcement issues', Press Release of 25 October 2001.

[174] See the ICN webpage at www.internationalcompetitionnetwork.org/index.php/en/about-icn.

[175] The members of the working groups mainly work by Internet, telephone, fax machine and videoconference.

[176] To give a characteristic example: at the last Conference of the ICN in Cape Town, a UK official from the Department of Trade and Industry flew to Cape Town for just one day to attend a regional workshop organised by a local NGO, TRALAC, which took place one day before the ICN annual conference. The official did not attend the ICN conference as he was not invited.

[177] See M.E. Janow (2003), 'Observations on Two Multilateral Venues: The International Competition Network (ICN) and the WTO' in Barry E. Hawk (ed.), *Annual Proceedings*

This has inevitably attracted criticism from trade officials. For instance, Bernard Hoekman from the World Bank, who has been one of the most influential commentators on the role of competition in the international trading system, has noted that 'the ICN is an inter-agency entity, not an inter-governmental body, reflecting a desire on the part of the "competition community" not to have to engage with trade and other officials on modalities of international cooperation (disciplines) in "their" area'.[178]

Secondly, the ICN does not exercise a rule-making function. According to the ICN website:

> where the ICN reaches consensus on recommendations, or 'best practices', arising from the projects, it is left to the individual competition authorities to decide whether and how to implement the recommendations, through unilateral, bilateral or multilateral arrangements, as appropriate.[179]

Thus, the ICN only produces soft law instruments, in the same way that such instruments are produced by bilateral enforcement cooperation agreements (discussed in Chapter 3), and similar to the OECD recommendations on hard-core cartels and enforcement cooperation. In practice, the various working groups have already issued a number of soft law instruments such as recommended practices and guiding principles in the fields that they cover.[180]

The ICN is one of the most characteristic examples of transgovernmentalism, also discussed in earlier chapters of the book.[181] Cooperation under transgovernmentalism involves specialised domestic officials cooperating with minimal supervision by foreign ministers, and is also based on networks since cooperation is based on 'loosely-structured, peer-to-peer ties developed through frequent interaction rather than formal negotiation'.[182] As Raustiala notes, the result of such networks is the

of the Fordham Corporate Law Institute Conference on International Antitrust Law and Policy (New York: Juris) 47, at 53.

178 See B. Hoekman and K. Saggi (2005), 'International Cooperation on Domestic Policies: Lessons from the WTO Competition Policy Debate' in S. Evenett and B. Hoekman (eds.), *Economic Development and Multilateral Trade Cooperation* (Palgrave Macmillan and World Bank) 456.

179 *Ibid.*

180 For details, see ICN (2006), *Statement of Mission and Achievements, Up Until May 2006*.

181 See Chapter 3. See also A.-M. Slaughter (2004), 'Sovereignty and Power in a Networked World Order' 40 *Stanford Journal of International Law* 283.

182 K. Raustiala (2002), 'The Architecture of International Cooperation: Transgovernmental Networks and the Future of International Law' 43 *Virginia Journal of International Law* 1, at 5.

diffusion of regulatory rules. Power still plays a role in these organisations; nonetheless, on such occasions power is 'soft power, which is defined as power to attract, which is different from traditional hard power, defined as the power to coerce'.[183] It would be rational to expect that the work of the ICN is led by industrialised countries such as the United States, the EU and Canada. While the ICN's current steering group includes representatives from South Africa, Russia, Mexico, Brazil and Turkey (with the rest of the representatives coming from industrialised rich states), none of these countries may be considered as truly developing as they are all states with considerable political power.

That said, in the absence of a multilateral agreement on competition and in view of the need for multilateral cooperation, forums such as the ICN and the OECD Global Forum on Competition definitely play an important role in the development of international competition norms. These forums develop mechanisms of cooperation and interaction between experts from competition authorities, academia and business worldwide, through which ideas and experiences are exchanged with the aim of reaching common understandings; they utilise soft law instruments without threatening a country's sovereignty.[184] Thus, the major development at the multilateral level in the last five years has been a shift from attempts to include competition law in a binding agreement to the creation of mechanisms (through UNCTAD, OECD and particularly the ICN) which contribute to the achievement of convergence on particular issues. Given the complexities of the operation of competition rules at the national level, as discussed in Chapter 2, this shift is to a certain extent reasonable, since only where such convergence is achieved can firmer international rules be adopted.

The recent history of multilateral cooperation/negotiations on competition shows that, officially, the EU shares this opinion. Having in practice to withdraw support for a WTO competition agreement, since it became clear that no consensus could be reached, the EU seems to have realised that at the multilateral level it must follow the second best scenario, i.e. participation in alternative multilateral fora, such as the ICN, which produce soft law instruments. As noted above, Mario Monti was from the very beginning a major proponent of the ICN, and since then, the Commission (in particular DG Competition, as DG Trade does not participate in the

[183] *Ibid.* at 51.

[184] See M. Bode and O. Budzinski (2005), *Competing Ways Towards International Antitrust: The WTO versus the ICN*, Marburg Papers on Economics 03/2005, at 14.

ICN) has been very active in the context of the works of this virtual organisation. The Commission co-chairs the Cartels Working Group, and has also co-chaired the Working Group on Competition Advocacy.[185] In addition, representation of the EU at the annual meetings of the ICN is at the highest level.[186]

6.5 Conclusion and evaluation of the role of the EU

This chapter has attempted to observe the development of multilateral talks on competition law and policy. It started by briefly discussing the debate initiated under the auspices of a number of international organisations, such as the League of Nations, where the issue was discussed in 1925, the proposed International Trade Organisation, where discussions took place in 1947, and UNCTAD, under the auspices of which the RBP Code was adopted in 1980. The major part of the chapter has been devoted to the talks on the adoption of a multilateral agreement at the WTO, with a focus on the development of the EU position, and the way that the United States and developing countries reacted to this proposal. Finally, and in view of the failure of the WTO talks, the chapter has discussed the operation of the ICN, which is currently the most active organisation in this field.

As seen, the debate over the possible adoption of a multilateral agreement on competition law is now almost a century old. Even though no agreement has been concluded to date, the long history of negotiations is a clear indication that this debate is an active one, and that some sort of multilateral agreement should be achieved some time in the near future. On the other hand, the examination of the development of the WTO negotiations has exposed the difficult problems that have to be addressed before such an agreement is concluded, as well as the various exogenous and endogenous dynamics that develop and have an influence on the position of particular countries in the context of the negotiations.

For instance, it has been suggested that in the EU, a network of influential academics and officials emerged in the early 1990s which, under the

[185] See the website of the ICN at www.internationalcompetitionnetwork.org.

[186] On the other hand, and with respect to the argument raised above that the community of trade experts has questioned the legitimacy of the operation of the ICN, it should be noted that within the European Commission there is a divergence in approaches as to the function of the ICN. In contrast to the attitude of competition officials, EU trade officials, at least informally, have expressed their dissatisfaction regarding their compulsory absence from ICN meetings and in general with the work of the ICN. Interview with European Commission official (Brussels, 22 July 2003).

leadership of Lord Brittan, expressed the position that the time had come for the conclusion of a binding international competition agreement. On the other hand, as argued in the chapter, varied and sometime diverse factors led to the development of this position, including the idea that the EU model of international governance should be expanded at an international level, the belief that a multilateral agreement on competition would open up foreign markets to EU firms, and finally, that the negotiations on competition would slow down the relevant talks on agriculture.

On the other side, the chapter has argued that the United States and a significant number of developing countries opposed the EU position for various and diverse reasons. In the United States, mainly because of its traditional position that a binding agreement on competition would be a threat to its sovereignty and because of the belief in the superiority of US competition law in relation to any other national law, it was felt that a multilateral agreement on competition could lead to the distortion of competition standards.

Developing countries also opposed the EU proposal, first of all because of the widespread concern that the adoption of such an agreement would undermine their ability to foster industrial policies capable of dealing with their dramatic economic problems, and more importantly to develop strong enterprises that would be able to compete at the international level. From a similar perspective, it has been argued that the adoption and application of competition law is not a priority for developing and least developed countries, since the enforcement of such laws would require the establishment of new institutions and the employment of qualified experts – a project arguably too expensive for states that suffer from poverty and a number of other socio-economic problems.

On the other hand, it has been argued that the reluctance of these states to proceed with the adoption of a WTO competition agreement is also linked to the reluctance of major industrialised countries to accept a prohibition on export cartels, which are exempted from their competition laws and harm the producers and consumers of the importing countries. As an even greater demand, the view was also expressed that a multilateral competition agreement should include a relevant prohibition for industrialised countries, while excluding from its application developing countries on the basis of flexibility, a notion which, along with progressiveness, technical assistance and capacity building, was extensively discussed in the context of negotiations at the WTO.

Finally, it has been suggested that the negotiations on competition law and policy have been influenced by the parallel negotiations on other trade issues, agriculture being the most directly linked. As observed, developing countries adopted the position that if no further commitments would be undertaken by industrialised states, and in particular by the EU, on agricultural subsidies, then they would not give their consent for the adoption of an agreement on competition. In fact, this *quid pro quo* nature of the WTO negotiations is an issue raised by the United States with regard to the inappropriateness of this institution to accommodate competition provisions. It has also been argued that the EU put the issue of competition on the table of negotiations in order to slow down the talks on agriculture, in view of the demand of developing countries for rapid reforms. Irrespective of the validity of these arguments, the fact that the controversy developed in the context of the negotiations on agriculture is a clear indication that the extent to which competition law could be formally incorporated in the broader international trading system in the future will to a certain extent depend on agreement on various other issues.

With regard to the content of such a possible agreement, among the various issues that were negotiated at the WTO, only hard-core cartels were finally promoted as a competition-related problem that may have an effect on the operation of international trade. Nonetheless, the notion of hard-core cartels, as in the case of the OECD recommendation on this issue, does not include export cartels, at least in the view of industrialised countries. In fact, this development reflects the concern developed mainly in the United States and expressed by the ICPAC Report that the real effects of anticompetitive practices on international trade have not yet been properly quantified. According to the Report:

> the level of quantitative and empirical economic analysis concerning private and government anticompetitive restraints that inhibit market access still remains quite limited ... The uneven quality of the evidence in many specific instances is also reflected in the corresponding absence of empirical analyses that determine or estimate the magnitude of the effects of these competition policy problems on global trade flows or the global economy. This very issue is itself a matter of debate.[187]

Apart from hard-core cartels, all the other issues that were included in the Doha Declaration (which as noted represented the peak of the negotiations at the WTO), relate to the application of core principles such as transparency, non-discrimination and procedural fairness in the application of competition law, the need for voluntary cooperation and, most

[187] See ICPAC Report, *supra* n. 95 at 224–5.

importantly, the support that has to be offered to developing countries in order to develop efficient competition policies. Nevertheless, even this minimum version of the competition agenda could not survive the negotiations, as at Cancun the negotiations reached a dead-end.

Apart from the reasons that led to the collapse of the WTO talks, the chapter has also discussed the alternative multilateral solutions, and in particular the ICN. As noted in various sections of the chapter, the ICN is the outcome of a proposal first put forward by the United States and supported mostly by the competition officials of a number of countries, including the EU. On the other hand, trade experts have been opposed to the work carried out by this virtual organisation. In this regard, it has been suggested that the interests of the particular groups that are developed in the context of multilateral talks on a given issue may vary considerably. This is the case within the European Commission where, as already noted, the preferences of DG Trade and DG Competition officials as to the most appropriate international organisation to host competition law negotiations are not identical and are in fact sometimes conflicting. Trade officials are keen on the adoption of competition law within the WTO context, while the competition officials support the ICN and the OECD. A similar situation has been identified with regard to the United States, where despite the long-lasting opposition by the competition officials to the possible adoption of a WTO competition agreement, the US trade representatives agreed to include competition law in the Doha Declaration.

Despite the emergence of different lobbies in the process of the negotiations for a multilateral agreement on competition, the chapter has also identified some of the main characteristics of the ICN as a form of international cooperation. In particular, it has been argued that even though the issues discussed at the ICN are similar to these discussed at the WTO, the major difference between the two institutions is that while the aim of the WTO talks was (is) the adoption of a binding agreement, the relevant aim of the ICN is the publication of best practices and recommendations which do not bind the participating countries. Thus, the ICN represents a more expanded version of transgovernmental cooperation as this has been described in the context of the discussion of bilateral enforcement cooperation agreements.

In view of its non-binding nature, the amount of the work that has been carried out at the ICN is significant, as a great number of reports, best practices and recommendations have been published on issues (such as mergers and the relationship between competition and sectoral regulation) which did not survive the relevant negotiations at the WTO. Hence, a lesson that has been learnt in the context of the analysis of multilateral talks on competition is that there can be no formal binding agreement on the issue before a common understanding has been reached on the issues that are to be included in such an agreement. In this regard, organisations such as the ICN, the OECD and UNCTAD are very important for the development of an international competition culture.

Reverting to the role that the EU has played in the field of multilateral talks on competition law and policy, it may be argued that the recent history of these talks has showed that the influence of the EU (as described in Chapters 4 and 5 has been significant in the formation and to a certain extent the application of competition law in the context of bilateral and plurilateral regional trade agreements) has not been as influential at the international level. The EU for more than ten years supported the inclusion of competition law and policy in the WTO. However, its proposal faced opposition from both the United States and developing countries for a number of reasons discussed above. Even though the official position of the EU (until the collapse of the negotiations in Cancun) was that the proposal for a WTO competition agreement was among its main aims, as the chapter has argued, in view of the opposition by a number of countries to the possible adoption of the agreement, the dynamics within the Commission changed over time, with DG Competition questioning the extent to which a competition agreement at the WTO was a feasible project.

In parallel, it has been argued that the United States put forward a more realistic proposal which supported the creation of a multilateral institution to serve as a forum for discussions on competition issues, a proposal which led to the establishment of the ICN. In view of the fact that DG Competition supported the establishment of the ICN and actively participates in its work, it could be argued that the EU has been a follower rather than the leader in the development of international competition law at the multilateral level, with the United States clearly taking the lead.

At the same time (as observed particularly in Chapter 4), the EU, in the context of its enlargement strategy, has shifted its interest to the adoption of bilateral trade agreements, which in practice require the co-signing parties to adopt and/or harmonise their competition regimes with the EU's own regime. Furthermore, as shown in Chapter 5, the EU has focused on the development of its own plurilateral system of competition, which has been the model followed by most of the other plurilateral agreements in the world.

7

Conclusions: Main Findings of the Study

7.1 General observations

This book has examined, through the lens of the EU, the process of internationalisation of competition rules by analysing different types of international agreements that include competition provisions. The book initially pointed out that competition law and policy co-exists with a number of other national policies which may also have an influence on the application of competition rules. Despite the identification of numerous factors upon which the particular application of competition law is dependent at national level, this book has not attempted to question the usefulness and validity of competition law and policy. In fact, statistics compiled for the purposes of the study show that competition law is a legal instrument adopted by more than half of the countries in the world, while most of them have adopted competition law in the last fifteen years. These statistics may themselves answer the question regarding whether competition law is considered an important instrument for the regulation of business practices in economies that are becoming increasingly liberalised.

On the other hand, the discussion developed in the second chapter of the book reminds us that competition rules are not a panacea, a solution for all the problems that may arise from the activities of private firms in the markets. In contrast, other public policies and sectoral regulations co-exist with competition laws on a national level and are employed to address the various issues related to the activity of such firms.

Furthermore, it should be kept in mind that competition policy and the co-related policies which deal with business activity encompass very important interests of the states which apply these policies, given that the role of private undertakings registered in particular states is very important for the states' economies, in view of the liberalisation of national markets. In fact, in liberalised economies such firms have on many occasions replaced state monopolies in the markets previously dominated by the state. In turn, in view of the liberalisation of international markets, and the fact that national firms have to compete internationally, the governments of particular states often apply competition rules in such a fashion as to try to give the national firms sufficient support to be able to survive in the international competitive environment. This observation is particularly relevant to developing countries, which as shown in various chapters have questioned the need for competition policy, and in any event have demanded preferential application of competition rules in order to be able to assist their domestic firms in becoming competitive in the international markets.

The argument that competition law deals with very sensitive aspects of national economies is also validated by the observation made in the context of this book that extraterritorial application of competition rules is a regular phenomenon in the field of competition. As also noted, the most frequent utiliser of competition rules in an extraterritorial manner has been the United States, which is the country with the most sophisticated competition regime in the world. Following the US example, the EU is also eager to utilise its competition rules extraterritorially, and this example has recently been followed by other countries.

Nonetheless, as also noted in various chapters, international problems need international solutions. The unilateral application of competition rules may provide temporary solutions to business practices that have an anticompetitive effect on multiple national markets; however, the increasing incidence of such practices indicates that some form of international cooperation is needed in order to overcome the problems that flow from these practices. In addition, it has also been stressed that, in view of the internationalisation of business activity, the varied and sometimes divergent characteristics of national competition rules may create problems in the future if no agreement is reached as to their optimum application, or at the least as to certain common standards on the application of competition rules.

In this regard, it has been suggested that international law is needed in order to put into context the cooperation of nation states on competition law and policy. To this end, the book has examined three types of agreements: bilateral and trilateral enforcement cooperation agreements on competition; bilateral trade agreements that include competition provisions; plurilateral regional trade agreements which include competition law; and finally, the book has attempted to analyse the process of negotiations that have taken place to date for the adoption of a multilateral agreement on competition. The following briefly sums up the main arguments developed in the process of the detailed analysis of these agreements.

7.2 Main findings of the study with regard to the operation of international agreements which are devoted to or include competition provisions

The first type of agreements discussed in the context of the present study were enforcement cooperation agreements. As mentioned, these agreements follow the relevant recommendations of the OECD, whose work has been substantial in the field of international competition law. The agreements do not harmonise the competition rules of the signing states, but do provide a number of cooperative mechanisms aimed at helping the signing countries to overcome problems that may arise where both jurisdictions review a particular business practice. As noted in the context of the detailed analysis of the agreements, mainly based on the agreements signed between the EU and the United States, this type of agreement may provide valuable solutions as regards the cooperation of the signing countries; they nonetheless have certain limitations. These limitations mainly arise from the fact that they do not provide for the exchange of confidential information; and more importantly the fact that they are soft law instruments which the signing parties apply on a discretionary basis. In this regard, it has been suggested that the second generation of agreements, which are agreements that are binding on the parties and provide for exchange of confidential information, are to be welcomed.

On the other hand, in the context of the examination of the agreements, it has been argued that soft law is a necessity in various regulatory fields where no consensus has been reached as to the optimum application of the legal instrument that regulate it. In view of the observation made in Chapter 2 that there does not as yet exist a universal common understanding about the optimum application of competition law and policy, the existence of soft law cooperation agreements, as well as other soft law instruments, such as the recommendations and best practices issued by the OECD, UNCTAD and the ICN, are important instruments towards the development of a common understanding of these concepts.

Following the examination of enforcement cooperation agreements, the book moved onto the examination of bilateral trade agreements that include competition provisions. The main characteristic of these agreements is that they have included competition provisions in a very broad context of provisions that relate to trade liberalisation, peace and security, and a number of other issues related and not related to competition law and policy.

Further to this general observation, as argued in Chapter 4, there are two different models of such agreements. The first model, followed by agreements signed by the United States and Canada, provide for cooperation of the signing parties on cases of mutual interest. In contrast to this model, bilateral trade agreements signed by the EU provide for the harmonisation of competition laws of the signing parties. It has been argued that, even though no dispute settlement mechanism is provided in these agreements for conflicts arising as to the application of competition rules by the signing parties, bilateral free trade agreements are much closer to hard law than the enforcement cooperation agreements.

Another important issue that has been raised in the context of the examination of bilateral agreements (both enforcement cooperation agreements and trade agreements that include competition law provisions) is that these agreements increase national power, in the sense that it is easier for the economically and politically stronger party to control and impose its preferences on their co-signing partners. As noted in Chapters 3 and 4, this is the reason why the United States has been the most prominent user of bilateral enforcement cooperation agreements, and this is also why the EU has pursued the conclusion of bilateral trade agreements that include competition provisions, mainly with neighbouring countries.

In contrast to bilateral agreements, plurilateral regional agreements secure a more balanced distribution of power among the participating countries. As noted in Chapter 5 which discussed these agreements, plurilateral regional trade agreements have certain similarities with the bilateral trade agreements that include competition law provisions, in the sense that they include competition law and policy in the context of a far broader nexus of regulations.

It has been shown that, as with the relevant bilateral agreements, there are two broad models followed by plurilateral agreements concerning competition law and policy. The first is the model followed by NAFTA and one of the agreements concluded by African states (SACU, and in part by SADC) which provides for enforcement cooperation of the contracting parties. In contrast to this model, and following the example of the EU, most of the other agreements reviewed in this study include substantive competition provisions that apply to cases where the business practices under consideration have an effect on the regional trade.

Further to this general observation, it has also been noted that in terms of institutional set-up there are also two main models followed by regional agreements. The first model is the one developed by the EU and followed by a number of other similar agreements, which provides for the establishment of a supranational body to apply the competition rules of the trading bloc. Some of those agreements also establish a regional judicial body to review the decisions issued by the supranational body. As opposed to this institutional setting, the regional competition rules in MERCOSUR are applied by two intergovernmental bodies that consist of representatives of the governments of the states that participate in the bloc. EAC is another such example, where an intergovernmental body has the competence to apply the rules.

What nevertheless should be taken into account is that the level of development of competition regimes in these trading blocs varies considerably. The EU is by far the most developed regional bloc in the world, while most of the other regional blocs have only recently adopted competition rules, and most of them have not yet applied these rules in practice, or have not even established the institutions that should apply these rules.

That said, as argued in the context of the examination of plurilateral regional agreements, the proliferation of such agreements, especially in view of the fact that attempts to adopt a multilateral agreement on competition law have not been fruitful, may mean that these agreements become of primary importance in the near future. This assumption is based on the argument that, following the example of the EU, a handful of regional blocs (rather than particular nation states) may participate in future multilateral negotiations.

This line of argument has been to a certain extent validated in the context of the discussion about the attempts to conclude a multilateral agreement on competition under the auspices of the WTO which was developed in Chapter 6. As shown in the chapter, developing countries have coordinated their actions and on particular occasions have expressed a common position in the negotiations, representing not only particular groups of states, but also regional blocs such as the African Union and CARICOM.

Apart from this general observation, the chapter reviewed the history of negotiations at the multilateral level with regard to the adoption of a competition agreement. The major part of the chapter was devoted to the examination of the negotiations that took place for almost ten years under the auspices of the WTO. In particular, the chapter reviewed the development of the proposal put forward by the EU for a WTO competition agreement, and the reactions that this proposal met from both the United States and the vast majority of developing countries.

This discussion brought to the surface a number of arguments developed in the context of the observations made in previous chapters. For instance, it exposed the traditional position of the United States that the unilateral application of competition rules is preferable in cases where an anticompetitive practice takes place in the territory of a state which has no competition law in place or is unwilling to apply the law. It also exposed the perception prevailing among the US competition community that US law is superior to other national competition laws, and therefore a multilateral agreement would not be desirable, as such an agreement could lead to the distortion of competition standards due to the *quid pro quo* nature of the WTO negotiations.

This last assumption, with regard to the nature of the negotiations at the WTO, simply restates the argument raised in previous chapters that competition law and policy is not an end in itself. As repeatedly noted, the particular application of competition law and policy at a national level takes into account other important policies, and in view of the absence of a multilateral agreement, this phenomenon is magnified at the international level where policies not directly linked to competition law, as well as the divergent policies of various countries, are encountered.

This was vividly illustrated in the context of the presentation of the reasons that led a number of developing countries to oppose the EU proposal for the adoption of a multilateral competition agreement at the WTO. In particular, it was noted that the proposal was rejected on the basis that these countries considered industrial policy to be a far more important policy than competition policy, since the application of industrial policy might assist them in creating firms strong enough to compete in the international markets. In addition, it was noted that the opposition of developing countries to the inclusion of competition and the other Singapore issues in the negotiations at the WTO was due to these countries' dissatisfaction with the process of negotiations on agriculture, which is another indication that multilateral negotiations on competition may depend upon the negotiations on issues not directly related to competition.

Irrespective of these arguments, the discussion on the WTO negotiations on competition also revealed that at least two policy networks have been developed in the process of the negotiations. In particular, it has been suggested that both in the EU and the United States, trade officials have been more sympathetic to the possible adoption of a competition agreement under the auspices of the WTO than their competition colleagues. This divergence in preferences has been more evident in the context of the work carried out at the ICN, which is dominated by competition experts and which excludes trade experts.

The analysis of the ICN's work has also validated the argument that in cases where there is no clear common understanding as to the optimum application of a legal instrument at the national level, soft law is employed to overcome the various problems that emerge with regard to the application of the legal instrument at the international level. As regards competition law and policy in particular, the fact that a common 'culture of competition' (that is, a common understanding on how competition operates, what the proper economic approach is, and to what extent the operation of competition law and policy may have an influence on international trade) has not emerged has made the contribution of the ICN to the field of international competition law, through a number of recommendations and best practices, of major significance. Of particular importance in this context has been the work carried out by the OECD and UNCTAD.

7.3 International dimension of EU competition law and policy

On the other hand, the examination of the various types of international agreements and the negotiations on the adoption of a multilateral competition agreement has provided some useful insights with regard to the central theme that this book has attempted to address, i.e. the international dimension of EU competition law and policy. A first principal argument that may be raised following the above analysis, is that the EU has been a prominent player – internationally – in the establishment and development of competition law and policy, as a tool for the effective regulation of economic activity in national markets. This argument is based on the fact that the EU has for fifty years consistently applied competition rules in the context of the supervision of its internal market. The choice of this model of governance of the markets (through the use of competition law and policy), in combination with the fact that the EU is economically and politically one of the most important powers in the world, has contributed enormously to the diffusion of the economic, political and legal concepts of competition law and policy, and the adoption of competition law by other countries.

Furthermore, and with regard to the discussion of the various types of agreements that include or are devoted to competition law, it has also become obvious from the above analysis that the EU has overall been one of the protagonists in the development of competition law and policy at the international level. This may be attributed first to the fact that the EU has applied competition law at a transnational level, since it is a regional agreement that comprises several Member States which retain their national sovereignty. In this regard, the fact that a common competition law has been developed throughout the region is by itself evidence of the contribution of the EU to the process of internationalisation of competition.

In addition, the EU has been actively involved in all the forms of international cooperation. More particularly, it has been active in all the international fora that include competition law in their agenda (WTO, OECD, ICN, UNCTAD), and has concluded with other countries or regional blocs a number of agreements that include competition rules. That said, the separate analysis of the various categories of agreements provided in previous chapters leads us to the conclusion – which is the main finding of this study – that depending on each particular type of agreement, the role of the EU in the formation and application of such agreements varies.

In particular, it has been argued that the EU's policy with regard to bilateral and trilateral enforcement cooperation agreements has generally been neutral, in the sense that the EU has signed agreements only with its most important partners, and it has not seemed eager to extend this nexus of cooperation to other states. This lack of enthusiasm of the EU towards entering into more agreements of this kind may be attributed to the fact that the EU's bureaucracy does not consider such semi-formal cooperation to be particularly effective, due to the discretionary nature of enforcement cooperation agreements. On the other hand, as noted, the EU has attempted to find ways which would allow it to conclude a second generation enforcement cooperation agreement with the United States, which could open up the way for the adoption of further agreements in the future. That said, as things now stand, it seems unlikely that the EU would proceed to the conclusion of more agreements of this type.

As opposed to enforcement cooperation agreements, the EU has invested significant resources in the negotiation and application of bilateral trade agreements which include competition provisions. In particular, it has been pointed out that it has used this type of agreement in order to expand its legal regime, including competition, to a large number of neighbouring countries, and to prepare the field for the accession of some of these countries to the EU. The first such agreements have already led to the accession of twelve countries, and considering how the EU has been expanded in the last fifty years, it seems safe to assume that more countries will join the EU in the future. In addition, the EU has actively pursued the smooth operation of these agreements by providing significant funding to its co-signing partners to assist them in drafting the necessary laws and in setting up enforcement institutions.

On the other hand, it has been noted that the closer the relationship of the EU with its co-signing partners, the more detailed the bilateral trade agreements become. This argument is also valid with regard to the competition provisions found in these agreements. As observed, the agreements signed with acceding and candidate countries, and to a certain extent also those with Mediterranean countries, imposed on these countries the harmonisation of their competition rules with those of the EU. In contrast, in the agreements with certain ex-USSR states, the relevant wording is far looser. In any event, it is beyond doubt that the EU has played a major role in both the formation and application of bilateral trade agreements which include competition provisions.

The EU has also had an influential role with regard to the establishment (or drafting) of competition regimes in other plurilateral regional blocs. This book has argued that such influence, at least in terms of competition, may be attributed primarily to the fact that a number of blocs have to a certain extent followed the EU competition regime, and less so to the attempts of the EU itself to impose its regime on these blocs. When the Treaty of Rome was signed in 1957, nobody could have anticipated the degree of influence that the newly established regional bloc would have in the field of international relations and international law. As noted above, one of the fields in which the EU has had a dramatic influence is competition law and policy. Chapter 5 on plurilateral regional trade agreements briefly reviewed the competition regime of the EU and argued that this regime has become the principal model for the development of the competition regimes of various other regional blocs around the world. The chapter also suggested that further research needs to be undertaken with regard to the development of the competition regimes of the other regional blocs in order to further quantify the extent to which the EU has influenced the development of these regimes.

By contrast, the discussion developed in Chapter 6 has revealed that in the field of multilateral competition negotiations, the EU has been the follower, and the United States the clear leader. This has been observed primarily in the context of the negotiations for a competition agreement in the WTO, where in the mid-1990s, the EU took the initiative to pursue the inclusion of a competition agreement within the international trade system, but faced fierce opposition both from the United States and from a number of developing countries, which eventually led to the collapse of the talks in Cancun. In addition, the secondary role of the EU has also been observed with regard to the formation of the ICN, which at the moment is the most active international (virtual) organisation in the field of competition law and policy. As pointed out, the original idea for the establishment of the ICN in fact came from the US bureaucracy, who proposed the creation of the ICN, at a time when the EU was very actively pursuing the inclusion of competition at the WTO, as a way, among other things, to escape a binding multilateral agreement. The EU, having come to realise that its proposal for a WTO competition agreement could not survive the difficult negotiations, felt compelled to support the proposal of the United States and the (admittedly very important) work of the ICN.

7.4 Final remarks

Marie-Laure Djelic has stated in relation to the process of internationalisation of competition law that:

> The case of antitrust is an illustration that something we can call 'globalization' is indeed happening. But it also shows that this globalization is very much a process in the making, partly open ended, quite complex and messy. Globalization is not, far from it, a state of things or a reality. Globalization is not 'the end of history' – rather it is our history in the making.[1]

This study has attempted to observe through the lens of the EU the internationalisation of competition rules, mainly by analysing international norms, which even though not unproblematic attempt to put into context this complex and messy process. The major finding of the book with regard to the international dimension of the EU, and in particular the role of the EU in the formation and application of international competition agreements, confirms Djelic's argument in the sense that, depending on the particular type of agreement, the influence of the EU varies.

The other main argument of the book is that, in view of the fact that competition law is a relatively new legal instrument, there is a considerable way to go before consensus is reached as to the optimum operation of competition law and policy, and probably even a longer distance to travel before countries agree to adopt a binding multilateral agreement on competition. Because as Gerber has very convincingly opined 'only when international obligations created an explicit alignment of the interests of the decision-makers did convergence achieve notable success'.[2]

[1] See M.-L. Djelic (2005), 'From Local Legislation to Global Structuring Frame: The Story of Antitrust' 5(1) *Global Social Policy* 55, at 71.

[2] D.J. Gerber (1999), 'The U.S.–European Conflict Over the Globalisation of Antitrust Law: A Legal Experience Perspective' 34(1) *New England Law Review* 123, at 133.

APPENDIX 1

Economic Theories Applied to Competition Law

A1.1 Classical theory

It was in the late seventeenth century when Adam Smith published his seminal work, *The Wealth of Nations*,[1] in which the theory of the market economy was invented. Smith, influenced by other major scholars of this era, such as Cantillon, Turgot and Hume, who had already tried to explain why competition appears in markets, or put simply, why an individual buyer wants to outbid his rivals,[2] was the first to use the concept of competition as a 'general organising principle of economic analysis and the economic society'.[3]

He considered individuals as egoistic creatures with no understanding of common interest or socially benefiting solutions, and described competition as a race by individuals which would make these individuals improve their production and force the price of the traded products to its 'natural level', or result in the lowering of profits to a minimum.[4] It follows that Smith saw competition as a process which would restrain individuals from colluding on prices at the expense of society.[5] Against this natural tendency of individuals, Smith did not propose the establishment of a competition or anti-monopoly policy, since on a theoretical level he actually paid no attention to monopolies.[6] Nonetheless, it has been suggested in the literature that Smith advocated some kind of

[1] A. Smith (1776), *An Inquiry into the Nature and Causes of the Wealth of Nations* (Dublin: Whitestone).

[2] O. Budzinski (2003), *Pluralism of Competition Policy Paradigms and the Call for Regulatory Diversity*, Philipps-University of Marburg Volkswirtschaftliche Beitraege No. 14/2003, available at http://papers.ssrn.com/sol3/papers.cfm?abstract_id=452900 (last visited on 2 December 2009).

[3] P.J. McNulty (1968), 'Economic Theory and the Meaning of Competition' 82(4) *Quarterly of Economics* 639, at 646–7.

[4] *Ibid.* at 643.

[5] According to one of his most quoted passages: 'People of the same trade seldom meet together … but the conversation ends in a conspiracy against the public, or in some contrivance to raise prices'. See Smith (1776), *supra* n. 1 at 183.

[6] The concept of monopoly and its effects was first challenged some seventy-five years after the publication of *The Wealth of Nations* by Dionysius Lardner. See Stigler (1982), 'The Economists and the Problem of Monopoly', at 1.

competition policy, since he proposed the following in order to maintain the process of competition: (i) the state must ensure that external institutional arrangements that define property rights would guarantee legal protection for market transactions, protect freedom of choice and prohibit unfair behaviour; (ii) there must be internal institutional arrangements which reduce unfair behaviour by moral rules; and (iii) he recommended that politicians should not follow any suggestions made by entrepreneurs.[7]

A1.2 Neoclassical economics

Almost 150 years after the emergence of the classical economic theory, another team of economists, including Cournot, Dupuit, Jevons, Edgeworth, Clark and Knight, added to Smith's theory by attempting to incorporate scientific methods, and in particular mathematics, in the analysis of markets. These new scientific tools offered them the opportunity to observe that market prices depend on the subjective relative value of goods (the marginal utility) rather than on objective values of the factors of production included in the goods (which was the classical understanding).[8]

What clearly makes this theory different from the classical theory is that it attempts to analyse the *effects* of competition, rather than considering competition as the ordering force. In doing so, neoclassical economists created 'price theory' and developed the standard models of monopoly, oligopoly and polypoly.[9] They further developed this analysis by creating the notion of 'perfect competition', which is the equilibrium of a polypolistic market.[10] This model is built upon two major theorems. The first indicates that under a situation of perfect competition, the market itself will generate a Pareto-efficient allocation of resources. The second states that if a king plans to achieve a certain distribution among his subjects, this distribution may be equally achieved by the market mechanism, provided that he is unimpaired in distributing initial resource endowment.[11]

The concept of perfect competition assumes that a large number of firms operate in a specific market; they produce identical products; there is a lack of innovation; both buyers and sellers have complete information about prices; and no firm is able to control prices. Should perfect competition prevail, then allocative and productive efficiency[12] will be achieved and this will bring

[7] Budzinski (2003), *supra* n. 2 at 4. [8] *Ibid.* at 4–5.

[9] McNulty (1968), *supra* n. 3 at 641.

[10] M. Furse (1996), 'The Role of Competition Policy: A Survey' 17(4) *European Competition Law Review* 250, at 251.

[11] J. Liesner and D. Glynn (1987), 'Does Anti-trust Make Economic Sense?' 8(4) *European Competition Law Review* 344, at 348.

[12] According to one of the most influential proponents of the neoclassical theory, Frank Knight, allocative efficiency is 'the assignment or allocation of the available productive

overall public welfare.[13] The opposite situation from perfect competition is a monopoly, where in its extreme form, there is a single seller in the market and many buyers. The assumption in a monopoly situation is that it is impossible for other firms to enter the market and the single seller is therefore able to control the prices (the monopolist is a 'price setter').[14] This model, even though it displays certain limitations, has been to a great extent the basis of most of the subsequent competition theories.

A1.3 Alternatives to the perfect competition model

It has been pointed out above that the model of perfect competition has certain limitations. A number of economists at the beginning at the twentieth century found that a number of phenomena in the market could not be explained under the perfect competition model. Such phenomena included the impact of advertising strategies on the choice of consumers, the fact that associations had by that time institutionalised information exchange and other forms of cooperation in the market, and also the fact that there was continual industry concentration in some markets.[15] Edward H. Chamberlain, in *The Theory of Monopolistic Competition*,[16] developed two main alternatives to the neoclassical model (perfect competition v. monopoly).

Monopolistic competition

The first alternative is the concept of 'monopolistic competition'. Monopolistic competition indicates a market where each seller chooses the best strategy, in the knowledge of the strategies followed by other sellers.[17] What the model of monopolistic competition added to the neoclassical model is the following: whereas, according to the neoclassical model, sellers have two options (either to sell at the market price or withdraw from it), and take industry demand as a fact, according to the monopolistic competition model, sellers

forces and materials among the various lines of industry', and productive efficiency is 'the effective coordination of the various means of production in each industry into such groupings as will produce the greatest result'. F. Knight (1933), *The Economic Organisation* (University of Chicago Press) 9.

13 For a comprehensive analysis of these notions, see F.M. Scherer and D.R. Ross (1990), *Industrial Market Structure and Economic Performance* (3rd edn, Houghton Mifflin) chs. 1, 2.

14 K. Mehta (1999), 'The Economics of Competition' in Faull and Nikpay (eds.), *The EC Competition Law of Competition* (Oxford University Press) paras. 1.58–1.61.

15 R.J.R. Peritz (1996), *Competition Policy in America, 1888–1992: History, Rhetoric, Law* (New York: Oxford University Press) 106.

16 E.H. Chamberlain (1933), *The Theory of Monopolistic Competition* (Harvard University Press) 55–69.

17 P. Smith and D. Begg (2000), *Economics* (6th edn, McGraw-Hill Publishing) ch. 10.

do not take demand as a fact but try to alter it by distinguishing their product from other sellers' similar products, either by offering something better for the same price, or by changing the buyer's impression about the product through advertisement.[18]

Oligopoly

The second and (in terms of the evolution of economic theory relevant to competition) more important of Chamberlain's inventions is the concept of 'oligopoly'. Oligopoly involves a market with few sellers, selling identical products, and each recognising that its own price depends not only on its own output, but also on the actions and strategies of other important competitors.[19] Chamberlain observed that in an oligopolistic market, if rivals act logically, the result is the same as it would be if there was a monopolistic agreement between them.[20] His theory was based on the ability of firms which operate in concentrated markets to react quickly to the strategies of the other firms in the same market. He therefore introduced an economic logic of cooperation between firms to explain the lack of price competition in markets with few firms, and by doing so he produced a model alternative to price competition in markets with many firms.[21]

A1.4 Workable competition and the Harvard School

Given the shortcomings of the theory of perfect competition, and based on the findings of Chamberlain, J.M. Clark introduced the concept of 'workable competition'.[22] According to this concept, since perfect competition is unattainable, governments should try to achieve the results which are closest to the perfect competition ideal.[23] In order to achieve this goal, a number of factors relating to the structure of the markets, conduct and performance of firms should be analysed to quantify the deviations of a particular industry from perfect competition.

Despite the fact that the concept of workable competition has certain limitations, and notably it is both difficult to select the particular criteria by which

[18] Peritz (1996), *supra* n. 15 at 108.

[19] Smith and Begg (2000), *supra* n. 17, ch. 10.

[20] G. Stigler (1964), 'A Theory of Oligopoly' 72(1) *Journal of Political Economy* 44.

[21] Peritz (1996), *supra* n. 15 at 108.

[22] J.M. Clark (1940), 'Toward a Concept of Workable Competition' 30(2) *American Economic Review* 241.

[23] In Clark's words, 'one may hope that government need not assume the burden of doing something about every departure from the model of perfect competition'. See Clark, *ibid.* at 256.

the workability of competition may be assessed and to weigh up whether these criteria have been fulfilled,[24] it was the central theoretical basis in the establishment of the principles of the Harvard Law School, which dominated the competition policy applied in the United States for more than thirty years. Despite its limitations, the European Court of Justice has made explicit reference to this theory and the definition of the notion of workable competition.[25]

Based on the static model (i.e. one that examines markets using an absolute distinction between monopoly and perfect competition), researchers of the Harvard School were the first to use data gathered in relation to different markets and apply them to specific industries.[26] According to their theory, it is the market structure which determines the conduct of firms and consequently the performance of the market. Thus, the major outcome of this line of thought was the creation of the structure–conduct–performance paradigm. Based on this paradigm, proponents of the Harvard School suggested that high concentration in a specific market is the main, if not the only, determinant of barriers to entry.[27] The aim of any competition policy should be to avoid concentrated markets and high entry barriers.[28] Hence, competition enforcement should be focused on structural remedies. As a consequence, the role of competition authorities and subsequently governments is very important. The theory of the Harvard School suggests that where the market structure is wrong, then the government must intervene in order to change this structure. If the conduct of market actors is wrong, then the government should intervene by, for instance, making sure that restrictive practices must be registered.[29]

24 A. Jones and B. Sufrin (2004), *EC Competition Law: Text, Cases and Materials* (Oxford University Press) 14. For an early comment on the concept, see S.H. Sosnick (1958), 'A Critique of Concepts of Workable Competition' 72(3) *Quarterly Journal of Economics* 380.

25 Moreover, the notion of workable competition has been used by the European Court of Justice in the *Metro* case: 'The powers conferred upon the Commission under Article [81(3)] show that the requirements for the maintenance of workable competition may be reconciled with the safeguarding of objectives of a different nature and to this certain restrictions on competition are permissible, provided that they are essential to the attainment of those objectives and they do not result in the elimination of competition for a substantial part of the Common Market'. See Case 26/76 *Metro SB* v. *Commission* [1977] ECR 1875, para. 20.

26 Furse (1996), *supra* n. 10 at 253.

27 For instance, Carl Kaysen and Donald Turner suggested that 'an unreasonable degree of market power as such must be illegal': C. Kaysen and D. Turner (1959), *Antitrust Policy* (Cambridge University Press) 111; Joe Bain defined barriers to entry as 'the advantages of established sellers in an industry over potential entrant sellers, these advantages being reflected in the extent to which established sellers can persistently raise prices above a competitive level without attracting new firms to enter the market': J.S. Bain (1956), *Barriers to New Competition* (Harvard University Press) 3.

28 Mehta (1999), *supra* n. 14, paras. 1.09–1.11.

29 Liesner and Glynn (1987), *supra* n. 11 at 356.

A1.5 The Chicago School

The proponents of the Chicago School came to question the structure–conduct–performance paradigm by showing that the causal link between concentration, entry barriers and monopoly profits was not very strong and at times even non-existent.[30] They thus gave a different definition of entry barriers. According to Stigler, entry barriers are costs that the new entrants have but the incumbents did not suffer, a definition obviously different from the one given by Bain.[31] According to Chicagoans, barriers to entry could exist either because of economies of scale and scope, or by the intervention of governments in the market, in the form of intellectual property laws, state aid, import tariffs, etc.[32]

Utilising the concepts of economies of scale and scope, they showed that the causal link is not between market concentration and high profit but between firm size leading to increased efficiency and sometimes to increased profits. The conclusion of this theoretical school was that governments should intervene in the markets only in cases of hard-core cartels and horizontal mergers that could either create a monopoly directly or facilitate cartelisation by drastically reducing the number of remaining sellers in the market.[33]

A1.6 Game theory model

These arguments by the proponents of Chicago School altered the Harvard structure–conduct–performance paradigm. Furthermore, a new line of economic thinking, also known as new industrial economics, has returned to the basic paradigm but also considers the conduct and performance of the market as important in the evaluation of the competitiveness of a market. By using game theory, this model mostly focuses on the conduct or strategic behaviour of firms in oligopolistic situations and tries to determine whether the possibility of collusion is likely or not.[34]

[30] Mehta (1999), *supra* n. 14, para. 1.12.

[31] G. Stigler (1968), 'Barriers to Entry, Economies of Scale and Firm Size' in R.D. Irwin (ed.), *The Organisation of Industry* (Homewood) 67–70.

[32] Mehta (1999), *supra* n. 14, para. 1.47.

[33] R. Posner (1979), 'The Chicago School of Antitrust Analysis' 127 *University of Pennsylvania Law Review* 925, at 928.

[34] G. Werden (2004), 'Economic Evidence on the Existence of Collusion: Reconciling Antitrust Law with Oligopoly Theory' 71 *Antitrust Law Journal* 719; R. Schmalense (1982), 'Antitrust and the New Industrial Economics' 72(2) *Papers and Proceedings of the Ninety-Fourth Annual Meeting of the American Economic Association* 24; for a comment, see A. Jacquemin (2000), *Theories of Industrial Organisation and Competition Policy: What are the Links?*, European Commission Forward Studies Unit Working Paper.

A1.7 Contestable markets

Another variant on perfect competition is the theory of contestable markets, developed in the last twenty-five years. According to William Baumol, who first developed the theory, a market is contestable if 'entry is absolutely free, and exit is absolutely costless'.[35] The theory of contestable markets is based on the distinction between fixed and sunk costs that a firm has to face in its attempt to enter the market. A fixed cost is a cost that cannot be recouped by a firm. To give a practical example, in the case of an airline, one fixed cost is the amount of money paid for the advertisement of the routes it provides. On the other hand, an aircraft is not necessarily a fixed cost, since it can be sold on the second-hand market.[36] If there is no second-hand market for aircraft, an airline which wants to terminate its operations would not be able to sell the aircraft, and would thus suffer, according to the contestability theory, sunk costs. The theory holds that if there were no sunk costs, the firm would be able to enter and exit the market at any time.

What the theory of contestability adds to economic thinking is that it no longer matters whether there are many firms in the market (as the model of perfect competition would suggest) in order for the market to be competitive. What matters is the existence of potential competition, that is the ability of a firm freely (i.e. without sunk costs) to enter or exit the market. Thus, competition law and policy should not be focused on issues relating to price, profits and behaviour of market players, but rather examine whether there are sunk costs in a market and, furthermore, whether these costs can be eliminated or recovered. This distinction is crucial since it shifts the interest of governments from the market itself to the perimeters of the market.[37]

Two points must be stressed with regard to the theory of contestability. The first is that it has been suggested in the literature that the theory lacks consistent assumptions and cannot be applied in real-world situations.[38] Secondly, the theory has very rarely been applied in competition cases.[39]

A1.8 Dynamic competition, innovation and technological efficiency

Joseph Schumpeter was the first economist to systematically study the relationship between competition and innovation.[40] Not satisfied with the static

[35] W.J. Baumol (1982), 'Contestable Markets: An Uprising in the Theory of Industry Structure' 72(1) *American Economic Review* 1.

[36] Liesner and Glynn (1987), *supra* n. 11 at 353. [37] *Ibid.* at 354.

[38] For a comprehensive criticism of the theory, see W.G. Shepherd (1984), 'Contestability vs. Competition' 74(4) *American Economic Review* 572.

[39] A. Oldale (2000), 'Contestability: The Competition Commission Decision on North Sea Helicopter Services' 21(8) *European Competition Law Review* 345.

[40] J. Schumpeter (1943), *Capitalism, Socialism and Democracy* (London: G. Allen & Unwin).

model of perfect competition,[41] Schumpeter emphasised dynamic technological efficiency, as opposed to the Pareto or allocative efficiency of the static analysis. He argued that what really matters in markets is not a price mechanism, which according to neoclassical economists would lead to static allocative and productive efficiency, but rather the pace of innovation.[42] Thus, what competition policy should be aiming at is to create the conditions in which technological innovation could reach maximum levels.

Based on this observation, he further argued that in highly competitive markets where many firms operate, these firms do not have the resources needed to innovate seriously. Instead, according to his theory a monopolist has the resources and he can also afford the risk of investing these resources in research and development projects. Thus, Schumpeter's contribution to the economic analysis of competition represented a breakthrough, since it opened up a new debate on the importance of innovation in estimating the level of competition in a market.

A1.9 The Austrian School

Another influential school of thought regarding the evolution of economic thinking on competition matters has been the Austrian School.[43] The Austrian School challenged neoclassical economics in both the methodological and political contexts and developed their theory about competition around two main arguments. The first is that markets should be analysed in dynamic terms. Like Schumpeter, they held that what really matters is the market process and not the notion of competitive equilibrium upon which neoclassical economics were built. The second central element of Austrian School analysis is that of entrepreneurship, which was defined as the alertness of traders to spot opportunities in the markets, not yet spotted by rivals.[44]

41 The static analysis totally ignores the time dimension, as it is looking at a situation of equilibrium. It is concerned solely with the allocation of resources, in the context of fixed technology and perfect information, and therefore does not take into account the effect that the dissemination of information and the product and process innovation may have in the markets. See Mehta (1999), *supra* n. 14, paras. 1.118–1.127. These assumptions have led commentators to argue that static analysis leads to a conceptually dubious 'Nirvana approach'. See H. Demsetz (1969), 'Information and Efficiency: Another Viewpoint' 12 *Journal of Law and Economics* 1, at 3.

42 In his words, 'The fundamental impulse that keeps the capitalist engine in motion comes from the new consumers' goods, the new methods of production and transportation, the new markets, the new forms of industrial organization that capitalist enterprise creates'. See Schumpeter (1943), *supra* n. 40 at 82.

43 Menger is considered the father of the Austrian School in the late nineteenth century. Nonetheless, Friedrich Hayek has been its most prominent advocate.

44 See Liesner and Glynn (1987), *supra* n. 11 at 362. See also I.M. Kirzner (1997), 'Entrepreneurial Discovery and the Competitive Market Process: An Austrian Approach' 35(1) *Journal of Economic Literature* 60.

Austrians, in particular Hayek, developed a theory based on the process of discovery and thus analysed competition from a behavioural point of view.[45] The main question of Hayek's research was about the 'division of knowledge', which according to his work was the central aspect of economics as a social science.[46] Hayek came to the conclusion that all aspects of knowledge division may be addressed by the markets themselves, where competition as a competitive process is the driving force of a system for information exchange.[47]

In sum, the Austrian School thought of competition as an active process centring at least as much on innovation as around price, and believed that the entrepreneurial quest for profits lay at the heart of the economy. Market process not only reveals information and knowledge about scarcities, but it also satisfies them in the best possible way. As a result, the role of the government should be twofold: first, to make sure that entrepreneurship, the market's most important driving force, is not hampered; secondly, to abstain from intervening directly in the market, as the market itself can create solutions that no human brain can invent.[48]

A1.10 Ordoliberalism

The notion of Ordoliberalism (constitutional liberalism) played a major part in the development of German competition law and subsequently of EU competition law.[49] It was developed at the University of Freiburg in the 1920s, initially by an economist, Walter Eucken, and two lawyers, Franz Bohn and Hanns Grossmann-Doerth.[50]

[45] On this point there is a similarity between the Austrian and the Chicago Schools.

[46] Three subsequent questions have to be addressed: (a) how do individuals acquire knowledge that may be useful to them?; (b) how is subjective knowledge disseminated?; and (c) how is knowledge controlled in order to reveal possible errors? M.E. Streit and M. Wohlgemuth (1997), *The Market Economy and the State: Hayekian and Ordoliberal Conceptions*, Max-Planck-Institut zur Erfoschung von Wirtschaftssystemen, Diskussionbeitrag 06–97, at 9, available at www.dundee.ac.uk/cepmlp/journal/assets/images/Streit-onHayek97.pdf (last visited on 2 December 2009).

[47] For a detailed analysis of these ideas, see F.A. Hayek (1978), *New Studies in Philosophy, Politics, Economics and the History of Ideas* (London: Routledge).

[48] See Liesner and Glynn (1987), *supra* n. 11 at 362.

[49] *Ibid.*; See also T.J. Horton and S. Schmit (2002), 'A Tale of Two Continents: The Coming Clash of the Conflicting Economic Viewpoints in Europe and the United States' 23(3) *University of Pennsylvania Journal of International Economic Law* 539. It is interesting to note that until the appointment of Philip Lowe, all the other Directors-General of the Directorate-General for Competition since the establishment of the European Commission came from Germany.

[50] This team was soon joined by a larger group of (mainly) younger legal and economic scholars. See D.J. Gerber (1994), 'Constitutionalising the Economy: German Neo-Liberalism, Competition Law and the "New" Europe' 42 *American Journal of Comparative Law* 25, at 28–9.

Ordoliberals brought together law and economics in order to overcome what has been described by Eucken as the 'great antinomy' in the history of economic knowledge. In the past, economists either examined economic phenomena from a theoretical point of view totally ignoring facts (theoretical economics), or, on the opposite side, their studies were solely based on facts, totally ignoring theory (this latter method was used by the historical school, which dominated German academia in the early twentieth century).[51] To overcome this intellectual gap, Eucken called for the integration of legal and economic knowledge. Ordoliberals considered economic freedom as part of political freedom and they sought an economy composed, to the extent possible, of small and medium-sized companies.[52]

Several characteristics differentiate Ordoliberalism from any other economic school that attempted to analyse the concept of competition. The most significant of these characteristics is the fact that it is based on humanist values rather than efficiency or other purely economic concerns. The aim of the ordoliberal society, as this was envisaged by its inventors, was to search for a 'third way' between democracy and socialism, between the US 'western' model and the Soviet 'eastern' one.[53] This model would create a social system where individuals would be as free as possible not only from political interference, but also from economic power. Competition would be the driving force which would secure sustained economic development and stability and would further control economic power, which allows infringements on the liberty of other people. Freedom of people in turn is regarded as the most significant precondition of moral behaviour.[54] Hence, ordoliberals argued that the crucial point with regard to competition law was not the market itself but the existence and acts of the largest firms in the market. They saw the existence of such firms as a threat to the economic and subsequently political freedom of people and thus proposed that the actions of such large firms should be controlled by the state.[55]

[51] *Ibid.* at 40–1.
[52] *Ibid.* at 37.
[53] *Ibid.* at 36.
[54] Streit and Wohlgemuth (1997), *supra* n. 46 at 7.
[55] See UNCTAD (2005), *Exclusionary Anti-competitive Practices: Their Effects on Competition and Development*, at 101.

APPENDIX 2

General Information about Plurilateral Regional Agreements

This appendix is supplementary to Chapter 5. The appendix is organised geographically and sets out some general information relating to key dates, membership and institutions for each of the agreements discussed.

A2.1 Europe

A2.1.1 The EU

The establishment of the EU goes back to 1951, when six countries[1] decided to enter the European Coal and Steel Community (ECSC). In 1957, these same states created the European Economic Community (EEC) and the European Atomic Energy Community (EURATOM). The aim of the EEC was the creation of a common market which would be achieved with the adoption of a common external tariff, the attainment of undistorted competition, the gradual coordination of the participating states' economic and monetary policies, and gradual harmonisation of their fiscal and social policies.[2] The EEC and EURATOM Treaties were merged in 1965, when the European Community was created.

The bloc has been built around four main institutions.[3] Two bodies have predominantly legislative functions: the Council of Ministers, which consists of governmental representatives of the Member States, and the European Parliament, which consists of members elected by the citizens of the Member States. The other institutions are: the (European) Court of Justice, which is the

[1] Belgium, France, Germany, Italy, Luxembourg and the Netherlands.

[2] See Articles A2 and A3 of the EC Treaty.

[3] On the complex legislative procedure in the EU as it stood until the entry into force of the Lisbon Treaty, see P. Craig and G. De Burca (2003), *EU Law: Text, Cases, and Materials* (Oxford University Press) 139–49. See also G. Tsebelis and G. Garrett (2001), 'The Institutional Foundations of Intergovernmentalism and Supranationalism in the European Union' 55(2) *International Organisation* 357. The structure of the EU, the competences of its institutions, the decision procedures and the relationship between the EU and its Member States are discussed in this study only to the extent that these arrangements directly relate to competition law and policy.

judicial body with the competence to decide upon cases based on EU law,[4] and the European Commission, which is the administrative body of the EU, with some quasi-judicial and legislative powers.

In the early years of its existence, the pace of cooperation and coordination in the EU was slow. In particular, the 1960s were characterised by tensions between the European Commission and the French government, led by the French President, Charles de Gaulle, which advocated that all decisions at the European level should be taken following a unanimous decision by the Member States,[5] thus slowing down law-making and heading to what was called 'euroschlerosis'.[6]

In the 1970s and 1980s, the EU was significantly enlarged. The six initial Member States had become ten by 1986, with the accession over time of Denmark, Ireland, the United Kingdom, Greece, Spain and Portugal. In 1986, the Single European Act (SEA), the first major amendment of the EC Treaty, was signed. The SEA provided for a number of important substantive and institutional changes in the EU system.[7] It reactivated the original ambition of creating a single internal market, where the free movement of goods, persons, services and capital would be ensured, by the end of 1992.

The second major amendment of the initial EC Treaty was the Treaty of Maastricht, signed in 1992, which established the European Union, and thus is called the Treaty of European Union (TEU). The TEU provided for the establishment of an economic and monetary union (EMU), and also introduced the three pillar structure of the Union. Apart from the Economic Communities pillar, which was included in the strategy of the EU since its conception, the Common Foreign and Security Policy pillar and the Justice and Home Affairs pillar were set up.[8] The Treaties of Amsterdam of 1997 and Nice of 2000, further expanded and deepened the cooperation between the Member States in the fields of security and defence, and judicial affairs, and also provided for changes in the judicial system and decision-making.[9] In parallel, in the last twenty years, the number of Member States of the EU has been more than

[4] Since 1989 various competences of the ECJ have been transferred to the Court of First Instance (CFI), and in 2004, the Civil Service Tribunal was established with the competence to examine cases relating to the civil service. See Article 225a EC.

[5] Known as the Luxembourg accords. See Craig and De Burca (2003), *supra* n. 3 at 13–14.

[6] See T. Sloot and P. Verschuren (1990), 'Decision-Making Speed in the European Community' 29(1) *Journal of Common Market Studies* 75.

[7] For a brief review of the amendments, see A. Campbell (1986), 'The Single European Act and its Implications' 35(4) *International and Comparative Law Quarterly* 932.

[8] As to the former, it included issues of foreign and security policy and enabled the Council to define common positions that should be followed by the Member States. As to the latter, it provided for cooperation on judicial and police issues as well as on international criminal matters. See Craig and De Burca (2003), *supra* n. 3 at 25–6.

[9] For a brief review, see *ibid.* at 28–52.

doubled. The first (small) wave of enlargement occurred in 1995, when Austria, Sweden and Finland joined the EU. On 1 May 2004, another ten countries joined the EU,[10] and on 1 January 2007, Bulgaria and Romania entered the Union, increasing the number of EU Member States to twenty-seven, and thus creating a Union with a population of more than 450 million inhabitants. Fifteen of the Member States use the euro as their common currency,[11] and in view of all these developments, the European Union has become a phenomenon unique in history.

This project is an ongoing one. The Treaty of Lisbon, which entered into force some days before the submission of this book, opens up new paths for the development of the EU. Both the EU and the EC Treaties have been amended, the latter being renamed the Treaty on the Functioning of the European Union (TFEU). More importantly, a number of novel elements have been incorporated into the workings of the EU. First, extended legislative powers have been granted to the European Parliament, which is empowered to co-decide with the Council of Ministers on certain areas, including the negotiation and adoption of international agreements.[12] Secondly, qualified majority voting in the Council (of Ministers) of the European Union is extended to new policy areas, such as immigration and culture; thirdly, the role of President of the European Council (which becomes a full EU institution) for an extended and renewable period of two and a half years has been created; fourthly, the position of High Representative of the Union for Foreign Affairs and Security Policy to present a united position on EU policies has been created, with the assistance of a new European External Action Service which is to provide back up and support to the High Representative. Fifthly, the Charter of Fundamental Rights has become legally binding.[13] While the practical consequences of these amendments are to be tested in the forthcoming years, what is beyond doubt is that the EU will continue to play an important role in the field of international law and international relations in more general in the foreseeable future.

[10] Cyprus, Czech Republic, Estonia, Hungary, Latvia, Lithuania, Malta, Poland, Slovakia and Slovenia.

[11] These include the states that entered the EU before 2000, with the exception of Denmark, Sweden and the United Kingdom. Slovenia has used the common currency from 1 January 2007, and Cyprus and Malta from 1 January 2008.

[12] This is of importance with regard to the topic discussed in this book. For analysis, see J. Wouters, J.D. Coppens and B. De Mesteer (2008), 'The European Union's External Relations' in S. Griller and J. Ziller (eds.), *The Lisbon Treaty: EU Constitutionalism without a Constitution Treaty?* (New York: Springer Wien) 143.

[13] See the website of the European Commission at http://europa.eu/lisbon_treaty/index_en.htm (last visited on 2 December 2009). For an analysis of the main changes that the the Treaty of Lisbon introduces to the EU, see Griller and Ziller (2008), *supra* n. 12.

A2.1.2 EFTA and EEA

The European Free Trade Association (EFTA) was created by seven countries (Austria, Denmark, Norway, Portugal, Sweden, Switzerland and the United Kingdom) in 1960, with the aim of liberalising trade among its Member States and at the same time of being a counter-balance to the European Economic Community.[14] Finland joined EFTA in 1961, Iceland in 1970, and Liechtenstein in 1991. Denmark, United Kingdom, Portugal, Austria, Finland and Sweden withdrew from EFTA at different stages in order to join the EU. Thus, EFTA currently has four Member States: Iceland, Liechtenstein, Norway and Switzerland, and it could be argued that while it has achieved its free trade goal and has been active for almost fifty years, it has certainly been overshadowed by the success of the EU. This is evident from the fact that most of its Member States eventually joined the EU. This trend has been recently followed by another EFTA Member State, Iceland, which recently applied for EU membership.

In parallel, EFTA and the EU have developed close formal cooperation through the Agreement on the European Economic Area (EEA), signed in 1992 between the EU and its Member States and Iceland, Liechtenstein and Norway, and which entered into force in 1994.[15] The EEA extends the EU internal market to the three EFTA states. It also provides for cooperation on horizontal issues such as environment, social policy and research and development; it does not, nevertheless, include areas such as the EU's common policies on external trade, agriculture and fisheries, monetary union or security and foreign affairs.[16]

In terms of institutions, EFTA is governed by the EFTA Council, an intergovernmental body which consists of representatives of the member states. The EFTA Secretariat is the supranational institution which deals with the day-to-day running of EFTA. At the EEA level, two other important bodies were set up in the context of the adoption of the EEA agreement. The first is the EFTA Surveillance Authority which consists of three Commissioners (each from every participating country) and functions independently of the EFTA states, and has the task to ensure that the EFTA member states respect their obligations undertaken in the EEA agreement. In addition, the EFTA Court of Justice has a role comparable to the European Court of Justice in the EU.

Finally, it should be noted that, in the last fifteen years, EFTA has created an extended network of bilateral free trade agreements. EFTA has signed eighteen

[14] See the website of EFTA at www.efta.int/content/about-efta/about-efta/aboutefta.

[15] Switzerland did not join the EEA since membership was rejected by referendum. The relationship between Switzerland and the EU is governed by bilateral agreements.

[16] See EFTA (2009), 'A Short Introduction to 50 Years of EFTA', available at www.efta.int/content/publications/fact-sheets/efta-general/efta-50-years.pdf (last visited on 2 December 2009).

such trade agreements with twenty-eight countries, and it is in the process of negotiating further similar agreements.[17]

A2.2 South America

A2.2.1 The Andean Community

In 1969, five of the members of the Latin America Free Trade Association, namely Bolivia, Colombia, Ecuador, Peru and Chile, signed the Cartagena Agreement, which set up the Andean Pact, a subregional organisation with its own distinct legal identity[18] with the aim of creating a customs union.[19] Venezuela entered the group in 1973, while Chile withdrew in 1976.[20] Although the institutions provided by the agreement were established,[21] developments over the creation of a customs union in this region were very slow in the 1970s, while in the 1980s negotiations were totally stagnant.[22]

The institutional set-up of the Andean Community was restructured in 1987 with the Protocol of Quito, which largely followed the structure of the EU.[23] Economic integration gained momentum in the 1990s, when intra-regional trade was substantially increased, partly due to the achievement in 1993 of a free trade area between four out of the five member states (with the exception of Peru), and the establishment of a common external tariff in

[17] *Ibid.* Note that these agreements include a bilateral agreement signed between EFTA and SACU.

[18] As stated in Cartagena Agreement, art. 48.

[19] See W.P. Avory (1972), 'Sub-Regional Integration in Latin America: The Andean Common Market' 11(2) *Journal of Common Market Studies* 85.

[20] For a brief history of the Andean Community, see the Community's website at www.comunidadandina.org/ingles/quienes/brief.htm (last visited on 2 December 2009).

[21] These institutions are the following: the General Secretariat, which is the executive body of the Andean Community and has the competence to initiate the legislative process, by formulating legislative proposals; legislation is adopted by the Council of Ministers, whose membership varies, in accordance with the subject; and finally the Andean Community Court of Justice (set up in 1969) is the regional judicial institution of the agreement. See R.M. Ferreira (2005), 'Regional Cooperation Agreement and Competition Policy: The Case of the Andean Community' in M. Mashayekhi and T. Ito (eds.), *Multilateralism and Regionalism: The New Interface* (Geneva and New York: UNCTAD) ch. 11, 145.

[22] See the website of the Andean Community.

[23] Two supranational bodies, the General Secretariat and the Commission, were given executive and rule-making powers (respectively), while at the top of the administrative hierarchy are the Presidential Council and the Council of Foreign Ministers. The Andean Court of Justice is the competent court to review cases relating to the regional legislation. See A. Malamud (2001), *Spillover in European and South American Integration: An Assessment*, Latin American Studies Association (LASA) 2001 Meeting Paper, at 11–13, available at http://lasa.international.pitt.edu/Lasa2001/MalamudAndres.pdf (last visited on 2 December 2009).

1995,[24] but also because of a number of acts of common legislation that were adopted at the time in a number of fields, such as agriculture, investment, intellectual property and competition.[25]

Regional integration slowed down in 2000 due to political and economic problems faced by the member states, but it regained momentum in 2003.[26] The free trade area was completed in January 2006, when Peru fulfilled the relevant obligations. Bolivia and Peru have not yet implemented the common external tariff; nonetheless, considerable recent attempts to strengthen further integration have been made. That said, in June 2006 Venezuela left the agreement with the aim of joining the rival regional grouping, MERCOSUR.

A2.2.2 MERCOSUR

MERCOSUR was established in 1989 by the Treaty of Asunción.[27] The driving force behind the adoption of the MERCOSUR agreement was similar to that of the establishment of the EU: the hope of limiting the possibilities of traditional military hostility between the major regional powers, Brazil and Argentina.[28] The founding members of the agreement were Brazil, Argentina, Uruguay and Paraguay. As noted, Venezuela is also in the process of entering MERCOSUR, while in the 1990s, Bolivia and Chile became associate members. MERCOSUR's initial aim was to create a customs union and a common market based on the four freedoms (free movement of goods, persons, services and capital).

In terms of institutional set-up, MERCOSUR is an intergovernmental and not a supranational organisation, in the sense that it has an administrative Secretariat but its competences are limited in comparison to the competences of the EU institutions. The MERCOSUR Council of the Common Market[29] resembles the Council of Ministers and the European Council of the EU,[30] and

[24] M. Bacquero Herrera (2004), 'The Andean Community: Finding her Feet within Changing and Challenging Multidimensional Conditions' 10 *Law and Business Review of the Americas* 577, at 583.

[25] See European Commission (2007), *Andean Community Regional Strategy Paper 2007–2013*, E/2007/678 (12 April 2007) 3–4.

[26] *Ibid.*

[27] Treaty Establishing a Common Market between the Argentine Republic, the Federal Republic of Brazil, the Republic of Paraguay and the Eastern Republic of Uruguay, www.sice.oas.org/trade/mrcsr/mrcsrtoc.asp (last visited on 2 December 2009).

[28] World Bank (2005), *Global Economic Prospects 2005: Trade, Regionalism and Development*, at 36.

[29] Which consists of the Ministers for Foreign Affairs and Economy and the Meetings of the Heads of State. In addition, there are Meetings of the Ministers of Agriculture and Industry, Justice and Internal and Social Affairs.

[30] See J.A.E. Vervaele (2005), 'MERCOSUR and Regional Integration in Latin America' 54 *International and Comparative Law Quarterly* 387, at 391. For a detailed analysis of the

the MERCOSUR Common Market Group, which consists of four officials (and four deputies) from each member state's ministry of foreign relations, ministry of the economy and central bank, is the main executive body of the institution, and also has the competence to conduct international negotiations based on the guidelines provided by the Council.[31]

The initial seven years of the operation of MERCOSUR were a great success, as trade and investment between Brazil and Argentina was quadrupled, and MERCOSUR became the third largest trading bloc in the world, after the EU and NAFTA.[32] Nonetheless, subsequent crises in the economies of Brazil and Argentina had an impact on the smaller and dependent economies of Paraguay and Uruguay, and this created major problems for the successful operation of MERCOSUR. This period was characterised by the regular use of trade protectionist measures by the participating countries, whose main aim was to resolve their domestic problems, and thus the negotiations on further regional integration were postponed.[33]

In general, MERCOSUR has achieved many of its initial objectives but is still some distance from achieving the goal of a common market. The customs union currently applies to 90 per cent of products; nevertheless, MERCOSUR members still utilise the 'safety clause' allowing them to temporarily impose high customs tariffs on selected products, such as cars, electronic equipment and chemicals.[34] In addition, there are no common market regulations in the agricultural sector, and regarding the four freedoms, improvement has been achieved only in relation to the free movement of goods.[35] The dispute settlement system of the bloc has not proved to be effective,[36] and furthermore, the MERCOSUR member states have shown reluctance on various occasions to adopt national rules compatible with the regional legislation.[37] It has also been suggested that this delay in the development of MERCOSUR may in particular be attributed to the reluctance of Brazil to support deeper integration, taking the view that the benefits associated with such a development are less than the costs that will occur from the loss of national sovereignty.[38]

institutional set-up of MERCOSUR, see R.A. Porrata Doria, Jr (2004), 'MERCOSUR: The Common Market of the Twenty First Century?' 32 *Georgia Journal of International and Comparative Law* 1, at 14–24.

31 See in detail, R. Bouzas and H. Soltz (2001), 'Institutions and Regional Integrations: The Case of MERCOSUR' in V. Bulmer-Thomas (ed.), *Regional Integration in Latin America and the Caribbean* (Institute of Latin American Studies, University of London).

32 See Porrata Doria (2004), *supra* n. 30 at 48. 33 *Ibid.* at 57.

34 See Vervaele (2005) supra n. 30 at 396. 35 See *ibid.* at 398.

36 See Porrata Doria (2004), *supra* n. 30 at 61–4.

37 As De Azevedo and Tavares De Araujo note, by 1999, Uruguay had incorporated into its national legislation only 50 per cent of the legislative instruments adopted by MERCOSUR. See A.F.Z. De Azevedo and M. Tavares De Araujo (2006), 'MERCOSUR Competition Law: Developments and Perspectives' (mimeo, on file with the author) 9.

38 *Ibid.*

A2.3 North America

A2.3.1 North American Free Trade Agreement

NAFTA, which was concluded by Canada, Mexico and the United States, entered into force in 1994.[39] Under NAFTA's provisions, within a period of fourteen years the signing parties must progressively eliminate tariffs imposed on goods imported from another signing party. The agreement includes detailed provisions relating to agricultural products, which are excluded from the provisions on tariff elimination. It also provides for the WTO compatible use of antidumping and countervailing duty measures.[40] NAFTA furthermore includes rules relating to investment, labour, intellectual property rights, financial services, telecommunications and public procurement, and detailed rules of origin. The agreement has been complemented by the North American Agreement for Environmental Cooperation,[41] and the North American Agreement on Labor Cooperation.[42]

It should be noted that none of the contracting parties entered the negotiations with the intention to create a political and social union. A political union would be in conflict with the traditional belief in the United States that such a union would considerably undermine the country's political autonomy. Canadian and Mexican governments were also concerned with the possible imbalances that could occur due to the bargaining power of the United States.[43] Such considerations had various implications. First, they had an impact on the type of the agreement, which took the form of a free trade agreement and not a customs union. Secondly, they had an impact on the institutional set-up provided by the agreement, since NAFTA does not provide for a supranational body to enforce its provisions. This role has been granted to the Free Trade Commission, which consists of government representatives,[44] and whose role is nevertheless strictly supervisory as it does not have the competence to adopt

[39] North American Free Trade Agreement, Canada–Mexico–United States, 8 December 1992, 32 ILM 289.

[40] Canada unsuccessfully attempted to negotiate the possible abolition of antidumping measures. See B. Hoekman (1998), *Free Trade and Deep Integration: Antidumping and Antitrust in Regional Agreements*, World Bank Policy Research Working Paper No. 1950, at 27–8.

[41] North American Agreement on Environmental Cooperation, Canada–Mexico–United States, 8 September 1993, 32 ILM 1480.

[42] North American Agreement on Labor Cooperation, 14 September 1993, 32 ILM 1499.

[43] F.M. Abbott (2000), 'NAFTA and the Legalisation of World Politics: A Case Study' 54(3) *International Organization* 519, at 522.

[44] The Commission is assisted by a Secretariat. See NAFTA, art. 2002.

secondary legislation. Thirdly, despite the fact that NAFTA's provisions are characterised by a high degree of precision and obligation, the parties were not willing to create a strong regional judicial institution similar to the ECJ. Instead, a moderate level of authority was granted to a dispute settlement mechanism.[45]

A2.3.2 CAFTA-DR

The most recent free trade agreement in the region is the Central American Free Trade Agreement, signed in 2004,[46] designed to eliminate tariffs between the United States and Costa Rica, El Salvador, Guatemala, Honduras and Nicaragua, plus the Dominican Republic. It is argued that the major proponents of the agreements were US clothing manufacturers, many of whom have been shifting their factories to Central America.[47] At the same time, Central American states were eager to enter such an agreement in order to ensure preferential treatment from the United States on the trade in textiles, compared to textiles from China.[48] The agreement also includes provisions on government procurement, services, investments and intellectual property rights, and has been implemented by the United States on a rolling basis, as countries make sufficient progress to meet the commitments imposed by the agreement.[49] On the other hand, it should be pointed out that the conclusion of CAFTA-DR raised major concerns both in the United States, where the agreement was passed by Congress by only a two-vote margin,[50] and also in Guatemala, El Salvador and Costa Rica,[51] which was the last country to ratify the agreement in 2007.

[45] See A.L.C. de Mestral (2006), 'NAFTA Dispute Settlement: Creative Experiment or Confusion?' in L. Bartels and F. Ortino (eds.), *Regional Trade Agreements and the WTO Legal System* (Oxford University Press), and Abbot (2000), *supra* n. 43.

[46] Dominican Republic–Central America–United States Free Trade Agreement, signed 5 August 2004, available at www.ustr.gov/trade-agreements/free-trade-agreements/cafta-dr-dominican-republic-central-america-fta/final-text (last visited on 2 December 2009).

[47] D. Dimon (2006), 'EU and US Regionalism: The Case of Latin America' XX(2) *International Trade Journal* 185, at 207–8.

[48] *Ibid.*

[49] See the export portal of the US government, at www.export.gov/fta/complete/CAFTA/index.asp?dName=CAFTA (last visited on 2 December 2009).

[50] The major concerns were raised by organised labour, the sugar industry and certain textile associations. See K.L. Balsanek, R.E. De Francesco, M.A. Frank, D.T. Hardin and M.R. Nicely (2006), 'International Legal Development in Review: 2005 Business Regulation' 40 *International Lawyer* 217, at 244.

[51] In fact there have been public protests in these countries, while Costa Rica has not yet ratified the Treaty. See E. Malkin (2006), 'Central American trade deal is being delayed by partners', *New York Times*, 2 March 2006.

A2.3.3 Free Trade Agreement of the Americas

Of the various regional projects in South and North America, the most ambitious one has been the negotiations over a Free Trade Agreement of the Americas (FTAA), launched in 1994. With the exception of Cuba, all countries in the Americas participated in the negotiations whose initial aim was the adoption of a very detailed free trade agreement and a free trade area by January 2005. Nine FTAA negotiating groups were created in the following areas: market access, investment, services, government procurement, dispute settlement, agriculture, intellectual property rights, subsidies, antidumping and countervailing duties, and competition policy. The aim of the FTAA project is to integrate the countries which participate in smaller regional blocs in North and South America (such as NAFTA, MERCOSUR, the Andean Community and CARICOM), and to this effect it includes elements from all these blocs.[52]

However, and despite the early optimism regarding the progress of the negotiations, a number of concerns raised primarily by Brazil[53] and other members of MERCOSUR[54] relating mainly to agricultural liberalisation, the use of antidumping measures and intellectual property rights,[55] led to the Ministerial Declaration, issued in November 2003 in Miami,[56] according to which particular countries may opt out from a number of areas, such as intellectual property, antidumping, agricultural subsidies, investment and competition.[57] Aside from this development, negotiations have slowed down and the goal of achieving a free trade area by 2005 has been postponed, and in general the future of the FTAA is in serious jeopardy, especially in view of the ongoing

[52] S.C. Smith (2006), 'The Free Trade Agreement of the Americas: Is there Still a Place for the World Trade Organisation?' 13 *Tulsa Journal of International and Comparative Law* 321, at 334.

[53] See A. Borges De Moura (2004), 'The Brazilian Perspective of the FTAA' 10 *Law and Business Review of the Americas* 695.

[54] In particular, in El Salvador in June 2003, these countries announced their decision to follow a three-track approach with regard to the issues under negotiation in the context of the FTAA. According to this view, certain issues would be dealt with at the multilateral level (agricultural subsidies, trade remedy disciplines, and a number of other issues that MERCOSUR was not eager to negotiate such as investment, aspects of services, intellectual property rights, competition policy and government procurement), the remaining issues at the FTAA level, and the market access negotiations on tariffs, agriculture and services would be addressed through a bilateral approach. See S.M. Stephenson and G.C. Hufbauer (2004), 'The Free Trade Area of the Americas: How Deep an Integration in the Western Hemisphere?', at 34, available at www.aeaweb.org/annual_mtg_papers/2005/0107_1015_1402.pdf (last visited on 2 December 2009).

[55] See J.A. Rivas-Campo and R. Tiago Juk Benke (2003), 'FTAA Negotiations: Short Overview' 6(3) *Journal of International Economic Law* 661, esp. 667–9.

[56] FTAA (2003), 'Free Trade Area of the Americas, Eighth Ministerial Meeting, Miami, USA, November 20, 2003, Ministerial Declaration', available at www.ftaa-alca.org/Ministerials/Miami/Miami_e.asp (last visited on 2 December 2009).

[57] *Ibid.* para. 10.

negotiations between the member states of MERCOSUR and the Andean Community leading to the establishment of the interregional South American Community of Nations.[58]

A2.4 Caribbean

A2.4.1 CARICOM

CARICOM was established by the Treaty of Chaguaramas, signed on 4 July 1973, and revised in 2001. It consists of fifteen member states,[59] most of which are small islands, and with the exception of Haiti and Suriname, former British colonies.[60] The objectives of CARICOM as identified in article 6 of the revised Treaty are wide-ranging,[61] and the revised Treaty also provides for the right of establishment, free movement of goods, services, persons and capital. In terms of trade, the aim of the contracting parties was to create a CARICOM single market and economy by December 2005. The single market was finally established in 2006, and is based on freedom of movement of goods, services, capital, business enterprise and labour within an area bounded by a customs union.[62] Currently, twelve member states participate in the single market.[63]

In terms of institutional set-up, the revised Treaty of Chaguaramas provides for the operation of a plethora of institutions, mainly intergovernmental.[64]

58 See the Presidential Declaration and Priority Agenda, issued at the First Meeting of Heads of State of the South American Community of Nations, Brasilia, 30 September 2005, available at www.comunidadandina.org/ingles/documentos/documents/casa_2005_4.htm (last visited on 2 December 2009).

59 The members are Antigua and Barbuda, the Bahamas, Barbados, Belize, Dominica, Grenada, Guyana, Haiti, Jamaica, Montserrat, Saint Lucia, St Kitts and Nevis, St Vincent and the Grenadines, Suriname and Trinidad and Tobago.

60 The total population of the member states is 14 million, while most of the CARICOM member states have a population that does not exceed 300,000 inhabitants.

61 The objectives include improvement of standards of living and work; achievement of full employment of labour and other factors of production; acceleration and coordination of sustained economic development and convergence; expansion of trade and economic relations with third states; achievement of enhanced levels of international competitiveness; organisation for increased production and productivity; achievement of a greater measure of economic leverage and effectiveness of member states in dealing with third states, groups of states and entities of any description; and the enhanced coordination of member states' foreign and economic policies and enhanced functional cooperation.

62 See N. Girvan (2007), 'Towards a Single Development Vision and the Role of the Single Economy', at 8, available at www.caricom.org/jsp/single_market/single_economy_girvan.pdf (last visited on 2 December 2009).

63 See SICE (2007), 'Establishment of the CARICOM Single Market and Economy: Summary of Status of Key Elements', available at www.sice.oas.org/TPD/CAR/csme_summary_key_elements_e.pdf (last visited on 2 December 2009).

64 See in detail, K.E. Bravo (2005), 'CARICOM, The Myth of Sovereignty, and Inspirational Economic Integration' 31 *North Carolina Journal of International Law and Commercial Regulation* 145, at 178–92.

According to the Treaty, the principal organs of CARICOM are the Conference of Heads of Government and the Community Council of Ministers.[65] The former, which consists of the member states' heads of governments, is the legislative organ of the organisation with the competence to provide policy direction, enter into treaties, establish the institutions of CARICOM, and take decisions regarding the financial affairs of the Community.[66] The Community Council of Ministers is responsible for the Community's strategy planning and the coordination of the three pillars of the Community: economic integration, functional cooperation and external relations.[67] These two institutions are assisted by four functional organs, established under article 10(2) of the revised Treaty. These include the Council for Finance and Planning (COFAD), the Council for Trade and Economic Development (COTED), the Council for Foreign and Community Relations (COFCOR), and the Council for Human and Social Development (COHSOD),[68] and several other bodies.

The main supranational administrative institution of CARICOM is the Secretariat, which has powers similar, but not equal, to the European Commission, as it does not have the competence to propose or adopt legislation, and it operates as a resource rather than an enforcing organisation.[69] Finally, in April 2005, the Caribbean Court of Justice was set up to serve both as the court with competence to decide upon issues relating to the provisions of the revised Treaty,[70] and as the court of final appeal for the member states' domestic, civil and criminal matters. These extended competences of the court are expected to lead to a harmonious development of jurisprudence in the region and thus assist the accomplishment of CARICOM's goals.[71]

A2.5 Africa

A2.5.1 West African Economic and Monetary Union

The Treaty establishing WAEMU was signed in January 1994 by seven countries[72] which had shared the same currency, the CFA franc, since 1960 through the

[65] See the revised Treaty of Chaguaramas, art. 10(1). [66] *Ibid.* arts. 11 and 12.

[67] *Ibid.* art. 13. [68] See also *ibid.* arts. 14–17.

[69] Bravo (2005), *supra* n. 64 at 187. [70] Revised Treaty of Chaguaramas, art. 211.

[71] For an analysis of the functions of the newly-established court and possible problems it may face, see S.A. McDonald (2004), 'The Caribbean Court of Justice: Enhancing the Role of International Organisations' 27 *Fordham International Law Journal* 930; L. Birdsong (2005), 'The Formation of the Caribbean Court of Justice: The Sunset of the British Colonial Rule in the English Speaking Caribbean' *University of Miami Inter-American Law Review* 197.

[72] Traite de l'Union Economique et Monetaire Ouest Africaine (UEMOA), available at www.uemoa.int/actes/traite/TraiteUEMOA.pdf (last visited on 2 December 2009). The member states of WAEMU are Benin, Burkina Faso, Ivory Coast, Mali, Niger, Senegal and Togo.

West African Monetary Union (WAMU).[73] It has been suggested that the underlying reason for the creation and strengthening of the regional bloc was the devaluation of the CFA franc by 50 per cent in 1994. The contracting parties felt that they had to supplement the monetary union with a customs union and a common market.[74] The EU model has been followed by WAEMU. In particular, the aim of the bloc is to achieve a single market based on the free movement of goods, persons, services and capital. The similarities of the WAEMU system with the EU is further exposed by the fact that there are five main regional institutions established, in accordance with the EU system: a Conference of Heads of States, a Council of Ministers, a Commission, a Court of Justice and an interparliamentary Committee.[75] As a general statement regarding the development of WAEMU, it could be argued that it has succeeded in the elimination of internal tariffs and its member states have applied a common external tariff since 2000. Nonetheless, there are still substantial obstacles both regarding internal trade and deviations from the common external tariff.[76]

A2.5.2 Economic Community of West African States

The Economic Community of West African States (ECOWAS) was established in 1975, with the adoption of the Treaty of Lagos (amended by the Treaty of Cotonou in 1993) with the aim of economically integrating the countries of this particular region. ECOWAS contains fifteen member states;[77] nonetheless, unlike WAEMU, whose members participate in ECOWAS, the process of integration has been particularly slow, due to the lack of political commitment in a region devastated by poverty and wars. To give a practical example, in 2006, the GDP of the fifteen member states was half that of Norway, while the average price for electricity was

[73] See A.S. Claeys and A. Sindzingre (2003), 'Regional Integration as a Transfer of Rules: The Case of the Relationship between the European Union and the West African Economic and Monetary Union (WAEMU)', paper presented at the Development Studies Association Annual Conference, Glasgow, University of Strathclyde, 10–12 September 2003, at 7–8. In 1997, Guinea Bissau joined the Union. All eight members of WAEMU are also members of a larger group of fifteen countries, the Economic Community of West African States (ECOWAS), discussed below.

[74] P. Van de Boogaerde and C. Tsangarides (2005), *Ten Years After the CFA Franc Devaluation: Progress Toward Regional Integration in the WAEMU*, IMF Working Paper No. WP/05/145, at 3–5.

[75] Claeys and Sindzingre (2003), *supra* n. 73 at 10.

[76] L.E. Hinkle and M. Schiff (2004), 'Economic Partnership Agreements Between Sub-Saharan Africa and the EU: A Development Perspective' 27(9) *The World Economy* 1321, at 1325.

[77] The member states are Benin, Burkina Faso, Cape Verde, Cote D'Ivoire, Gambia, Ghana, Guinea, Guinea Bissau, Liberia, Mali, Niger, Nigeria, Senegal, Sierra Leone and Togo. Mauritania was also a member of ECOWAS until 1999, when it withdrew from the agreement.

four and a half times the average charges of OECD countries, and international calls were four times the average prices charged in OECD countries.[78]

In terms of institutional set-up, article 6(1) of the Treaty provides for the establishment of a number of intergovernmental and supranational institutions. In particular, the article provides for the creation of '(a) the Authority of Heads of State and Government; (b) the Council of Ministers; (c) the Community Parliament; (d) the Economic and Social Council; (e) the Community Court of Justice; (f) the Executive Secretariat; (g) the Fund for Cooperation, Compensation and Development; (h) Specialised Technical Commissions; and (i) Any other institutions that may be established by the Authority'. Thus, the institutional set-up provided by the ECOWAS Treaty is similar to the one provided by the EU Treaty.

A2.5.3 East African Community

The East African Community encompassed five African states, namely Burundi, Kenya, Rwanda, Uganda and Tanzania.[79] Initially, the EAC agreement was signed in 1967, but it collapsed ten years later.[80] It was revived in 1999 under the Treaty of East African Cooperation, which was signed in Arusha by Kenya, Uganda and Tanzania. On 1 January 2005, the Protocol on the establishment of the EAC Customs Union entered into force.[81] According to the Treaty establishing the EAC, the member states further aim to create a common market and a monetary union.

With regard to trade remedies, and on the basis of article 75 of the Treaty, the Protocol establishing the customs union contains a number of provisions addressing issues related to antidumping, countervailing duties and safeguard measures.[82] These provisions do not abolish these trade measures; nonetheless, they provide that the member states will cooperate with other member states and the regional institutions in the process of investigation relating to these measures.[83] In terms of institutional set-up, the basic structure of the EAC is

[78] See S. Kaplan (2006), 'West African Integration: A New Development Paradigm?' 29(4) *Washington Quarterly* 81, at 84.

[79] Burundi and Rwanda entered the EAC relatively recently, in 2007.

[80] See A.T. Mugomba (1978), 'Regional Organisations and African Underdevelopment: The Collapse of the East African Community' 16(2) *Journal of Modern African Studies* 261; C. Kirkpatrick and M. Watanabe (2005), 'Regional Trade in Sub-Saharan Africa: An Analysis of East African Trade Cooperation 1970–2001' 73(2) *The Manchester School* 141.

[81] See M.A. McIntyre (2005),'*Trade Integration in East African Community: An Assessment for Kenya*, IMF Working Paper No. 05/143, at 9–12.

[82] See arts. 16–19 of the Protocol on the Establishment of the East African Customs Union.

[83] The Protocol also provides for the establishment of an intergovernmental Committee on trade remedies (in art. 24) and a dispute settlement procedure (art. 41) to resolve disputes

similar to the structure of the EU. The main institutions provided by the Treaty are the Assembly, which is the legislative organ of the Community, the Council of Ministers, which has the competence to take the political decisions as to the development of the Community and to adopt secondary legislation (regulations, directives and decisions), the EAC Court of Justice, and the Secretariat, a supranational organisation which has the responsibility to implement the articles of the Treaty, as well as regulations and directives adopted by the Council.[84]

A2.5.4 COMESA

The Common Market of Eastern and Southern Africa (COMESA) was established by a Treaty signed on 5 November 1993 in Kampala, Uganda, and ratified a year later in Lilongwe, Malawi. COMESA was formed in order to replace the former preferential trade area (PTA) which had been in existence since 1982,[85] and is one of the largest regional blocs in Africa, as it includes nineteen member states,[86] covers 42.6 per cent of the total African surface area, and accounts for 44.6 per cent of the total population of the continent and 32 per cent of the total GDP.[87]At the same time, COMESA's member states are characterised by strong differences in their economic and social backgrounds, while the region in general is characterised by low growth rates, political instability and is severely economically affected by the spread of HIV, as well as by volatile international agricultural prices.[88]

The Treaty provides for the creation of a free trade area, a customs union, and the gradual creation of a monetary union. On the other hand, antidumping measures and countervailing duties are not abolished by the Treaty. Nonetheless, it is provided that the member states must cooperate in the investigation of cases of dumping and subsidies.[89] The free trade area was launched in 2000, with eleven of the nineteen member states participating and the other

that may arise relevant to these trade remedies. See A.K. Mullei (2005), 'Integration Experience of East African Countries', paper presented at the Symposium Marking the 30th Anniversary of Banco de Mozambique, Maputo, Mozambique, 17 May 2005, at 10–14, available at www2.centralbank.go.ke/downloads/gov_speeches/Mozambique-paper.pdf (last visited on 2 December 2009).

84 See the website of EAC at www.eac.int/institutions.htm.

85 See P. Khandelwal (2004), 'COMESA and SADC: Prospects and Challenges for Regional Trade Integration', at 8.

86 COMESA's member countries are Burundi, Comoros, Democratic Republic of Congo, Djibouti, Egypt, Eritrea, Ethiopia, Kenya, Libya, Madagascar, Malawi, Mauritius, Rwanda, Seychelles, Sudan, Swaziland, Uganda, Zambia, Zimbabwe.

87 See F. Carmignani (2005), 'The Road to Regional Integration in Africa: Macroeconomic Convergence and Performance in COMESA' 15(2) *Journal of African Economies* 212, at 213.

88 *Ibid.* at 213–18.

89 See COMESA Treaty, arts. 51–4.

nine trading on preferential terms, while the customs union was lanched in June 2009.[90]

With regard to the institutional set-up of the group, the Treaty provides for the operation of four organs with decision-making powers. These include the COMESA Authority, which consists of the heads of governments of the member states, the COMESA Council of Ministers, the Committee of Governors of Central Banks, and the regional Court of Justice (operational since 1998).[91] Hence, as in the case of a number of African regional blocs, the institutional set-up of COMESA is similar to that of the EU.

A2.5.5 Southern African Customs Union

The Southern African Customs Union includes five member states: South Africa, which is economically and politically the major force in the region; Botswana, Lesotho, Namibia and Swaziland (called the 'BLNS countries'). The agreement was first signed in 1910, and provided for free movement of manufactured goods, a common external tariff and a revenue sharing formula.[92] Since then, the agreement has been amended twice, first in 1969, and more recently in 2002. Today, SACU operates as a full customs union.

In terms of institutional set-up, the main institutions of SACU are the Council of Ministers, which has legislative powers, and the Commission, which is a supranational body responsible for the implementation of the provisions of the agreement, as well as the decisions of the Council.[93] The new SACU agreement also provides for the creation of an ad hoc tribunal to decide upon any dispute that may arise with regard to the application of the agreement's provisions. The tribunal is to be set up at the request of the Council and will be composed of three members.[94] The Tribunal is not yet operational.[95]

SACU is characterised by the high level of dependence of the smaller SACU member countries on South Africa, which accounts for 90 per cent of total SACU GDP. In addition, as a result of the most recent amendment of the agreement, it has assumed absolute discretion over external trade policy, and in particular decisions on antidumping, safeguard measures and countervailing

90 See COMESA's website at www.comesa.int.

91 See COMESA Treaty, chs. 4 and 5, arts. 7–44.

92 R. Gibb (1997), 'Regional Integration in Post-Apartheid Southern Africa: The Case of Renegotiating the Southern African Customs Union' 23(1) *Journal of Southern African Studies* 67, at 73–5.

93 On the operation of and problems faced by SACU, see R. Kirk and M. Stern (2005), 'The New Southern African Customs Union Agreement' 28(2) *The World Economy* 169.

94 See SACU Agreement, art. 13.

95 See G. Mandigora (2007), *Dispute Settlement Mechanisms in Bilateral and Regional Trade Arrangements*, Tralac discussion paper.

duties that should be applied to non-members of the agreement.[96] In contrast to the 1969 agreement, the new SACU agreement provides for the establishment of supranational bodies to review the application of such trade measures.[97]

A2.5.6 Southern African Development Cooperation

The Southern African Development Cooperation was created in 1992, when eleven countries signed the Declaration and Treaty establishing the SADC, in Windhoek, Namibia (amended in 2001), with the aim of promoting peace and development in the region.[98] The origins of SADC go back to 1980, when the frontline states[99] signed the Treaty of Arusha, with the aim of resisting the influence of South Africa in the region.[100] To date, SADC includes fifteen member states,[101] and is a good example of the overlapping membership that characterises African regional trade agreements. All the five SACU members are also members of SADC, while eight of SADC's members are members of COMESA,[102] and one of SADC's members (Tanzania) is also a member of EAC.

With regard to trade, a Protocol was signed in 1996 which led to the establishment of a free trade area in 2000, in which all the member states participate except Angola and the Democratic Republic of Congo.[103] Currently, 85 per cent of all intra-SADC trade has been liberalised and the aim of SADC's member states is to fully liberalise trade by 2012. In addition, SADC has announced its intention to have a common external tariff, and thus become a customs union, by 2010, and to establish a central bank by 2016.[104]

[96] See Kirk and Stern (2005), *supra* n. 93 at 169–75.

[97] See N. Joubert (2004), 'The Reform of South Africa's Anti-Dumping Regime', WTO, Managing the Challenges of WTO Participation, Case Study No. 38.

[98] On the objectives of SADC, see art. 5 of the Amended Declaration and Treaty Establishing the Southern Africa Development Community, signed and entered into force on 14 August 2001 in Blantyre, Malawi, available at www.sadc.int/index/browse/page/120 (last visited on 2 December 2009).

[99] Angola, Botswana, Lesotho, Malawi, Mozambique, Swaziland, Tanzania, Zambia and Zimbabwe.

[100] Following the collapse of apartheid, South Africa eventually joined SADC in 1994. See Khandelwal, *supra* n. 85 at 12.

[101] Angola, Botswana, Democratic Republic of Congo, Lesotho, Madagascar, Malawi, Mauritius, Mozambique, Namibia, South Africa, Seychelles, Swaziland, United Republic of Tanzania, Zambia and Zimbabwe.

[102] Democratic Republic of Congo, Madagascar, Malawi, Mauritius, Seychelles, Swaziland, Zambia and Zimbabwe.

[103] See Khandelwal, *supra* n. 85 at 12.

[104] See *ibid.* at 12–13; see also P. Kalenga (2004), *Implementation of the SADC Trade Protocol: Some Reflections*, Trade Law Centre for Southern Africa, Stellenbosch Trade Brief.

In terms of the institutional set-up of the bloc, the supreme policy-making and legislative organ is the Summit, which consists of the heads of state of all the member states.[105] The Council of Ministers is another important institution provided by the Treaty, which has the competence to oversee the functioning and development of SADC and to recommend to the Summit the establishment of other institutions and organs.[106] The Council is assisted by another two intergovernmental organs, the Committee of Ministers and the Committee of Officials,[107] while the Secretariat is a centralised supranational organ that has the competence to apply the Decisions of the Summit.[108] Finally, article 16 of the SADC Treaty provides for the creation of a regional Tribunal, which has been operational since November 2005.[109]

A2.6 Asia

A2.6.1 ASEAN

The Association of South East Asian Nations (ASEAN) was first established in 1967, when the five original member countries[110] signed the Bangkok Declaration, with the aim of pursuing peace and political stability in the region. Following a PTA signed in 1977, members of ASEAN finally signed a free trade agreement in 1995.[111] The expressed aim of the ASEAN members is to have a fully integrated free trade area by 2010 for the five original member states, plus Brunei (ASEAN-6), and by 2015 for the remaining four members.[112] In addition, ASEAN members have agreed to create an economic community by 2020.[113]

[105] See art. 10 of the Amended Declaration and Treaty Establishing the Southern Africa Development Community.

[106] See *ibid.* art. 11. [107] See *ibid.* arts. 12 and 13.

[108] See *ibid.* arts. 14 and 15.

[109] See *ibid.* arts. 16 and 32, and the website of the African International Courts and Tribunals at www.aict-ctia.org/courts_subreg/sadc/sadc_home.html (last visited on 2 December 2009).

[110] Indonesia, Malaysia, the Philippines, Singapore and Thailand. Brunei Darussalam joined ASEAN in 1984, Vietnam in 1995, Laos and Myanmar in 1997, and Cambodia in 1999.

[111] For an analytical overview of the ASEAN project until the conclusion of the FTA, see L.H. Tan (2005), 'Will ASEAN Economic Integration Progress Beyond a Free Trade Area?' 53 *International and Comparative Law Quarterly* 935, at 936–9.

[112] Nonetheless, note that a sensitive list of products, primarily agricultural products, is excluded from the list. In addition, recent research has shown that tariffs have been eliminated by the ASEAN-6 countries only for 65 per cent of the products on the inclusion list. Thus, the 2010 and 2015 deadlines will need to be extended. See L. Cuyvers, P. De Lombaerde and S. Verhestraeten (2005), *From AFTA Towards an ASEAN Economic Community … and Beyond*, Centre for ASEAN Studies Working Paper (January 2005) 5, 7.

[113] *Ibid.* 9 *et seq.*

In terms of institutional set-up, ASEAN is an intergovernmental organisation, whose highest decision-making institution is the ASEAN Summit, which consists of the heads of governments and convenes on an annual basis. The body responsible for the application of the ASEAN Free Trade Agreement (AFTA) is the Council of Ministers, which includes ministerial level representatives from each member state, plus the Secretary General of ASEAN. Thus, the role of the ASEAN Secretariat, which is an independent supranational body, has been limited (as intended) mainly due to concerns that it would threaten the sovereignty of the member states.[114]

A2.7 Cross-regional

A2.7.1 APEC

The Asia-Pacific Economic Cooperation (APEC) was set up in 1989, and is an informal forum that promotes economic liberalisation comprising twenty-one countries.[115] As already mentioned, APEC is a cross-regional organisation, as it includes member states from four continents. The aim of APEC's founding members at the time of its establishment was to bring the WTO Uruguay Round negotiations to a successful end. In particular, it has been argued that the United States has used the adoption of this cross-regional arrangement as leverage for the difficult negotiations with the EU.[116] The official aim of APEC's participating countries is freer trade for the industrialised countries by 2010 and for developing member countries by 2020.

[114] See M. Hunt (2002), 'From "Neighbourhood Watch Group" to Community? The Case of ASEAN Institutions and the Pooling of Sovereignty' 56(1) *Australian Journal of International Affairs* 99.

[115] The Members of APEC are Australia, Brunei Darussalam, Canada, Chile, the People's Republic of China, Hong Kong, China, Indonesia, Japan, Republic of Korea, Malaysia, Mexico, New Zealand, Papua New Guinea, Peru, the Philippines, the Russian Federation, Singapore, Chinese Taipei, Thailand, the United States and Vietnam.

[116] See S.-H. Park (2005), 'Increasing Sub-regionalism within APEC and the Bogor Goals: Stumbling Block or Building Block?', at 3, available at www.apec.org.au/docs/koreapapers2/SX-SHP-Paper.pdf (last visited on 2 December 2009).

BIBLIOGRAPHY

Books, Book Chapters, Articles, Working Papers and speeches

Abbott, F.M. (2000), 'NAFTA and the Legalisation of World Politics: A Case Study' **54**(3) *International Organisation* 519

Abbott, K.W. and D. Snidal (2000), 'Hard and Soft Law in International Governance' **54**(3) *International Organisation* 421

Abbott, K., R. Keohane, A. Moravcsik, A.-M. Slaughter and D. Snidal (2000), 'The Concept of Legalisation' **54**(3) *International Organisation* 401

Abeyratne, R. (2001), 'Competition and Liberalisation in Air Transport' **24**(4) *World Competition* 607

Accominotti, O. and M. Flandreau (2005), *Does Bilateralism Promote Trade? Nineteenth Century Liberalisation Revisited*, CEPR Discussion Paper No. 5423

Adedeji, A. (2002), *'History and Prospects for Regional Integration in Africa', speech delivered at the Third Meeting of the African Development Forum, Addis Ababa*, 5 March 2002, available at www.uneca.org/eca_resources/Speeches/2002_speeches/030502adebayo.htm

Akbar, Y. and G. Suder (2006), 'The New EU Merger Regulation: Implications for EU–US Merger Strategies' **48**(5) *Thunderbird International Business Review* 667

Albers, M. (2002), 'Energy Liberalisation and EC Competition Law' **25** *Fordham International Law Journal* 909

Alter, K.J. (1998), 'Who are the "Masters of the Treaty"? European Governments and the European Court of Justice' **52**(1) *International Organisation* 121

Amato, G. and L. Laudati (eds.) (2001), *The Anticompetitive Impact of Regulation* (Edward Elgar Publishing)

Anderson, K. (2003), *How Can Agricultural Reform Reduce Poverty?*, Centre for International Economic Studies Discussion Paper No. 0321

Anderson, K. and W. Martin (eds.) (2005), *Agricultural Trade Reform and the Doha Development Agenda* (World Bank and Palgrave Macmillan)

Anderson, R.D. and P. Holmes (2002), 'Competition Policy and the Future of the Multilateral Trading System' **5**(2) *Journal of International Economic Law* 531

Archibugi, D. and C. Pietrobelli (2002), 'The Globalisation of Technology and its Implications for Developing Countries: Windows of Opportunity or Further Burdens?' **70**(9) *Technological Forecasting and Social Change* 861

Atwood, J.R. (1993), 'Positive Comity: Is it a Positive Step?' in Barry Hawk (ed.), *1992 Annual Proceedings of the Fordham Corporate Law Institute International Antitrust Law and Policy Conference* (New York: Fordham Corporate Law Institute)

Aubert, C. (2003), '*Competition Policy for Countries with Different Development Levels*', paper presented at the CEPR Competition Policy in International Markets Workshop, 17–18 October 2003, available at www.cepr.org/meets/wkcn/6/6613/papers/Aubert.pdf

Avory, W.P. (1972), 'Sub-Regional Integration in Latin America: The Andean Common Market' **11**(2) *Journal of Common Market Studies* 85

Bacquero Herrera, M. (2004), 'The Andean Community: Finding her Feet within Changing and Challenging Multidimensional Conditions' **10** *Law and Business Review of the Americas* 577

Bain, J.S. (1956), *Barriers to New Competition* (Harvard University Press)

Bakhoum, M. (2006), 'Delimitation and Exercise of Competence between the West African Economic and Monetary Union (WAEMU) and its Member States in Competition Policy' **29**(4) *World Competition* 653

Baldwin, M. (2006), 'EU Trade Politics: Heaven or Hell?' **13**(6) *Journal of European Public Policy* 526

Baldwin, R. and M. Cave (1999), *Understanding Regulation: Theory, Strategy and Practice* (New York: Oxford University Press)

Balsanek, K.L., R.E. DeFrancesco, M.A. Frank, D.T. Hardin and M.R. Nicely (2006), 'International Legal Development in Review: 2005 Business Regulation' **40** *International Lawyer* 217

Banks, J.D. (1998), 'The Development of the Concept of Extraterritoriality under European Merger Law and its Effectiveness under the Merger Regulation following the Boeing/McDonnell Douglas Decision 1997' **19**(5) *European Competition Law Review* 306

Barnet, S.E. (2004), 'Conflicts of Jurisdiction and International Comity in Extraterritorial Antitrust' **18** *Emory International Law Review* 555

Baumol, W.J. (1982), 'Contestable Markets: An Uprising in the Theory of Industry Structure' **72**(1) *American Economic Review* 1

Bavasso, A. F. (1998), 'Boeing /McDonnell Douglas: Did the Commission Fly Too High?' **19**:4 *European Competition Law Review*, 243

Bebr, G. (1953), 'The European Coal and Steel Community: A Political and Legal Innovation' **63** *Yale Law Journal* 1

Beckford, D.S. (2009), '*CARICOM: Perspectives on Challenges to Meeting Regional and Multilateral Obligations*', paper presented at UNCTAD Regional Seminar on Trade and Competition: Prospects and Future Challenges for Latin America and the Caribbean, SP/SRCC– PFDALC Di No. 18–09

Beghin, J.C. and A. Aksoy (2003), *Agricultural Trade and the Doha Round: Lessons from Commodity Studies*, Centre for Agricultural and Rural Development, Iowa State University Briefing Paper No. 03-BP 42

Bellis, J.-F. (1997), 'The Treatment of Dumping, Subsidies and Anticompetitive Practices in Regional Trade Agreements' in P. Demaret, J.-F. Bellis and G. García Jiménez (eds.), *Regionalism and Multilateralism after the Uruguay Round: Convergence, Divergence and Interaction* (Brussels: European Interuniversity Press)

Benidickson, J. (1993), 'The Combines Problem in Canadian Legal Thought' **43**(4) *University of Toronto Law Journal* 799

Bercero, I.G. and S. Amarasinha (2001), 'Moving the Trade and Competition Debate Forward' **4**(3) *Journal of International Economic Law* 481

Berg, W. (2004), 'The New EC Merger Regulation: A First Assessment of its Practical Impact' **24** *Northwestern Journal of International Law and Business* 683

Bhattacharjea, A. (2004), 'Export Cartels: A Developing Country Perspective' **38**(2) *Journal of World Trade* 331

(2006), 'The Case for a Multilateral Agreement on Competition Policy: A Developing Country Perspective' **9**(2) *Journal of International Economic Law* 293

Bilal, S. (2004), '*Can the EU Be a Model and a Driving Force for Regional Integration in Developing Countries?*', paper presented at the Second Annual Conference of the Euro-Latin Study Network on Integration and Trade, Florence, Italy, 29–30 October 2004, available at www.ecdpm.org

Biondi, A., P. Eeckhout and J. Flynn (eds.) (2004), *The Law of State Aids in the European Union* (Oxford University Press)

Birdsong, L. (2005), 'The Formation of the Caribbean Court of Justice: The Sunset of the British Colonial Rule in the English Speaking Caribbean' *University of Miami Inter-American Law Review* 197

Bliss, M. (1991), 'The Yoke of the Trusts: A Comparison of Canada's Competitive Environment in 1889 and 1989' in R.S. Khemani and W.T. Stanbury (eds.), *Historical Perspectives on Canadian Competition Policy* (Halifax NS: Institute for Research on Public Policy)

Bode, M. and O. Budzinski (2005), *Competing Toward International Antitrust: The WTO vs. the ICN*, Marburg Papers on Economics No. 03/2005

Boeder, T.L. and G.J. Dorman (2000), 'The Boeing/McDonnell Douglas Merger: The Economics, Antitrust Law and Politics of the Aerospace Industry' **XLV**(1) *Antitrust Bulletin* 119

Borges De Moura, A. (2004), 'The Brazilian Perspective of the FTAA' **10** *Law and Business Review of the Americas* 695

Bouzas, R. and H. Soltz (2001), 'Institutions and Regional Integrations: The Case of MERCOSUR' in V. Bulmer-Thomas (ed.), *Regional Integration in Latin America and the Caribbean* (Institute of Latin American Studies, University of London)

Brady, R.A. (1945): 'The Role of Cartels in the Current Cultural Crisis' **35**(2) *American Economic Review* 312

Braithwaite, J. and P. Drahos (2000), *Global Business Regulation* (Cambridge University Press)

Braudel, F. (1979), *The Wheels of Commerce: Civilization and Capitalism 15th –18th Century* (New York: Harper & Row) vol. II

Bravo, K.E. (2005), 'CARICOM, The Myth of Sovereignty, and Inspirational Economic Integration' **31** *North Carolina Journal of International Law and Commercial Regulation* 145

Brittan, L. (1999), '*The Need for a Multilateral Framework of Competition Rules*', paper presented at OECD Conference on Trade and Competition, Paris, 29–30 June 1999, reproduced in OECD, *Trade and Competition Policies: Exploring the Ways Forward* (Paris: OECD)

(1992), *Competition Policy and International Relations* (Brussels: Centre for European Policy Studies)

Brown, O., F. Haq Shaheen, S. Rafi Khan and M. Yusuf (2005), *Regional Trade Agreements: Promoting Conflict or Building Peace?*, International Institute for Sustainable Development Working Paper

Budzinski, O. (2003), *Pluralism of Competition Policy Paradigms and the Call for Regulatory Diversity*, Philipps-University of Marburg Volkswirtschaftliche Beitraege No. 14/2003

Burley, A.-M. (1992), 'Law Among Liberal States: Liberal Internationalism and the Act of State Doctrine' **92**(8) *Columbia Law Review* 1907

Burnside, A. and Y. Botteman (2004), 'Networking Amongst Competition Agencies' **10**(1) *International Trade Law and Regulation 9*

Burnside, A. and H. Crossley (2005), 'Cooperation in Competition: A New Era' **30**(2) *European Law Review* 234

Byers, M. and G. Nolte (2003), *United States Hegemony and the Foundations of International Law* (Cambridge University Press)

Byrne, B., S. Goodman and E. Shapiro (2006), 'Extending the Long Arm of US Antitrust Law: The Ian Norris Extradition Battle', *Global Competition Review*, December 2005/January 2006

Cacciato, C. (1996), 'Subsidies, Competition Laws, and Politics: A Comparison of the EU and USA', Centre for West European Studies, University of Pittsburgh Policy Paper No. 2

Calvani, T. (2005), 'Conflict, Cooperation, and Convergence in International Competition' **72** *Antitrust Law Journal* 1127

Campbell, A. (1986), 'The Single European Act and its Implications' **35**(4) *International and Comparative Law Quarterly* 932

Carmignani, F. (2005), 'The Road to Regional Integration in Africa: Macroeconomic Convergence and Performance in COMESA' **15**(2) *Journal of African Economies* 212

Cernat, L. (2005), 'Eager to Ink but Ready to Act? RTA Proliferation and International Cooperation on Competition Policy' in P. Brusick, A.M. Alvarez and L. Cernat (eds.), *Competition Provisions in Regional Trade Agreements: How to Assure Development Gains* (Geneva and New York: UNCTAD)

Chamberlain, E.H. (1933), *The Theory of Monopolistic Competition* (Harvard University Press)

Claeys, A.S. and A. Sindzingre (2003), '*Regional Integration as a Transfer of Rules: The Case of the Relationship Between the European Union and the West African Economic and Monetary Union (WAEMU)*', paper presented at the Development Studies Association Annual Conference, Glasgow, University of Strathclyde, 10–12 September 2003

Clark, J.M. (1940), 'Toward a Concept of Workable Competition' **30**(2) *American Economic Review* 241

Clough, S.B. and C.W. Cole (1941), *Economic History of Europe* (Boston MA: D.C. Heath)

Coase, R.H. (1979), 'Adam Smith's View of Man' **19**(3) *Journal of Law and Economics* 529

Cocuzza, C. and M. Montini (1998), 'International Antitrust Co-operation in a Global Economy' **19** *European Competition Law Review* 156

Commanor, W. and P. Rey (1997), 'Competition Policy Towards Vertical Restraints in Europe and the United States' **24** *Empirica* 37

Cosma, H.A. and R. Whish (2003), 'Soft Law in the Field of EU Competition Policy' **14**(1) *European Business Law Review* 25

Craig, P. and G. De Burca (2003), *EU Law: Text, Cases, and Materials* (Oxford University Press)

Crampton, P.S. and B.A. Facey (2002), 'Revisiting Regulation and Deregulation Through the Lens of Competition Policy' **25**(1) *World Competition* 25

Crampton, P.S. and C.L. Witterick (1997), 'Trade Distorting Private Restraints and Market Access: Learning to Walk Before We Run' **24** *Empirica* 53

Cremona, M. (2003), 'State Aid Control: Substance and Procedure in the Europe Agreements and the Stabilisation Association Agreements' **9**(3) *European Law Journal* 265

Cuyvers, L., P. De Lombaerde and S. Verhestraeten (2005), *From AFTA Towards an ASEAN Economic Community ... and Beyond*, Centre for ASEAN Studies Working Paper

Dabbah, M. (2003), *The Internationalisation of Antitrust Policy* (Cambridge University Press)

Damro, C. (2006), 'The New Trade Politics and EU Competition Policy: Shopping for Convergence and Co-operation' **13**(6) *Journal of European Public Policy* 867

Dana, W.F. (1902), 'The Supreme Court and the Sherman Anti-Trust Act' **16**(3) *Harvard Law Review* 178

Danzon, P. and Li-Wei Chao (2000), 'Does Regulation Drive out Competition in Pharmaceutical Markets?' **XLIII** *Journal of Law and Economics* 311

Daugbjerg, C. (1999), 'Reforming the CAP: Policy Networks and Broader Institutional Structures' **37**(3) *Journal of Common Market Studies* 407

De Bievre, D. (2006), 'The EU Regulatory Trade Agenda and the Quest for WTO Enforcement' **13**(6) *Journal of European Public Policy* 851

Demsetz, H. (1969), 'Information and Efficiency: Another Viewpoint' **12** *Journal of Law and Economics* 1

De Noronha Goyos, D. (1997), 'The Globalisation of Competition Law: A Latin American Perspective' **3**(1) *International Trade Law Review* 20

Desta, M.G. and N J. Barnes (2006), 'Competition Law and Regional Trade Agreements' in L. Bartels and F. Ortino (eds.), *Regional Trade Agreements and the WTO Legal System* (Oxford University Press)

Devuyst, Y., J. Kankanen, P. Lindberg, I. Orssich and G. Roebling (2002), 'EU Enlargement and Competition Policy: Where are We Now?' **1** *Competition Policy Newsletter* 3

DiMaggio, P.J. and W.W. Powell (1983), 'The Iron Cage Revisited: Institutional Isomorphism and Collective Rationality in Organizational Fields' **48** *American Society Review* 147

Dimon, D. (2006), 'EU and US Regionalism: The Case of Latin America' **XX**(2) *International Trade Journal* 185

Dinan, D. (2004), *Europe Recast: A History of the European Union* (Lynne Rienner)

Dixit, A (1984), 'International Trade Policies for Oligopolistic Competition' **94** *Economic Journal* 1

Dixit, A. and J.E. Stiglitz (1977) 'Monopolistic Competition and Product Diversity' **67**:3 *The American Economic Review*, 297

Djelic, M.-L. (2005), 'From Local Legislation to Global Structuring Frame: The Story of Antitrust' **5**(1) *Global Social Policy* 55

Dobson, P. (2005), *Vertical Restraints Policy Reform in the European Union and United Kingdom*, Loughborough University Research Series Paper No. 2005:2

Doern, G. and S. Wilks (eds.) (1996), *Comparative Competition Policy: National Institutions in a Global Market* (Oxford University Press)

Ehlermann, C.-D. (1992), 'The Contribution of EC Competition Rules to the Single Market' **29** *Common Market Law Review* 257

(1994), 'The International Dimension of Competition Policy' **17** *Fordham International Law Journal* 833

(2000), 'The Modernization of EC Antitrust Policy: A Legal and Cultural Revolution' **37** *Common Market Law Review* 537

Ehlermann, C.-D. and J. Rattlif (2005), *Mario Monti's Legacy for Competition Policy in Article 82*, Wilmer Cutler Pickering Hale and Dorr Antitrust Series Paper No. 50

Eichengreen, B. and J.A. Frankel (1995), 'Economic Regionalism: Evidence from Two 20th Century Episodes' **6**(2) *North American Journal of Economics and Finance* 89

Elgstrom, O. (2007), 'Outsiders' Perceptions of the European Union in International Trade Negotiations' **45** *Journal of Common Market Studies* 949

Elhauge, E. and D. Geradin (2007), *Global Competition Law and Economics* (Hart Publishing)

Emmert, F., F. Kronthaler and J. Stephan (2005), *'Analysis of Statements Made in Favour of and Against the Adoption of Competition Law in Developing and Transition Economies*, paper presented at the project on Competition Policy Foundations for Trade Reform, Regulatory Reform, and Sustainable Development, Brussels, 19 and 20 April 2005

Evenett, S.J. (2005), 'What Can We Learn from the Competition Provisions of RTAs?' in P. Brusick, A.M. Alvarez and L. Cernat (eds.), *Competition Provisions in Regional Trade Agreements: How to Assure Development Gains* (Geneva and New York: UNCTAD)

Evenett, S.J., M.C. Levenstein and V.Y. Suslow (2001), 'International Cartel Enforcement, Lessons from the 1990s' **24**(9) *World Economy* 1221

Fabiosam, J., J. Beghin, S. de Cara, A. Elobeid, C. Fang, M. Isik, H. Matthey, A. Saak, P. Westhoff, D. Scott Brown, B. Willot, D. Madison, S. Meyer and J. Kruse (2005), 'The Doha Round of the World Trade Organisation and Agricultural Markets Liberalisation: Impacts on Developing Economies' **27**(3) *Review of Agricultural Economics* 317

Ferreira, R.M. (2005), 'Regional Cooperation Agreement and Competition Policy: The Case of Andean Community' in M. Mashayekhi and T. Ito (eds.), *Multilateralism and Regionalism: The New Interface* (Geneva and New York: UNCTAD)

Fikentscher, W. (1994) 'Competition Rules for Private Agents in the GATT/WTO System' **49** *Swiss Review of International Economic Relations*, 281

(2001) 'Market Anthropology and Global Trade' **1**:1 *The Gruter Institute Working Papers on Law, Economics, and Evolutionary Biology*

Finckenstein, K. von (2001), *'International Antitrust Cooperation: Bilateralism or Multilateralism?'*, speech delivered in Vancouver, 31 May 2001, available at www.apeccp.org.tw/doc/Canada/Policy/1a.htm

Finger, J.M. and Ph. Schuler (2000), 'Implementation of Uruguay Round Commitments: The Development Challenge' **23**(4) *The World Economy* 511

Finger, J.M. and L.A. Winters (2002), 'Reciprocity in the WTO' in B. Hoekman, A. Mattoo and P. English (eds.), *Development, Trade and The WTO* (World Bank)

Finnemore, M. and S.J. Toope (2001), 'Alternatives to "Legalization": Richer Views of Law and Politics' **55**(1) *International Organisation* 743

Forrester, I.S. and A.P. Komninos (2006), *EU Administrative Law: Competition Law Adjudication*, Sectoral Report on Adjudication in the Competition Field, American Bar Association, European Union Administrative Law Project

Fox, E.M. (1995), 'Competition Law and the Agenda for the WTO: Forging the Links of Competition and Trade' **4** *Pacific Rim Law and Policy* 1

(1997), 'Toward World Antitrust and Market Access' **91**(1) *American Journal of International Law* 1

(1999), 'Competition Law and the Millennium Round' **2**(4) *Journal of International Economic Law* 665

(2003), 'Antitrust and Regulatory Federalism: Races Up, Down, and Sideways' **75** *New York University Law Review* 1781

(2006), 'The WTO's First Antitrust Case – *Mexican Telecom*: A Sleeping Victory for Trade and Competition' **9** *Journal of International Economic Law* 271

(2006), 'Monopolization, Abuse of Dominance and the Indeterminacy of Economics: The US/EU Divide' *Utah Law Review* 725

Fox, E.M. and J.A. Ordover (1995), 'The Harmonisation of Trade Law and Competition Law: The Case for Modest Linkages of Law and Limits to Parochial State Action' **19**(2) *World Competition Law and Economics* 5

Fox, E.M. and L.A. Sullivan (1987), 'Antitrust – Retrospective Prospective: Where are We Coming From? Where are We Going?' **62** *New York University Law Review* 936

Freeman, L.N. (1995), 'US–Canadian Information Sharing and the International Antitrust Enforcement Assistant Act of 1994' **84** *Georgetown Law Journal* 339

Friederiszick, H.W., L.-H. Roller and V. Verouden (2006), 'European State Aid Control: An Economic Framework' in P. Buccirossi (ed.), *Advances in the Economics of Competition Law* (MIT Press)

Furnish, A. (1970), 'A Transnational Approach to Restrictive Business Practices' **4** *International Lawyer* 317

Furse, M. (1999), 'Competition Law and the WTO Report Japan – Measures Affecting Consumer Photographic Film and Paper' **20**(1) *European Competition Law Review* 9

(2004), *Competition Law of the EC and the UK* (4th edn, Oxford University Press)

Galindo-Rodriguez, B. (2007), '*European Competition Policy: Development and Protectionism*, speech delivered at the Sixth Annual ICN Conference, Moscow, available at www.icn-moscow.org/get_file.php?id=187

Galindo Sanchez, R. (2005), '*New Antitrust ANDEAN Regulation*', available at www.brigardurrutia.com.co/figuras/funciones/documento.asp?ruta=/publicaciones/87/NewAntitrustAndean2005_rgs.pdf

Gellhorn, E. and W.E. Kovacic (1994), *Antitrust Law and Economics in a Nutshell* (West Publishing)

Geradin, D. (ed) (2004), *Modernization and Enlargement: Two Major Challenges for EC Competition Law* (Intersentia)

Geradin, D. and N. Petit (2004), 'Competition Policy in South Mediterranean Countries' **3**(1) *Review of Network Economics* 65

Gerber, D.J. (1994), 'Constitutionalising the Economy: German Neo-Liberalism, Competition Law and the "New" Europe' **42** *American Journal of Comparative Law* 25

(1999), 'The US–European Conflict Over the Globalisation of Antitrust Law: A Legal Experience Perspective' **34**(1) *New England Law Review* 123

(2000), *Law and Competition in the Twentieth Century: Protecting Prometheus* (Oxford University Press)

Gibb, R. (1997), 'Regional Integration in Post-Apartheid Southern Africa: The Case of Renegotiating the Southern African Customs Union' **23**(1) *Journal of Southern African Studies* 67

Gilpin, R. (1987), *The Political Economy of International Relations* (Princeton University Press)

Giotakos, D., L. Petit, G. Garnier and P. De Luyck (2001), 'General Electric/Honeywell: An Insight into the Commission's Investigation and Decision' **3** *Competition Policy Newsletter* 5

Girvan, N. (2007), 'Towards a Single Development Vision and the Role of the Single Economy', available at www.caricom.org/jsp/single_market/single_economy_girvan.pdf

Glenn, J.K. (2004), 'From Nation-States to Member States: Accession Negotiations as an Instrument of Europeanization' **2** *Comparative European Politics* 3

Goodnow, F.J. (1897), 'Trade Combinations at Common Law' **12**(2) *Political Science Quarterly* 212

Gottschalk, K. and S. Schmidt (2004), 'The African Union and the New Partnership for Africa's Development: Strong Institutions for Weak States?' **4** *Internationale Politik und Gesellschaft* 138

Goyder, E.C. (2003), *EC Competition Law* (4th edn, Oxford University Press)

Graham, E. (2002), 'The Relationship Between International Trade Policy and Competition Policy' in Z. Drabek (eds.), *Globalization Under Threat: The Stability of Trade Policy and Multilateral Agreements* (Edward Elgar Publishing)

Grewlich, A.S. (2001), 'Globalisation and Conflict in Competition Law: Elements and Possible Solutions' **24**(3) *World Competition* 367

Griffin, J.P. (1994), 'EC and US Extraterritoriality: Activism and Cooperation' **17** *Fordham International Law Journal* 353

(1998), 'Antitrust Aspects of Cross-Border Mergers and Acquisitions' **19**(1) *European Competition Law Review* 12

(1999), 'What Business People Want from a World Antitrust Code' **34**(1) *New England Law Review* 39

Griffin, J.M. (2000), *'An Inside Look at a Cartel at Work: Common Characteristics of International Cartels'*, paper presented at the American Bar Association Section of Antitrust Law Forty-eighth Annual Spring Meeting, Washington DC, 6 April 2000, available at www.usdoj.gov/atr/public/speeches/4489.htm

Gross, L. (1948), 'The Peace of Westphalia, 1648–1948' **42**(1) *American Journal of International Law* 20

Gugler, K., D.C. Muller, B.B. Yurtoglu and C. Zulehner (2003), 'The Effects of Mergers: an International Comparison' **21** *International Journal of Industrial Organisation* 625

Ham, A.D. (1993), 'International Cooperation in the Anti-trust Field and in particular the Agreement Between the United States of America and the Commission of the European Communities' **30** *Common Market Law Review* 571

Hammond, S. (2006), '*Charting New Waters in International Cartel Prosecution*', speech delivered at the Twentieth Annual National Institute on White Collar Crime, 2 March 2006, available at www.justice.gov/atr/public/speeches/214861.htm

Hawk, B. (1995), 'System Failure: Vertical Restraints and EC Competition Law' **32** *Common Market Law Review* 973

Hayek, F.A. (1978), *New Studies in Philosophy, Politics, Economics and the History of Ideas* (London: Routledge)

Held, D., D. Golblatt, A.G. McGrew and J. Perraton (1999), *Global Transformations: Politics, Economics and Culture* (Stanford University Press)

Hertel, T.W., B.M. Hoekman and W. Martin (2002), 'Developing Countries and a New Round of WTO Negotiations' **17**(1) *World Bank Research Observer* 113

Higgott, R. (2005), *The Theory and Practice of Global and Regional Governance: Accommodating American Exceptionalism and European Pluralism*, GARNET Working Paper No. 01/05

Himelfarb, A.J. (1996), 'The International Language of Convergence: Reviving the Antitrust Dialogue Between the United States of America and the European Union with a Uniform Understanding of Extraterritoriality' **17**(3) *University of Pennsylvania Journal of International Economic Law* 909

Hinkle, L.E. and M. Schiff (2004), 'Economic Partnership Agreements Between Sub-Saharan Africa and the EU: A Development Perspective' **27**(9) *The World Economy* 1321

Hoekman, B. (1997), *Competition Policy in the Global Trading System: A Developing Country Perspective*, World Bank Policy Research Working Paper No. 1735

(1998), *Free Trade and Deep Integration: Anti-Dumping and Antitrust in Regional Agreements*, World Bank Policy Research Working Paper No. 1950

Hoekman, B. and P. Holmes (1999), 'Competition Policy, Developing Countries and the WTO' **22**(6) *The World Economy* 875

Hoekman, B. and P.C. Mavroidis (2002), *Economic Development, Competition Policy and the World Trade Organisation*, World Bank Policy Research Working Paper No. 2917

Hoekman, B. and K. Saggi (2005), 'International Cooperation on Domestic Policies: Lessons from the WTO Competition Policy Debate' in S. Evenett and B. Hoekman (eds.), *Economic Development and Multilateral Trade Cooperation* (Palgrave Macmillan and World Bank)

Hoj, J. and M. Wise (2004), *Product Market Competition and Economic Performance in Japan*, OECD Economics Department Working Paper No. 387, ECO/WKP(2004)

Holmes, P., J. Mathis, T.C.A. Anant and S.J. Evenett (2003), 'The EU and India on Competition Policy at the WTO: Is there a Common Ground?' in L.A. Winters and P.S. Mehta (eds.), *Bridging the Differences: Analyses of Five Issues of the WTO Agenda* (Jaipur: CUTS)

Holmes, P., H. Müller, A. Papadopoulos and A. Sydorak (2006), *A Taxonomy of International Competition Cooperation Provisions*

Holmes, P., A. Papadopoulos, O. Kayali and A. Sydorak (2005), 'Trade and Competition in Regional Trade Agreements: A Lost Opportunity?' in P. Brusick, A.M. Alvarez and L. Cernat (eds.), *Competition Provisions in Regional Trade Agreements: How to Assure Development Gains* (Geneva and New York: UNCTAD)

Holscher, J. and J. Stephan (2004), 'Competition Policy in Central Eastern Europe in the Light of EU Accession' **42**(2) *Journal of Common Market Studies* 321

Horna, P.M. and B.O. Kayali (2007), 'National Implementation of Competition-Related Provisions in Bilateral and Regional Trade Agreements' in A.-M. Alvarez and L. Wilse-Samson (eds.), *Implementing Competition-Related Provisions in Regional Trade Agreements: Is It Possible to Obtain Development Gains?* (Geneva and New York: UNCTAD)

Horton, T.J. and S. Schmit (2002), 'A Tale of Two Continents: The Coming Clash of the Conflicting Economic Viewpoints in Europe and the United States' **23**(3) *University of Pennsylvania Journal of International Economic Law* 539

Howse, R. (2002), 'From Politics to Technocracy – and Back Again: The Fate of the Multilateral Trading Regime' **96**(1) *American Journal of International Law* 94

Hufbauer, G.C. and B. Kotschwar (1998), *The Future of Regional Trading Arrangements in the Western Hemisphere*, paper prepared for the Michigan State University Tenth Anniversary Conference, Institute of International Economics Paper, available at www.iie.com/publications/papers/paper.cfm?ResearchID=318

Hufbauer, G.C., and Y. Wong (2005), *Prospects for Regional Free Trade in Asia*, IIE Working Paper No. WP 05–12

Hughes, E.J. (1999), 'The Left Side of Antitrust. What Fairness Means and Why it Matters' **77** *Marquette Law Review* 265

Hunt, M. (2002), 'From "Neighbourhood Watch Group" to Community? The Case of ASEAN Institutions and the Pooling of Sovereignty' **56**(1) *Australian Journal of International Affairs*, 99

Hurt, S.R. (2003), 'Co-operation and Coercion? The Cotonou Agreement Between the European Union and ACP States and the End of the Lomé Convention' **24**(1) *Third World Quarterly* 161

Irwin, D. (1993), 'Multilateral and Bilateral Trade Policies in the World Trading System: An Historical Perspective' in J. De Melo and A. Panagariya (eds.), *New Dimensions in Regional Integration* (New York: Cambridge University Press)

Ivaldi, M. and O. Bertrand (2006), *'European Competition Policy in International Markets'*, available at http://papers.ssrn.com/sol3/papers.cfm?abstract_id=951594

Iyori, H. (1997), 'Japanese Cooperation in International Antitrust Law Enforcement' in H. Ulrich (ed.), *Comparative Competition Law: Approaching an International System of Antitrust Law* (Baden-Baden: Nomos Verlagsgesellschaft)

Jacoby, N.H. (1975), 'Multinational Corporations and National Sovereignty' in P.M. Boarman and H. Schollhammer (eds.), *Multinational Corporations and Governments: Business-Government Relations in an International Context* (New York: Praeger Publishers)

Jacquemin, A. (2000), *Theories of Industrial Organisation and Competition Policy: What are the Links?*, European Commission Forward Studies Unit Working Paper

James, C. (2001), *'International Antitrust in the Bush Administration'*, paper presented at Canadian Bar Association on Competition Law, Ottawa, Canada, 21 September 2001, available at www.usdoj.gov/atr/public/speeches/9100.pdf

Janow, M.E. (2000), 'Transatlantic Cooperation on Competition Policy' in S.J. Evenett, A. Lehman and B. Steil (eds.), *Antitrust Goes Global: What Future for Transatlantic Cooperation?* (Brookings Institution Press)

(2003), 'Observations on Two Multilateral Venues: The International Competition Network (ICN) and the WTO' in Barry Hawk (ed.), *Annual Proceedings of the Fordham Corporate Law Institute Conference on International Antitrust Law and Policy* (New York: Juris)

Janow, M.E. and C.R. Lewis (2001), 'International Antitrust and the Global Economy: Perspectives on the Final Report and Recommendations of the International Competition Policy Advisory Committee to the Attorney General and the Assistant Attorney General for Antitrust' **24**(1) *World Competition* 3

Jatar, A.J. and L. Tineo (1998), 'Competition Policy in the Andean Countries: Ups and Downs of a Policy in Search of its Place' in M. Rodriguez Mendoza, P. Correa and B. Kotschwar (eds.), *The Andean Community and the United States: Trade and Investment Relations in the 1990s* (Organization of American States)

Jayasuriya, K. (2001), 'Globalisation, Sovereignty, and the Rule of Law: From Political to Economic Constitutionalism?' **8**(4) *Constellations* 443

Jenny, F. (2001), 'Globalisation, Competition and Trade Policy: Convergence, Divergence and Cooperation' in Yang-Ching Chao, Gee San, Chang Fa Lo and Jiming Ho (eds.), *International and Comparative Competition Law and Policies* (Kluwer Law International)

Jenny, F. and P. Horna (2005), 'Modernization of the European System of Competition Law Enforcement: Lessons for Other Regional Groupings' in P. Brusick, A.M. Alvarez and L. Cernat (eds.), *Competition Provisions in Regional Trade Agreements: How to Assure Development Gains* (Geneva and New York: UNCTAD)

Jones, A. and B. Sufrin (2004), *EC Competition Law: Text, Cases and Materials* (Oxford University Press)

Jordana, J. and D. Levi-Faur (2004), 'The Politics of Regulation in the Age of Governance' in J. Jordana and D. Levi-Faur (eds.), *The Policy of Regulation: Institutions and Regulatory Reforms for the Age of Governance* (Edward Elgar Publishing)

Joubert, N. (2004), *The Reform of South Africa's Anti-Dumping Regime*, Managing the Challenges of WTO Participation Case Study No. 38

Kaczorowska, A. (2000), 'International Competition Law in the Context of Global Capitalism' **21**(2) *European Competition Law Review* 117

Kalenga, P. (2004), *Implementation of the SADC Trade Protocol: Some Reflections, Stellenbosch Trade Law Centre for Southern Africa Trade Brief*

Kalijarvi, T.V. (1963), 'Obstacles to European Unification' **348** *Annals of the American Academy of Political and Social Science, The New Europe: Implications for the United States* 46

Kallaugher, J. and B. Sher (2004), 'Rebates Revisited: Anti-competitive Effects and Exclusionary Abuse under Article 82' **25**(5) *European Competition Law Review* 263

Kaplan, S. (2006), 'West African Integration: A New Development Paradigm?' **29**(4) *Washington Quarterly* 81

Kaysen, C. and D. Turner (1959), *Antitrust Policy* (Cambridge University Press)

Kenwood, A.G. and A.L. Lougheed (1971), *The Growth of International Economy* (London: Allen & Unwin)

Khandelwal, P. (2004), *COMESA and SADC: Prospects and Challenges for Regional Trade Integration*, IMF Working Paper No. WP/04/227

Kiriazis, G. (2001), '*Jurisdiction and Cooperation Issues in the Investigation of International Cartels*', available at http://ec.europa.eu/competition/speeches/text/sp2001_010_en.pdf

Kirk, R. and M. Stern (2005), 'The New Southern African Customs Union Agreement' **28**(2) *The World Economy* 169

Kirkpatrick, C. and M. Watanabe (2005), 'Regional Trade in Sub-Saharan Africa: An Analysis of East African Trade Cooperation 1970–2001' **73**(2) *The Manchester School* 141

Kirzner, I.M. (1997), 'Entrepreneurial Discovery and the Competitive Market Process: An Austrian Approach' **35**(1) *Journal of Economic Literature* 60

Klein, J.I. (1996), '*A Note of Caution with respect to a WTO Agenda on Competition Policy*', speech delivered at the Royal Institute of International Affairs, Chatham House, London, 18 November 1996, available at www.usdoj.gov/atr/public/speeches/0998.htm

(1999), *Luncheon address delivered at the Anti-Cartel Enforcement Conference, Westin Grand Hotel*, Washington, DC, 30 September 1999, available at www.usdoj.gov/atr/public/speeches/3727.htm

(1999), '*A Reality Check on Antitrust Rules in the World Trade Organization, and a Practical Way Forward on International Antitrust*', speech delivered at OECD Conference on Trade and Competition, Paris, 29–30 June 1999, reproduced in OECD, *Trade and Competition Rules: Exploring the Ways Forward* (Paris: OECD)

(2000), '*Time for a Global Competition Initiative?*', speech delivered at the EC Merger Control Tenth Anniversary Conference, Brussels, 14 September 2000, available at www.usdoj.gov/atr/public/speeches/6486.pdf

Knight, F. (1933), *The Economic Organisation* (University of Chicago Press)

Kolasky, W. (2004), 'What is Competition? A Comparison of US and Europe Perspectives' **49**(1/2) *Antitrust Bulletin* 29

(2005), 'Mario Monti's Legacy: A US Perspective' **1**(1) *Wilmer Cutler Hale and Dorr LLP* 159

Kovacic, W.E. and C. Shapiro (2000), 'Antitrust Policy: A Century of Economic and Legal Thinking' **14**(1) *Journal of Economic Perspectives* 43

Krisch, N. (2005), 'International Law in Times of Hegemony: Unequal Power and the Shaping of the International Legal Order' **16**(3) *European Journal of International Law* 369

Kroes, N. (2005), '*Preliminary Thought on Policy Review of Article 82*', speech delivered at the Fordham Corporate Law Institute, 23 September 2005, speech 05/537

(2005), '*The First Hundred Days*', speech delivered at the Fortieth Anniversary of the Studienvereinigung Kartellrecht 1965–2005, International Forum on European Competition Law, Brussels, speech 05/205

(2009), '*Tackling Cartels: A Never-ending Task*', *speech delivered at Anti-Cartel Enforcement: Criminal and Administrative Policy Panel Session, Brasilia, 8 October 2009*, speech/09/454

Krueger, A.O. (2000), 'NAFTA's Effects: A Preliminary Assessment' **23**(6) *The World Economy* 761

Krugman, P. (1983), 'New Theories of Trade Among Industrial Countries' **73**(2) *American Economic Review* 343

(1991), '*The Move to Free Trade Zones*' *in Policy Implications of Trade and Currency Zones* (Federal Reserve Bank of Kansas City)

(1997), 'What Should Trade Negotiators Negotiate About?' **35**(1) *Journal of Economic Literature* 113

Kurzer, P. (2001), *Markets and Moral Regulation: Cultural Change in the European Union* (Cambridge University Press)

Laird, S., R. Peters and D. Vanzetti (2004), *Southern Discomfort: Agricultural Policies, Trade and Poverty*, Centre for Research in Economic Development and International Trade, University of Nottingham Working Paper No. 04/02

Lee, K.Y. (2005), *The WTO Dispute Settlement and Anti-competitive Practices: Lessons Learnt from Trade Disputes*, University of Oxford Centre for Competition Law and Policy Working Paper No. (L)10/05

Leonard, M. (2005), *Why Europe Will Run the 21st Century* (Fourth Estate)

Levenstein, M. and V.Y. Suslow (2004), 'Contemporary International Cartels and Developing Countries: Economic Effects and Implications for Competition Policy' **71** *Antitrust Law Journal* 801

Levenstein, M.C. and V. Suslow (2005), 'The Changing International Status of Export Cartel Exemptions' **20** *American University International Law Review* 785

Levenstein, M., V. Suslow and L. Oswald (2003), *International Price Fixing Cartels and Developing Countries: A Discussion of Effects and Policy Remedies*, William Davidson Working Paper No. 538

Levy, N. (2005), 'Mario Monti's Legacy in EC Merger Control' **1**(1) *Competition Policy International* 99

Lianos, I. (2007), 'The Contribution of the United Nations to the Emergence of Global Antitrust Law' **15**(2) *Tulane Journal of International and Comparative Law* 2

Lie, J. (1997), 'Sociology of Markets' **23** *Annual Review of Sociology* 341

Liesner, J. and D. Glynn (1987), 'Does Anti-trust Make Economic Sense?' **8**(4) *European Competition Law Review* 344

Lipimile, G.K. and E. Gachuiri (2005), 'Allocation of Cases Between National and Regional Competition Authorities: The Case of COMESA' in P. Brusick, A.M. Alvarez and L. Cernat (eds.), *Competition Provisions in Regional Trade Agreements: How to Assure Development Gains* (Geneva and New York: UNCTAD)

Litan, R.E. and C. Shapiro (2001), *Antitrust Policy During the Clinton Administration*, Competition Policy Centre, University of California, Berkeley Working Paper No. CPC01–22

Litwack, J.M. (1992), 'Legality and Market Reform in Soviet-Type Economies' **5**(4) *Journal of Economic Perspectives* 77

Lloyd, P.J. (2002), 'Competition Policy in the Asia-Pacific Region' **14**(2) *Asian-Pacific Economic Literature* 1

Maher, I. (2002), 'Competition Law in the International Domain: Networks as a New Form of Governance' **29**(1) *Journal of Law and Society* 112

Malaguti, M.-C. (1998), 'Restrictive Business Practices in International Trade and the Role of the World Trade Organisation' **32**(3) *Journal of World Trade* 117

Malamud, A. (2001), *Spillover in European and South American Integration: An Assessment*, Latin American Studies Association Meeting Paper, available at http://lasa.international.pitt.edu/Lasa2001/MalamudAndres.pdf

Malkin, E. (2006), *'Central American trade deal is being delayed by partners'*, New York Times, 2 March 2006

Mancero-Bucheli, G. (1998), 'Anticompetitive Practices by Private Undertakings in Ancom and Mercosur: An Analysis from the Perspective of EC Law' **47** *International and Comparative Law Quarterly* 149

Mandigora, G. (2007), *Dispute Settlement Mechanisms in Bilateral and Regional Trade Arrangements*, Tralac Discussion Paper, available at www.tralac.org/cgi-bin/giga.cgi?cmd=cause_dir_news_item&cause_id=1694&news_id=42876&cat_id=1090

Mansfield, E.D. and E. Reinhardt (2003), 'Multilateral Determinants of Regionalism: The Effects of GATT/WTO on the Formation of Preferential Trading Agreements' **57** *International Organisation* 829

March, J.G. and J.P. Olsen (1998), 'The Institutional Dynamics of International Political Orders' **52**(4) *International Organisation* 943

Marcos, F. (2007), *Downloading Competition Law from a Regional Trade Agreement: A New Strategy to Introduce Competition Law to Bolivia and Ecuador*, Berkeley Program in Law and Economics, Latin American and Caribbean Law and Economics Association (ALACDE) Annual Paper No. 50107-8

Markert, K.E. (1968), 'Recent Developments in International Antitrust Co-operation' **13** *Antitrust Bulletin* 355

Marsden, F. (2003), *A Competition Policy for the WTO* (Cameron May)

(2004), 'WTO Decides First Competition Case with Disappointing Results' *Competition Law Insight* (May) 3

Marsden, P. (ed.) (2007), *Handbook of Research in Trans-Atlantic Antitrust* (Edward Elgar Publishing)

Mathis, J. (2005), *The Southern African Custom Union (SACU) Regional Cooperation Framework on Competition Policy and Unfair Trade Practices* (Geneva and New York: UNCTAD)

Matoo, A. and A. Subramanian (2004), 'The WTO and the Poorest Countries: The Stark Reality' **3**(3) *World Trade Review* 385

Maur, J.-M. (2005), 'Exporting Europe's Trade Policy' **28**(11) *The World Economy* 1565

Maxton, G.P. and J. Wormald (2004), *Time for a Model Change: Re-engineering the Global Automotive Industry* (Cambridge University Press)

McCrudden, C. (2006), 'Legal Research and the Social Sciences' **122** *Law Quarterly Review* 632

McDavid, J.L. and L.K. Marshall (2001), 'Antitrust Law: Global Review Regimes' *National Law Journal* 1

McDonald, S.A. (2004), 'The Caribbean Court of Justice: Enhancing the Role of International Organisations' **27** *Fordham International Law Journal* 930

McGowan, L. (2007), 'Theorising European Integration: Revisiting Neofunctionalism and Testing its Suitability for Explaining the Development of EC Competition Policy?' **11**(3) *European Integration Online Papers* 1

McGowan, L. and M. Cini (1999), 'Discretion and Politization in EU Competition Policy: The Case of Merger Control' **12**(2) *Governance* 175

McIntyre, M.A. (2005), *Trade Integration in East African Community: An Assessment for Kenya*, IMF Working Paper No. 05/143

McNulty, P.J. (1968), 'Economic Theory and the Meaning of Competition' **82**(4) *Quarterly of Economics* 639

Mertikopoulou, V. (2007), 'DG Competition's Discussion Paper on the Application of Article 82 of the EC Treaty to Exclusionary Abuses: The Proposed Economic Reform from a Legal Point of View' **28**(4) *European Competition Law Review* 241

Mestral A.L.C. de (2006), 'NAFTA Dispute Settlement: Creative Experiment or Confusion?' in L. Bartels and F. Ortino (eds.), *Regional Trade Agreements and the WTO Legal System* (Oxford University Press)

Metzer, J.-M. (2000), 'Seattle: Failure or New Departure?', *OECD Observer*, July 2000

Meunier, S. and K. Nicolaïdis (2006), 'The European Union as a Conflicted Trade Power' **13**(6) *Journal of European Public Policy* 906

Meyer, J.W., J. Boli, G.M. Thomas and F.O. Ramirez (1997), 'World Society and the Nation State' **103**(1) *American Journal of Sociology* 144

Miller, D.L. and J. Davidow (1982), 'Antitrust in the United Nations: A Tale of Two Codes' **18**(2) *Stanford Journal of International Law* 347

Mogens, P.C. (2001), '*Towards Basic Rules on Trade Related Competition Policy*', speech delivered in Brussels, 2 March 2001, available at http://trade.ec.europa.eu/doclib/docs/2004/november/tradoc_120130.pdf

Monti, G. (2002), 'Article 81 and EC Public Policy' **39** *Common Market Law Review* 1057

(2007), *EC Competition Law* (Cambridge University Press)

Monti, M. (2000), '*Cooperation Between Competition Authorities: A Vision for the Future*', speech delivered at the Japan Foundation Conference, Washington DC, 23 June 2000, speech/00/234

(2000), '*The Main Challenges of a New Decade of EC Merger Control*', speech delivered at the EC Merger Control Tenth Anniversary Conference, Brussels, 14–15 September 2000, speech 00/311

(2001), '*The Future for Competition Policy in the European Union*', speech delivered at Merchant Taylor Hall, London, 9 July 2001, speech/01/340

(2002), '*A Global Competition Policy?*', speech delivered at European Competition Day, Copenhagen, 17 September 2002, speech 02/399

(2004), '*A Reformed Competition Policy: Achievements and Challenges for the Future*', speech delivered at the Center for European Reform, Brussels, 28 October 2004, speech 04/477

Morawetz, V. (1910), 'The Sherman Anti-trust Act' **11**(1) *American Economic Association Quarterly* 321

Morris, D. (2003), '*Dominant Firm Behaviour under UK Competition Law*', paper presented at the Fordham Corporate Law Institute Thirtieth Annual Conference on International Antitrust Law and Policy, New York, 23–24 October 2003

Moschel, W. (2002), 'The Relationship Between Competition Authorities and Sector Specific Regulators' in D. Tzouganatos (eds.), *EU Competition Law and Policy: Developments and Priorities, Proceedings from Athens Conference, April 19th 2002* (Nomiki Vivliothiki SA)

Motta, M. and A. De Streel (2003), 'Exploitative and Exclusionary Excessive Prices in EU Law' in C.-D. Ehlermann and I. Atanasiu, *European Competition Law Annual 2003: What Is an Abuse of a Dominant Position?* (Hart Publishing)

Muchoki Njoroge, P. (2008), *Capacity Building and Technical Assistance Activities on Competition Law and Policy: COMESA's Case*

Mugomba, A.T. (1978), 'Regional Organisations and African Underdevelopment: The Collapse of the East African Community' **16**(2) *Journal of Modern African Studies* 261

Muhara, L. (2007), '*Brief on Progress and Challenges of the Competition and Fair Trading Commission in Malawi*', paper delivered at the Eighth Session of the Intergovernmental Group of Experts, UNCTAD, Geneva, 17–19 July 2007

Mullei, A.K. (2005), '*Integration Experience of East African Countries*', paper presented at the Symposium Marking the Thirtieth Anniversary of Banco de Mozambique, Maputo, Mozambique, 17 May 2005, available at www2.centralbank.go.ke/downloads/gov_speeches/Mozambique-paper.pdf

Murphy, G. (2001), 'Canada, Australia and New Zealand Competition Authorities Sign Cooperation Arrangement' **22**(8) *European Competition Law Review* 322

Narlikar, A. and J. Odell (2003), '*The Strict Distributive Strategy for a Bargaining Coalition: The Like Minded Group in the World Trade Organization*', paper presented at a Conference on Developing Countries and the Trade Negotiation Process, UNCTAD, Geneva, 6–7 November 2003

Narlikar, A. and D. Tussie (2004), 'The G20 at the Cancun Ministerial: Developing Countries and their Evolving Coalitions in the WTO' **27**(7) *The World Economy* 947

Nazzini, R. (2006), 'Article 81 EC: Between Time Present and Time Past: A Normative Critique on "Restriction of Competition" in EU Law' **43**(2) *Common Market Law Review* 497

Nicolaides, P. (2000), 'An Essay on Economics and the Competition Law of the European Community' **27** *Legal Issues of Economic Integration* 7

Noonan, Ch. (2007), *Emerging Principles of International Competition Law* (Oxford University Press)

Nordlander, C. (2004), 'Discovering Discovery: US Discovery of EC Leniency Statements' **25**(10) *European Competition Law Review* 646

Nyirabu, M. (2004), 'Appraising Regional Integration in Southern Africa' **13**(1) *African Security Review* 21

Odudu, O. (2006), *The Boundaries of EC Competition Law: The Scope of Article 81* (Oxford University Press)

Oldale, A. (2000), 'Contestability: The Competition Commission Decision on North Sea Helicopter Services' **21**(8) *European Competition Law Review* 345

O'Rourke, K.H. and G. Williamson (2004), 'Once More: When Did Globalisation Begin?' **8** *Journal of European Economic History* 109

Ostry, S. (1995), 'New Dimensions for Market Access: Challenges for the Trading System' in *OECD, New Dimensions in Market Access in a Globalising World Economy* (Paris: OECD) 25

Papadopoulos, A. (2007), 'Bilateral Enforcement Cooperation' in P. Marsden (ed.), *Handbook of Research in Trans-Atlantic Antitrust* (Edward Elgar Publishing)

Parisi, J.J. (1999), 'Enforcement Co-operation Among Antitrust Authorities' **20**(3) *European Competition Law Review* 133

Park, S.-H. (2005), '*Increasing Sub-regionalism Within APEC and the Bogor Goals: Stumbling Block or Building Block?*', available at www.apec.org.au/docs/koreapapers2/SX-SHP-Paper.pdf

Parker Willis, H. (1912), 'Political Obstacles to Anti-Trust Legislation' **20**(6) *Journal of Political Economy* 588

Pate, H. (2004), '*Antitrust in a Transatlantic Context: From the Cicada's Perspective*', speech delivered at Antitrust in a Transatlantic Context Conference, Brussels, 7 June 2004, available at www.usdoj.gov/atr/public/speeches/203973.pdf

Patterson, D.E. and C. Shapiro (2001), 'Trans-Atlantic Divergence in GE/Honeywell, Causes and Lessons' *Antitrust* 18

Paul, J.R. (1991), 'Comity in International Law' **32**(1) *Harvard International Law Journal* 2

Pauwelyn, J. (2001), 'The Role of Public International Law in the WTO: How Far Can We Go?' **95**(3) *American Journal of International Law* 534

Pelkmans, J. and P. Brenton (1999), 'Free Trade with the EU: Driving Forces and the Effects' in O. Memedovic, A. Kuyvenhoven and W. Molle (eds.), *Multilateralism and Regionalism in the Post-Uruguay Round Era: What Role for the EU?* (Boston MA: Kluwer)

Peritz, R.J.R. (1996), *Competition Policy in America, 1888–1992: History, Rhetoric, Law* (New York: Oxford University Press)

Petersmann, E.-U. (1994), 'Proposals for Negotiating International Competition Rules in the GATT-WTO World Trade and Legal System' *49 Swiss Review of International Economic Relations* 231

(1999), 'Legal Economic and Political Objectives of National and International Competition Policies: Constitutional Functions of WTO "Linking Principles" for Trade and Competition' **34**(1) *New England Law Review* 145

Philpott, D. (1995), 'Sovereignty: An Introduction and Brief History' **48** *Journal of International Affairs* 353

Piccioto, S. (1998), '*Globalisation, Liberalisation, Regulation*', paper presented at Conference on Globalisation, the Nation-State and Violence, Sussex University, 16 April 1998, available at www.lancs.ac.uk/staff/lwasp/glibreg.pdf

Pitofski, R. (1999), 'Competition Policy in a Global Economy: Today and Tomorrow' **2**(3) *Journal of International Economic Law* 403

Porrata Doria, Jr, R.A. (2004), 'MERCOSUR: The Common Market of the Twenty First Century?' **32** *Georgia Journal of International and Comparative Law* 1

Posner, R. (1979), 'The Chicago School of Antitrust Analysis' **127** *University of Pennsylvania Law Review* 925

Potter, P.B. (1943), 'Universalism Versus Regionalism in International Organisation' **37**(5) *American Political Science Review* 850

Preub, U. (1999), 'Political Order and Democracy: Carl Schmitt and His Influence' in Ch. Mouffe (ed.), *The Challenge of Carl Schmitt* (New York: Verso)

Prosser, T. (1997), *Law and The Regulators* (New York: Oxford University Press)

Raustiala, K. (2002), 'The Architecture of International Cooperation: Transgovernmental Networks and the Future of International Law' **43** *Virginia Journal of International Law* 1

Reinker, K.S. (2004), 'Case Comment: Roche vs. Empagran' **28** *Harvard Journal of Law and Public Policy* 297

Reismann, W.M. (1991), 'A Hard Look at Soft Law: Panel Report', **82** *American Society of International Law* 371

Riley, A. (1995), 'The Jellyfish Nailed? The Announcement of the EC/US Competition Co-operation Agreement' **16**(3) *European Competition Law Review* 185

Rill, J.F. and C.C. Wilson (2000), 'The A.C. Nielsen Case' in S.J. Evenett, A. Lehman and B. Steil (eds.), *Antitrust Goes Global: What Future for Transatlantic Cooperation?* (Brookings Institution Press)

Rivas-Campo, J.A. and R. Tiago Juk Benke (2003), 'FTAA Negotiations: Short Overview' **6**(3) *Journal of International Economic Law* 661

Rodger, B. (2000), 'Competition Policy, Liberalism and Globalization A European Perspective' **6** *Columbia Journal of European Law* 289

Rodger, B. and A. McCulloch (2004), *Competition Law and Policy in the EC and UK: An Introduction to Practice and Policy* (3rd edn, Cavendish Publishing)

Rodrik, D. (1999), 'How Far Will International Economic Integration Go?' **14**(1) *Journal of Economic Perspectives* 177

Rosch J.T. (2007), '*I Say Monopoly, You Say Dominance: The Continuing Divide on the Treatment of Dominant Firms, Is It the Economics?*', speech delivered at the International Bar Association Antitrust Section Conference, Florence, 8 September 2007, available at www.ftc.gov/speeches/rosch/070908isaymonopolyiba.pdf

Rostow, E. (1960), 'British and American Experience with Legislation Against Restraints of Competition' **23**(5) *Modern Law Review* 477

S.B.T. (1966), 'Petrol Solus Agreements: British Common Law of Restraint of Trade in a New Context' **52**(4) *Virginia Law Review* 690

Sapir, A. (2000), 'Trade Regionalism in Europe: Towards an Integrated Approach' **38** *Journal of Common Market Studies* 151

Sceres, K. (2007), 'Multi-Jurisdictional Competition Law Enforcement: The Interface Between European Competition Law and the Competition Laws of the New Member States' **3**(2) *European Competition Journal* 465

Scherer, F.M. and R.S. Balous (1994), *Unfinished Tasks: The New International Trade Theory and Post Uruguay Round Challenges*, British-North American Committee Issues Paper No. 3

Scherer, F.M. and D.R. Ross (1990), *Industrial Market Structure and Economic Performance* (3rd edn, Houghton Mifflin)

Schimmelfennig, F. (2008), 'EU Political Accession Conditionality after the 2004 Enlargement: Consistency and Effectiveness' **15**(6) *Journal of European Public Policy* 918

Schmalense, R. (1982), 'Antitrust and the New Industrial Economics' **72**(2) *Papers and Proceedings of the Ninety-Fourth Annual Meeting of the American Economic Association* 24

Schmidt, A. (2001), *Non-Competition Factors in the European Competition Policy: The Necessity of Institutional Reforms*, Centre for Globalisation and Europeanisation of the Economy Discussion Paper No. 13

Schmidt, C.A.J. (2002), '*The Defence of Competition in the MERCOSUR*', available at www.seae.fazenda.gov.br/central_documentos/textos_artigos/2002–1/3-pdfwin32

Schumpeter, J. (1943), *Capitalism, Socialism and Democracy* (London: G. Allen & Unwin)

Schutze, R. (2006), 'Supremacy Without Pre-emption? The Very Slowly Emergent Doctrine of Community Pre-Emption' **43** *Common Market Law Review* 1023

Shaw, M. (2004), *International Law* (5th edn, Cambridge University Press)

Shelton, J.R. (1999), 'Competition Policy: What Chance for International Rules?' **1**(2) *OECD Journal of Competition Law and Policy* 51

Shepherd, W.G. (1984), 'Contestability vs. Competition' **74**(4) *American Economic Review* 572

Sierra, J.L.B. (2000), *Exclusive Rights and State Monopolies under EC Law: Article 86 (Former Article 90) of the EC Treaty* (Oxford University Press)

Singh, A. (2003), *Competition and Competition Policy Development in Emerging Markets: International and Developmental Dimensions*, ESRC Working Paper No. 246

Slaughter, A.-M. (1993), 'International Law and International Relations Theory: A Dual Agenda' **87** *American Journal of International Law* 205

(2000), 'Governing the Global Economy through Government Networks' in M. Byers (ed.), *The Role of Law in International Politics: Essays in International Relations and International Law* (Oxford University Press)

(2004), 'Sovereignty and Power in a Networked World Order' **40** *Stanford Journal of International Law* 283

Sloot, T. and P. Verschuren (1990), 'Decision-making Speed in the European Community' **29**(1) *Journal of Common Market Studies* 75

Smith, A. (1776), *An Inquiry into the Nature and Causes of the Wealth of Nations* (Dublin: Whitestone)

Smith, K.E. (2005), 'The Outsiders: The European Neighbourhood Policy' **81**(4) *International Affairs* 757

Smith, P. and D. Begg (2000), *Economics* (6th edn, McGraw-Hill Publishing)

Smith, S.C. (2006), 'The Free Trade Agreement of the Americas: Is there Still a Place for the World Trade Organisation?' **13** *Tulsa Journal of International and Comparative Law* 321

Sokol, D.D. (2007), *Why is This Chapter Different from All the Others? An Examination of Why Countries Enter into Non-Enforceable Competition Policy Chapters in Free Trade Agreements*, Legal Studies Research Paper No. 2007–13

Spaak, F. and J.N. Jaeger (1961), 'The Rules of Competition Within the European Common Market' **26**(3) *Law and Contemporary Problems* 485

Springman, C. (2005), 'Fix Prices Globally, Get Sued Locally? US Jurisdiction Over International Cartels' **72** *University of Chicago Law Review* 265

Stark, C. (2000), '*Improving Bilateral Antitrust Cooperation*', speech delivered in Washington DC, 23 June 2000, at 2, available at www.usdoj.gov/atr/public/speeches/5075.htm

Steinberg, R.H. (2002), 'In the Shadow of Law or Power? Consensus-Based Bargaining and Outcomes in the GATT/WTO' **56**(2) *International Organisation* 339

Stephenson, S.M. and G.C. Hufbauer (2004), '*The Free Trade Area of the Americas: How Deep an Integration in the Western Hemisphere?*', available at www.aeaweb.org/annual_mtg_papers/2005/0107_1015_1402.pdf

Stewart, T. (2001), '*Challenges of Developing a Competition Regime in CARICOM*', available at www.iadb.org/sds/doc/IFM-Taimoon_Stewart-E.pdf

Stigler, G. (1968), 'Barriers to Entry, Economies of Scale and Firm Size' in R.D. Irwin (ed.), *The Organisation of Industry* (Homewood)

(1971), 'The Theory of Economic Regulation' **2**(1) *Bell Journal of Economics and Management* 1

(1982), 'The Economists and the Problem of Monopoly' **72**(2) *American Economic Review* 1

Streit, M.E. and M. Wohlgemuth (1997), *The Market Economy and the State Hayekian and Ordoliberal Conceptions*, Max-Planck-Institut zur Erfoschung von Wirtschaftssystemen, Diskussionbeitrag No. 06–97, available at www.dundee.ac.uk/cepmlp/journal/assets/images/Streit-onHayek97.pdf

Subbioto, R. and F. Amato (2002), 'Reform of the European Competition Policy Concerning Vertical Restraints' **69**(1) *Antitrust Law Journal* 147

Szepesi, S. (2004), *Comparing EU Free Trade Agreements: Competition Policy and State Aid*, ECDPM InBrief 6(E) (ECDPM, Maastricht)

Tallberg, J. (2002), 'Delegation to Supranational Institutions: Why, How, and with What Consequences?' **25**(1) *West European Politics* 23

Tan, L.H. (2005), 'Will ASEAN Economic Integration Progress Beyond a Free Trade Area?' **53** *International and Comparative Law Quarterly* 935

Tavares de Araujo, Jr, J. (2000), '*Competition Policy and the EU-MERCOSUR Trade Negotiations*', paper presented at the Working Group on EU–MERCOSUR Trade Negotiations, Paris, 12–13 May 2000, available at www.sice.oas.org/compol/Articles/cpeumerc.doc)

Taylor, M.D. (2006), *International Competition Law: A New Dimension for the WTO?* (Cambridge University Press)

Timberg, S. (1973), 'An International Antitrust Convention: A Proposal to Harmonise Conflicting National Policies Towards the Multinational Corporation' **8** *Journal of International Law and Economics* 157

Trebilcock, M. (1986), *The Common Law of Restraint of Trade* (Toronto: Carswell)

Trebilcock, M. and R. Howse (1999), *The Regulation of International Trade* (2nd edn, Routledge)

Truli, E. (2009), 'Competition in the Telecommunications Sector: Delineation of Competences Between the NCA and the NRA – the Example of Greece' **8** *Competition in the Telecommunications Sector* 188

Tsebelis, G. and G. Garrett (2001), 'The Institutional Foundations of Intergovernmentalism and Supranationalism in the European Union' **55**(2) *International Organisation* 357

Vachudova, M.A. (2002), 'The Leverage of the European Union on the Reform in Post Communist Europe', paper presented at the Workshop on Enlargement and European Governance, ECPR Joint Session Workshops, Turin, 22–27 March 2002, available at www.essex.ac.uk/ecpr/events/jointsessions/paper-archive/turin/ws4/Vachudova.pdf

Van de Boogaerde, P. and C. Tsangarides (2005), *Ten Years After the CFA Franc Devaluation: Progress Toward Regional Integration in the WAEMU*, IMF Working Paper No. WP/05/145

Van Kraay, F.G.A. (1977), 'Proposed EEC Regulation on the Control of Mergers' **26**(2) *International and Comparative Law Quarterly* 468

Van Miert, K. (1998), 'International Cooperation in the Field of Competition: A View from the EC' in Barry Hawk (ed.), *1997 Fordham Corporate Law Institute*

International Antitrust Law and Policy Conference (New York: Fordham Corporate Law Institute)

Venit, J. (2003), 'Brave New World: The Modernisation and Decentralisation of Enforcement under Articles 81 and 82 of the EC Treaty' **40** *Common Market Law Review* 545

Vervaele, J.A.E. (2005), 'MERCOSUR and Regional Integration in Latin America' **54** *International and Comparative Law Quarterly* 387

Vickers, J. (2005), 'Abuse of Market Power' **115** *Economic Journal* 244

Walker, F. (1905), 'The Law concerning Monopolistic Combinations in Continental Europe' **20**(1) *Political Science Quarterly* 13

Walker, W.K. (1992), 'Extraterritorial Application of US Antitrust Laws: The Effect of the European Community–United States Agreement' **33** *Harvard International Law Journal* 583

Waller, S.W. (1997), 'Internationalisation of Antitrust Enforcement' **77** *Boston University Law Review* 343

Weatherill, S. (2005), *EU Consumer Law and Policy* (Edward Elgar Publishing)

Weil, P. (1983), 'Towards Relative Normativity in International Law?' **77** *American Journal of International Law* 413

Weiler, J.H.H. (1991), 'The Transformation of Europe' **100**(8) *Yale Law Journal* 2403

Werden, G. (2004), 'Economic Evidence on the Existence of Collusion: Reconciling Antitrust Law with Oligopoly Theory' **71** *Antitrust Law Journal* 719

Whish, R. (2003), *Competition Law* (4th edn, Butterworths)

Willimsky, S.M. (1997), 'The Concept(s) of Competition' **18**(1) *European Competition Law Review* 53

Wionczek, M.S. (1970), 'The Rise and Decline of Latin American Economic Integration' **9**(1) *Journal of Common Market Studies* 49

Wood, D.P. (1995), 'The Internationalisation of Antitrust Law: Options for the Future' **44** *De Paul Law Review* 1289

(1999), 'Is Cooperation Possible' **34**(1) *New England Law Review* 103

Woolcock, S. (2004), *The Singapore Issues in Cancun: A Failed Negotiation Ploy or a Litmus Test for Global Governance?*, LSE Working Paper, available at www2.lse.ac.uk/internationalRelations/centresandunits/ITPU/docs/woolcocksingaporeissues.pdf

Yang, Y. and S. Gupta (2005), *Regional Trade Arrangements in Africa: Past Performance and the Way Forward*, IMF Working Paper No. WP/05/36

Yntema, H. (1966), 'The Comity Doctrine' **65**(1) *Michigan Law Review* 9

Yong, O.K. (2006), *'Opening Remarks' at the Second ASEAN Conference on Competition Policy and Law*, Bali, Indonesia, 14–16 June 2006, available at www.aseansec.org/18507.htm

Young, A.R. and J. Peterson (2006), 'The EU and the New Trade Politics' **13**(6) *Journal of European Public Policy* 795

Young, O.R. (1991), 'Political Leadership and Regime Formation: On the Development of Institutions in International Society' **45** *International Organisation* 281

Zach, R. (1998), 'International Cooperation Between Antitrust Enforcement Agencies: A View from a Small Country' in H. Ulrich (ed.), *Comparative Competition Law: Approaching an International System of Antitrust Law* (Baden-Baden: Nomos Verlagsgesellschaft)

Zanettin, B. (2002), *Cooperation Between Antitrust Agencies at the International Level* (Hart Publishing)

Zedillo, E. (2006), '*The WTO's Biggest Problem at 10: Surviving the Doha Round*', speech delivered at Conference on WTO at 10: Governance, Dispute Settlement and Developing Countries, Columbia University, 7 April 2006, available at www.ycsg.yale.edu/center/forms/doha.pdf

Official Documents and reports, Press Releases

ABA Antitrust Division (2003), '*Comments and Recommendations on the Competition Elements of the Doha Declaration*', available at www.abanet.org/antitrust/at-comments/2003/05–03/doha.pdf

AEPLAC (2007), *Assessment of Institutional Standing in the Fields of Competition and State Aid*, report presented in the context of the TACIS programme, available at http://old.aeplac.eu/pdf/2007/Compet/Compet.pdf

African Union (2007), 'African Union in a Nutshell', available at www.africa-union.org/root/au/AboutAu/au_in_a_nutshell_en.htm

Andean Community, 'European cooperation for harmonizing rules on free competition in the Andean region', Press Release of 8 June 2001, available at www.comunidadandina.org/INGLES/press/press/np8–6–01.htm

APEC (1999), 'APEC Principles to Enhance Competition and Regulatory Reform', available at www.oecd.org/dataoecd/48/52/2371601.doc

APEC Committee on Trade and Development (2006), *Annual Report to the Ministers*, APEC#206-CT-01.6

Council (EC), '2640th Council Meeting, General Affairs and External Relations', Press Release 6419/0521 of 21 February 2005

Council and European Commission (2002), Joint Statement of the Council and the Commission on the Function of the Network of Competition Authorities, available at http://ec.europa.eu/comm/competition/ecn/joint_statement_en.pdf

Croatian Competition Agency (2006), *Annual Report of the Croatian Competition Agency for 2005*, available at www.aztn.hr/eng/pdf/izvjesca/ANNUAL%20REPORT%20aztn%202005%20eng.pdf

Danish Competition Authority (2004), 'Wider Nordic antitrust cooperation', Press Release of 2 March 2004, available at www.ks.dk/english/news/press-releases/2004/wider-nordic-antitrust-cooperation/

EAC (2006), 'Regional Cooperation on Competition Policy and Law: The Experience of the East African Community', available at www.unctad.org/sections/wcmu/docs/c2clp_ige7p25_en.pdf

EAC Secretariat (2006), 'Role of EAC in Promoting Competition in the Region' (Dr Flora Mndeme Musonda, Director of Trade, EAC) available at www.cuts-international.org/7up3/Role_EAC.pdf

ECOWAS, 'Regional Competition Policy Framework', available at www.ecowas.int/publications/en/actes_add_commerce/1.Regional_Competition_Policy_Framework-final-P.pdf

EFTA (2009), 'A Short Introduction to 50 Years of EFTA', available at www.efta.int/content/publications/fact-sheets/efta-general/efta-50-years.pdf

European Commission (1995), *Report of the Group of Experts, Competition Policy in the New Trade Order: Strengthening International Competition and Rules*, COM(95)359 final

(1996), *Communication to the Council, An International Framework of Competition Rules*, COM(96)284

(1996), *How a Unified Strategy Can Help European Business, Background Note on the Market Access Strategy*, MEMO/96/108

(1998), *EC Commission Report to the Council and the European Parliament on the Application of the Agreement Between the European Communities and the Government of the United States of America regarding the application of their competition laws, 1 January to 31 December 1997* (Brussels, 11 May 1998)

(1999), *White Paper on the Modernisation of the Rules Implementing Articles 85 and 86 of the EC Treaty*, Commission Programme 99/027 (Brussels, 28 April 1999)

(2002), *Communication to the Council and the European Parliament, Trade and Development: Assisting Developing Countries to Benefit from Trade*, COM(2002) 513 final (18 September 2002)

(2002), 'Glossary of Terms Used in EU Competition Policy', available at http://ec.europa.eu/competition/publications/glossary_en.pdf

(2003), *Report from the Commission to the Council and the European Parliament on the Application of the Agreements Between the European Communities and the Government of the United States of America and the Government of Canada regarding the Application of their Competition Laws, 1 January 2002 to 31 December 2002*, available at http://europa.eu.int/comm/competition/international/bilateral/canada/2002_report_en.pdf

(2003), *Wider Europe – Neighbourhood: A New Framework for Relations with our Eastern and Southern Neighbours*, COM(2003)104 final (Brussels, 11 March 2003)

(2003), *Technical Assistance Programmes and Projects Provided by the European Community and its Member States in the Field of Trade and Competition Policy*, WT/WGTCP/W/223

(2004), *Communication from the Commission, European Neighbourhood Policy: Strategy Paper*, COM(2004)373 final (Brussels, 12 May 2004)
(2004), *European Neighbourhood Policy: Strategy Paper*, COM(2004)373 final
(2005), *Discussion Paper on the Application of Article 82 of the EC Treaty to Exclusionary Abuses*, Public Consultation Document
(2005), *Country Report: Egypt*, SEC(2005)287/3 (Brussels, 2 March 2005)
(2005), *Country Report: Lebanon*, SEC(2005)289/3 (Brussels, 2 March 2005)
(2005), *Country Report: Armenia*, SEC(2005)285/3 (Brussels, 2 March 2005)
(2005), *Country Report: Azerbaijan*, SEC(2005)286/3 (Brussels, 2 March 2005)
(2005), *Country Report: Georgia*, SEC(2005)288/3 (Brussels, 2 March 2005)
(2005), *State Aid Action Plan: Less and Better Targeted State Aid: A Roadmap for State Aid Reform 2005–2009*, COM(2005)107 final (Brussels, 7 June 2005)
(2006), *ENP Progress Report: Jordan*, SEC(2006)1508/2 (Brussels, 4 December 2006)
(2006), *ENP Progress Report: Tunisia*, SEC(2006)1510 (Brussels, 4 December 2006)
(2006), *ENP Progress Report: Ukraine*, SEC(2006)1505/2 (Brussels, 4 December 2006)
(2006), 'The Fight Against Cartels', available at http://europa.eu.int/comm/competition/citizen/cartel_stats.html
(2006), 'Screening Report: Turkey – Chapter 8, Competition Policy', available at http://ec.europa.eu/enlargement/pdf/turkey/screening_reports/screening_report_08_tr_internet_en.pdf
(2006), 'Screening Report: Croatia – Chapter 8, Competition Policy', available at http://ec.europa.eu/enlargement/pdf/croatia/screening_reports/screening_ report_08_hr_internet_en.pdf
(2006), *Commission Staff Working Paper accompanying the Communication from the Commission to the Council and the European Parliament on Strengthening the European Neighbourhood Policy; ENP Progress Report, Morocco*, COM(2006)final
(2007), *A Strong European Neighbourhood Policy*, COM(2007)774 final
(2007), *Andean Community Regional Strategy Paper 2007–2013*, E/2007/678 (12 April 2007)
(2007), Country Report: Armenia, SEC(2008)392/3 (Brussels, 3 April 2008)
(2008), 'Vademecum Community Rules on State Aid', available at http://ec.europa.eu/competition/state_aid/studies_reports/vademecum_on_rules_09_2008_en.pdf
(2008), *Communication to the Council, Western Balkans: Enhancing the European Perspective*, COM(2008)127 final
(2008), *Implementation of the European Neighbourhood Policy in 2008*, COM(2009)188(3)
(2008), *Financial Assistance to the Western Balkans: Donor Cooperation*, Memo/08/144

(2008), *Country Report: Azerbaijan*, SEC(2008)391 (Brussels, 3 April 2008)
(2008), *Albania 2008 Progress Report*, SEC(2008)2692
(2008), *Bosnia and Herzegovina 2008 Progress Report*, SEC(2008)2693
(2008), *Kosovo (under UNSCR 1244/99) 2008 Progress Report*, SEC(2008)2697
(2008), *Montenegro 2008 Progress Report*, SEC(2008)2696
(2008), *Serbia 2008 Progress Report*, SEC(2008)2698
(2008), *Guidance on the Commission's Enforcement Priorities in Applying Article 82 of the EC Treaty to Abusive Exclusionary Conduct by Dominant Undertakings*, COM(2009)864 final
(2009), *Country Report: Egypt*, SEC(2009)523/2 (Brussels, 23 April 2009)
(2009), *Country Report: Georgia*, SEC(2009)513/2 (Brussels, 3 April 2009)
(2009), *Progress Report: Jordan*, SEC(2009)517/2 (Brussels, 23 April 2009)
(2009), *Country Report: Lebanon*, SEC(2009)518/2 (Brussels, 23 April 2009)
(2009), *Rapport de Suivi Maroc*, SEC(2009)520/2 (Brussels, 23 April 2009)
(2009), *ENP Progress Report: Tunisia*, SEC(2009)521/2 (Brussels, 23 April 2009)
European Commission, 'Following an undertaking by Microsoft to change its licensing practices, the European Commission suspends its action for breach of the competition rules', Press Release IP/94/653 of 17 July 1994
'Kodak-Fuji case – EU to join the WTO/GATT panel: statement by the European Commission', Press Release IP/96/931
'Commission clears the merger of Halliburton and Dresser in the area of oilfield services', Press Release IP/98/643 of 8 July 1998
'Commission opens procedure against Air France for favouring Amadeus reservation system', Press Release IP/99/171 of 15 March 1999
'Commission acts to prevent discrimination between airline computer reservation systems', Press Release IP/00/835 of 25 July 2000
'The Commission prohibits GE's acquisition of Honeywell', Press Release IP/01/939 of 3 July 2001
'EU–Chile Association Agreement to be signed today in Brussels', Press Release IP/02/1696 of 18 November 2002
FTAA (2003), 'Free Trade Area of the Americas Eighth Ministerial Meeting Miami, USA, November 20, 2003, Ministerial Declaration', available at www.ftaa-alca.org/Ministerials/Miami/Miami_e.asp
Group of 77 (2003), 'Declaration of the Group of 77 and China on the Fifth WTO Ministerial Conference, Cancun, Mexico, 10–14 September 2003', available at www.g77.org/main/docs/FinalG77Decl-22aug-5thWTO.pdf
International Chamber of Commerce (1996), *ICC Statement on International Cooperation Between Antitrust Authorities*, Doc. 225/450 Rev 3 (28 March 1996)
(1999), *ICC Recommendations to the International Competition Policy Advisory Committee (ICPAC) on Exchange of Confidential Information Between Competition Authorities in the Merger Context*, Commission on Law and Practices relating to Competition, Document 225/525 (21 May 1999)

ICN (2003), *A Report on the First Annual Conference of the International Competition Network, Naples, 28–29 September 2002*

(2004), *Report of the Working Group on Antitrust Enforcement in Regulated Sectors to the Fourth ICN Annual Conference, Bonn, June 2005*, available at www.internationalcompetitionnetwork.org/media/library/conference_4th_bonn_2005/Interrelations_Between_Antitrust_and_Regulation.pdf

(2007), *Cartels Working Group Report, Cooperation Between Competition Agencies in Cartel Investigations*, presented at the ICN Annual Conference, Moscow, May 2007, available at www.icn-moscow.org/get_file.php?id=115

International Competition Policy Advisory Committee (2000), '*ICPAC Final Report to the Attorney General and the Assistant Attorney General for Antitrust*, available at www.usdoj.gov/atr/icpac/finalreport.htm

Kenya (2003), *Comments by Kenya on the Second Revision of the Draft Cancun Ministerial Text*, WT/MIN(03)/W/21 (14 September 2003)

OECD (1994), *Merger Cases in the Real World: A Study of Merger Control Procedures* (Paris: OECD)

(1999), *CLP Report on Positive Comity*, DAFFE/CLP(99)

(1999), *Trade and Competition Policies for Tomorrow* (Paris: OECD)

(2001), *Trade and Competition Policies: Options for a Greater Coherence* (Paris: OECD)

(2001), 'Promoting Competition in Postal Services' 3(1) *OECD Journal of Competition Law and Policy* 7

(2002), *Fighting Hard-Core Cartels: Harm, Effective Sanctions and Leniency Programme* (Paris: OECD)

(2002), 'Regulatory Reform for Greece' 3(4) *OECD Journal of Competition Law and Policy* 7

(2004), *Competition Law and Policy in Russia: An OECD Peer Review* (Paris: OECD)

(2005), *Hard Core Cartels: Third Report on the Implementation of the 1998 Recommendation* (Paris: OECD)

(2006), *Competition Provisions in Regional Trade Agreements*, COM/DAF/TD(2005)3/final, OECD Trade Policy Working Paper No. 31

(2008), *Note by the US to the Latin America Competition Forum*, DAF/COMP/LACF/WD(2008)1

OECD Competition Committee (2004), *Regulating Market Activities by Public Sector*, DAF/COMP(2004)36

OECD Global Forum on Competition (2002), *OECD Global Forum on Competition: Contribution by UEMOA*, CCNM/GF/COMP/WD(2002)30

(2003), *The Objectives of Competition Law and Policy, OECD Secretariat Note*, CCNM/GF/COMP(2003)3

(2004), *Regulatory Reform: Stock-taking of Experience with Reviews of Competition Law and Policy in OECD Countries and the Relevance of Such Experience for Developing Countries*, CCNM/GF/COMP(2004)

(2004), *Challenges/Obstacles Faced by Competition Authorities in Achieving Greater Economic Development through the Promotion of Competition: Contribution from Algeria*, CCNM/GF/COMP/WD(2004)21

OECD Joint Group on Trade and Competition (2001), *The Role of 'Special and Differential Treatment' at the Trade, Competition and Development Interface*, COM/TD/DAFFE/CLP(2001)21/final

SADC Secretariat (2007), 'SADC Expert Group Meeting on Competition Law and Policy', available at www.sadc.int/attachments/calendar/251/1892_Expert%20Group%20Meeting%20on%20Competition%20Law%20&%20Policy%20Record%20(Draft).pdf

UNCTAD (2003), *WTO Core Principles and Prohibition: Obligations relating to Private Practices, National Competition Laws and Implications for a Competition Policy Framework*, UNCTAD/DITC/CLP/2003/2

(2004), 'Communication Submitted by Brazil Ministry of Justice, Cooperation and Dispute Mediation Mechanism in MERCOSUR related to Competition Law and Policy', available at http://r0.unctad.org/en/subsites/cpolicy/docs/IGE1104/Brazil_cooperation.pdf

(2005), *Exclusionary Anti-competitive Practices: Their Effects on Competition and Development*, UNCTAD/DITC/CLP/2005/4

(2005), *Review of Recent Experiences in the Formulation and Implementation of Competition Law and Policy in Selected Developing Countries*, UNCTAD/DITC/CLP/2005/2

(2005), 'Communication Submitted by Turkey to the Fifth United Nations Conference to Review All Aspects of the Set of Multilaterally Agreed Equitable Principles and Rules for the Control of Restrictive Business Practices', available at www.unctad.org/sections/wcmu/docs/tdrbpconf6p043_en.pdf

(2006), *Voluntary Peer Review of Competition Policy: Tunisia*, UNCTAD/DITC/CLP/2006/2

(2006), *COMPAL Global Annual Report 2005*, UNCTAD/DITC/CLP/2006/1

(2007), 'Submission by Romania to the Inter-governmental Group of Experts, Criteria for Evaluating the Effectiveness of Competition Authorities', available at www.unctad.org/sections/wcmu/docs/c2clp_ige8p15Romania_en.pdf.

(2008), *Voluntary Peer Review of Competition Policies of WAEMU, Benin and Senegal* (New York and Geneva: United Nations)

UNICE (1999), *Preliminary UNICE Comments on the Commission Discussion Paper: Trade and Competition: WTO Framework on Competition Rules*, UNICE Paper No. 1/30/1

US Department of Justice (1998), 'Department of Justice clears WorldCom/MCI merger after MCI agrees to sell its Internet business', Press Release of 15 July 1998

(2001), 'Justice Department requires divestitures in merger between General Electric and Honeywell', Press Release of 2 May 2001

(2001), 'Statement by Assistant Attorney General Charles A. James on the EU's decision regarding the GE/Honeywell acquisition', Press Release of 3 July 2001

(2001), 'Department of Justice and Microsoft Corporation reach effective settlement on antitrust lawsuit', Press Release of 2 November 2001

(2001), 'US and foreign antitrust officials launch International Competition Network: new international venue will assist in global convergence on important antitrust enforcement issues', Press Release of 25 October 2001

(2009), 'Justice Department withdraws report on Antitrust Monopoly Law: Antitrust Division to apply more rigorous standard with focus on the impact of exclusionary conduct on consumers', Press Release of 11 May 2009

World Bank (2005), *Global Economic Prospects 2005: Trade, Regionalism and Development*

WTO (1996), *Singapore Ministerial Conference of the Parties to the WTO, Singapore Ministerial Declaration*, WT/MIN(96)/DEC

(2001), *2001 Doha Ministerial Declaration*, WT/MIN(01)/DEC/1

(2004), *Decision Adopted by the General Council on 1 August 2004*, WT/L/579

(2006), *Trade Policy Review, Report by the Secretariat: East African Community*, WT/TPR/S/171

WTO Working Group on the Interaction Between Trade and Competition Policy (1999), *The Fundamental Principles of Competition Policy*, WT/WGTCP/W/127

WTO Working Group on Trade and Investment (1998), *Bilateral, Regional, Plurilateral, and Multilateral Agreements*, WT/WGTI/W/22

Submissions to the WTO Working Group on Trade and Competition

EU

Communication from the European Community and its Member States, WT/WGTCP/W/1, of 11 June 1997

Communication from the European Community and its Member States, WT/WGTCP/W/45, of 24 November 1997

Communication from the European Community and its Member States, WT/WGTCP/W/62, of 5 March 1998

Communication from the European Community and its Member States, WT/WGTCP/W/115, of 29 May 1999

Communication from the European Community and its Member States, WT/WGTCP/W/130, of 12 July 1999

Communication from the European Community and its Member States, WT/WGTCP/W/140, of 8 June 2000

Communication from the European Community and its Member States, WT/WGTCP/W/152, of 25 September 2000

Communication from the European Community and its Member States, WT/WGTCP/W/184, of 22 April 2002
Communication from the European Community and its Member States, WT/WGTCP/W/193, of 1 July 2002
Communication from the European Community and its Member States, WT/WGTCP/W/222, of 19 November 2002
Communication from the European Community and its Member States, WT/WGTCP/W/234, of 26 June 2003

United States

Communication from the United States, WT/WGTCP/W/6, of 19 June 1997
Communication from the United States, WT/WGTCP/W/116, of 25 May 1999
Communication from the United States, WT/WGTCP/W/203, of 15 August 2002

Other

Communication from India, WT/WGTCP/W/216, of 26 September 2002
Communication from Mauritius, WT/MIN(03)/W/17, of 12 September 2003

INDEX